Henry Moore

at Dulwich Picture Gallery

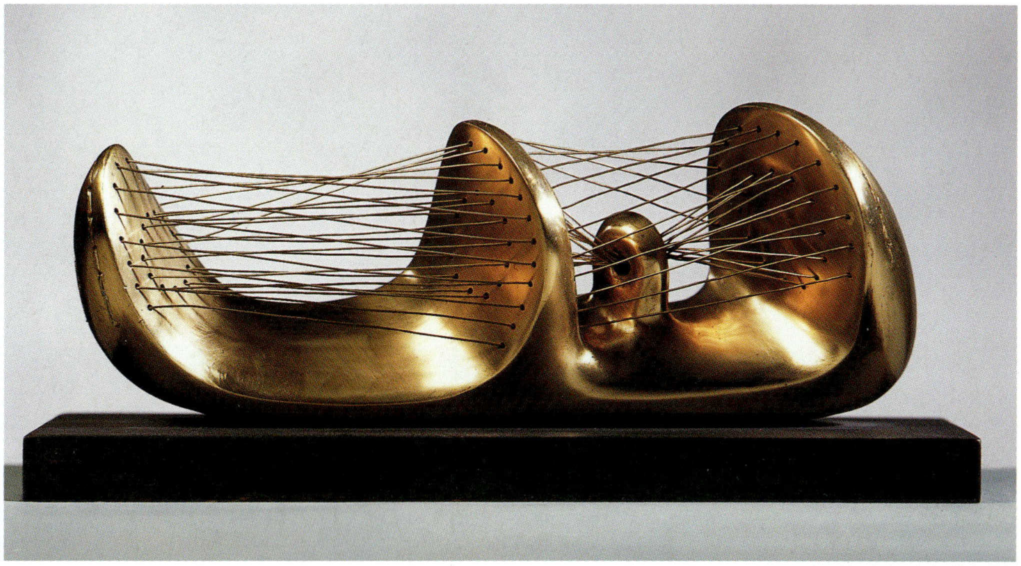

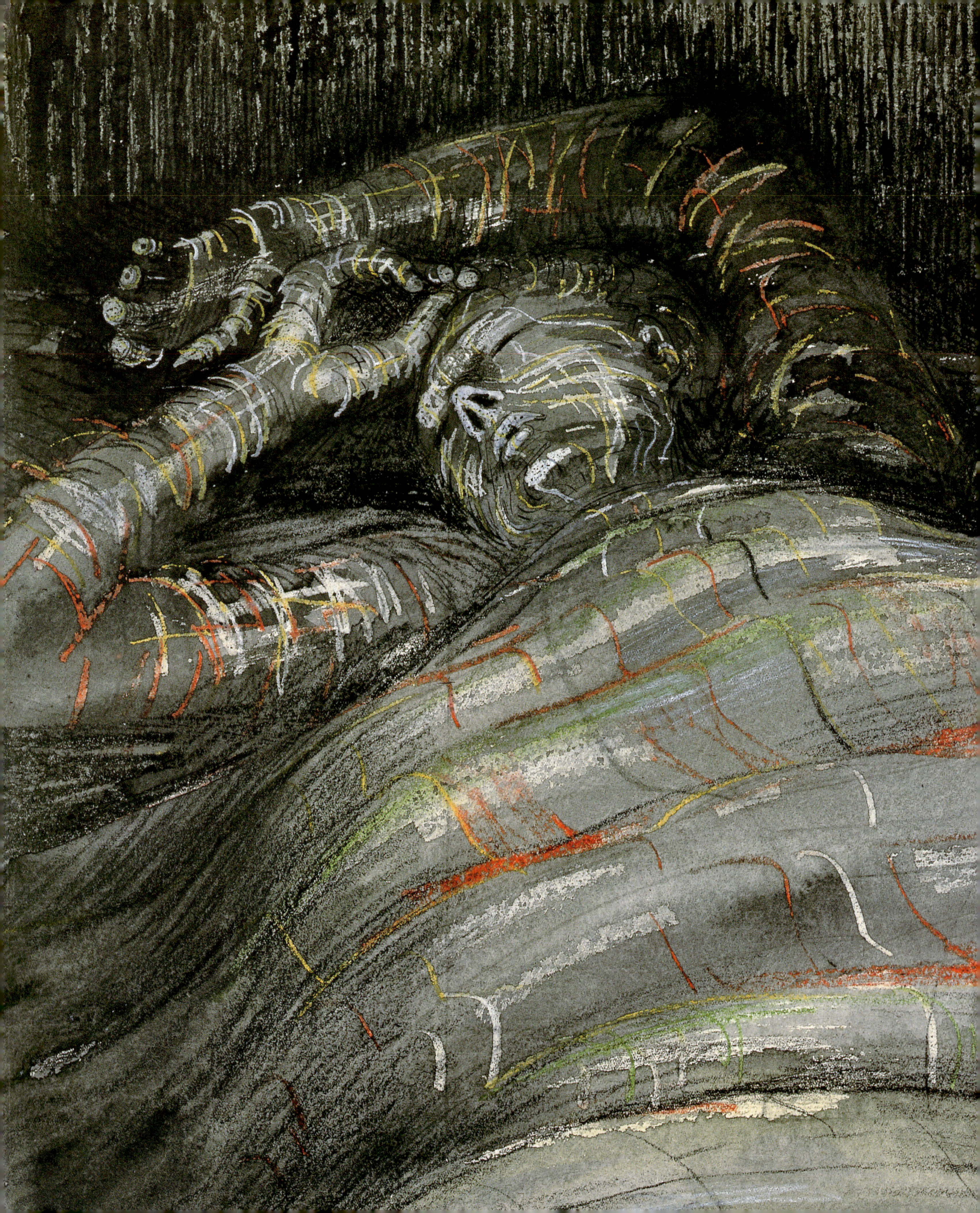

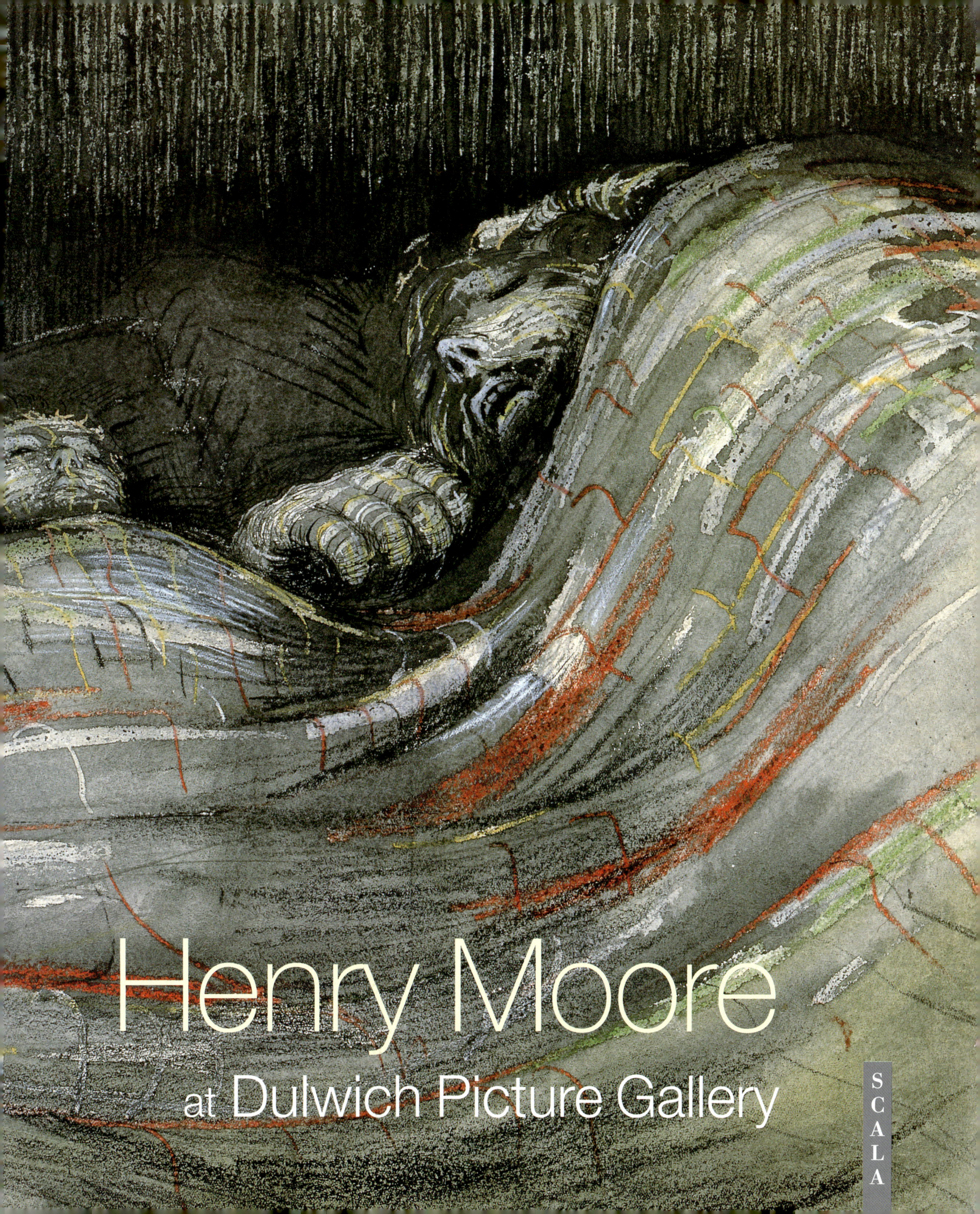

Henry Moore

at Dulwich Picture Gallery

SCALA

Dedicated to the memory of Robert Sainsbury

First published in 2004 by
Scala Publishers Ltd
Northburgh House
10 Northburgh Street
London EC1V 0AT

ISBN 1 85759 352 9

Published on the occasion of the exhibition
Henry Moore at Dulwich Picture Gallery,
12 May–12 September 2004

Edited by Colin Grant
Designed by Nigel Soper
Printed in Italy

Sponsored by Lady Lisa Sainsbury

p. 1: *Reclining Stringed Figure*, 1939 (cat. 26)
Frontispiece: *Sleeping Shelterers: Two Women and a Child* (detail), 1940 (cat. 64)

Note on the dimensions and identification of works

Dimensions of works are as supplied by the lenders. In the catalogue entries dimensions of works on paper are arranged as height x width, and those of the sculpture as height x width (or length) x depth when all three measurements are available. Otherwise individual dimensions are given using the conventional abbreviations.

Henry Moore's works are often numbered using one or more of the following abbreviations:

AG Numbers from the seven-volume catalogue raisonné of drawings edited by Anne Garrould and published by Lund Humphries

CGM Numbers from the four-volume catalogue raisonné of graphics edited by Gérald Cramer, Alistair Grant and David Mitchinson and published by Gérald Cramer

HMF The Henry Moore Foundation drawing archive

LH Numbers from the six-volume catalogue raisonné of sculpture edited by David Sylvester (vol. 1) and Alan Bowness (vols 2–6) and published by Lund Humphries

Contents

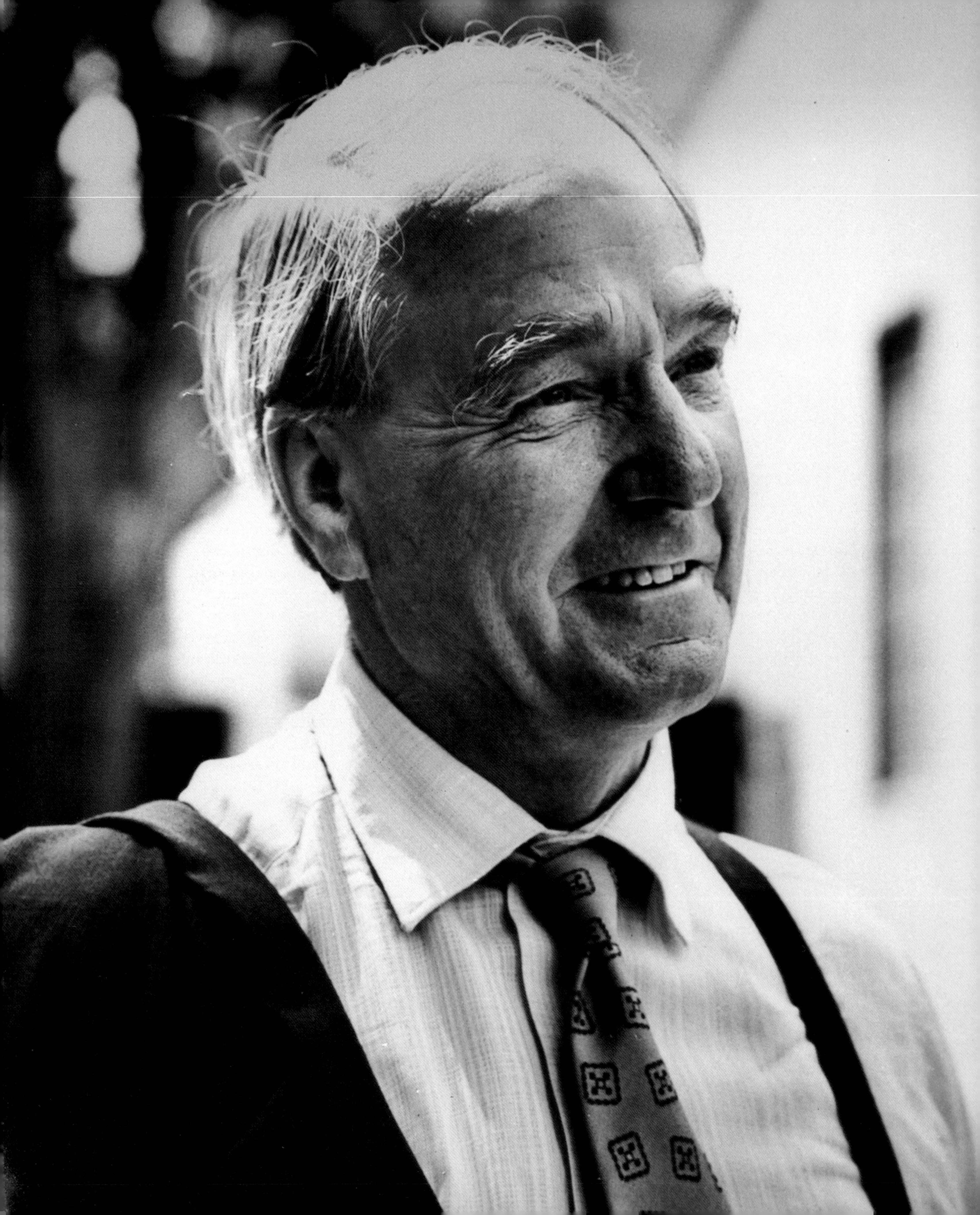

Foreword

Desmond Shawe-Taylor

DIRECTOR, DULWICH PICTURE GALLERY

OF ALL THE EXHIBITIONS that we have mounted at Dulwich Picture Gallery, *Henry Moore* is the most ambitious. From the start we have been very fortunate in the extraordinary support that we have received from all those who agreed with us that a Moore exhibition in London is long overdue. But the one person whose enthusiasm and generosity converted this idea into a reality is Lisa Sainsbury.

Bob and Lisa Sainsbury were friends of Henry Moore and his wife Irina, and their magnificent gift to the nation – the Sainsbury Centre in Norwich – features twenty-two of his greatest works, housed in a famous Norman Foster building. When I first mentioned the project to Lisa she agreed on the spot to lend the entire collection of the Sainsbury Centre in Norwich and to fund the exhibition. She conceived the project as a tribute to Henry Moore and to her husband, who died in 2000; Lisa and Bob's inspired collection forms the core of the show. Lady Sainsbury has been joined in her commitment by her son (and Henry Moore's godson) David, Lord Sainsbury of Turville. Many thanks are due also to David Sainsbury's agent, Christopher Stone, for his role in facilitating the arrangement. It is rare that a gallery can hope for so generous an act of patronage and sponsorship as this.

Nonetheless, the exhibition could have gone no further without the wholehearted support of the current owners of the Sainsbury Collection, the University of East Anglia. Fortunately for us, Nichola Johnson, the Director of the Sainsbury Centre for Visual Arts, graciously agreed to the proposal with characteristic enthusiasm. It was Nichola's suggestion that the exhibition be co-curated by Ian Dejardin of Dulwich and Amanda Geitner of the Sainsbury Centre, who head the collections and exhibitions departments of their respective institutions. They were fortunate indeed to be joined in the planning and research of the show by Ann Garrould, Henry Moore's niece and the editor of the seven-volume catalogue raisonné of his drawings, who also wrote the introductory essay to this book. Our special thanks must go to her for her enthusiasm in what has been a lifetime's involvement with, and championship of, her uncle's work.

Our next debt of gratitude is to The Henry Moore Foundation. At a time when large-scale exhibitions of Moore's work are opening all over the world, our approach to the Foundation as potential lenders could not have come at a more difficult time. Nonetheless, so rich is their collection that they were able to support the show with thirty-five important works, some rarely seen before and all of the finest quality. Our thanks go to Tim Llewellyn, the Director, and the Trustees for this generosity. David Mitchinson, the Head of Collections and Exhibitions, and Anita Feldman Bennet, Curator, could not have been more helpful; and we are most grateful to Anita for her fascinating contribution to the catalogue. Malcolm Woodward, Head Conservator, gave generous advice, particularly with regard to the potentially hair-raising installation of the huge *Large Two Forms* in the grounds, and Emma Stower gave invaluable help with photographic material. The Foundation is also, of course, holder of the copyright in Moore's work, and without their support we simply could not have proceeded. The response of other lenders to our requests for loans was most generous – to all of the lenders to the show we are exceptionally grateful. A special thank you is owed to one of our key lenders, Tate, for a generous change of mind.

At Dulwich Ian Dejardin's commitment to the project has been crucial. To him fell the greatest burden of the work in the early stages, and he is also the author of that part of the catalogue that discusses the various themes of Moore's work. Ian's team in the exhibitions department, Vicky Norton, exhibitions officer, and Eloise Stewart, exhibitions assistant, have provided their usual sterling professional support, while Emma Hazell ably facilitated matters at the Sainsbury Centre.

We have been particularly fortunate in securing the services of George Sexton Associates as designers of the exhibition. The Gallery's exhibition rooms have never looked so extraordinary; and – more importantly – George and his team's sensitivity both to Henry Moore's work and to the integrity of Soane's famous gallery was obvious from the outset. Despite his transatlantic commitments, George's personal input has been inspiring, and we owe a particular vote of thanks to his representative in this country, Joseph Geitner. At Dulwich James Hall brought his own considerable design skills to bear as liaison point for George and his team. The installation of this ambitious project could not have been contemplated without the hard-won expertise of Momart plc – our thanks to them. Finally, many thanks to Scala, publishers of the catalogue, in particular Colin Grant, who managed the project, and the book's designer, Nigel Soper.

Fig. 1
Henry Moore in Berlin on the completion of the casting of *Reclining Figure*, 1963–5 (LH519), destined for the Lincoln Center, New York.

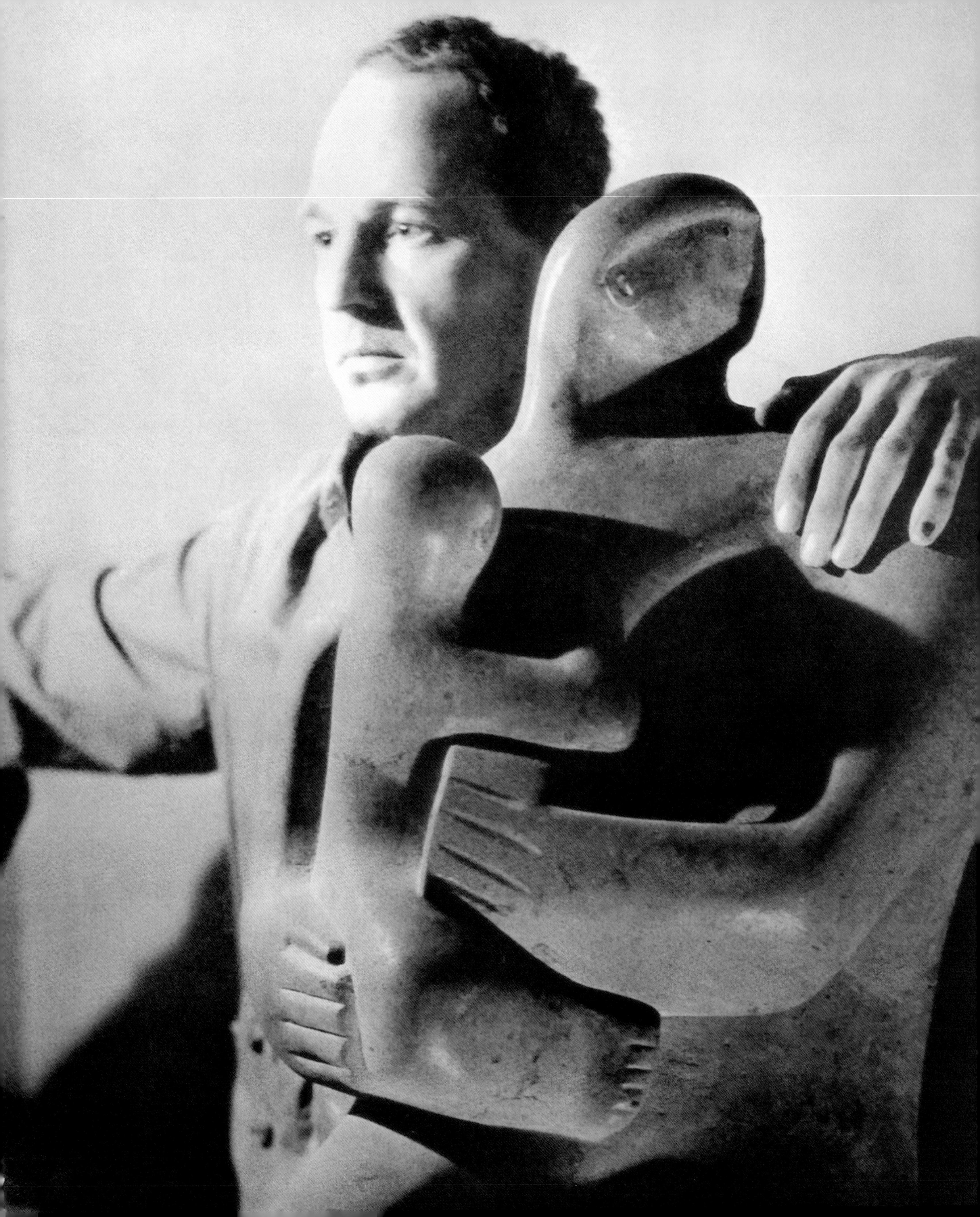

Henry Moore and the Sainsbury Family

Ann Garrould

THIS EXHIBITION CELEBRATES A BOND OF FRIENDSHIP between four people that began in 1933 and was to last for more than half a century. Sadly, only one of those four is still living and so for her the exhibition is both a tribute to and a commemoration of three other lives. Lisa Sainsbury, ninety-two in March 2004, has been the guiding spirit during the preparation of this show, which includes drawings and sculptures hitherto unseen by the general public.

The friendship began when a young man with a passionate interest in modern art went to the Leicester Galleries in London late in 1933. Bob Sainsbury, in a tape-recorded interview with Steven Hooper,[1] recalled going with a friend, the painter and engraver Blair Hughes-Stanton, who introduced him to the sculptor whose work was being exhibited there. Bob and Henry Moore liked each other immediately; their friendship deepened and, when Bob and Lisa's son David was born in 1940, Henry was asked to be his godfather. As the years passed, Henry, conscious of his eight years' seniority in age, began, possibly as early as 1948, addressing Bob as 'my boy', an affectionate form of address he continued to use until his death in 1986. By this time Bob, too, was in his eighties.

In 1933, at the Leicester Galleries, Bob probably mentioned to Henry that he had bought a small sculpture of a baby's head and two drawings by the highly controversial artist Jacob Epstein. Henry would have spoken very warmly of Epstein as the artist who had borne the brunt of the scathing attacks of art critics, thus making life a little easier for those who came immediately after him (Epstein was eighteen years older than Henry). If the conversation turned to Bob's interest in art and his reason for acquiring works by an artist vilified in the press, Henry would have been both impressed and intrigued by Bob's confidence in his own judgement, particularly if Bob had told him that his parents had no interest in modern art and had indeed ridiculed his choice of the Epstein sculpture and drawings. Knowing Henry, I am sure it was not long before he suggested to Bob that he should go to the British Museum to see the collection of ethnographic art, a collection Henry had studied and sketched in his student days (1921–4) at the Royal College of Art.

Bob bought Henry's *Mother and Child* (fig. 2, cat. 8), carved out of Green Hornton stone in 1932, from the Leicester Galleries. On his way home to his flat in Westmoreland Street, Bob panicked, thinking that he had bought a sculpture too large to go through his front door. Considering it more calmly, he realized that it would be perfectly possible to turn the figure through ninety degrees and carry it through on its back.

Once placed in the Westmoreland Street flat, not only his parents but also many of Bob's friends regarded the sculpture 'with about as much ridicule as Epstein's figures … and as subsequent purchases of primitive art'. That ridicule went on when the sculpture was in 'the hall at our house in Smith Square'.[2] Bob was a young businessman; he had trained as an accountant, not as an art historian. How could he know, his friends and parents asked, what was good or bad in contemporary art? His parents did not visit art galleries or museums. At Cambridge Bob had never once visited the Fitzwilliam Museum, a few yards down the road from his own college. Why was he wasting money on what the art critics had derided as 'monstrosities'?

Bob encountered similar criticism of his taste by his father-in-law. Talking to Steven

Fig. 2
Henry Moore with *Mother and Child* (cat. 8), now in the Robert and Lisa Sainsbury Collection, University of East Anglia.

Hooper in 1996, Lisa describes her father's visit to Smith Square and his reaction, 'I mean when he saw the Henry Moore *Mother and Child* in the hall he thought this was the absolute end.' Lisa's father was mollified when he discovered that Bob had made a catalogue of his own acquisitions: 'You've got a catalogue, the sort of thing businessmen don't have?'[3]

In contrast to Bob's non-existent art education, Lisa told Steven Hooper that her 'father had taken art education extremely seriously … we had been dragged round every famous museum in the world … we were told what we must like and what we mustn't like … I saw a lot of art and really rebelled against it.' Lisa had moved from Geneva to Paris with her parents in 1920 or 1921. They lived near the Boulevard Montparnasse, so Lisa attended the nearby École Alsacienne, walking to school daily. On her way there she looked in the windows of 'every little art shop and Afro art shop as one does at that age' (Lisa was eight or nine at this time). What also excited her were the galleries showing 'Picasso and so on … and of course Modigliani at that stage was selling his drawings just around the corner. So one lived in that sort of [world] … of course Father thought it was rubbish.' Lisa, however, had discovered art that delighted her.

Despite being second cousins, Lisa Van den Bergh and Bob Sainsbury did not meet until early 1933. Their first encounter was at a charity ball arranged to raise funds for the Princess Beatrice Hospital in London, a particular interest of Bob's mother. At this time Lisa was living in Kensington Palace Gardens with her great-uncle Henry. After the ball Bob invited Lisa to dinner. Talking to Lisa in the summer of 2003, she told me she believed the charity ball was close in date to her twenty-first birthday on 3 March 1933. Clearly she and Bob quickly discovered their mutual interest in art because she said that, although memory can play tricks seventy years after the event, she thinks she was with Bob when he actually bought the *Mother and Child* carving from Henry. What had stayed in Lisa's memory is the fact that after the sale Henry commented that the price (£158) Bob paid for the sculpture was equivalent to approximately half Henry's annual salary at Chelsea School of Art.

In 1933 Henry still came into the category of 'struggling young artist'. He had arrived in London in September 1921 with a scholarship (actually called a Royal Exhibition) of £90 per annum.[4] Out of that he had to pay for lodgings and breakfast – finnan haddock every morning – his bus fares and books. He rarely got home to see his parents and younger siblings while they were still in Yorkshire. When his father fell dangerously ill in the summer of 1922 and was advised to move away from the industrial North, my mother (fig. 3), as the eldest unmarried daughter, took it upon herself to move her parents to Wighton in Norfolk. My grandfather died five or six weeks after the move south and is buried in Wighton churchyard. My grandmother (fig. 4) continued to live with my mother so Henry would come to Norfolk during his college vacations. My mother's snapshots, taken with an old 'box-Brownie' camera, of Henry carving in the Wighton garden in 1922 or 1923 still exist. After my mother married in 1925, my six-foot-tall father used to pass on his old trousers to his new brother-in-law, four inches shorter than he, so that Henry would not cover his own trousers with stone dust. My father also remembered Henry taking back empty beer bottles (two pence each) in order to be able to buy full ones. Life was certainly not easy for a sculptor who had chosen to follow modern trends in art.

When my parents moved to Colchester in 1926, Henry's visits became more frequent. Three sitters were available to him – my mother (cat. 76),[5] my father and my grandmother (fig. 5). The stone mask carved in 1927 (cat. 5)[6] with its long straight nose and ears set close to the head is effectively a portrait of my father. In their early years many artists

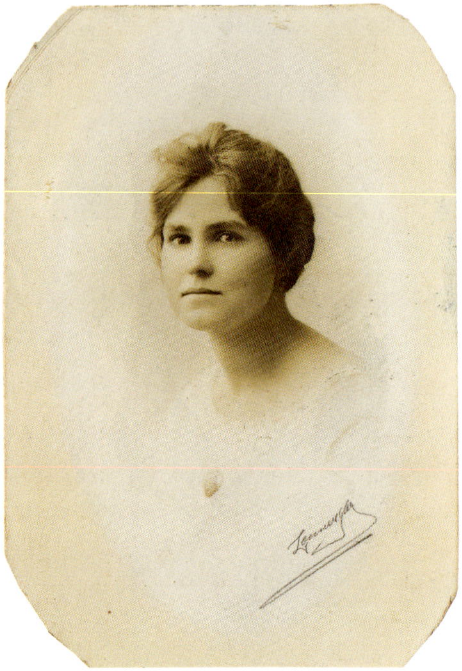

Fig. 3 (above)
Mary Garrould,
the artist's sister.

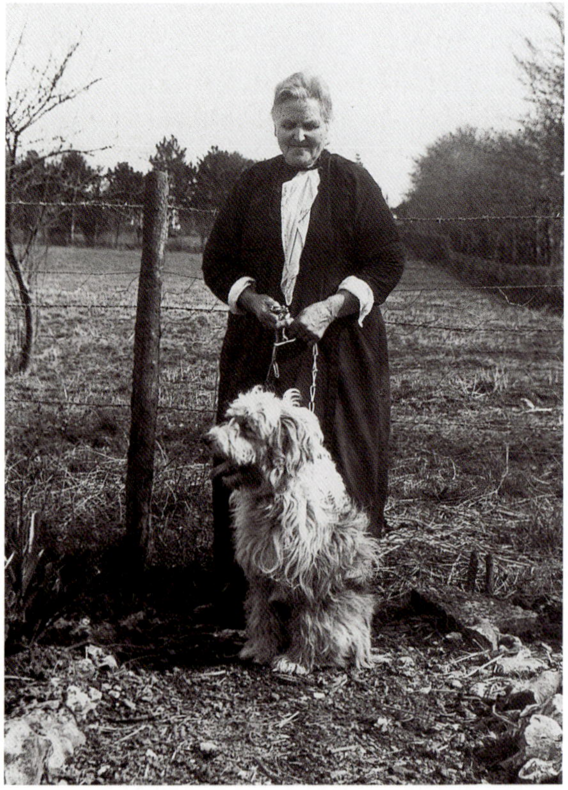

Fig. 4 (left)
Mrs Mary Moore,
the artist's mother,
with her dog Pongo.

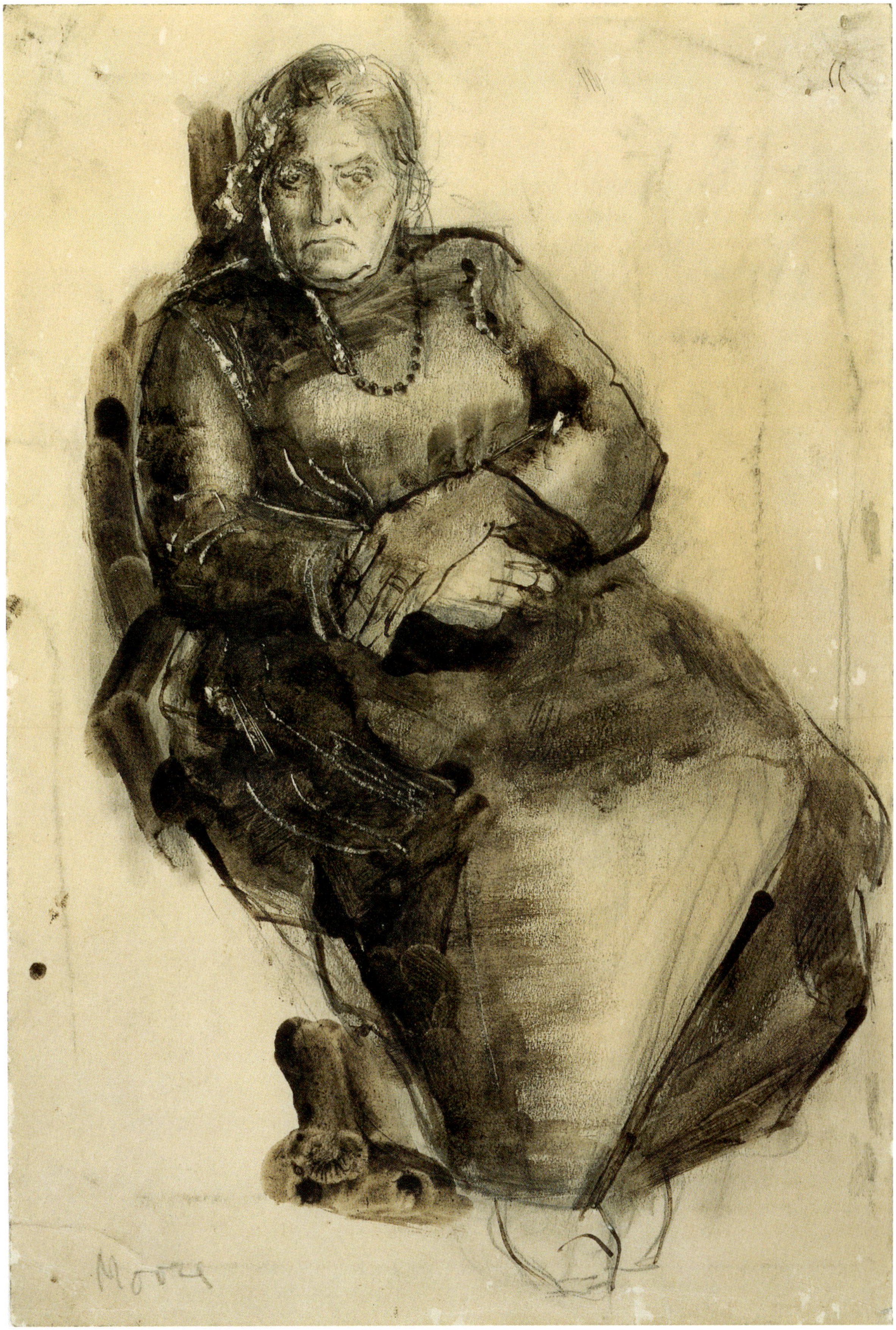

Fig. 5 (right)
The Artist's Mother, 1927
(AG 27.3), pencil (rubbed),
pen and ink;
The Henry Moore
Foundation: gift of Mary
Moore Danowski 1979.

appreciated the willingness of family members to pose for them – Rembrandt had Saskia and Hendrickje, Cézanne his father, and Manet and Monet their wives.

Henry married Irina Radetsky in July 1929; within days she was posing for him, at first rather shyly, clad in a petticoat (cat. 78), but in 1935 in the nude (cat. 88). Irina was born in Kiev on 26 March 1907 to a Russian father and a mother who was mainly Russian but with Polish ancestors. As a small child, I can remember being very impressed by an aunt who spoke Russian, Polish, French and English – she retained an endearing Russian accent to the end of her life, pronouncing 'with' as 'wiz'. Shortly after Irina's birth her parents moved north, living in Moscow and St Petersburg and spending the summers in fashionable resorts such as Yalta. When Irina's father disappeared during the 1917 revolution, her mother dispatched her ten-year-old daughter to Kiev to live with her grandmother. Irina's mother was evacuated with other White Russians, eventually ending up in Paris where she married a British army officer, Norman Bult-Francis. By this time Irina's grandmother had died in Kiev, and Irina was being cared for by a teacher of deaf and dumb children. When the teacher deemed it safe to return to Moscow, she set out on an arduous journey across Russia, with Irina, probably eleven years old at this stage, helping her to care for the children. In Moscow the Polish Embassy managed to trace Irina and she was smuggled out of Russia on a Polish passport. Once in Paris, Irina attended a French school until she was fifteen or sixteen when her mother and Bult-Francis decided to send her to live with his parents in their large house in Buckinghamshire. They frequently entertained their 'real' grandchildren, so Irina, as a step-grandchild, often felt excluded, especially since her childhood had been so different from those of the other children.

Irina spoke very rarely of her early life, even to Henry. After he died, she told me of some events of the journey from Kiev to Moscow and also of other happier memories. As I listened, I found it intensely moving that a child not yet in her teens had experienced the loss of her father, separation from her mother and total uncertainty about her own future. Very few people got to know Irina really well. Fearful of being hurt yet again, she built a well nigh impenetrable wall around herself. I shall always remember her fierce sense of independence, her very perceptive judgement of character and her gentle sense of humour.

In the autumn of 1926 Irina enrolled as a student-painter at the Royal College of Art where Henry had been teaching in the Sculpture School since 1924. However, they did not meet until the autumn term of 1928 when Henry saw her and decided to ask her to a college dance. He also invited her to go and watch him carving his first public commission on the facade of the London Transport Headquarters at 55 Broadway, close to St James's Park; Irina remembered being very impressed seeing Henry carving while standing on high scaffolding but what impressed her more was the bitterly cold weather – she thought she had not been so cold since leaving Russia.

By 1929 Bob Sainsbury had already become a collector. While he was at Cambridge (1924–7), he had begun collecting private press books. College vacations were often spent with his parents in their central London flat. His mother enjoyed going to horse races where she would put a small sum of money on a horse. One day she remarked that she had been given a wonderful tip and asked whether Bob would also like to put a bet on the horse. As Bob said, 'solely to please my mother I said, "yes". The horse came home at 20 to 1 and I (now) had five pounds.'[7] He spent the money on what would become a treasured possession – a remaindered copy of Flaubert's *Three Tales*, seen in a bookseller's window. After graduating in history, Bob studied accountancy; as the grandson of the founder (in

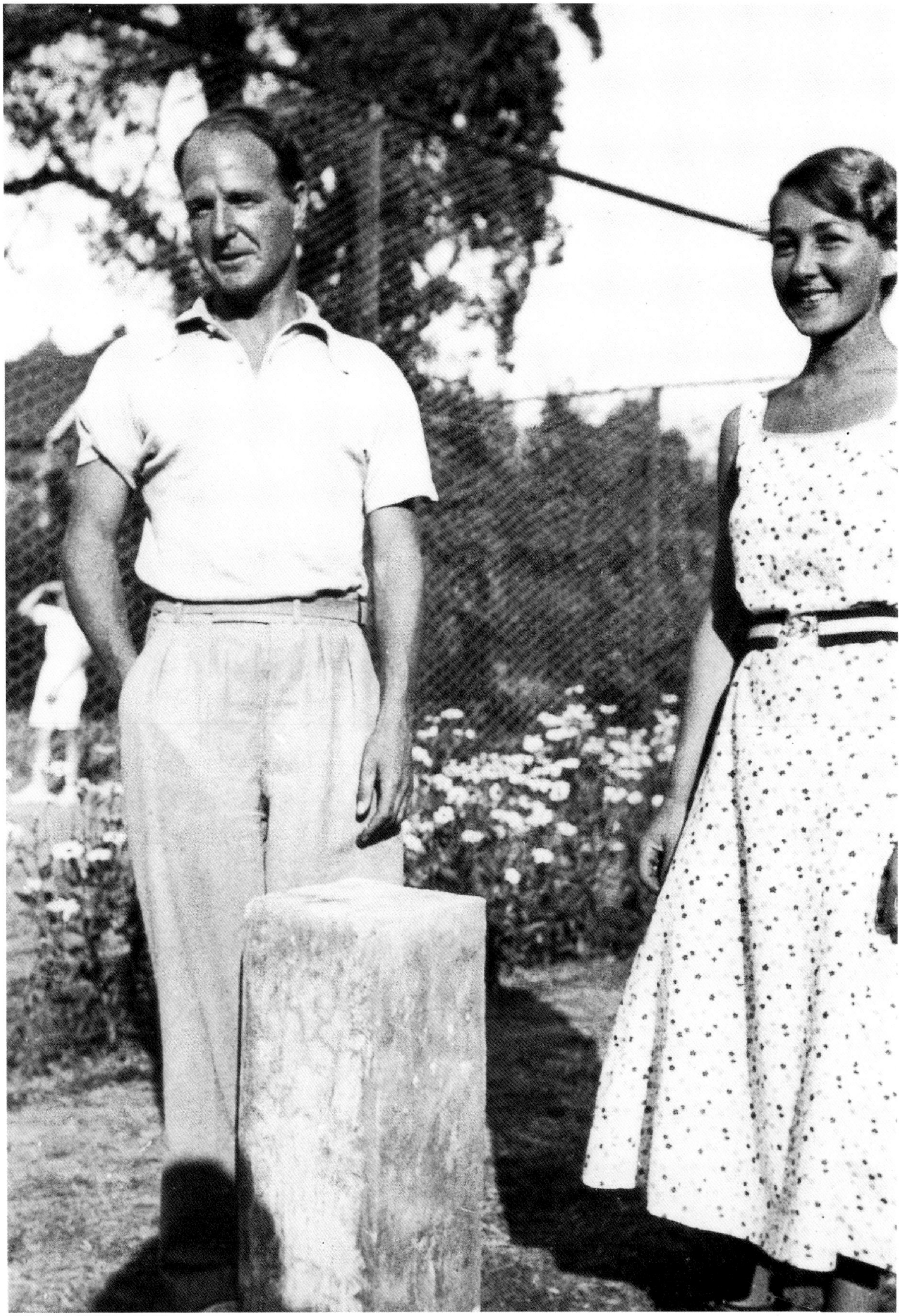

Fig. 6
Henry and Irina Moore
at The Glack, near Deal,
Kent, 1931.

1869) of the Sainsbury company, he would join the company in 1930. His interest in collecting fine books continued and he used to go on Saturday afternoons (his only time off) to Zwemmer's, the bookshop and art gallery. In about 1931 Bob made his first purchases of modern art – the sculpture and two drawings by Epstein already mentioned. Around the same time he met Blair Hughes-Stanton, the artist who introduced him to Henry Moore and also became co-founder with Bob of the Gemini Press. It was Bob's first venture into another aspect of his interest in the arts; he financed the venture, leaving the technical side to Hughes-Stanton. Bob later told Steven Hooper:

> I helped create something. That is the significance of it ... Lisa and I have never handed things over to people and just taken the consequences. We always have tried to work with them and I worked with Blair – he did all the technical side and had the ideas but I was free to criticise.[8]

As Hooper himself says, this experiment 'established a pattern of critical and productive patronage which (Bob) and Lisa have continued to the present'.[9] They have always been 'hands on' patrons, as much with their chosen architect as with their garden designers.

Besides buying Henry's *Mother and Child* in 1933, Bob also acquired a drawing by Henri Gaudier-Brzeska, a painting by Matthew Smith and, perhaps more importantly, four pieces of Chinese porcelain of the Tang dynasty – the first non-European, non-modern works in his and Lisa's collection. Bob always insisted that he bought works of art because he liked them, just as he had liked the small seashells he had collected during his school holidays on the east coast of England. When he bought his first two examples of African art in 1935, he said: 'I knew nothing about African art. I had never seen it consciously before. I didn't appreciate it, I didn't understand it or know anything about it. I straightforward liked it in sensual terms.'[10] Liking a sculpture, a piece of porcelain, a drawing, acquiring it and possessing it and thus being able to study it, hold it whenever one wished, have been the guiding principles of Bob and Lisa's choice of acquisitions.

In 1935 Bob and Lisa acquired a *Reclining Figure* (cat. 22) carved by Henry from an ironstone pebble he had picked up on the beach at Sizewell in Suffolk. This was one of seven sculptures he carved out of ironstone, which proved over the years to be very friable, breaking apart in flakes if touched. In 1962 Henry asked Bob if he and Lisa would allow the reclining figure to be cast in bronze before the small carving was irreparably damaged. They agreed and so two casts were made, one for them (cat. 23) and one for Irina.

The following November (1936) Henry had a one-man exhibition at the Leicester Galleries in London. Among the nineteen sculptures and sixteen drawings shown was a sculpture called *Square Form* (cat. 42), which Henry had carved earlier in the year. Arguing that the *Square Form* seemed to have little to do with the human form, critics have always regarded this work as belonging to his 'abstract period' (a phrase Henry disliked). Between 1933 and 1935 Henry had been one of the leading members of Unit One, a group of avant-garde sculptors, painters and architects. In a statement written for Unit One in 1934, Henry explained that his intention was:

> to combine as intensely as possible the abstract principles of sculpture along with the realisation of my idea. All art is an abstraction to some degree: in sculpture the material forces one away from pure representation and towards abstraction. Abstract qualities of design are essential to the value of a work but

to me of equal importance is the psychological human element.

Bob and Lisa bought *Square Form* in 1936.

Apropos of the titles Henry gave his works – *Seated Nude*, *Mother and Child*, *Reclining Figure*, *Square Form* – I asked him many years ago why he chose such simple descriptions for his sculptures and drawings. His reply was

> All art should have a certain mystery and should make demands on the spectator. Giving a sculpture or a drawing too explicit a title takes away part of that mystery so that the spectator moves on to the next object, making no effort to ponder the meaning of what he has just seen. Everyone thinks that he or she looks but they don't really, you know.

In her conversation with Steven Hooper in 1996 Lisa complained about 'being dragged round every famous museum in the world … made worse by the fact that my father approached [art] in a completely […] … he didn't look but he knew what one should like and what one shouldn't like … He went by the labels.'

Bob and Lisa got married on Lisa's twenty-fifth birthday, 3 March 1937. They chose their mutual wedding present together – Modigliani's *Portrait of Baranowsk*i, painted in 1918. They had chosen, together of course, the present given to them by Bob's elder brother Alan – an oil painting by Pierre Bonnard of a scene that would have been very familiar to Lisa, *Paris: Les Grands Boulevards*, executed in 1898. Steven Hooper's introduction to the Robert and Lisa Sainsbury Collection summarizes the situation perfectly: 'Coming from opposite ends of the art spectrum, they both developed a passion for what was, at that time, the unconventional in art and each broadened the horizons of the other.'[11] Bob always said that Lisa introduced him to Paris, her home city: 'The Rue de Seine was as natural to her as the Charing Cross Road was to me … We had developed a rapport in matters of art by the time we got married and, therefore, the whole of our married life we have been together in the collection.' Lisa added, 'If you look at the collection there are two very strong approaches. I mean, Bob is much more interested in sculpture. I think if the collection hadn't been affected by me it would be all sculpture and drawings and I've always had a passion for colour. But we meet in the middle.'[12]

Shortly after their marriage Bob and Lisa moved into the house that was to be their home for the next fifty-eight years. The five floors of a Georgian house in Smith Square, Westminster, provided them with infinitely more space than Bob's former flat in Westmoreland Street; one senses that they both enjoyed the re-hanging and re-siting of works of art. Henry's *Mother and Child* was placed in the curve of the stairwell in the hall and remained there, apart from loans to various exhibitions, until it went to the Sainsbury Centre for the Visual Arts at the University of East Anglia, which opened in 1978.

Lisa and Bob continued acquiring works of art: a Renoir bought in 1937 out of a small legacy to Lisa; a Degas *Little Dancer* purchased in 1938 together with another Tang figure; Oceanic pieces bought in 1939 from a dealer in Paris, from whom they also bought a small Picasso drawing *Head of a Woman*, hesitating to do so while in Paris but changing their minds on their return to England. The Paris dealer sent it to them in an unregistered envelope. They also commissioned a portrait of Lisa from Jacob Epstein in the same year. One day, while Lisa was sitting for her portrait, Epstein showed her a letter he had received in his mail that morning; it was a demand from Sainsbury's threatening to stop his credit unless he paid his bill. Epstein never knew that, from that day on, Bob personally guaranteed his credit. As an accountant, Bob also tried to advise Epstein on the control of his finances. He met with scant success – Epstein signed documents before asking Bob about the wisdom of so doing. As a result, Bob loaned him a sum of money.

The Second World War broke out on 3 September 1939. Bob and Lisa already had a daughter, Elizabeth, born the previous year; Lisa had gone back to work as an almoner at St Thomas's Hospital south of the Thames. When she became pregnant with their second child, it was clear that there could be complications with the birth so she and Elizabeth went to Toronto since Hitler had started his blitz on London in September 1940. After David's birth in October that year, Lisa returned to London leaving both children in Canada. For the rest of the war she worked at St Thomas's. Bob, as the only director available to visit shops that had been bombed, was often called out at night. Their own home in Smith Square, uncomfortably close to the Houses of Parliament – a prime target for German bombers – suffered bomb damage. Lisa says she and Bob moved eleven times during the war.

None of these inconveniences stopped them acquiring more art. However, it was decided to store drawings and paintings outside London. The drawings went to Bob's parents' house and were put in a cupboard. Fortunately, Bob and Lisa decided to visit them one day and Bob started to look at his drawings. All was well until he reached the Picasso *Head* at the bottom of the pile; this 'had come out in yellow spots', to quote Bob. The foxing was removed by a skilled restorer. The paintings and drawings were taken from the damp cupboard to drier storage in Oxford, but they had to be moved elsewhere when the Germans started bombing Oxford.

Two drawings by Henry were probably in the same cupboard, since they had been acquired in 1939. One is of the twenty-two-year-old Irina seated in a Windsor chair (cat. 78) in the flat in Parkhill Road, Belsize Park, to which she and Henry had returned after their honeymoon. The Windsor chair remained in the Moore household for many years, moving first to Kent where I can clearly remember it in their cottage, Burcroft, and then to the sun room in Hoglands, Hertfordshire, where it still was in 1986 when Henry died. Irina had the ability to sit motionless for what, at least to me as a child, seemed unconscionably long periods. She radiated a sense of tranquillity, of serenity.

The second drawing, also of Irina (cat. 88), dates from 1935, the last year in which she posed nude for Henry (later sketches always show her fully clothed). If Henry's memory is to be trusted, this sketch was also done in the Parkhill Road flat, which consisted of a ground-floor studio full of carvings, a bathroom and two small rooms on the first floor. The dimensions of the room dictated the close viewpoint.

In 1940 Bob and Lisa bought two more of his drawings. One was *Sculptural Object in a Landscape* (cat. 38), a major drawing done in the summer of 1939, a few months before war broke out. This drawing was developed from a tiny sketch, one of thirteen on a single sheet of paper. Henry always wanted his over-lifesize sculptures to be placed outdoors and seen against nature. Early in the 1930s he had decided to keep photographic records of his sculpture. One photograph, reproduced in the fifth edition (1988) of Lund Humphries' *Henry Moore: Complete Sculptures*, volume I, was of a 13in/33cm-long maquette of a reclining figure he had done in 1938 (fig. 7). This he placed on a base out in his Kent garden in front of the landscape with its distant trees and hedges. By moving the camera very close to the maquette, Henry achieved a photograph of what seemed to be a monumental reclining figure set in a landscape devoid of human beings

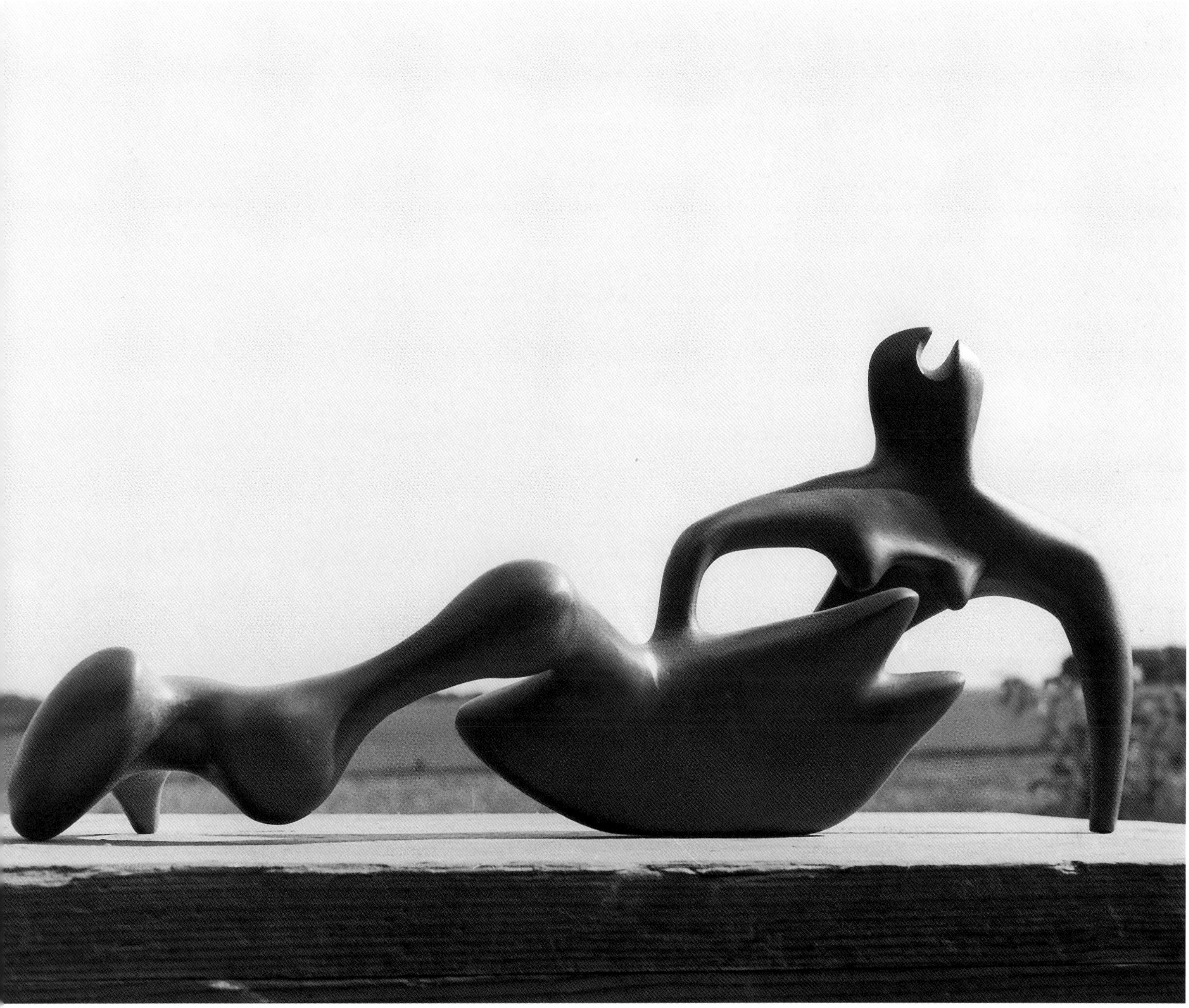

Fig. 7
Reclining Figure, 1938 (LH192), lead; Museum of Modern Art, New York: purchased 1939.

and their habitations. Comparison of the angle of the hedge in the background of Bob and Lisa's drawing with that in the photograph taken by Henry in 1938 persuades me that, when he did the drawing, Henry was sitting very close to the spot from which he had taken the photograph in the previous year. The second drawing acquired was *Reclining Figures for Metal Sculpture* (cat. 27) in subdued grey-blues and sand colour.

When war was declared Henry, at forty-one, was too old to fight again for his country. He dared not start any new carvings, not knowing what the future might hold. The area of Kent where he lived was designated a restricted area, making travelling difficult, and he and Irina realized they would probably have to move further inland. Henry turned to drawing, recording hundreds of ideas for sculptures. Besides the *Reclining Figures for*

Metal Sculpture mentioned above, Bob and Lisa also bought *Standing Figures: Studies for Sculpture* (cat. 96), drawn perhaps when Henry was in a less despondent mood, given its cobalt blue and bright reds. It is a page from a drawing book or sketch pad that Henry took apart in order to sell individual drawings. The book or pad was probably first used in 1939 and then laid aside before being taken up again in 1940; Henry often did this.

The following year, 1941, Henry's *Group of Shelterers* (cat. 63) entered the Sainsbury Collection. This drawing is based on a much smaller sketch in the First Shelter Sketchbook; it is the central section of page 29 in that book (fig. 8).

In 1942 Lisa and Bob bought a sculpture and a drawing by Henry. The sculpture was *Half Figure No. 2* of 1929 (cat. 81) in concrete. Henry wrote of his experiments using concrete as a medium for sculpture between 1926 and 1934: 'In their material they are experiments I tried … in concrete – of special mixtures and colour – reinforced and built up first and then carved finally like any stone.' When he first began to use concrete in 1926, Henry was living in London on what he earned for teaching two days a week at the Royal College of Art. He needed to eat; he needed to pay rent for his flat; money, or more accurately, the lack of it, was a problem. Marble cost money. Henry used to go to quarries and buy or, better still, be given small offcuts of stone. This of course accounted for the small size of many of his early carvings. Concrete cost much less. His earliest venture in concrete in July 1926, the 5in (12.7cm)-high *Baby's Head*, was done for his sister Betty. The unwitting model was her not quite three-months-old daughter. By 1929, the date of the Sainsbury *Half Figure*, Henry was more confident of his ability to work in concrete – the sculpture is over 17in (39cm) high. In all, there are twenty-one sculptures in concrete.

The drawing Lisa and Bob bought in 1942 was *Sleeping Shelterers: Two Women and a Child* (cat. 64; entitled *Shelter Sleepers* in the catalogue raisonné). As with *Group of Shelterers* (AG 40.89), this drawing was also based on a smaller sketch from the Second Shelter Sketchbook (cat. 60) probably executed late in 1940. Unable to work on sculpture since December 1939, Henry relied totally on the sale of his drawings in 1940 and 1941, enlarging several sketches from the two small (208 x 165mm) Shelter Sketchbooks. The large finished drawings were then placed in the hands of London dealers.

As Henry began to lose interest in sketching shelterers in more orderly surroundings (for instance, bunk beds were installed, doing away with haphazard groups of men, women and children huddled in overcoats or blankets trying to sleep on the bare platforms), Herbert Read suggested to Henry that he might draw members of Britain's underground army – the miners. Henry was officially commissioned to do a series of drawings by the War Artists' Advisory Committee. These he did just before and just after Christmas 1941. The Sainsbury Collection *Miner Drilling (Miner with Lamp)* (cat. 67; entitled *Miner Drilling in Drift* in the catalogue raisonné) is a splendid enlargement of one of the smaller sketches done a mile underground in the Wheldale Colliery in Yorkshire. Henry commented afterwards that if he were to describe what hell might be like, his memory of standing at the coal-face deafened by the noise of the coal-cutting machine and covered by thick black coal dust would be a very adequate description.

Over the years Bob and Lisa bought four other drawings by Henry. One was the *Shelter Drawing* (cat. 66), which in the Sainsbury Collection bears the title *Shelter Drawing (Mother and Child with Reclining Figures)*. *Odysseus in the Cave of the Naiads* (cat. 72) is an enlargement of a preliminary sketch for illustrations to *The Rescue* by Edward Sackville-West. The last two drawings that Bob and Lisa acquired have very personal connotations. The *Family Group* (cat. 19) is one of many studies for possible sculpture for schools in

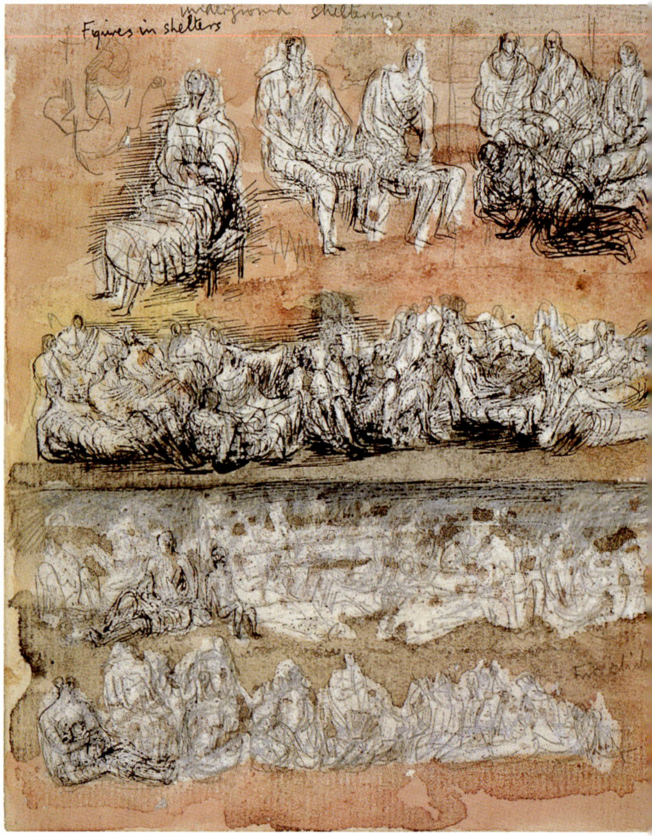

Fig. 8
Figures in Shelters (First Shelter Sketchbook, p.29), 1940–41 (AG 40-41.29), pencil, wax crayon, watercolour wash, pen and ink; The British Museum, London: bequest of Jane Clark.

Impington and Stevenage, both near Henry's home in Hertfordshire. This is true from an art-historical point of view; for Henry's closest relatives, it is also a deep-felt expression of his yearning for a living family group of his own. Irina had suffered two or three miscarriages in the early part of the war, one brought on by helping Henry push their car out of a ditch into which he had driven during the blackout. Each time Henry asked my mother to go over to Hoglands to look after her. In the drawing *Two Women Seated at a Table* (cat. 89) the figures are based on Henry's memory of my mother knitting and Irina looking at a book. Bob and Lisa bought this drawing directly from Henry, who had been shocked when they told him of the prices for similar drawings being charged by the London art-dealers.

This drawing and *Odysseus in the Cave of the Naiads* were two of the early acquisitions made out of the Art Account that Bob and Lisa set up in 1946, initially limiting themselves to spend no more that £1,000 per annum on works of art. In 1953 they doubled the limit and in 1957 it was increased to £3,000. Later, Bob was to justify the limit he and Lisa had chosen to impose upon themselves in the post-war years, saying that he had 'absolutely no regrets about the Art Account and the limitations it put on the collection'.[13] In 1958 Lisa persuaded her accountant husband to remove the limit on what they might spend on art. Bob agreed, since their finances were secure, and at fifty-two he 'was hardly a young man'.[14] Although the 6in (15.5cm)-high *Madonna and Child* (cat. 12) bronze, cast from the definitive maquette for the *Madonna and Child* in St Matthew's Church, Northampton (fig. 9), and the 1946–7 *Reclining Figure* (cat. 28) were bought when the limitations of the Art Account were still in place, the last two purchases of sculpture by Henry, in 1960 and 1962, fell outside the £3,000 limit imposed in 1957.

Bob and Lisa had acquired the bronze *Madonna and Child* in 1945 when their son David was still a small child. One wonders whether his familiarity with this sculpture was a reason for his choice, at the age of thirteen, of a drawing of the same subject (cat. 13). Henry sometimes gave his godson drawings as birthday presents and on one occasion David recalls going alone to Henry's house to choose one. Henry was in the sitting room with several cardboard boxes by his chair. He selected drawings from each of the boxes, laid them out on the floor and invited David to make his choice. When David had decided which drawing he would like, Henry wrote on it, 'To David, October 24th, 1953'. David says, 'I went home clutching the drawing to myself.' This drawing and four others, also gifts from Henry, are shown in public for the first time at this exhibition.

David remembers Henry as a great communicator with people of all ages from the very young to the very old. One of David's childhood memories is of Henry urging him to run his hand up and down the back of the *Mother and Child* that stood in the curve of the staircase of his parents' house in Smith Square. Another is of Henry enthusing about various artefacts in the African section of the British Museum and in particular about the tactile qualities of a carved stool. Enjoying the company of children as much as he did, Henry would have listened gravely and answered all David's questions, taking great care not to talk down to him.

From the mid-1930s Bob and Lisa's circle of friends included many people who also knew Henry and Irina. Among them were Kenneth Clark, appointed in 1933 as the youngest Director of the National Gallery, with his beautiful wife Jane; Kenneth's successor at the National Gallery, Philip Hendy, and his wife Cicely who became one of Lisa's great friends; Barbara Hepworth and Ben Nicholson; Jacob Epstein; Lee Miller the photographer and Roland Penrose, artist, collector and writer on art; the Russian-born Véra Russell and her art-critic husband John, who would always write very favourably of Henry's exhibitions;

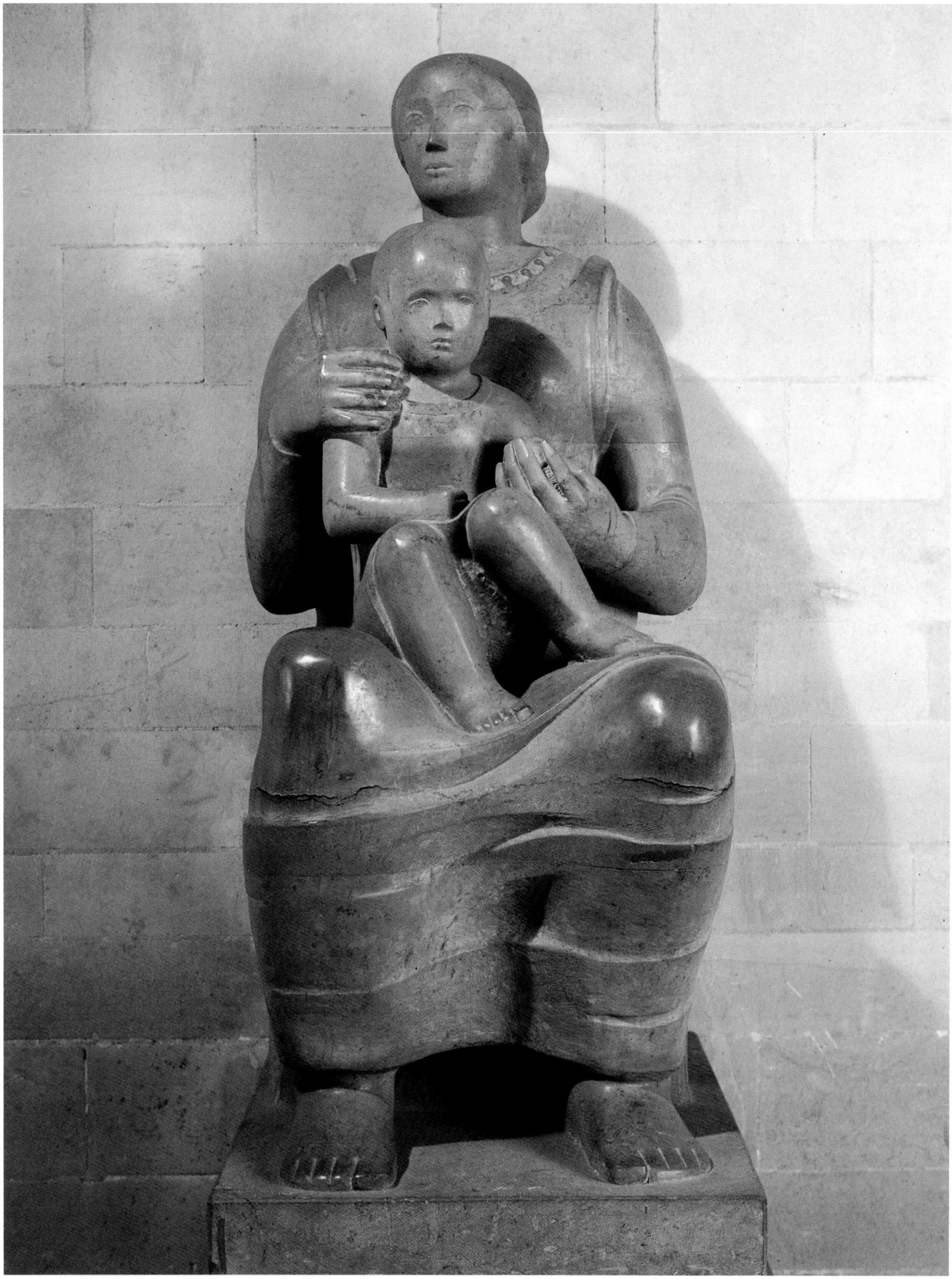

Fig. 9 (left)
Madonna and Child,
1943–4 (LH 226),
Brown Hornton stone;
St Matthew's Church
Northampton (donor:
Canon J. Rowden Hussey).

David Sylvester, another art critic; and Graham Sutherland and his wife Kathleen. Lisa cannot, after almost sixty years, be certain whether she met other friends of Henry and Irina – Stephen Spender and his wife Natasha, for example. She is fairly sure that she and Bob did not meet W.H. Auden, whose poems Henry would later illustrate. As she said to me in summer 2003, 'We weren't really part of the literary circle.'

Naturally, the Sainsburys met many art dealers. One with whom they became particularly friendly in about 1938 was Erica Brausen at the Storran Gallery in London. From her they acquired Chaim Soutine's oil painting of 1931, *Lady in Blue*, formerly in the collection of Paul Guillaume. Lisa had wanted to buy two other Soutine paintings in the 1939 exhibition but was told by Bob that they could not afford them. However, the meeting with Erica Brausen was to have a very fortunate outcome, for when she moved to the Hanover Gallery, she introduced Bob and Lisa to an impoverished young artist whom the gallery had decided to represent. His name was Francis Bacon; in 1955 Lisa and Bob became his patrons. In his introductory remarks on Bacon in volume 1 of the *Robert and Lisa Sainsbury Collection* Graham Beal commented:

> They consistently acquired paintings, supplied financial help and Lisa commissioned a portrait of her husband. Lisa herself was asked by the artist to sit as a model. With one exception all the works in the Collection date from between 1952 and 1960 and as a group these twelve paintings present a coherent picture of the artist's development during this critical period.[15]

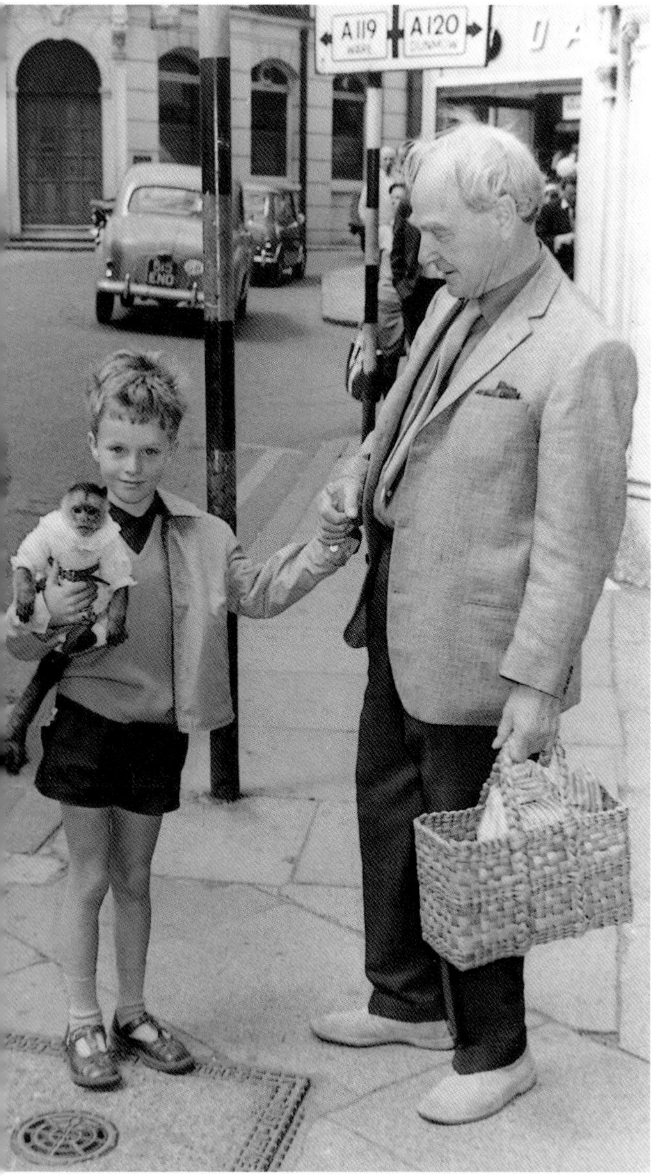

Fig. 10
Henry Moore and his
great-nephew Charles
with a monkey.

The portrait of Bob that Lisa had commissioned was paid for by the sale of a 1913 Renoir painting *Femme au Corset* that Lisa had bought in 1937. She had decided:

> I was getting really tired of the Renoir. To the horror of Henry who had decided that Renoir never painted a bad picture, I sold it for £3,000. Henry was absolutely furious. One of the things I did with it was to pay Francis (Bacon) £425 for a portrait of Bob.[16]

The Sainsburys gave Bacon immense support, commissioning several works from him and helping him with loans when he was desperately short of money. A short while after this Bob and Lisa established the Sainsbury Awards to help young, newly graduated artists. Worth about £500 each, they were of invaluable assistance to painters or sculptors who lacked studios and dealers.

In 1959 Bob was invited to become a Trustee of the Tate Gallery, arriving on the Board three years after Henry stood down in 1956, having spent fourteen years as a Trustee. Bob also was a Trustee for fourteen years, the last four as Chairman. He and Lisa were therefore very much aware of new artists both in Britain and abroad. Some artists were not well known and needed considerable financial help, such as the Turkish painter Mübin Orhon. In 1971 they met John Davies (a Sainsbury Award winner in 1970); one year later they funded an exhibition of the twenty-six-year-old artist's work at the Whitechapel Gallery in London.

The collection continued to grow and the house at Smith Square was no longer big enough. Bob and Lisa decided to give the collection away, finally settling on the University of East Anglia in Norwich as the extraordinarily fortunate recipient. Their son David would pay for a building that would house the collection and also the School of Fine Arts. Bob

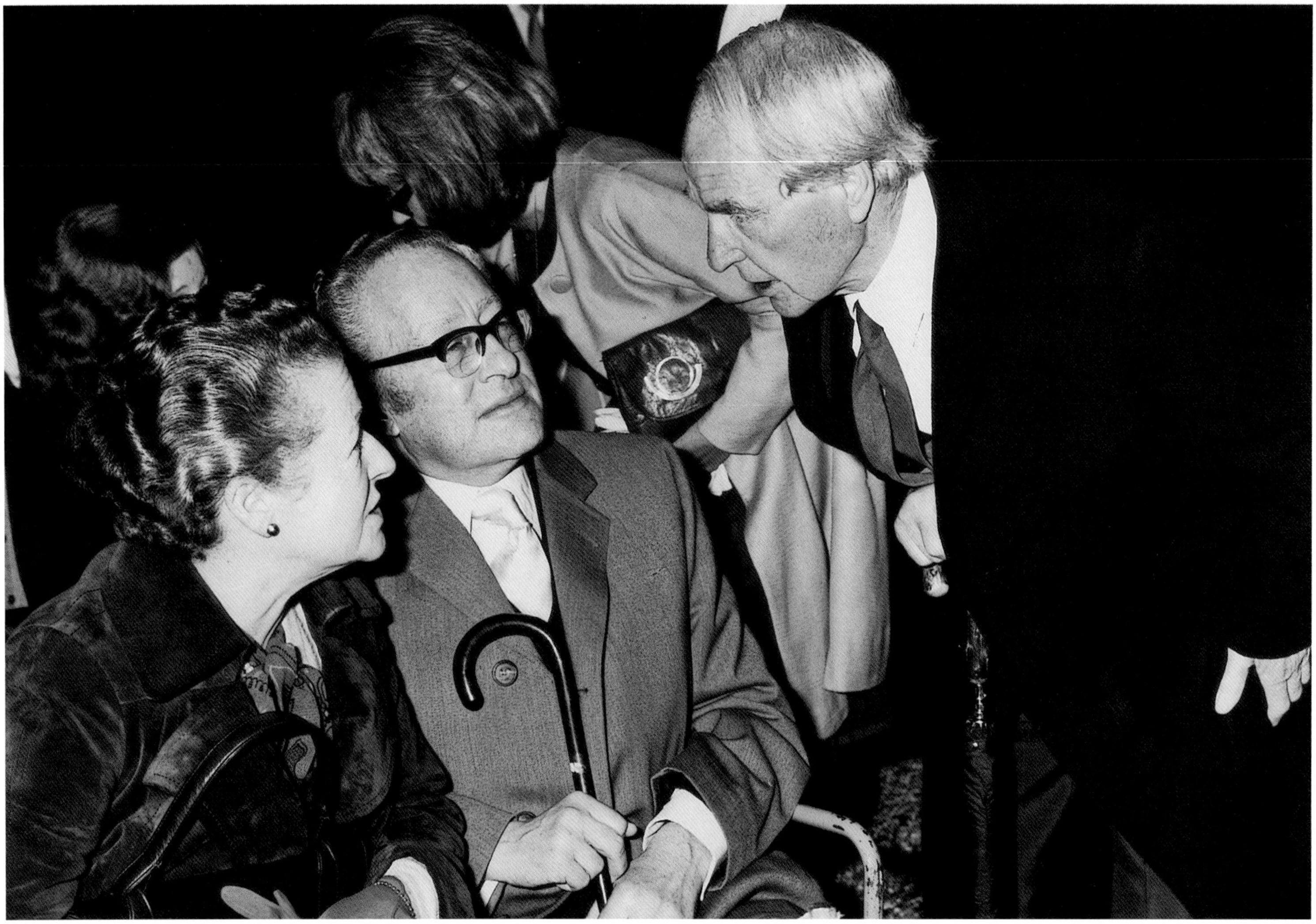

and Lisa chose a young architect to design the new building; his name was Norman Foster. The Sainsbury Centre for the Visual Arts opened in 1978 and Bob himself prepared the checklist catalogue for the opening exhibition. Thirteen years later, the collection had been extended to the point where Norman Foster was asked to design the Crescent Wing. As chance would have it, Lisa had invited me to lunch on 11 November 2003, the very day that *The Times* published an article on Foster with the announcement that he had won the competition to design a new terminal for Beijing airport for the 2008 Olympic Games. Lisa's pleasure at Norman Foster's success was manifest.

Henry fell ill in June 1983 and was admitted to Addenbrooke's Hospital in Cambridge on 8 August. Bob and Lisa visited him two or three times before his admission. On one occasion Lisa arrived with a special back-support cushion that temporarily alleviated the pain in his lower back. On Henry's return home they came to see him and Irina, who was still moving round the house with a Zimmer frame, having fractured the neck of her femur earlier. A week or so before Henry died on 31 August 1986 Bob and Lisa visited him. We all realized that the end could not be far off; physically he was much weaker and his memory for facts and faces was almost gone. While Henry's nurse attended to his needs, Lisa, Bob and I went to sit in the garden. Practical as ever, Lisa was concerned about Henry's palliative care – I believe I was able to reassure her. At the time of Henry's funeral

Fig. 11
Moore with Bob and Lisa Sainsbury in Rome, 1972.

on 4 September Bob and Lisa were abroad but they were able to attend the Memorial Service held for him in Westminster Abbey on 18 November 1986.

Irina retreated into her shell, seeing only close members of her family. As my son shared her birthday (26 March), we went to spend the afternoon with her on her eighty-second birthday in 1989. Nine days later she died; she is buried at Henry's side in the small churchyard of St Thomas's Church, Perry Green.

1998 was the centenary of Henry's birth. The main celebration of that event in Great Britain was an exhibition of his work at the Sainsbury Centre for the Visual Arts. Henry would have been very touched by his friends' affectionate tribute.

The Sainsbury Collection now embraces ceramics by Hans Coper and Lucie Rie – ceramics are Lisa's passion; works on paper by the Basque sculptor Eduardo Chillida; Japanese screens and lacquerware; and paintings by two Russian artists, Boris Zaborov, who completed a portrait of Lisa reminiscent of the works of Odilon Redon, and Yuri Kuper, whose works include still lives in oil and mixed media as well as lithographs. Bob and Lisa's immense generosity to the University of East Anglia was recognized on 23 June 1999 when the Freedom of the City of Norwich was conferred upon them both. The City Hall was filled with their friends. It was a memorable occasion; those of us privileged to share it with Bob and Lisa were very conscious of the depth of affection felt for them both.

Bob died on 2 April 2000. At a service in St John's Smith Square on 3 October to celebrate Bob's life, tributes were paid by friends – David Attenborough, Norman Foster, Steven Hooper and Guenter Treitel, who had been one of a group of Jewish children whom Bob and Lisa had arranged to have brought out of Eastern Europe before the Second World War began. It was an immensely moving service for a much loved man.

Lisa continues to add to the collection, acquiring *objets d'art* for the same reason Bob had given fifty years earlier – 'I straightforward liked it in sensual terms'. Lisa's enthusiasm and delight in her latest acquisitions are vividly conveyed when she describes them, giving the lie to the figures written on her birth certificate.

On 11 November Lisa showed me a letter dated 2 November 2003 from the Japanese Ambassador. He wrote that 'the Government of Japan … has bestowed upon you the Order of the Rising Sun, Gold Rays and Neck Collar in recognition of your distinguished contribution to the relationship between our two countries'. This recognition is in part for the foundation of the Sainsbury Institute for the Study of Japanese Arts and Cultures (SISJAC), which had its beginnings in a telephone call made by Lisa on her eighty-sixth birthday. SISJAC opened in October 2001 in a beautiful Georgian building in Norwich Cathedral Close. Very recently the Japanese Government granted Lisa permission to acquire two magnificent Japanese paintings, now displayed in the Sainsbury Centre for the Visual Arts at the University of East Anglia in Norwich.

Bob disliked the word 'collector', preferring to call himself a 'passionate acquirer'. Between them, Bob and Lisa, over the course of sixty years, acquired an astonishingly wide-ranging collection of wonderful artefacts. Lisa reminded me that they were not always in agreement as to what they should choose or indeed who were the great artists; in fact they quite often argued. Their differing views have enriched the collection; their generosity in making it available for public enjoyment has enriched us, giving us time 'to stand and stare' in this frenetic twenty-first century.

Fig. 12
Ann Garrould and Moore at Hoglands.

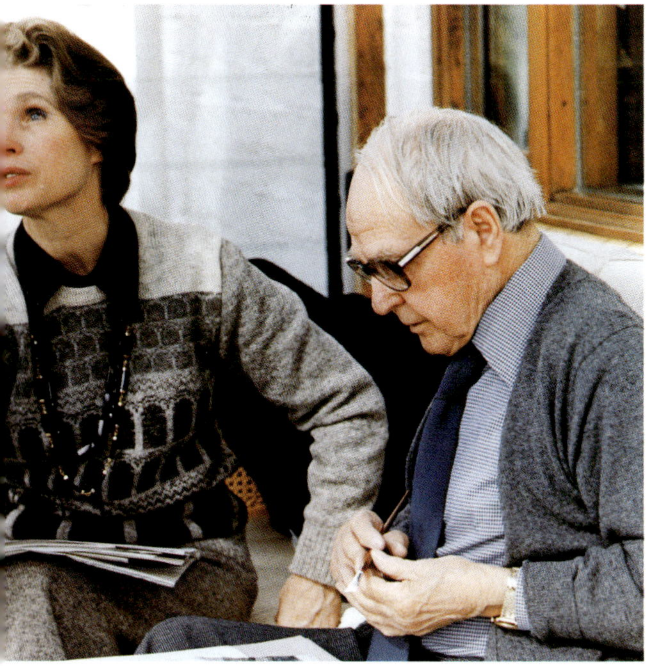

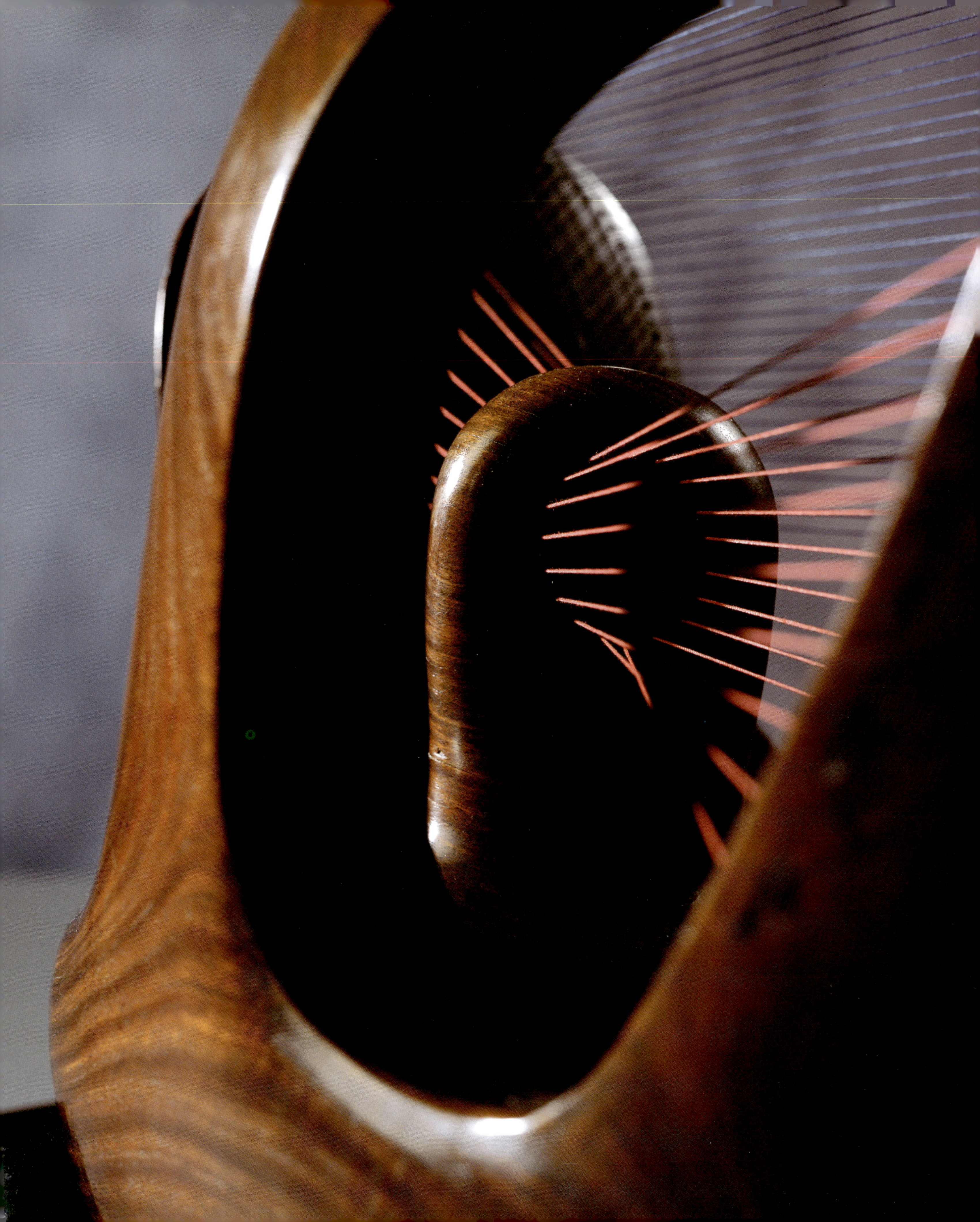

Anita Feldman Bennet

THIS EXHIBITION IN DULWICH marks the first time that Moore's *Bird Basket* (cat.46) has been exhibited in the United Kingdom since 1978, when it could be seen at Cartwright Hall in Bradford as part of a retrospective to mark the artist's eightieth birthday. The reason for this gap of twenty-six years is largely because the carving, arguably the most important of all Moore's stringed sculptures, was one of only a few pieces of his own work that the artist and his family kept and lived with in their home. Following an initial run of exhibitions shortly after the work was made, including *Surrealism Today* at The Zwemmer Gallery, London, in 1940 and the 1946 Moore retrospective at the Museum of Modern Art, New York, *Bird Basket* was removed from Hoglands only for a few exhibitions.[1] In cleaning and restringing *Bird Basket* in 1994, the conservators of The Henry Moore Foundation rediscovered the brilliant red and blue colours of the original strings (fig. 13), which had been completely discoloured over the years, but were still vibrant in unexposed sections of the work. Two years ago the sculpture was allocated to the Foundation, and since then the carving has been on display at the Henry Moore Institute in Leeds.

Moore's stringed sculptures in particular were the result of his exploration of how one form can be seen inside another, an essential part of his emerging interest in the internal/external idea. This concept was not limited to abstract forms, but is also frequently manifest in the mother and child theme with arms protectively encircling a child, or in numerous figures in which an internal element is exposed. It further relates to ideas of enclosure in the helmet series, where an outer form protects an inner form, and also to studies of figures in caves or shelters. Concern for depicting volume in space, and the desire to open out form beyond the limitations inherent in materials such as wood or stone, were the driving forces that led Moore to the innovation of using strings. The negative space created by these open forms reveals unexpected vistas through the work and continually shifting perspectives, lending a sense of mystery. An inscription on a transformation drawing of 1932 reads: 'design the spaces instead of concentrating on lumps … enlarge and widen the scope of sculpture.'[2] Pure form and the aesthetic of truth to materials were not enough – Moore found it necessary to open out sculpture more fully and relate forms to one another. For practical reasons this was achieved earlier in drawing than in sculpture, as wood and stone presented inherent limitations in shape, scale, flexibility and strength. Although Moore never stopped carving, eventually he found that using lead or bronze allowed more freedom of form invention.

The genesis of the stringed carvings stems from Moore's exploration of internal/external forms present in nature as well as in ethnographic works of art. In his series of transformation drawings organic forms such as bones and seashells metamorphose into figures. One example, *Studies of Bones*, 1932 (HMF 942),[3] includes a sketch in which the starting point is a New Ireland carving that Moore had seen in the British Museum; he was especially interested in the manipulation of forms within other forms present in Oceanic carvings. A closely related drawing, *Studies of Bones, Shell and Mushroom*, 1932 (HMF 947, fig. 14), depicts a series of holes derived from a shell penetrated by a spiral rod and viewed from different perspectives. The earliest anticipation

Fig. 13
Bird Basket (detail), 1939 (cat.46), lignum vitae and string; The Henry Moore Foundation: accepted by HM Government in lieu of inheritance tax and allocated in 2002.

Surrealism, Space and String: Henry Moore's *Bird Basket*

of the use of strings or wire to connect and visually penetrate sculptural forms comes from another of the 1932 transformation drawings, which Moore inscribed, 'Build up spatial sculpture bird cage sculpture with concrete & wire one form inside another … sort of spear-head inside sheath hole upwards'.[4] He rephrased this more clearly years later in a 1968 interview: '[it was the] ability to look through the strings as with a birdcage and to see one form within another which excited me.'[5]

Studies of sculptural forms connected by linear drawing resembling strings appear in Moore's sketchbooks as early as the No. 2 Drawing Book of 1930–34.[6] By 1936 Moore was filling sheets of paper with ideas for stringed sculptures, many closely connected to studies for carvings of square forms. The sketch centre left in *Ideas for Sculpture: Stone Forms* (fig. 15) anticipates the shape of *Bird Basket* and links it to the stone carvings he was working on simultaneously at his cottage, Burcroft, in Kent. In drawings of the following year stringed forms are seen from various perspectives, and even as upright or reclining stringed figures in architectural settings.[7]

Although sketches of seemingly related forms can be found,[8] suddenly *Bird Basket* appears in a 1937 drawing seen from two different angles, more or less completely resolved and already placed on a pedestal (fig. 16). Even the strings are depicted as they would eventually be realized, in red and blue, in order to further distinguish the internal forms. Despite many compositions bearing titles such as 'Ideas for Sculpture', we know that especially during the late 1930s Moore often drew already existing sculptures in invented settings, changing their scale and placing them among other sculptures both real and imaginary. The problem of dating Moore's work is further compounded by the fact that the artist signed and frequently misdated many of his drawings years after they were originally executed. Thus *Bird Basket* was carved in 1939 but appears in a number of compositions dating from 1937 to1940. In *Landscape Drawing with Figures*, 1938 (fig. 17), the sweeping arc of *Bird Basket* is echoed by similar yet disparate shapes surrounding it, such as a hooked gourd, a reclining figure and a rounded mother and child; even the body and legs of a winged insect as well as the spikes of a garden fork and rake invite comparison. Lower right we can imagine what *Bird Basket* might have looked like had the

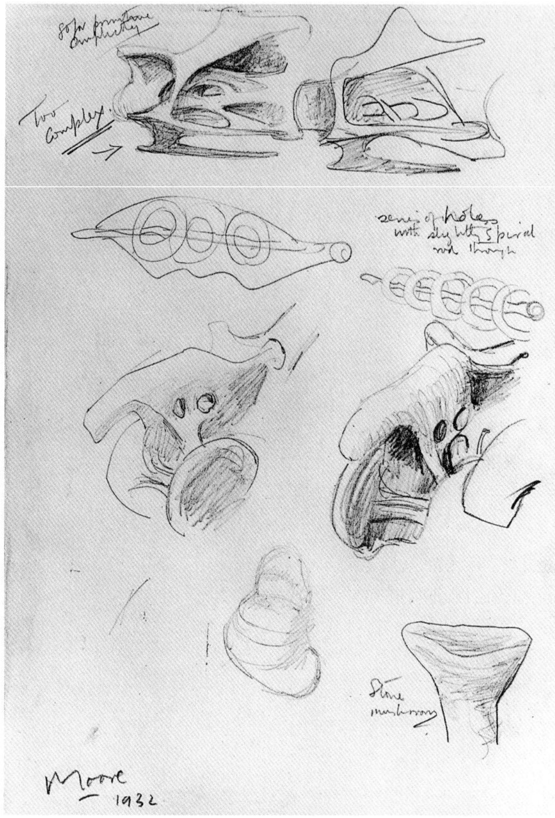

Fig. 14
Studies of Bones, Shell and Mushroom, 1932 (AG 32.58, HMF 947), pencil; The Arts Council Collection, London: purchased from the artist 1963.

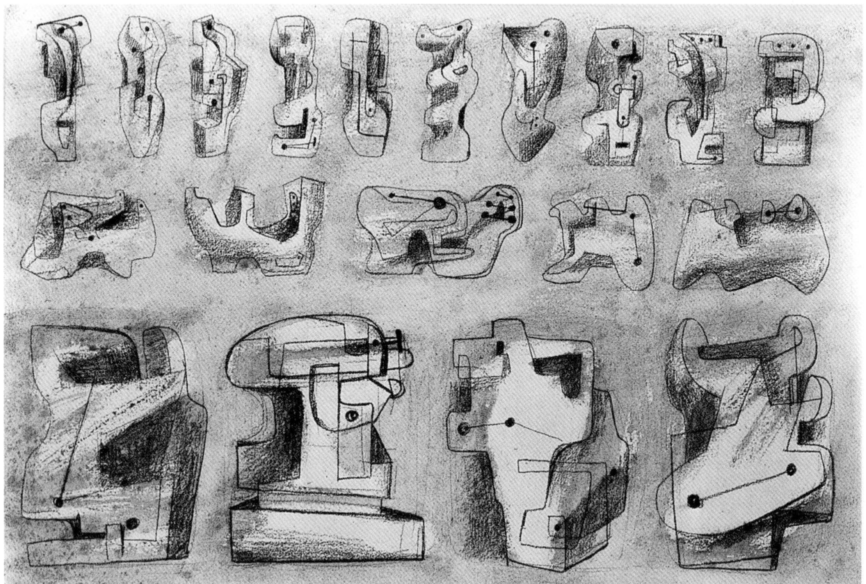

Fig. 15
Ideas for Sculpture: Stone Forms, 1936
(AG 36.12, HMF 1249), chalk and wash;
The Board of Trustees of the Victoria and Albert Museum, London.

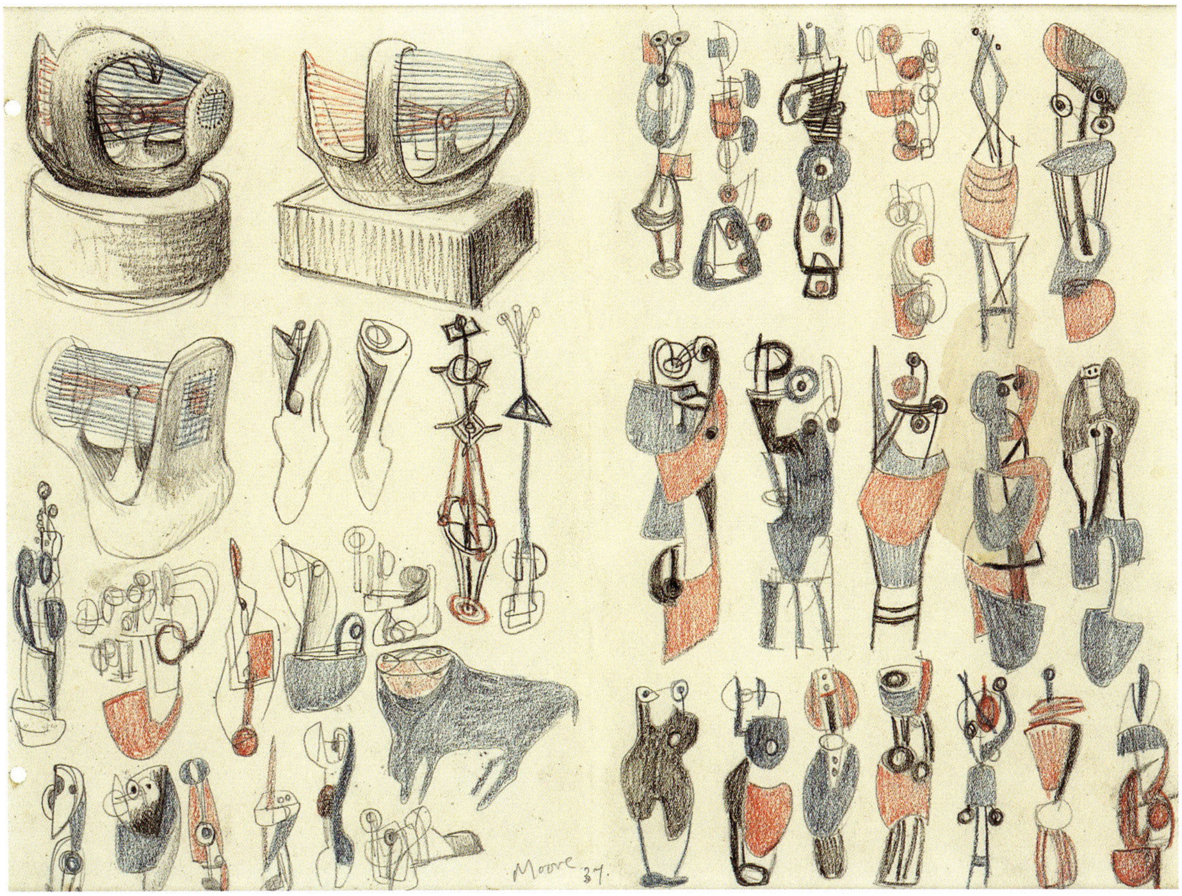

Fig. 16
Ideas for Sculpture (Bird Basket), 1937 (AG 37.64, HMF 1338a), pencil and chalk; private collection, USA.

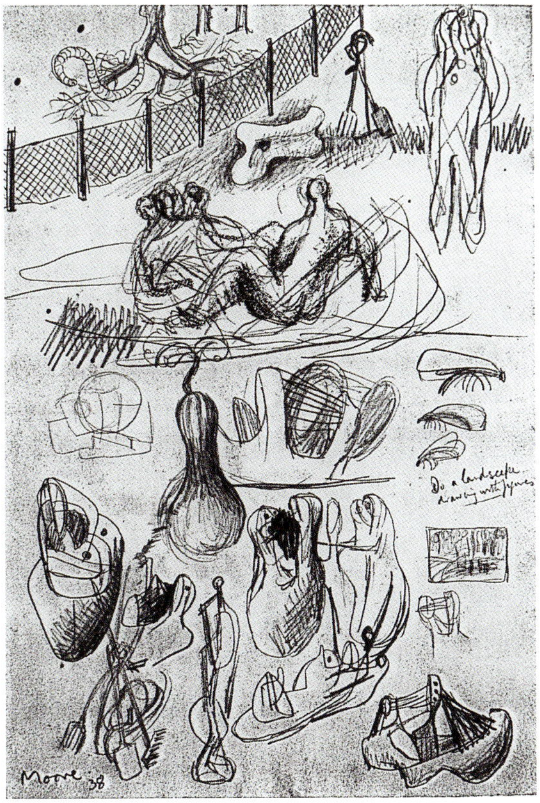

Fig. 17
Landscape Drawing with Figures, 1938 (AG 38.29, HMF 1414a), pencil, crayon and wax crayon; private collection, Germany.

form been opened out to extreme lengths, twisted, and the smaller internal form made dominant. A fence also serves, like the strings, to dissect the composition as well as to enable one to see through it.

A similar fence later appears in *Drawing for Spanish Prisoners' Appeal*, 1939 (AG 39.31, HMF 1467), conceived as an idea for a lithograph to be sold in aid of the Spanish Republicans who fled Spain only to be imprisoned in France.[9] In the final lithograph the chain link fence has been replaced by barbed wire (fig. 18). Moore had visited the Altamira caves in Spain in 1934. Two years later, horrified by the catastrophic events befalling the country, he signed the Surrealist manifesto calling for an end to the British policy of non-intervention. In the summer of 1937 Moore accompanied Roland Penrose to Paris and, with Alberto Giacometti, Paul Eluard, André Breton and Max Ernst, visited Picasso in his studio to see *Guernica* in progress. Moore's political involvement culminated with the design of the broadsheet of the 1938 Surrealist declaration *We Ask your Attention* (fig. 19). Here, a line emanates from the eye of a profile head, taking on a life of its own as eyeglasses hooked on an imagined ear and unifying the text with the image in its equal treatment of positive and negative space. The document is a call for action based on the unity of various parties of the United Front to 'intervene as poets, artists and intellectuals by violent or subtle subversion'. Moore attempted to visit Spain the same year as part of a delegation of writers and artists opposing Fascism but was refused permission to travel by the British government, possibly because of his membership of the left wing Artists' International Association.[10] The same year Moore and Herbert Read became the primary supporters of the first British Artists' Congress, established to promote art education in

Britain as well as artists' trade unions. In interviews years later Moore played down his earlier political commitments, yet as England came closer to another horrific war, his anxiety was publicly expressed:

> We are witnessing in Europe, in Africa, in Asia, three large-scale wars which are being carried on, despite the deeply shocked protests of the whole civilized world, with an inhuman totalitarian ferocity which may well make us despair …
> Are we to stand aside while these forces complete the wreck of our civilization?[11]

By this time Hampstead, where Moore and Irina had been living since 1929, had become a refuge for intellectuals and artists fleeing continental Europe. Herbert Read coined the

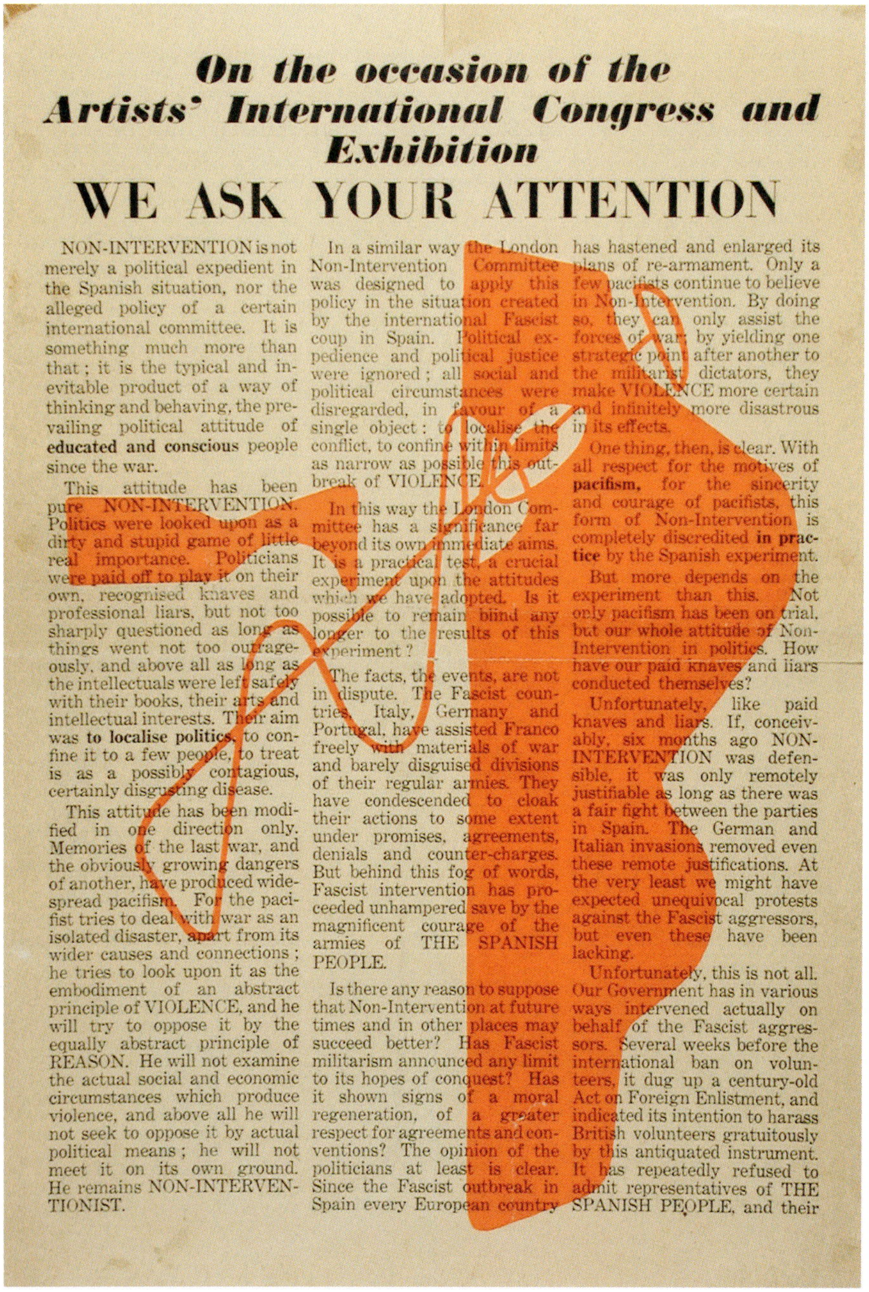

On the occasion of the Artists' International Congress and Exhibition

WE ASK YOUR ATTENTION

NON-INTERVENTION is not merely a political expedient in the Spanish situation, nor the alleged policy of a certain international committee. It is something much more than that; it is the typical and inevitable product of a way of thinking and behaving, the prevailing political attitude of **educated and conscious** people since the war.

This attitude has been pure NON-INTERVENTION. Politics were looked upon as a dirty and stupid game of little real importance. Politicians were paid off to play it on their own, recognised knaves and professional liars, but not too sharply questioned as long as things went not too outrageously, and above all as long as the intellectuals were left safely with their books, their arts and intellectual interests. Their aim was **to localise politics**, to confine it to a few people, to treat is as a possibly contagious, certainly disgusting disease.

This attitude has been modified in one direction only. Memories of the last war, and the obviously growing dangers of another, have produced widespread pacifism. For the pacifist tries to deal with war as an isolated disaster, apart from its wider causes and connections; he tries to look upon it as the embodiment of an abstract principle of VIOLENCE, and he will try to oppose it by the equally abstract principle of REASON. He will not examine the actual social and economic circumstances which produce violence, and above all he will not seek to oppose it by actual political means; he will not meet it on its own ground. He remains NON-INTERVENTIONIST.

In a similar way the London Non-Intervention Committee was designed to apply this policy in the situation created by the international Fascist coup in Spain. Political expedience and political justice were ignored; all social and political circumstances were disregarded, in favour of a single object: to localise the conflict, to confine within limits as narrow as possible this outbreak of VIOLENCE.

In this way the London Committee has a significance far beyond its own immediate aims. It is a practical test, a crucial experiment upon the attitudes which we have adopted. Is it possible to remain blind any longer to the results of this experiment?

The facts, the events, are not in dispute. The Fascist countries, Italy, Germany and Portugal, have assisted Franco freely with materials of war and barely disguised divisions of their regular armies. They have condescended to cloak their actions to some extent under promises, agreements, denials and counter-charges. But behind this fog of words, Fascist intervention has proceeded unhampered save by the magnificent courage of the armies of THE SPANISH PEOPLE.

Is there any reason to suppose that Non-Intervention at future times and in other places may succeed better? Has Fascist militarism announced any limit to its hopes of conquest? Has it shown signs of a moral regeneration, of a greater respect for agreements and conventions? The opinion of the politicians at least is clear. Since the Fascist outbreak in Spain every European country has hastened and enlarged its plans of re-armament. Only a few pacifists continue to believe in Non-Intervention. By doing so, they can only assist the forces of war; by yielding one strategic point after another to the militarist dictators, they make VIOLENCE more certain and infinitely more disastrous in its effects.

One thing, then, is clear. With all respect for the motives of **pacifism**, for the sincerity and courage of pacifists, this form of Non-Intervention is completely discredited **in practice** by the Spanish experiment.

But more depends on the experiment than this. Not only pacifism has been on trial, but our whole attitude of Non-Intervention in politics. How have our paid knaves and liars conducted themselves?

Unfortunately, like paid knaves and liars. If, conceivably, six months ago NON-INTERVENTION was defensible, it was only remotely justifiable as long as there was a fair fight between the parties in Spain. The German and Italian invasions removed even these remote justifications. At the very least we might have expected unequivocal protests against the Fascist aggressors, but even these have been lacking.

Unfortunately, this is not all. Our Government has in various ways intervened actually on behalf of the Fascist aggressors. Several weeks before the international ban on volunteers, it dug up a century-old Act on Foreign Enlistment, and indicated its intention to harass British volunteers gratuitously by this antiquated instrument. It has repeatedly refused to admit representatives of THE SPANISH PEOPLE, and their

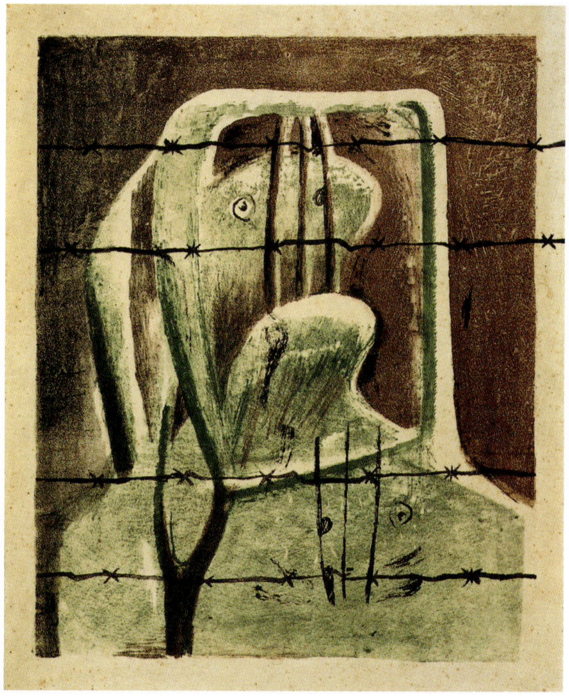

Fig. 18
Spanish Prisoner, *c.*1939 (CGM 3), uneditioned lithograph; The Henry Moore Foundation: gift of the artist 1977.

Fig. 19
We Ask Your Attention, 1938, broadsheet of the Surrealist Declaration designed by Henry Moore; The Henry Moore Foundation Archive.

remarkably British understatement, 'a nest of gentle artists',[12] for a group that was as diverse and determined as it was politically aware. In addition to his previously existing friendships with Barbara Hepworth, John Skeaping, Ben Nicholson, Paul Nash and Roland Penrose, Moore was exchanging ideas with Marcel Breuer, Walter Gropius, Piet Mondrian, E.L.T. Mesens, Lázló Moholy-Nagy and Naum Gabo. This intellectual climate produced an unparalleled period of artistic experimentation in London. In 1935 David Gascoyne published *A Short Survey of Surrealism*, the first study in English on the subject, although ironically his *First Manifesto of English Surrealism* was published six months earlier but only in French. Several English writers and artists then joined forces to promote Surrealism in Britain, culminating with the *International Surrealist Exhibition* held in London at the New Burlington Galleries. Along with Read, Nash, Hugh Sykes Davies and Humphrey Jennings, Moore served on the organizing committee and also exhibited three drawings and four sculptures. One of these, *Reclining Figure*, 1931, in lead (LH 101, bronze illustrated fig. 20), reveals a piercing of the body with parallel apertures echoing Picasso's recurring motif of the female figure as a guitar and anticipating Moore's sculptural use of strings. The exhibition was extremely popular, attracting 23,000 visitors and an appearance at a related lecture by Salvador Dali in a diving suit (all the more auspicious in retrospect, given Moore's first helmet at the end of the decade).[13] Although Moore is often portrayed as peripheral to the English Surrealist movement, in part due to his parallel interest in the opposing movement of Constructivism and Abstraction, there is no doubt that many of the fundamental concepts in Moore's work, most notably transformation and use of found objects, were indebted to Surrealism. The catalogue for the *International Surrealist Exhibition* contained a preface by André Breton, and an introduction by Read proclaiming: '[the artist] will oppose the conscious and the unconscious, the deed and the dream, truth and fable, reason and unreason, and out of these opposites he will create a new synthesis.'[14]

Moore repeatedly stated that his inspiration for stringed sculptures came from models he had seen in the British Museum:

Fig. 20
Reclining Figure, 1931 (LH 101), bronze edition of six cast 1963.

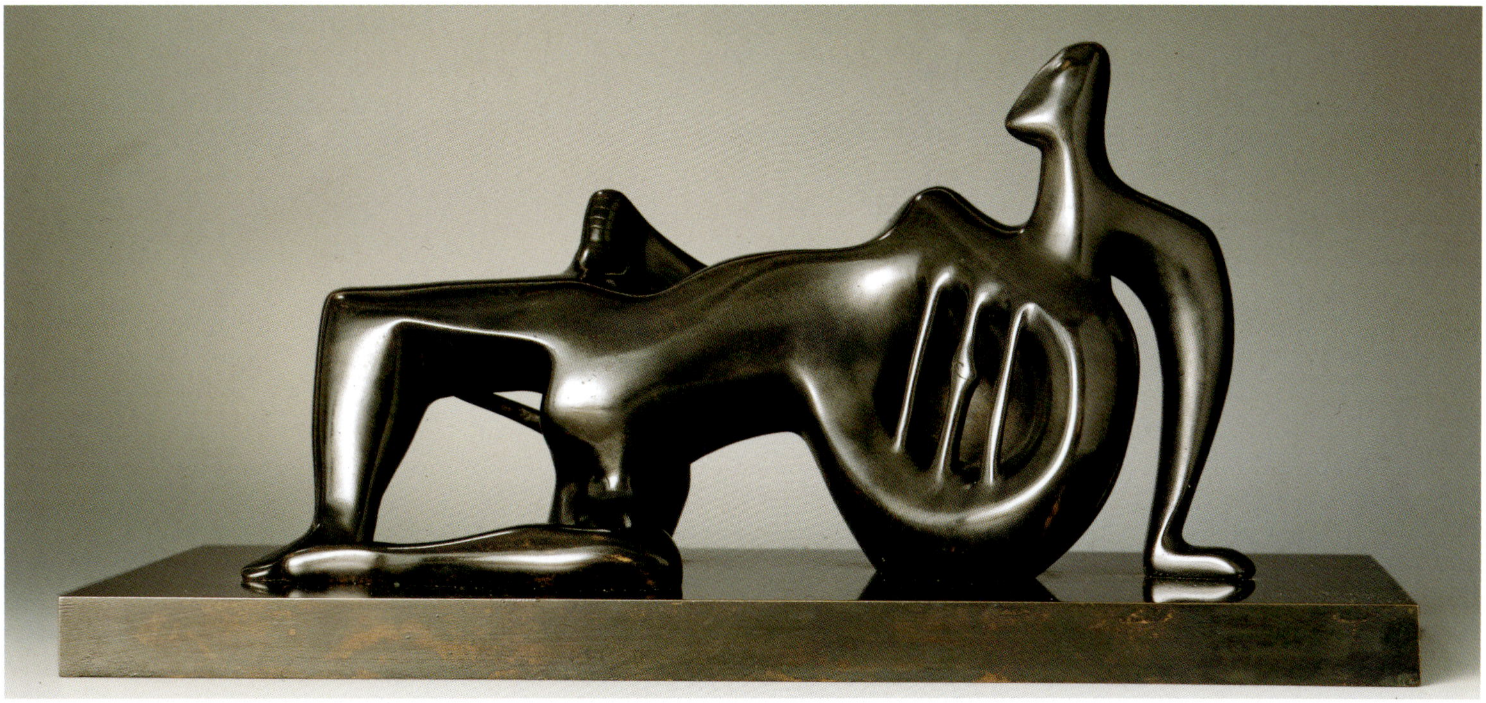

I was fascinated by the mathematical models I saw there which had been made to illustrate the difference of the form that is halfway between a square and a circle … One end could be twisted to produce forms that would be terribly difficult to draw on a flat surface.'[15]

But the impetus for Moore's visits to see these mathematical models first hand may have come from photographs of similar models by Man Ray reproduced in *Cahiers d'Art* in 1936; although Moore knew the periodical well, whether or not he had seen these photographs is uncertain.[16] Even more influential was the arrival of Naum Gabo in London from Germany in 1935, a decade after he and his brother Antoine Pevsner issued the Constructivist Manifesto in Russia, dedicated to the exploration of space through the manipulation of new forms and materials. This corresponded to the utopian Bauhaus philosophy of a classless, machine-age synthesis of all the arts. Miriam Gabo recalled that in the late 1930s, after seeing one of Moore's stringed figure sculptures in his studio, Gabo declared: 'Strings, I'll show them what to do with strings.'[17] Moore's approach was always more organic, however, and intrinsically related to his excavation of internal forms. He explained:

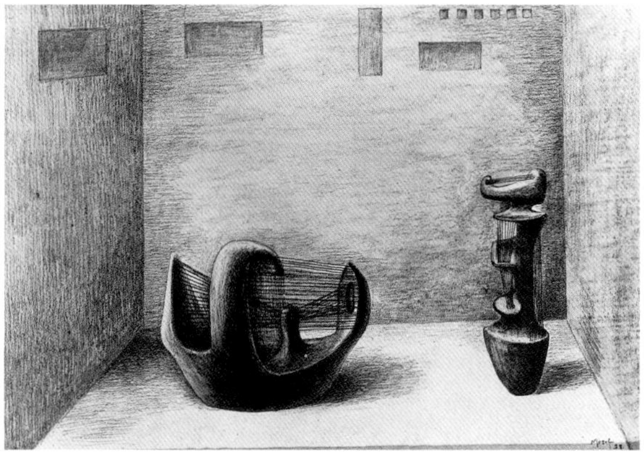

Fig. 21
Two Stringed Figures in a Setting, 1938
(AG 38.38, HMF 1371),
crayon, chalk and wash;
private collection, UK.

He [Gabo] developed this string idea so that his structure always became space itself, whereas I like the contrast between the solid and the strings. The string and the 'open' idea was the side I was trying to relate and develop. This perhaps was the culmination of that process in which I was making an outside shape a sculpture in its own right (Interior/Exterior Forms), yet one which was not completed until each part was connected to the other. When I connected one side to the other you could see through *and* inside.[18]

Thus Moore found himself with a foot in both camps: that of the Surrealists with an emphasis on metamorphosis, biomorphic forms and found objects; as well as that of the Constructivists and Abstractionists, seeking to purify form and develop sculpture spatially. But for Moore one approach did not necessarily negate the other, and to a large extent *Bird Basket* can be understood as a synthesis of the two. He explained:

The *Bird Basket* to me is one of the special stringed figures that I made. It has got an organic form to it although the strings are abstract straight lines. It is called *Bird Basket* because it has the handle of a basket over the top and strings that show the little inner space as a bird inside a cage – at one end is the head and at the other end the tail. The title is a mixture of the two forms and the two words 'Bird' and 'Basket' are significant because they were arrived at in a practical way. What also makes me treat it as something special in my mind is that lignum vitae is one of the hardest woods in nature, and it can take a very beautiful surface and very thin edges like those at the left-hand side. Also it was more like carving a stone and at that time I still preferred stone to any other material.[19]

Moore and Gabo exhibited together in 1936, in *Abstract and Concrete*, which toured Oxford, London, Liverpool and Cambridge and also featured the work of Nicholson, Piper, Mondrian, Léger and Calder. The journal *Axis* sponsored the exhibition and published Moore's 'Notes on Sculpture'[20] the following year in a collection of essays entitled *The*

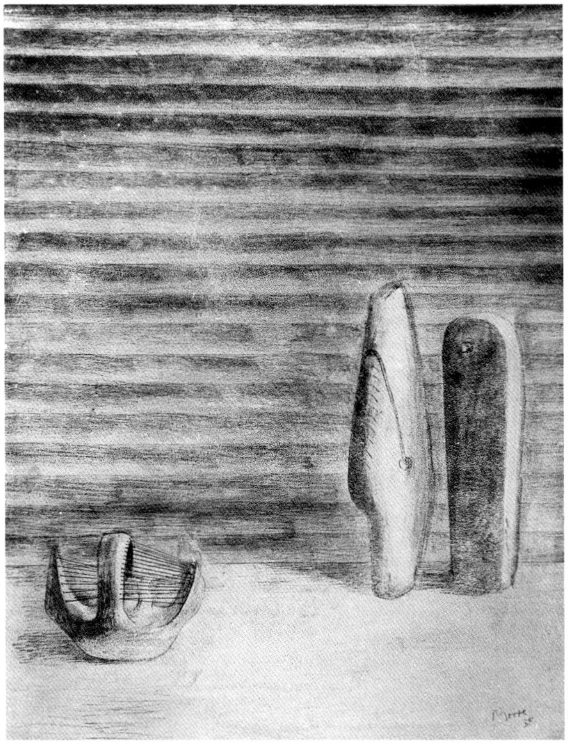

Fig. 22
Ideas for Sculpture, 1938
(AG 38.35, HMF 1368),
pencil, chalk (washed);
private collection, UK.

Fig. 23
Bird Basket photographed
by the artist in the open air
at Burcroft, 1939.

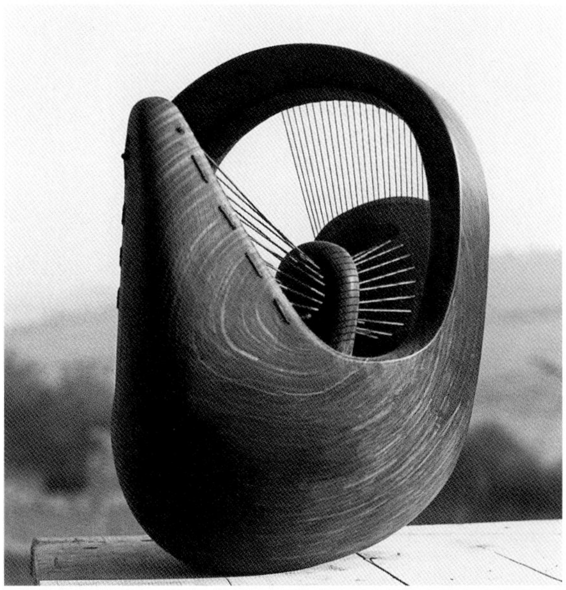

Painter's Object, which also included the writings of Léger, Kandinsky and Moholy-Nagy. This collaboration was strengthened the following year with the launch by Gabo, Nicholson and Leslie Martin of *Circle: International Survey on Constructive Art*, committed to promoting abstract art by association with other fields such as architecture, science and technology, and with the view that clarity of design reflected an ideal social organization. Contributors reflected the diverse brief and, in addition to Moore, included Mondrian and Read; Le Corbusier, Marcel Breuer and Maxwell Fry on architecture; Siegfried Giedion on engineering; Jan Tschichold on typography; and Léonide Massine on choreography.

Moore's coupling of Surrealist and Abstract/Constructivist concepts also pervades his drawings of the late 1930s, many of which feature *Bird Basket*. The Surrealist tendency to place a recognizable object in an unfamiliar surrounding, or reconsider one object through juxtaposition with others, plus arbitrary change of scale, is combined with austere architectural settings. In *Two Stringed Figures in a Setting*, 1938 (fig. 21), Moore's *Stringed Figure*, 1938 (LH 190), looms over *Bird Basket*, although in reality the upright figure is smaller, with a height of 35cm (13¾ in). The two lignum vitae carvings, like prisoners, occupy a tightly confined room without windows, only relieved by recurring geometric motifs that break up the space high above them. The idea is reworked in another drawing of the same year (fig. 22) in which *Bird Basket* appears to be watched over by two upright forms against a stark unrelenting corrugated wall. These imagined claustrophobic spaces recur in many of Moore's drawings from 1938 and doubtless reflect the tension and growing sense of anxiety as political events in Europe steered England inevitably closer to war.

Yet depictions of *Bird Basket* in these confined architectural settings belie the fact that the work was created in completely the opposite surroundings, carved in the open air at the artist's cottage in Kent. There Moore took photographs of the sculpture against a vista of sweeping countryside that eliminated all sense of the work's true scale. He used photography not only to manipulate the sense of monumentality, but also to reveal unusual views of the sculpture, photographing it end-on with the point shooting straight up like a ship's prow (fig. 23). Seeing a vulnerable wood carving in the open air exposed to the elements seems as unlikely a place to find the sculpture as the imagined architectural panoramas. Such unexpected contrasts are explored in *Pictorial Ideas and Settings for Sculpture*, 1939 (fig. 24), a page from one of the most accomplished and inventive sketchbooks of Moore's career. *Bird Basket* reappears far left in one of thirty-seven compositions contained on a single sheet. In these compositions both organic and abstract forms transform into disconcerting figures arranged in alienated groupings contemplated by or hidden from others. Subjects are further related to both extremes of confined architectural spaces and open landscape. The settings are sometimes arbitrary; one image of objects against a stark wall is inscribed 'or blue sky'. The sculptural forms blur boundaries of reality as both actual and imagined works co-exist. This sense of recognition yet confusion, a sort of déjà vu, adds both mystery and a sense of apprehension.[21]

As one of the final and most complex of Moore's stringed sculptures, *Bird Basket* marked the end of an era. Outbreak of war forced Moore to evacuate his cottage in Kent. The bombing of his Hampstead studio in 1940 led to his move to Hoglands, in the Hertfordshire hamlet of Perry Green, which remained his home for the rest of his life. Partially due to a lack of materials during the war, Moore concentrated on drawing. He not only stopped making stringed sculptures after 1939, he stopped creating sculpture altogether for three years. He resumed sculpting in 1943 with the seemingly radical

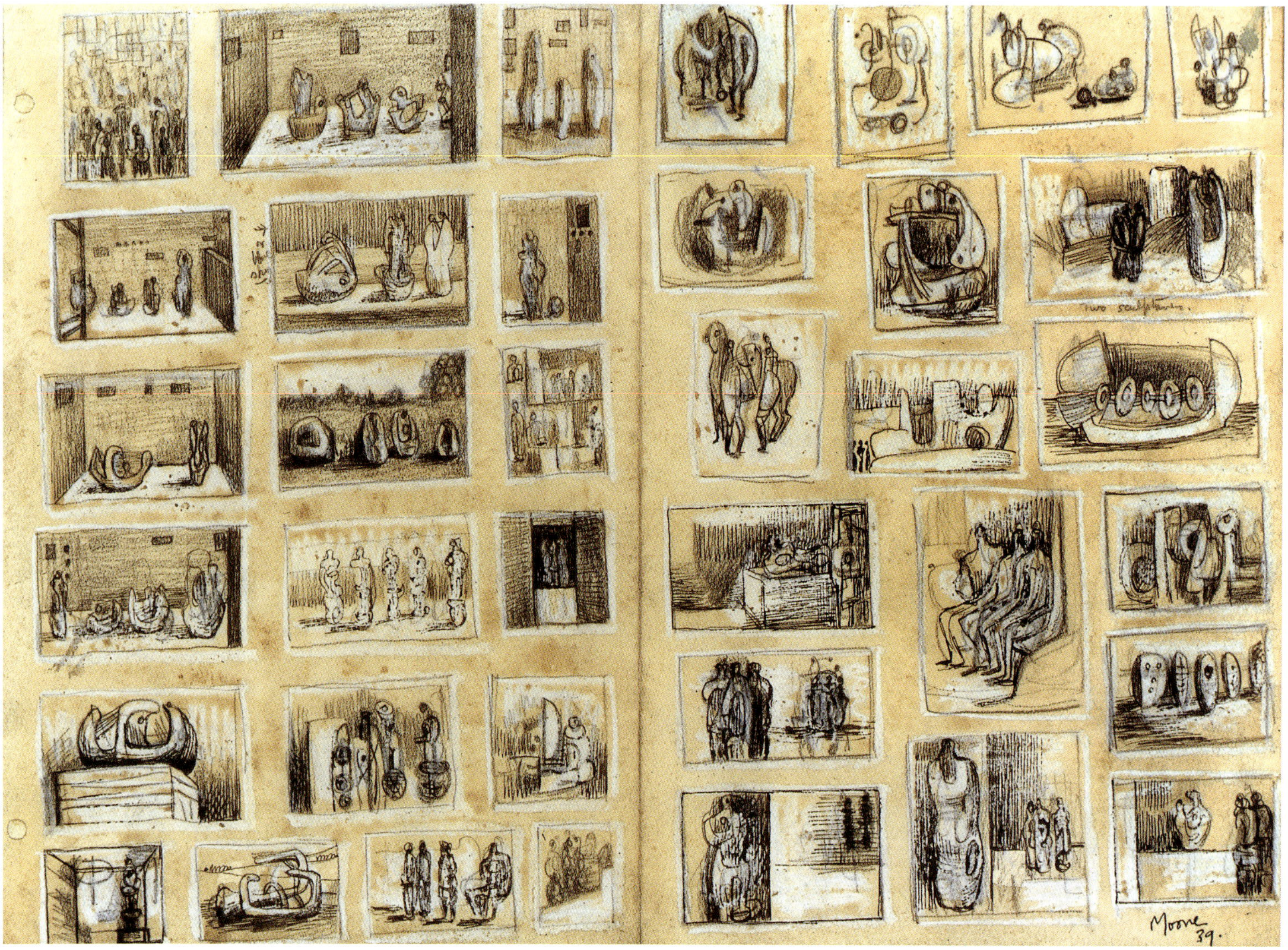

departure of the maquettes (cats 11, 12) for the Northampton *Madonna and Child* 1943–4 (fig. 9), and was consequently rejected by the Surrealist group for producing 'sacerdotal images'.[22] Moore explained his change of direction by the fact that '[stringed works] were too much in the nature of experiments to be truly satisfying … It becomes a matter of ingenuity rather than a fundamental human experience.'[23]

With Moore's move to Perry Green, *Bird Basket* also found a new home. Although he stopped depicting the sculpture in his drawings, the work reappears in numerous photographs of the artist at home, as testament to the affinity of modern, and indeed all, art forms with daily life. In fact, *Bird Basket* is one of only a few pieces of his own work that Moore chose to live with – a notable other being *Maquette for King and Queen* 1952 (LH 348). These could be found among artworks from many non-Western cultures as well as found objects, and paintings by artists such as Cézanne, Courbet and Degas. Usually *Bird Basket* was displayed alongside a twisted, gnarled vine on a side table with Millet's black crayon drawing *La Baratteuse* hanging above (fig. 25). The careful juxtaposition of such disparate objects, each with forms echoed in the others, can be seen to summarize Moore's personal vision of continuity and affirmation of life and nature.

Fig. 24
Pictorial Ideas and Settings for Sculpture, 1939 (AG 39.15, HMF 1456), pencil, wax crayon, wash, pen and ink; private collection, UK

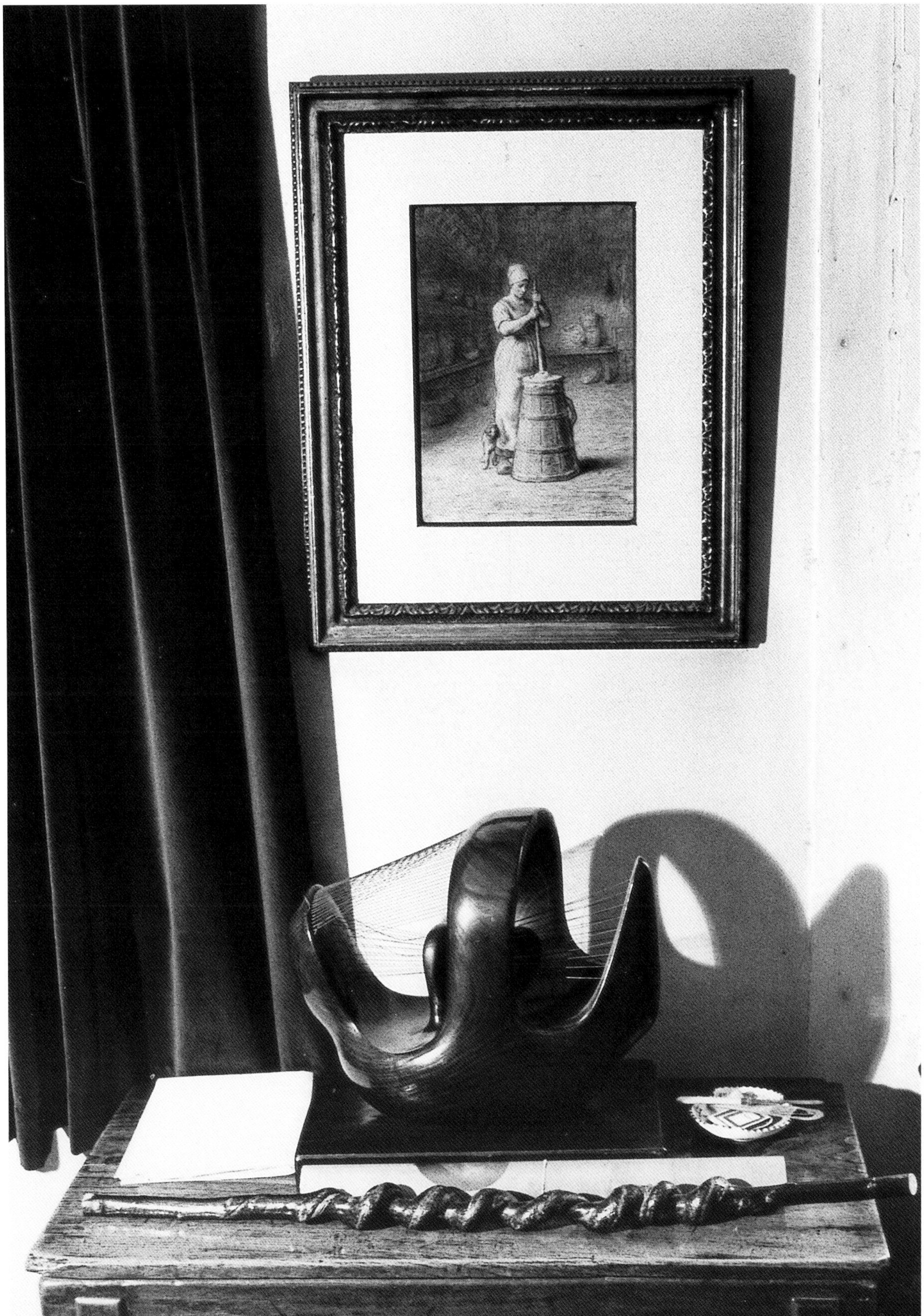

Fig. 25
Bird Basket in Hoglands, with twisted branch and Jean-François Millet's *La Baratteuse* (1852–5).

Catalogue

Ian Dejardin

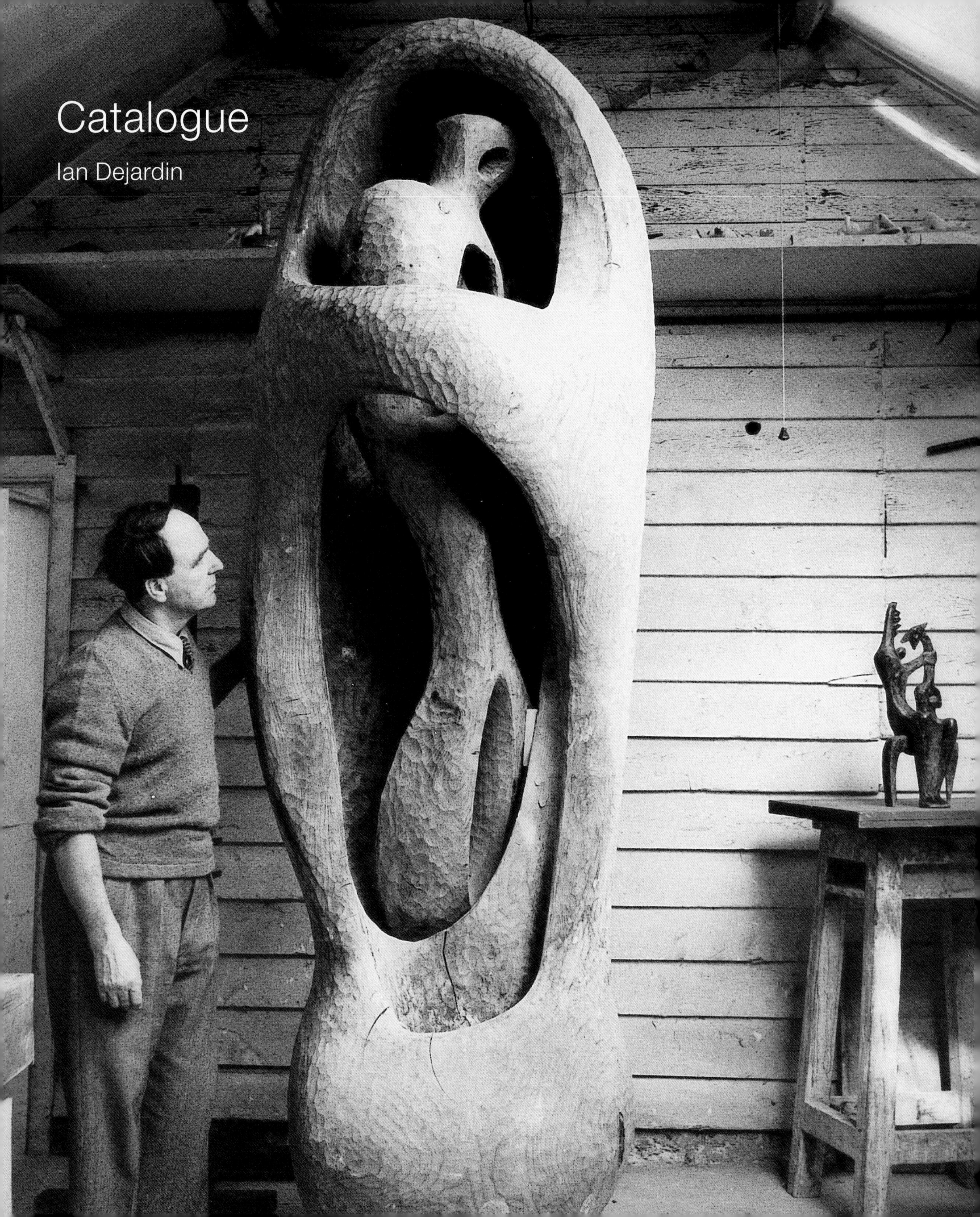

HENRY MOORE'S REPUTATION as an artist has been affected in many ways by the manner in which he presented himself in that role. He was an instinctive master of the 'soundbite' long before the term was invented, and seems to have made himself readily available for comment and interview, to the extent that his hospitality was often abused in later years by strangers turning up at his home, Hoglands. Moore himself provided many stories that fed his personal 'myth', even volunteering (in the manner of his day) 'obsessions' or 'fixations' to elucidate certain works, something that many modern and contemporary artists avoid at all costs. It is absolutely characteristic that he should let it be known that the impetus that made him want, as a boy, to be a sculptor came from a story about Michelangelo. It is also absolutely characteristic that it was not the *moral* of the story (Michelangelo accepts the advice of a passing old man, knocking out teeth from a sculpted satyr to make the sculpture's appearance more realistic – i.e. there is no source so lowly that you cannot learn from it) but the sheer verbal éclat of its description of the artist as 'the greatest sculptor in the world' that captured him.

Henry Moore was a driven artist, endlessly prolific and experimental, and was profoundly serious about his calling. In this he was helped by some important and stalwart supporters, of whom Herbert Read and Sir Kenneth Clark were probably the most influential. He was a true twentieth-century celebrity, with a respect for celebrity's value. He seems to have been devoid of that defining characteristic of his twenty-first-century equivalents – irony. His self-belief seems to have been more or less total. Not only that but he had a solid, Northern working-class concept of duty that meant that the trappings of glory that came thick and fast after the war – the honorary degrees, the Order of Merit, the trusteeships – were taken on by him not in a vainglorious fashion but simply as his due, a just reward, not just to him but to Art itself. In 1981 he was to say:

> If there is one thing which perhaps pleases me about my career as a sculptor, it is that interest in my work may have helped towards the enormous growth in the appreciation and also the practice of sculpture in the last half century. When I began at Leeds School of Art they had to start a sculpture school specially for me and I was the only student ...[1]

His childhood inner ear had set him on the right track; he was indeed widely trumpeted as 'the greatest sculptor in the world', just like Michelangelo. His life story has a Vasarian perfection about its final triumphant arc in which he certainly colluded, but with pride rather than vanity. Rarely has an artist provided so much material for biographers and interviewers, perhaps the lingering instinct of the long-term teacher that he was for over fifteen years. Books about him and his work flowed in a constant stream after the very first, with text by Read. was published by Zwemmer in 1934.[2]

The backlash was inevitable. As he entered his final, all-dominating phase, when every major plaza, every new architectural hot-spot, seemed to sprout its accompanying Henry Moore; as the photo opportunities blossomed – Henry Moores in front of the Santa Croce in Florence, Henry Moores presiding over Scottish moors, Henry Moores in front of great new art galleries in Toronto or Washington DC, Henry Moores in Greece, Henry Moores in front of the Houses of Parliament and along the Embankment – a younger generation of rising artists (some, like Anthony Caro, former assistants) very swiftly developed a frankly bitter sense of oppression alongside their respect, and by the time of his death in 1986, two years before what was to have been his ninetieth-birthday show at the Royal Academy, it might be said that even the public had begun to share the sense of satiety. The centenary of his birth in 1998 passed with only a handful of smaller shows in this country, unlike the recent crop of celebrations for the 'class of 1903' – Barbara Hepworth, John Piper, Eric Ravilious *et al.*

A re-assessment has often been heralded, but is it really necessary? Henry Moore's legacy is surely safe, even if audiences have occasionally looked elsewhere. His Foundation is at the centre of sculptural endeavour; his sculptures are still all around us, all over the world; the Japanese still make their pilgrimages; he is still a household name.

Fig. 26
Henry Moore in his studio at Hoglands with elmwood *Upright Internal/External Figure*, carved 1953–4 (LH 297, now in the collection of the Albright–Knox Art Gallery, Buffalo), and *Mother and Child* (LH 315).

Introduction

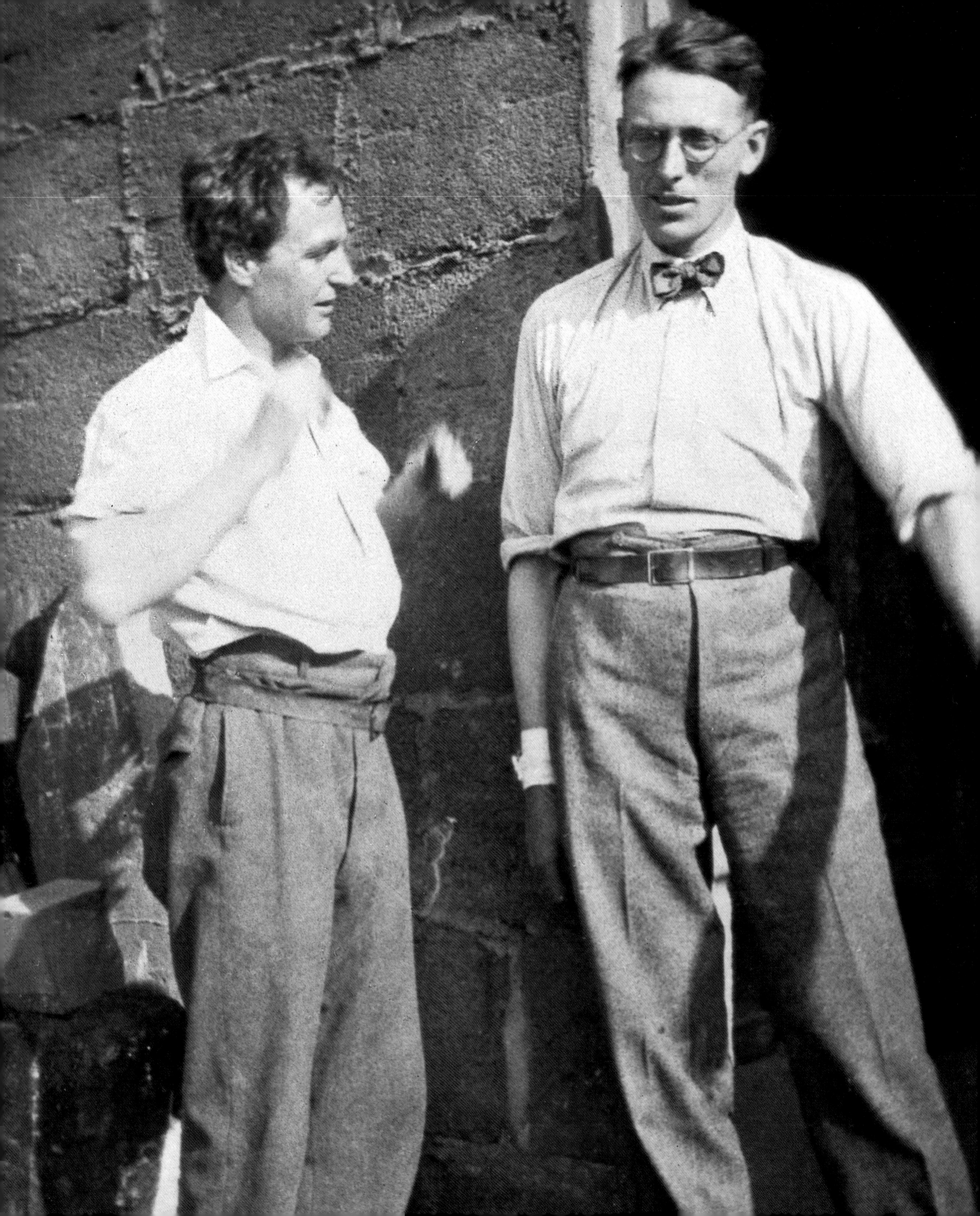

‘Feeding on garbage’ – the British Museum

This student has been feeding on garbage, anyone can see that.
BERESFORD PITE,
Professor of Architecture, Royal College of Art[3]

THE EARLIEST OBJECTS IN THE EXHIBITION date from 1922, the second year of Henry Moore’s period as a student (on a ‘Royal Exhibition Scholarship’) at the Royal College of Art in London. He was, of course, lucky to be alive – he had served at the front in the First World War, and been temporarily invalided out after being gassed. He had gone on to Leeds College of Art in September 1919. The academic teaching he received there had not managed to stifle his profound interest in the latest developments in sculpture. He had seen Sir Michael Sadler’s collection – one of the seminal influences on the artists of Moore’s generation – which included not only great works of ‘modern art’ (Cézanne, Matisse, Van Gogh, Gauguin, Kandinsky) but also of African art. Anyone with even a slight interest in the European art scene would have known that such works of so-called ‘Primitive’ art had been exciting and influencing the leading artists for a couple of decades. He was also a voracious reader, and had devoured Roger Fry’s *Vision and Design* (published in 1920), which translated that excitement into inspiring prose, inculcating in the young sculptor the quasi-moral enthusiasm of the time for carving as opposed to modelling, and for ‘truth to materials’ (a mantra for decades). Many of his defining attitudes were already in place. His blazing energy and drive had always been there. He was raring to engage with the contemporary cutting edge.

London, then, was intoxicating: ‘For the first year I was in a dream of excitement … at night I had my books, and I knew that not far away I had the National Gallery and British Museum and the Victoria and Albert with the reference library where I could get any book I wanted.’[4] Paris followed, either in 1922 or 1923, although he was too shy to make use of his introduction there to Aristide Maillol, provided by William Rothenstein, Principal of the Royal College of Art. Back at the college he was ruffling feathers in the academic establishment. The Professor of Sculpture was Derwent Wood, a fine enough sculptor (i.e. modeller), but of the old school, a pillar of the Royal Academy. However, Moore was too canny simply to be negative, and the baby was not thrown out with the bath water; he quickly realized that not all academic training was bunk. In Leon Underwood, for instance, he was fortunate to have a really talented teacher of drawing, and the catalogue raisonné of Moore’s drawings attests to how seriously he took the life class. Barry Hart (fig. 27), teacher of carving, was also a kindred spirit, to the extent of being best man at Moore’s wedding. And, not least, William Rothenstein was extremely supportive.

Derwent Wood, meanwhile, was less than ecstatic in his end of first year report: ‘His life work shows improvement. Design not much to my liking. Is much interested in carvings.’[5] One of Wood’s exercises that Moore balked at was the exact reproduction of the head of the Virgin from the marble relief of *The Virgin and Child* by Domenico Rosselli at the Victoria and Albert Museum (cat. 2). The method that Wood wished him to employ involved making a plaster model and then reproducing that using the mechanical technique of ‘pointing’ – the standard procedure of Victorian sculptors, whose main creative endeavour lay in creating the original plaster, leaving its exact reproduction in marble, considered mere craft skill, to their assistants. Henry Moore managed to persuade Barry

Fig. 27
Henry Moore with Barry Hart (his stone-carving instructor at the Royal College of Art), photographed outside Hart Bros. stone carving works in 1922.

Hart to let him carve the copy directly. He even went so far as to mark the surface with little holes to represent the marks made by the pointing machine, to deceive Wood (cat. 2).

Moore quickly realized that there would have to be a difference between his college and his private work. Nothing could be more different from his Rosselli copy than the little white marble *Dog* (cat. 1) produced in the same year, but this is far more representative of his taste. He had taken to visiting the British Museum twice a week, and was almost overwhelmed by what he saw there – the place was to be a lifelong obsession. He quickly developed a real passion for Mexican carving and this almost architectural piece looks like it could have been chipped off an Aztec temple. A hint of gargoyle in its crouching form seems appropriate:

> Mexican sculpture, as soon as I found it, seemed to me true and right, perhaps because I at once hit on similarities with some eleventh-century carvings I had seen as a boy on Yorkshire churches. Its 'stoniness', by which I mean its truth to material, its tremendous power without loss of sensitiveness, its astonishing variety of form-invention and its approach to a full three-dimensional conception of form, made it unsurpassed in my opinion by any other period of stone sculpture.[6]

A work such as the slate *Relief Head* of 1923 (cat. 3) might have been influenced by African sculpture, or even by Gauguin. William Rothenstein had introduced Henry to his brother Charles Rutherston, who became a good friend and early purchaser, of two smallish wood carvings. Rutherston's own collection, containing ancient Chinese, African, Scythian, Siberian, Archaic Greek and Egyptian work, not to mention modern works by Jacob Epstein (1880–1959) and Frank Dobson (1886–1963), was to prove another source of inspiration.

Throughout his period as a student and beyond (see cats 4, 5, 6) Moore's skills blossomed, but his own 'voice' was still a little muffled, as he tried to absorb and make personal the powerful influences of the British Museum. At the end of the summer of 1924 he achieved his diploma, qualifying him as an art teacher. Wood was a little more generous in his final report, though still hardly effusive: 'Has shown great improvement in all branches, hard-working, his life-work shows promise, altogether a good student.'[7] Even better, he won a six-month travelling scholarship. However, at that point Wood left; and Rothenstein asked Moore to 'look after' the sculpture school meanwhile. Ernest Cole was appointed Wood's successor, – and Moore was given a seven-year appointment as assistant in the sculpture department. Teaching, at the college or, from 1931, at the Chelsea School of Art, was to provide the bulk of his 'bread and butter' until 1939.

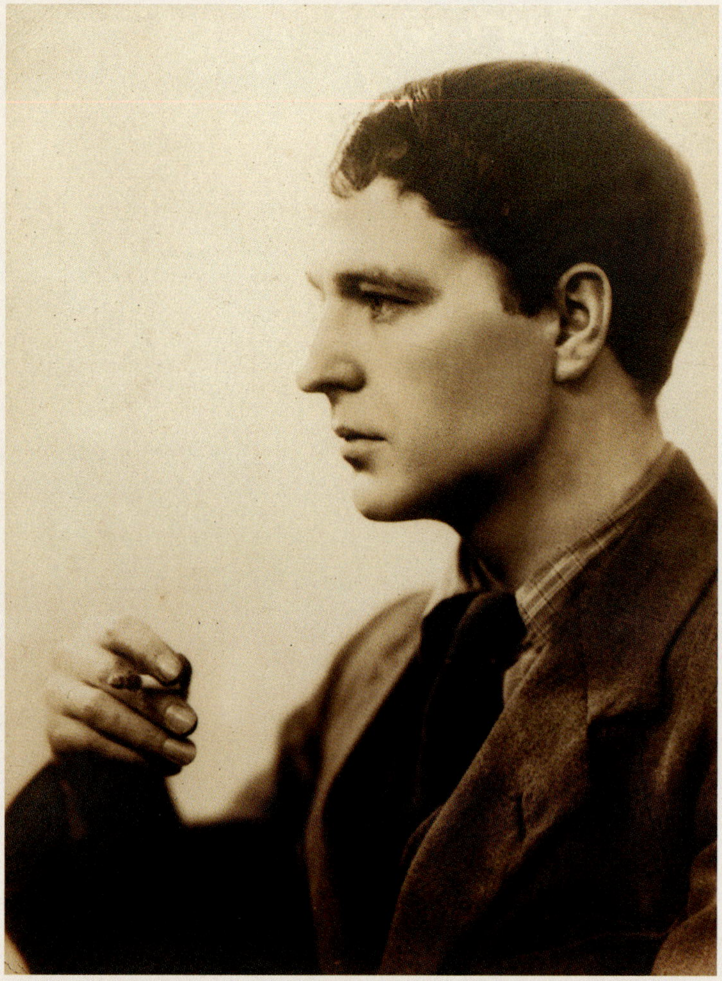

Fig. 28
Henry Moore in *c.*1923–4.

1.
Dog 1922
Marble
h.178mm
The Henry Moore Foundation: gift of the artist 1977
LH 2

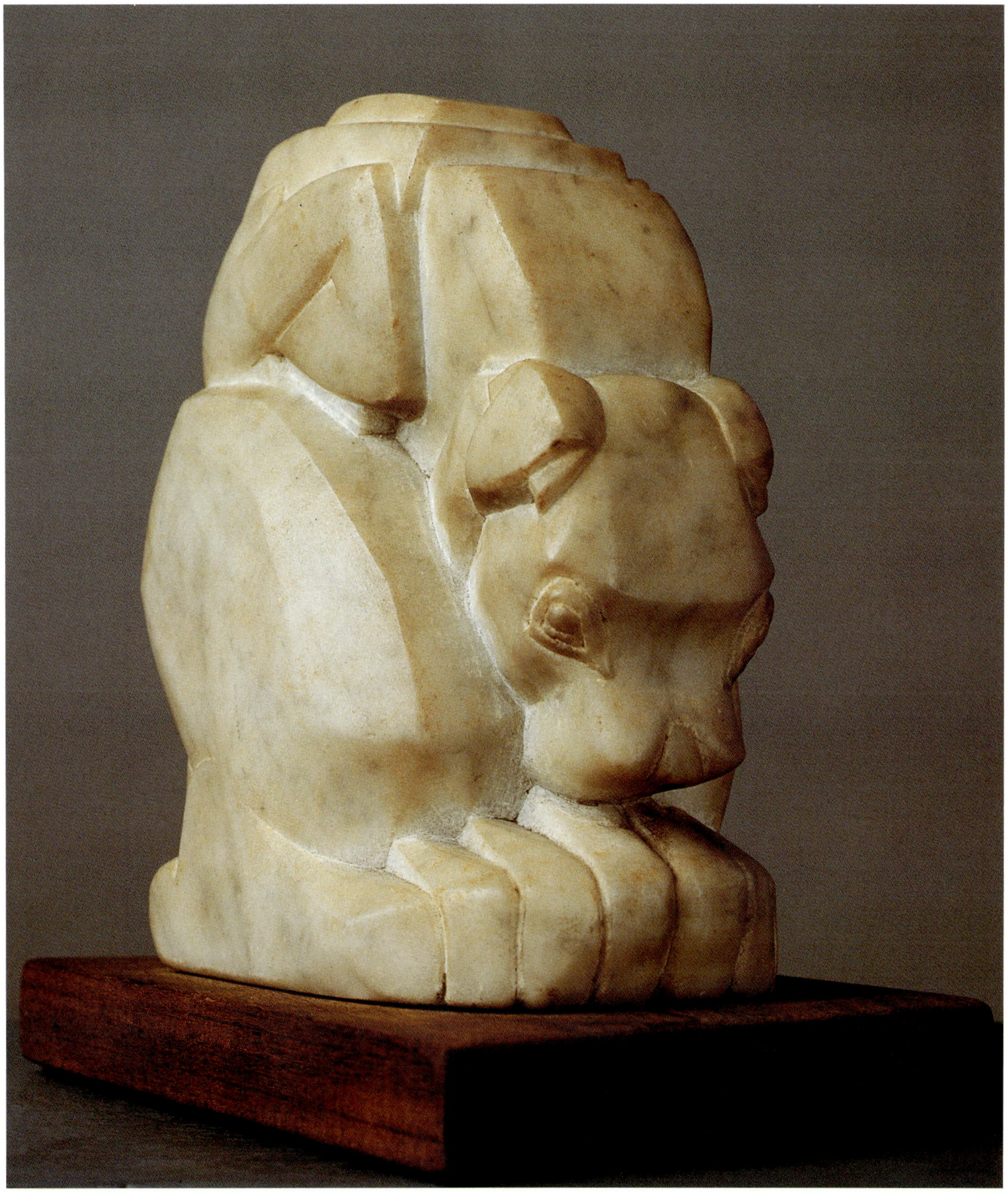

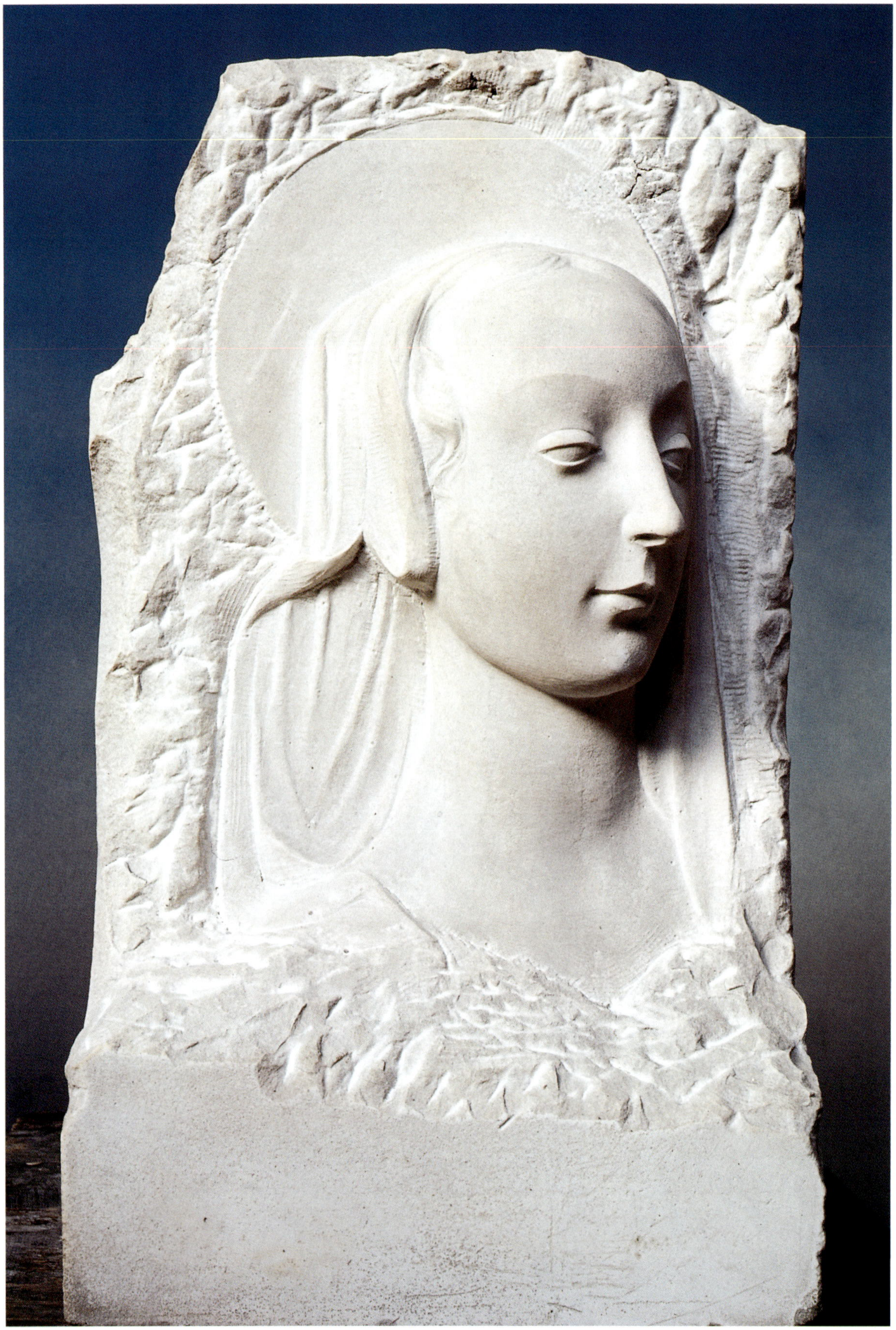

2.
Head of the Virgin 1922
After the marble relief
The Virgin and Child
by Domenico Rosselli
(*c.*1439–97/8)
in the Victoria and
Albert Museum
Marble
h.532mm
The Henry Moore
Foundation:
acquired 1988
LH 6

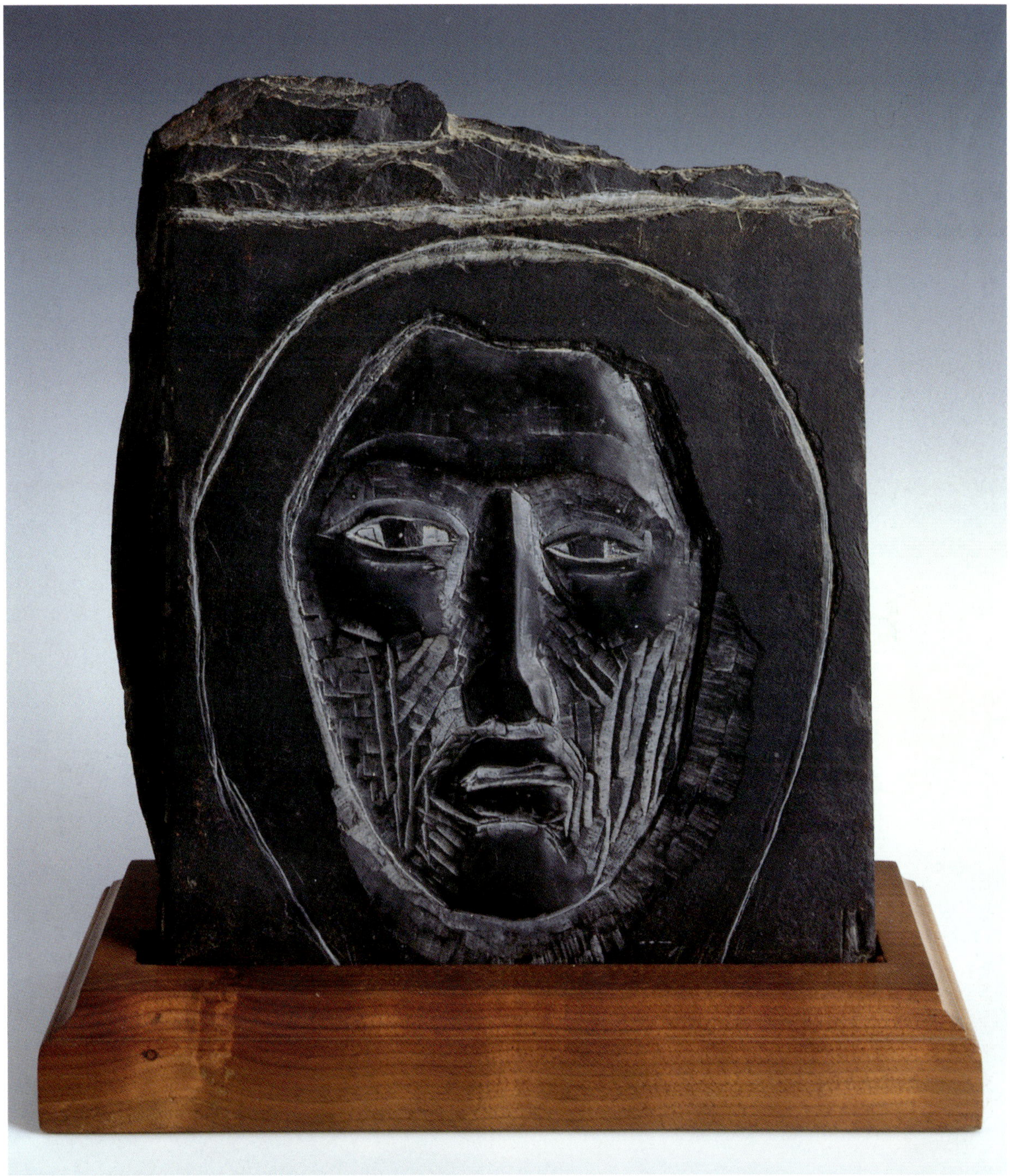

3.
Relief Head 1923
Slate
314 x 278 x 30mm
Private Collection,
Switzerland
LH 9

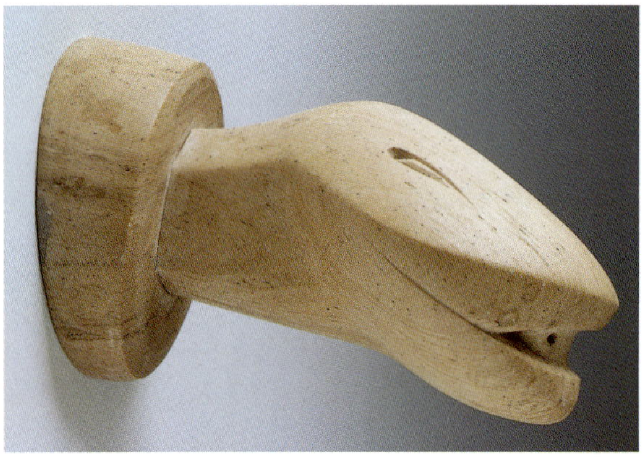

4.
Head of Serpent 1927
Stone
180 x 114 x 114mm
Private Collection,
Switzerland
LH 45

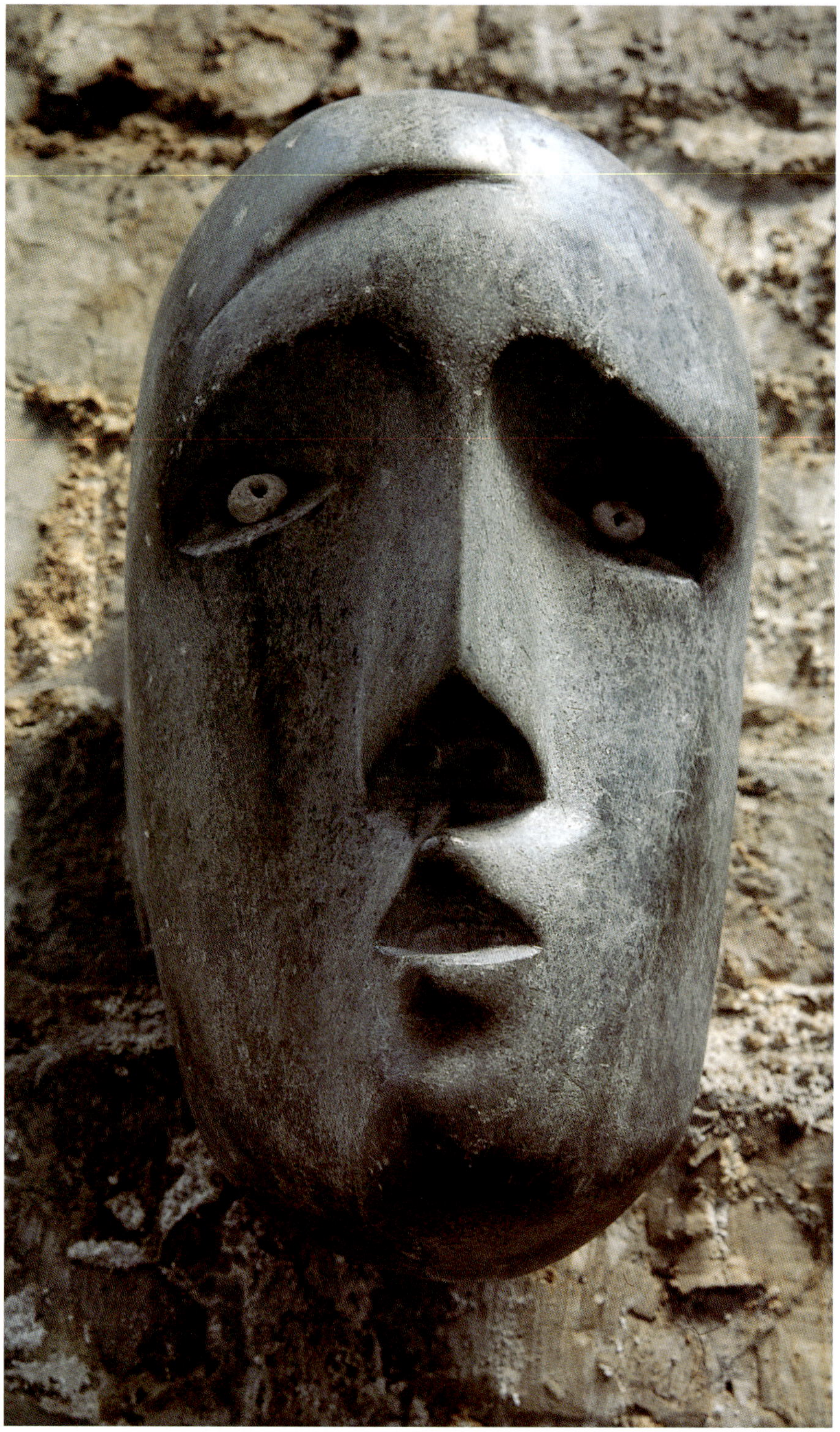

5.
Mask 1927
Green stone
h.210mm
The Henry Moore
Foundation: acquired 1997
LH 46

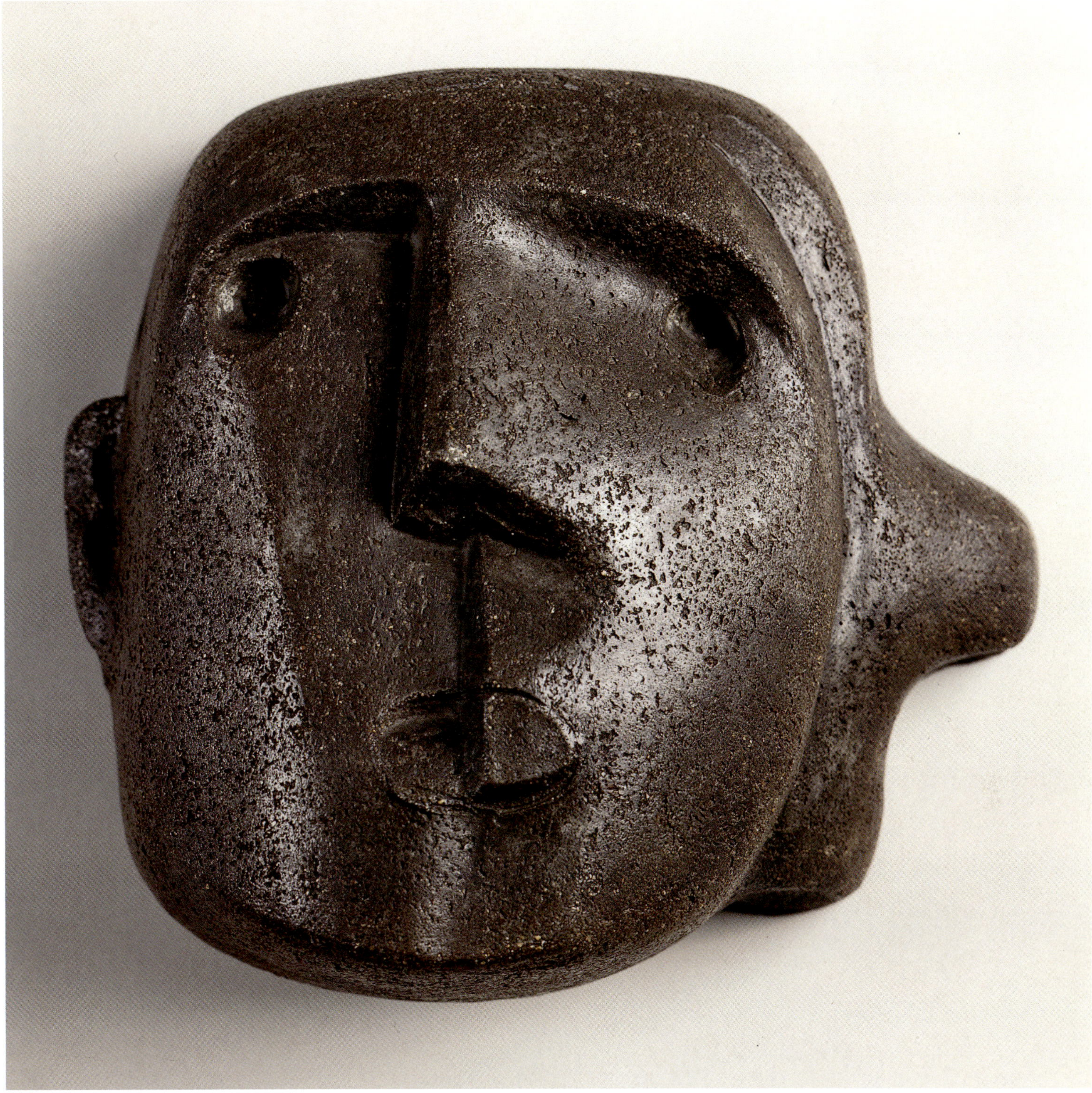

6.
Mask 1929
Cast concrete
240 x 210 x 123mm
Leeds Museum and Art Galleries (City Art Gallery)
LH 62

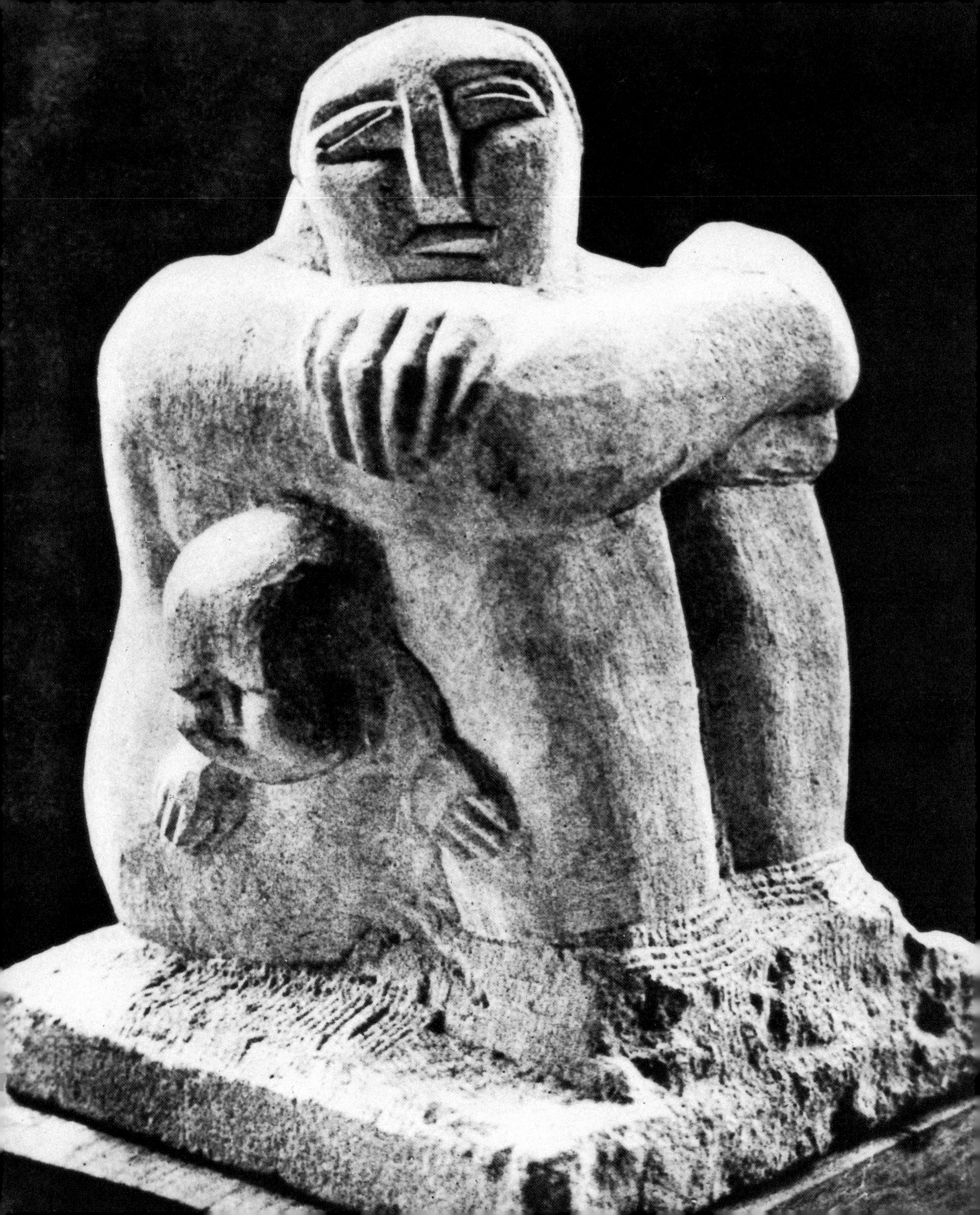

> From very early on I have had an obsession with the Mother and Child theme. It has been a universal theme from the beginning of time and some of the earliest sculptures we've found from the Neolithic Age are of a Mother and Child … I suppose it could be explained as a 'Mother' complex.[8]

WHILE MOORE COULD AT TIMES be a little too eager to appeal to the lay psychologist in his interviewers, there is no doubt that, mother complex or not, the mother and child theme in his oeuvre was both early to appear and long-lasting. To some extent it was a complex borrowed from the British Museum, as his quote above hints. His earliest versions (figs 29, 30) also owe a clear debt to Jacob Epstein, whose importance for Moore was considerable. Epstein was not only an inspiring iconoclast with a visible enthusiasm for African art, he was the forerunner, and as such had taken the brunt of the brickbats and abuse that 'modern art' inevitably attracted from traditionalist quarters. Some critics indeed were routinely vicious at Moore's expense also for years, but Epstein had always been there first. He had even seen his sculpture mutilated on Charles Holden's British Medical Association building in response to public outrage, a kind of philistine insult that Moore never had to endure (although his work has attracted its fair share of 'common-or-garden' vandalism).

Fig. 30 (below)
Mother and Child, 1924–5 (LH 26), Green Hornton stone; Manchester City Galleries.

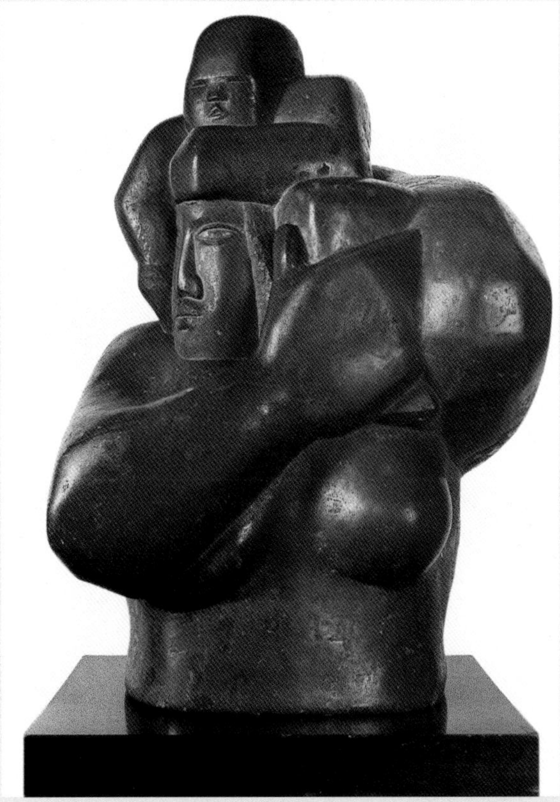

The early mother and child sculptures are solid, blockish affairs celebrating the unity of the two figures, with Herculean infant emerging from strange places (fig. 29) or balanced on its mother's head (fig. 30). 'Truth to materials' and the 'British Museum tendency' are clearly in evidence here, but by 1930 his tiny *Mother and Child* (cat. 7), carved from an ironstone pebble, shows him manipulating his still monumental figures into positive delicacy through the sheer virtuosity of his carving – even penetrating the pebble beneath the child's outreaching arm, while the mother's enfolding arm echoes the movement and creates a spiralling, enclosing form like the petals of a rose.

There follows, in 1932, one of the masterpieces of the early period, the Sainsbury *Mother and Child* in beautiful Green Hornton stone (cat. 8). It was bought by Robert Sainsbury in 1933, who recorded that its position of honour in the hall of his house did not necessarily guarantee admirers: 'There is no doubt that it was the exception for anyone to like it. Most people thought it was funny – and these were educated people …'[9] The exaggerated shoulder, cliff-face back, and twist of the legs to the side beautifully evoke the inner muscular feel of this mother's protectiveness, while the baby itself is on a far more diminutive and consequently vulnerable scale than previously. In that sense this is a more naturalistic work than the monumental mothers of the previous decade.

During the 1930s Moore could hardly avoid being involved in that decade's obsessions with abstraction and, later, surrealism, in which debates friends like Barbara Hepworth (1903–75), her (second) husband Ben Nicholson (1894–1982), John Piper (1903–93) and Paul Nash (1889–1946) were passionately involved. Surrealism surfaced in Moore's art most particularly in the form of his stringed figures, an idea that Hepworth

Fig. 29 (left)
Mother and Child, 1922 (LH 3), Portland stone; private collection.

The Mother and Child

and Hans Arp (1887–1966) were also very much involved with, and which are very often near abstract as well. The *Mother and Child* of 1938 in lead and yellow string (cat. 9) shows Moore using the string not merely as a visual interpretation of tension but as a psychological indicator. The strings function to lock the eyes of mother and child together while simultaneously making clear the nurturing bond, with the strings leading from baby's face to mother's breasts. Here the use of strings, rather different from his practice elsewhere, is in danger perhaps of being overly literal in an 'X marks the spot' kind of way. In *Stringed Figure: Bowl* (1938, cat. 45) the strings tension the abstract shape, providing the visual stimulation of a stretched membrane. In *Bird Basket* (1939, cat. 46) a smaller form is glimpsed through the strings like a bird in a cage, an early precursor of the later internal/external form type with all its resonances of protection and vulnerability. Moore was certainly only partially comfortable with the technique; between 1937 and 1939 he produced twenty-seven stringed figures but soon gave it up, admitting: 'I could have done hundreds. They were fun, but too much in the nature of experiments to be really satisfying.'[10] Unlike for Hepworth, where the use of string created an extra dynamic of delicate balance and tension that was very much an extension of her sculptural language, for Moore the string felt foreign to his art – almost frippery.

One of the galvanizing factors that led Moore to make his famous wartime shelter drawings was that the spectacle of so many people sheltering from the Blitz in the Tube stations of London seemed to throw up so many instant 'Henry Moores', most obviously rows of reclining figures. But he was quick to spot variations on his mother and child theme also (cat. 64), and the discomfort and distress of the situation add a new empathetic edge to the relationship. In this example mother and child are asleep, but the enveloping blanket suggests both shroud and flowing river – not waving, but drowning, as it were. A later shelter drawing (also acquired by the Sainsburys, cat. 66) shows Moore actively developing his themes away from the shelter context, and includes in the bottom right-hand corner a mother and child which is in fact closer in form to a Renaissance Madonna and Child.

The shelter drawings were exhibited during the war, along with other war artists' work, at the National Gallery. There they happened to be seen in 1942 by the Revd Walter Hussey who by a lucky chance was looking for an artist to fulfil a sculptural commission for his church, St Matthew's in Northampton, in honour of the church's fiftieth anniversary in 1943. The result was to be Moore's most famous sculpture so far, the Northampton *Madonna and Child* (fig. 9). Here, more than in any previous sculpture, the influence of Moore's travelling scholarship of eighteen years before suddenly bore fruit.

In February 1925 Moore had finally taken up his scholarship and with mixed feelings set off for Italy, no doubt expecting to feel nothing but contempt for the decadent products of the Renaissance and Baroque. Of course the experience turned out to be rich – overwhelmingly so, sufficient to cause a very miserable period of derailed self-confidence on his return. Some extremely positive impressions were made, however. He had expected to like Giotto, and he did, emphatically: 'Giotto's painting is the finest sculpture I've met in Italy', he wrote.[11] In the same letter his fashionable prejudices (and some casual 1920s male chauvinism) got in the way of a proper appreciation of Donatello: 'in the influence of Donatello I see the beginning of the end – Donatello was a modeller, and it seems to me that it is modelling that has sapped the manhood out of Western sculpture.' Misguided perhaps (and, in fairness, Moore certainly appreciated Donatello later in life, when he used regularly to rate the Florentine sculptor in his 'top ten greatest artists ever'[12]), but the lessons learned from Giotto, and from Masaccio, the other major seminal discovery of his Italian trip, are clear to see in the monumental form and serene simplicity of the Northampton *Madonna*, which was installed on 10 February 1944, and dedicated and unveiled ten days later. It seems extraordinary that this work, surely the most accessible of all Moore's masterpieces, should have unleashed the critical firestorm that it did. The clay models made for it became sought after in their own right, and one, in order to avoid offending Revd Hussey and Sir Kenneth Clark, to both of whom Moore had inadvertantly promised it, was cast in bronze – a practice that became a financially rewarding commonplace (cats 11 and 12) for Moore, attracting criticism from some quarters. Moore was later to explain his development into a modeller (among other things, of course) of the effete Donatellesque tendency:

> When I began to make sculpture thirty years ago, it was very necessary to fight for the doctrine of truth to material (the need for direct carving, for respecting the particular character of each material, and so on). So at that time many of us tended to make a fetish of it. I still think it is important, but it should not be the criterion of the value of a work – otherwise a snowman made by a child would have to be praised at the expense of a Rodin or a Bernini. Rigid adherence to the doctrine results in domination of the sculpture by the material. The sculptor ought to be master of his material. Only, not a cruel master.[13]

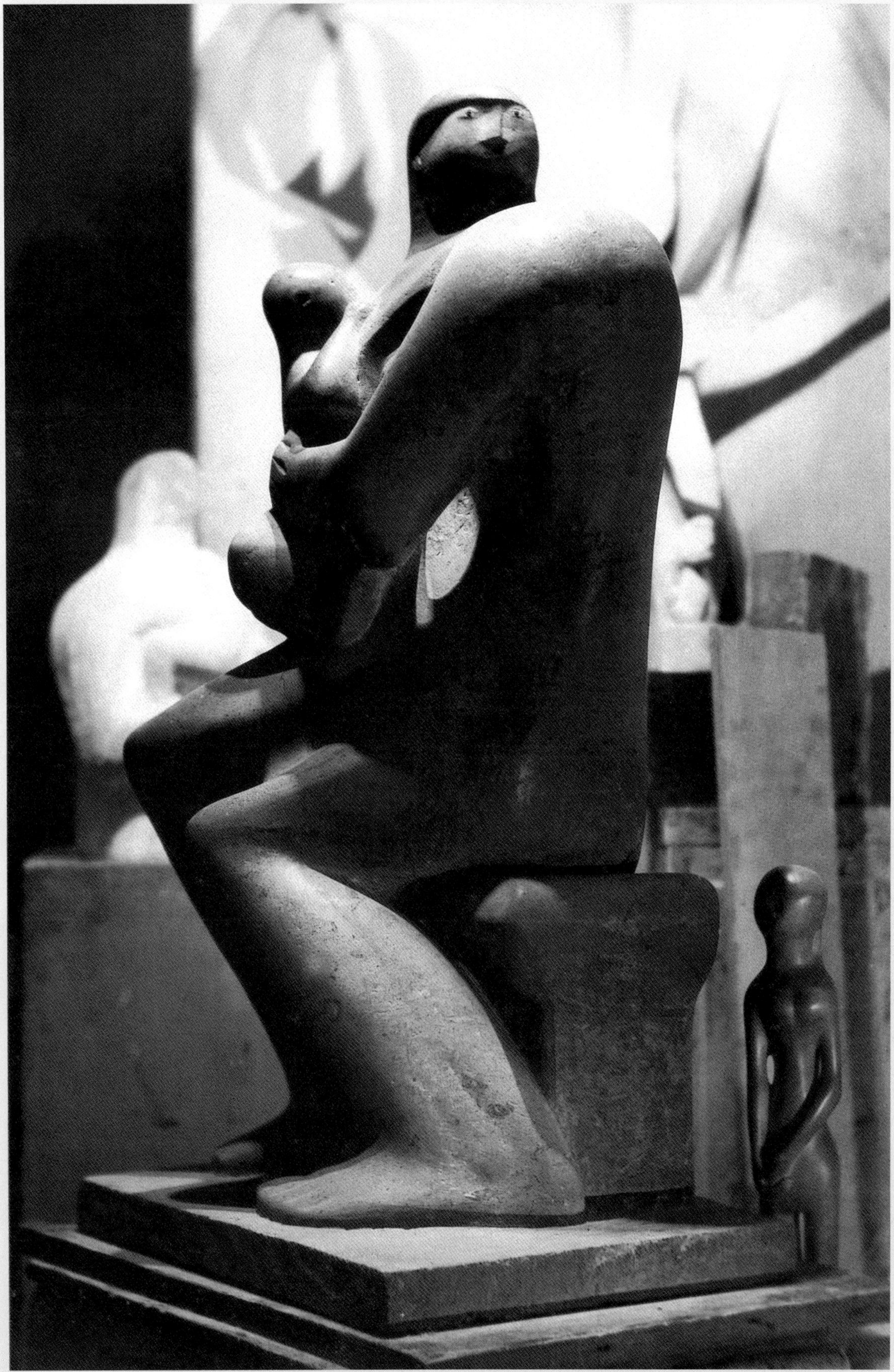

Fig. 31
Henry Moore's studio at 11a Parkhill Road, Belsize Park, showing *Mother and Child* (cat. 8) and boxwood *Figure* (LH 112).

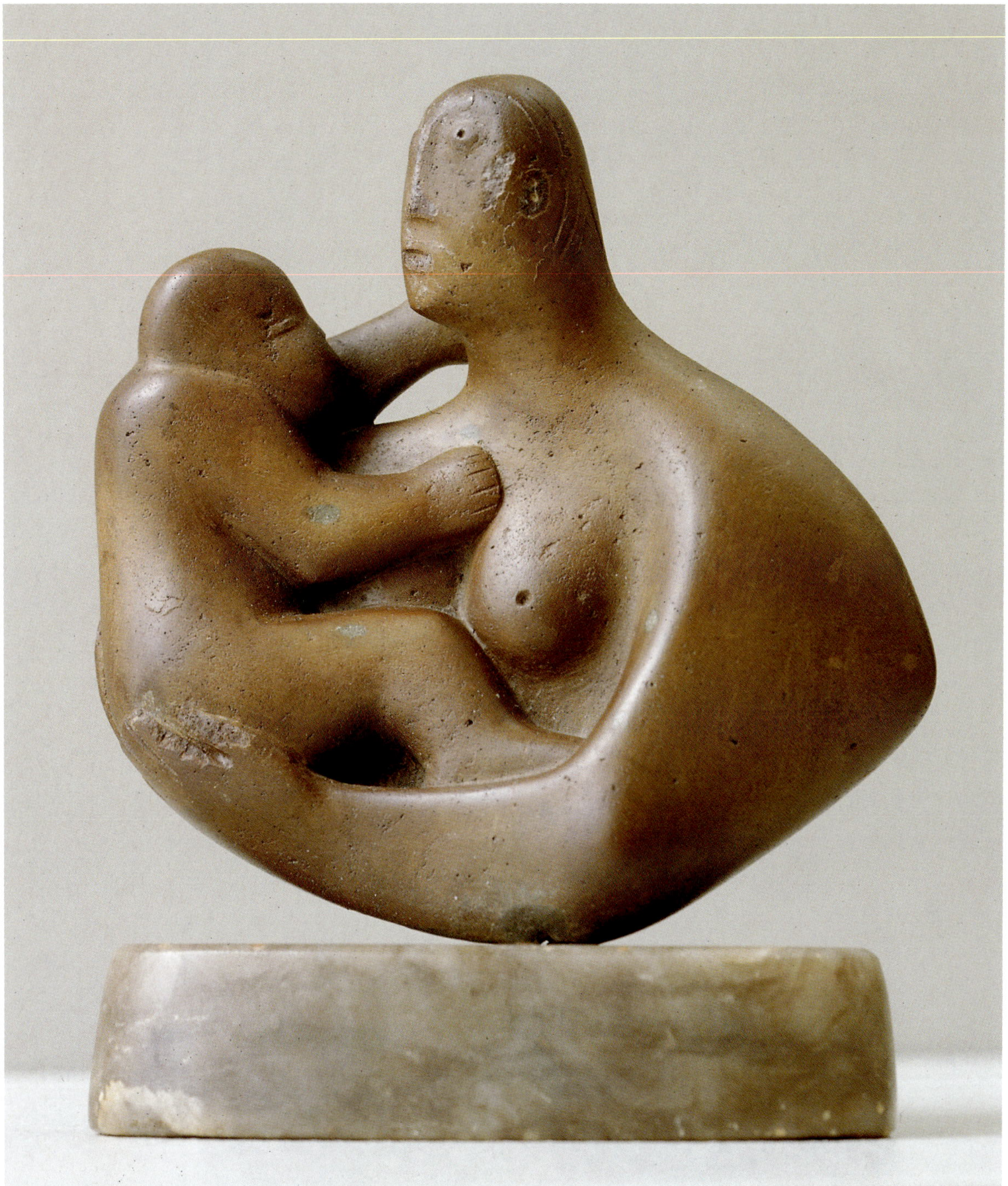

7.
Mother and Child 1930
Ironstone
h.150mm
The Henry Moore
Foundation: acquired 1998
LH 86

8.
Mother and Child 1932
Green Hornton stone
995 x 535 x 380mm
Robert and Lisa Sainsbury
Collection, University of
East Anglia, UEA 82
LH 121

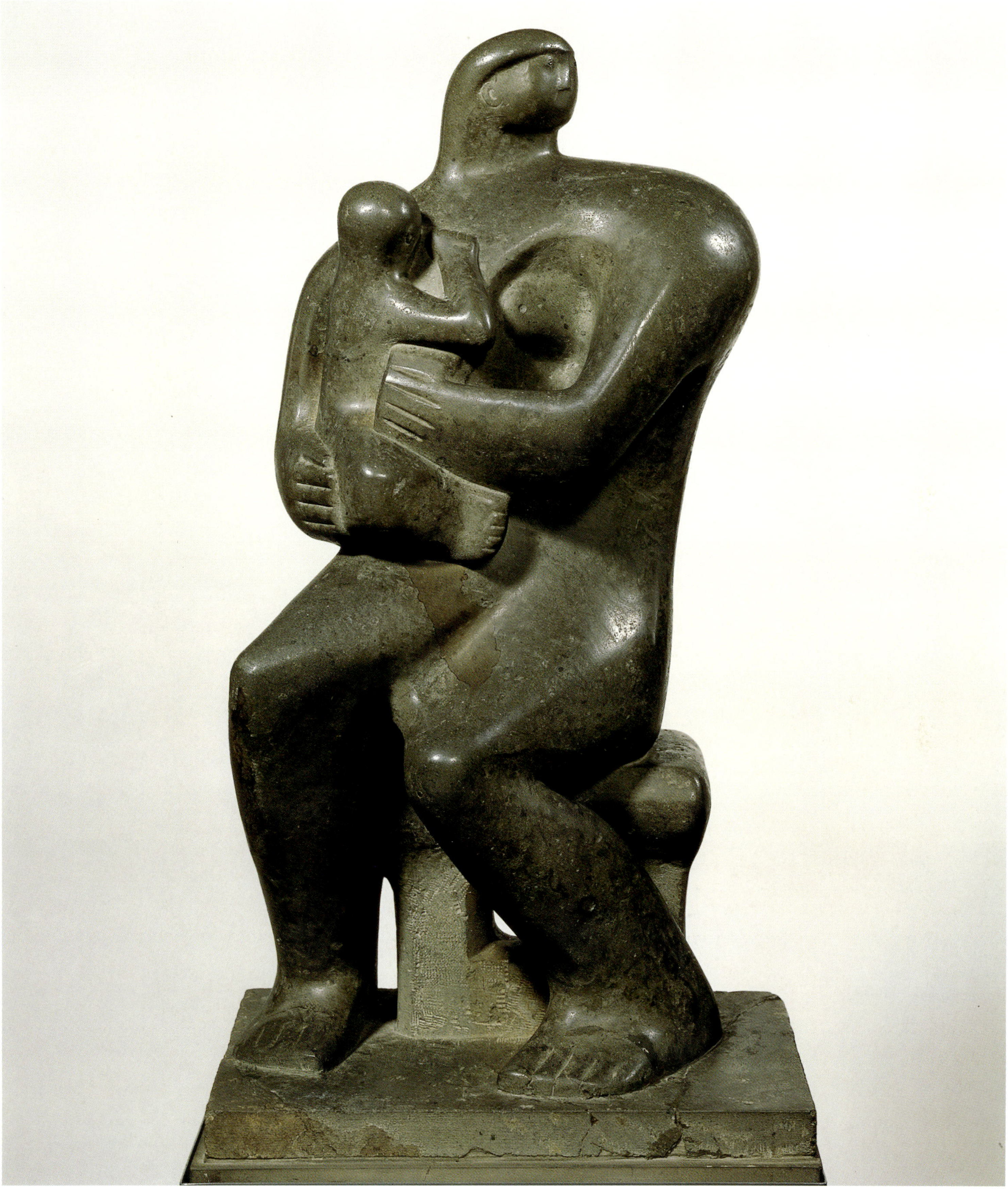

8.
Mother and Child 1932
Other views: side, back and detail of front.

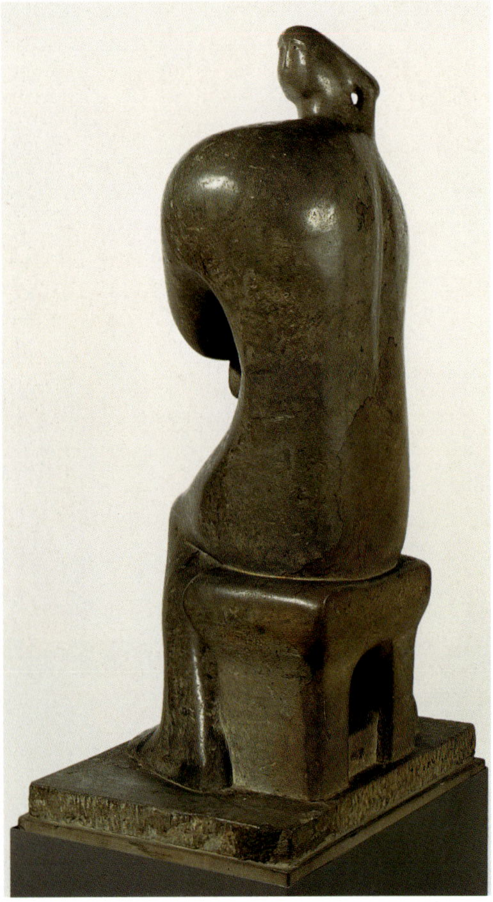

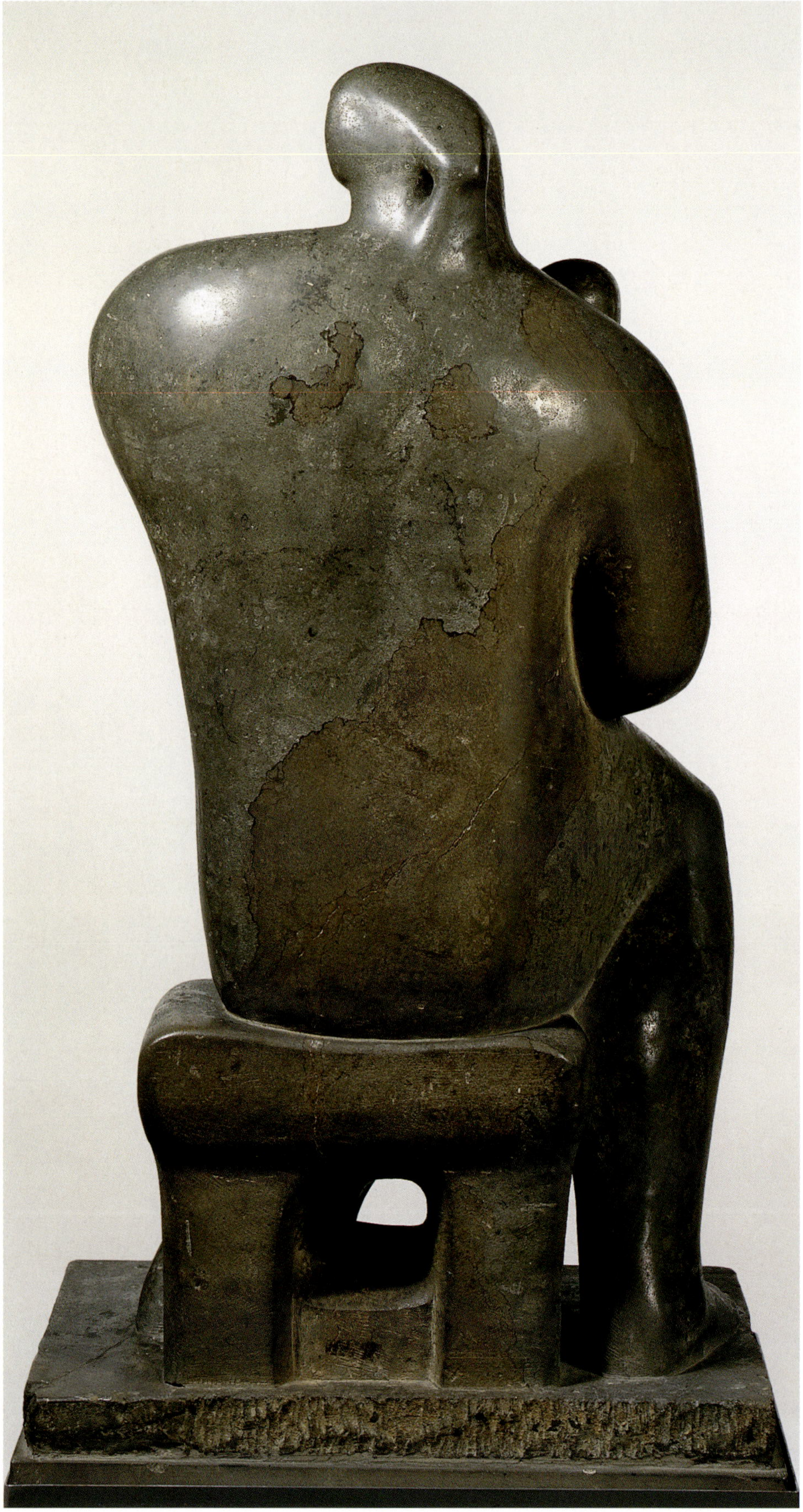

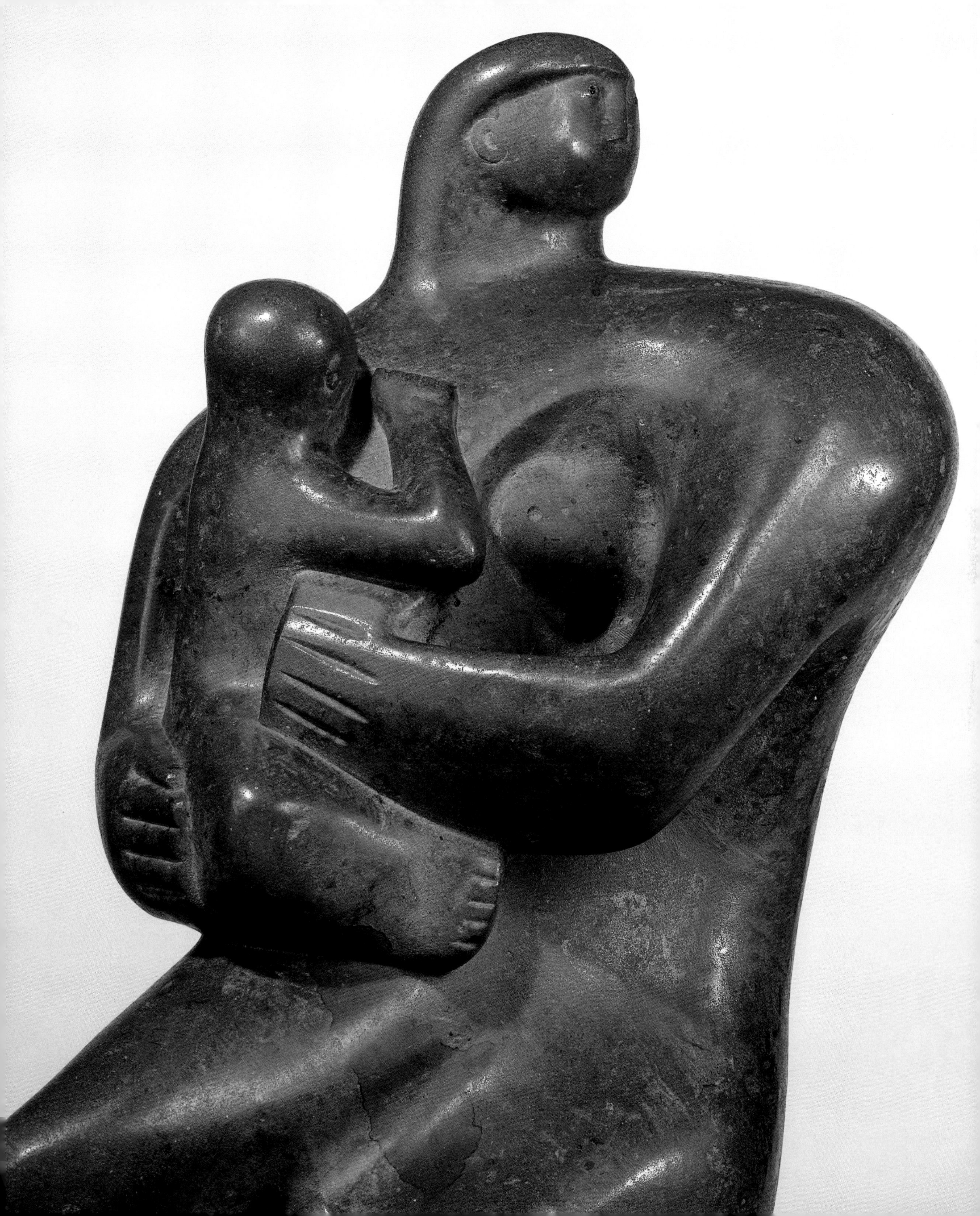

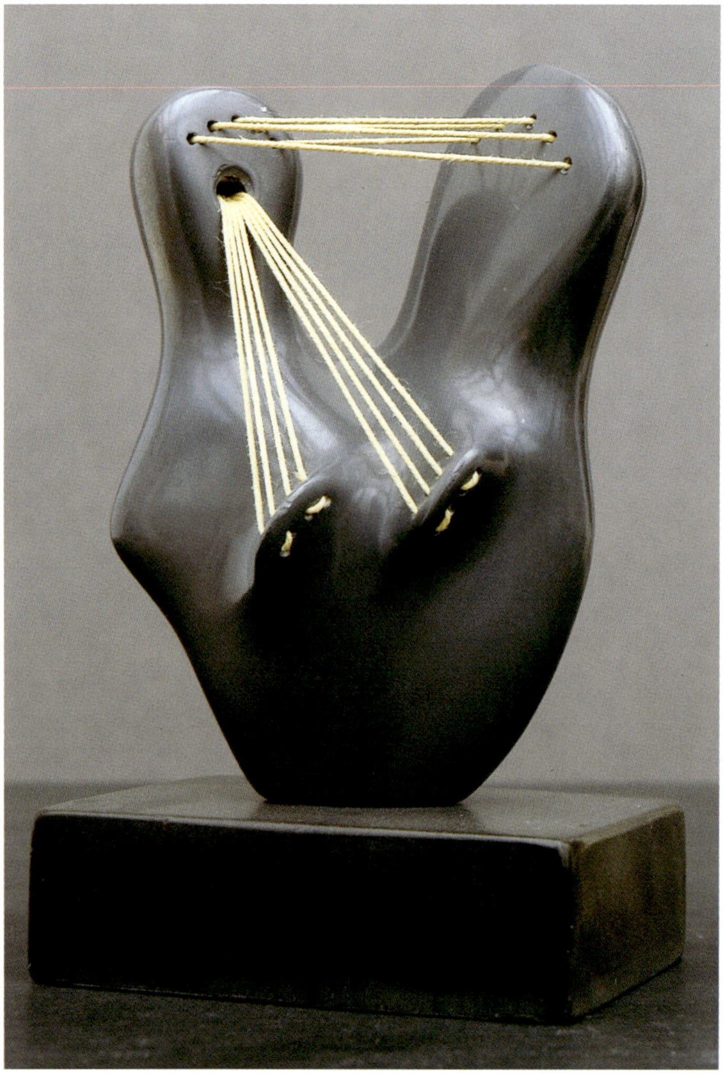

9.
Mother and Child 1938
Lead and yellow string
h.95mm
The Henry Moore Foundation: acquired by exchange 1996
LH 186

10.
Madonna and Child Studies 1943
Coloured crayon, wax crayon, watercolour wash, pen and ink
217 x 167mm
Signed and dated lower right: 'Moore / 43'
Northampton Central Museum and Art Gallery, D.236.1986.1
AG 43.85, HMF 2175a

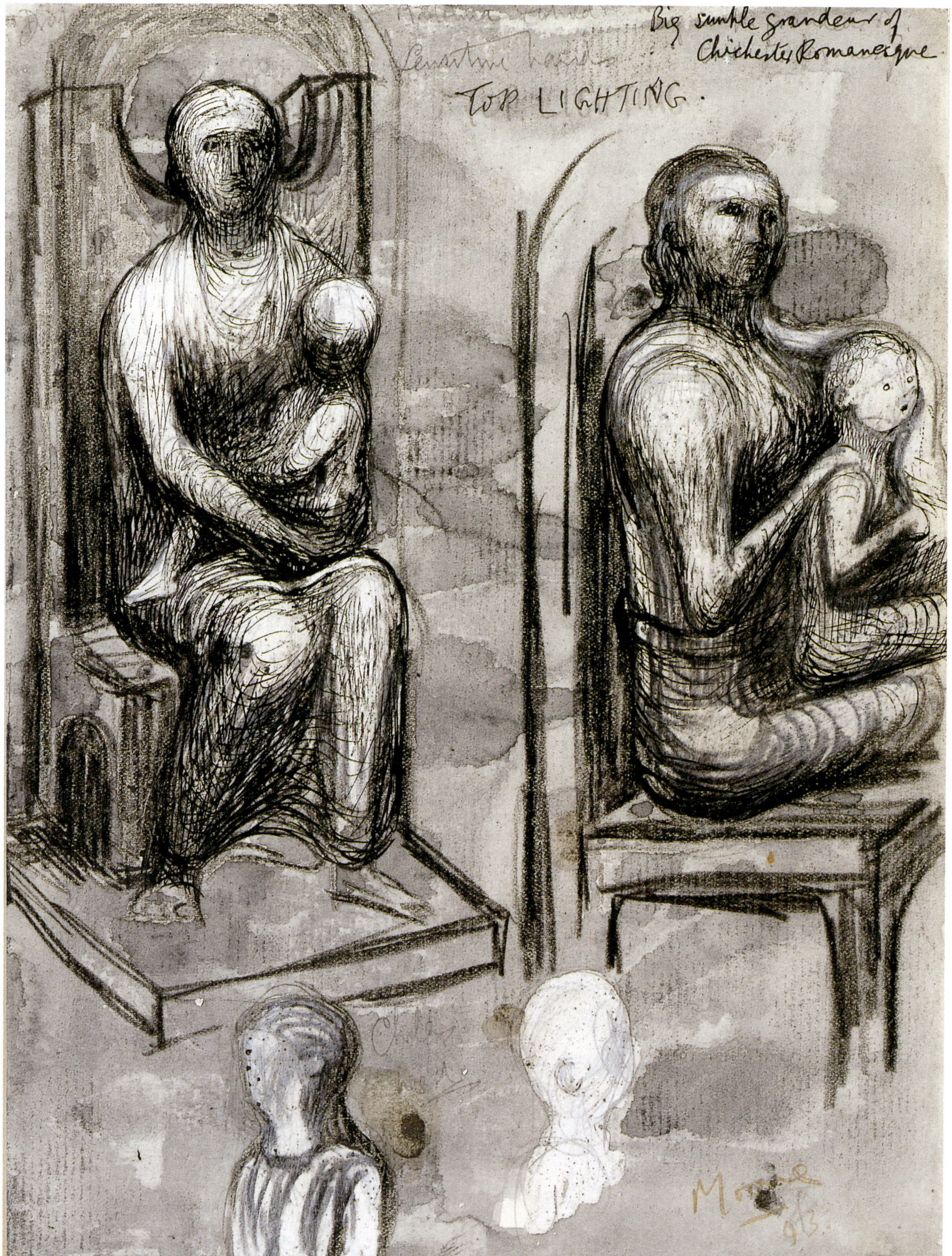
Big simple grandeur of
Chichester Romanesque
TOP LIGHTING.
Moore
43.

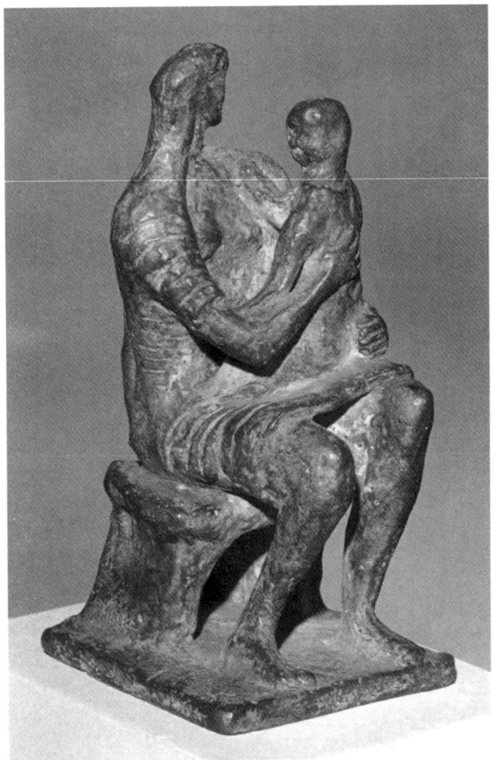

11.
Madonna and Child
1943
Bronze
140 x 76 x 76mm
Tate, purchased 1950,
NO5600
LH 223

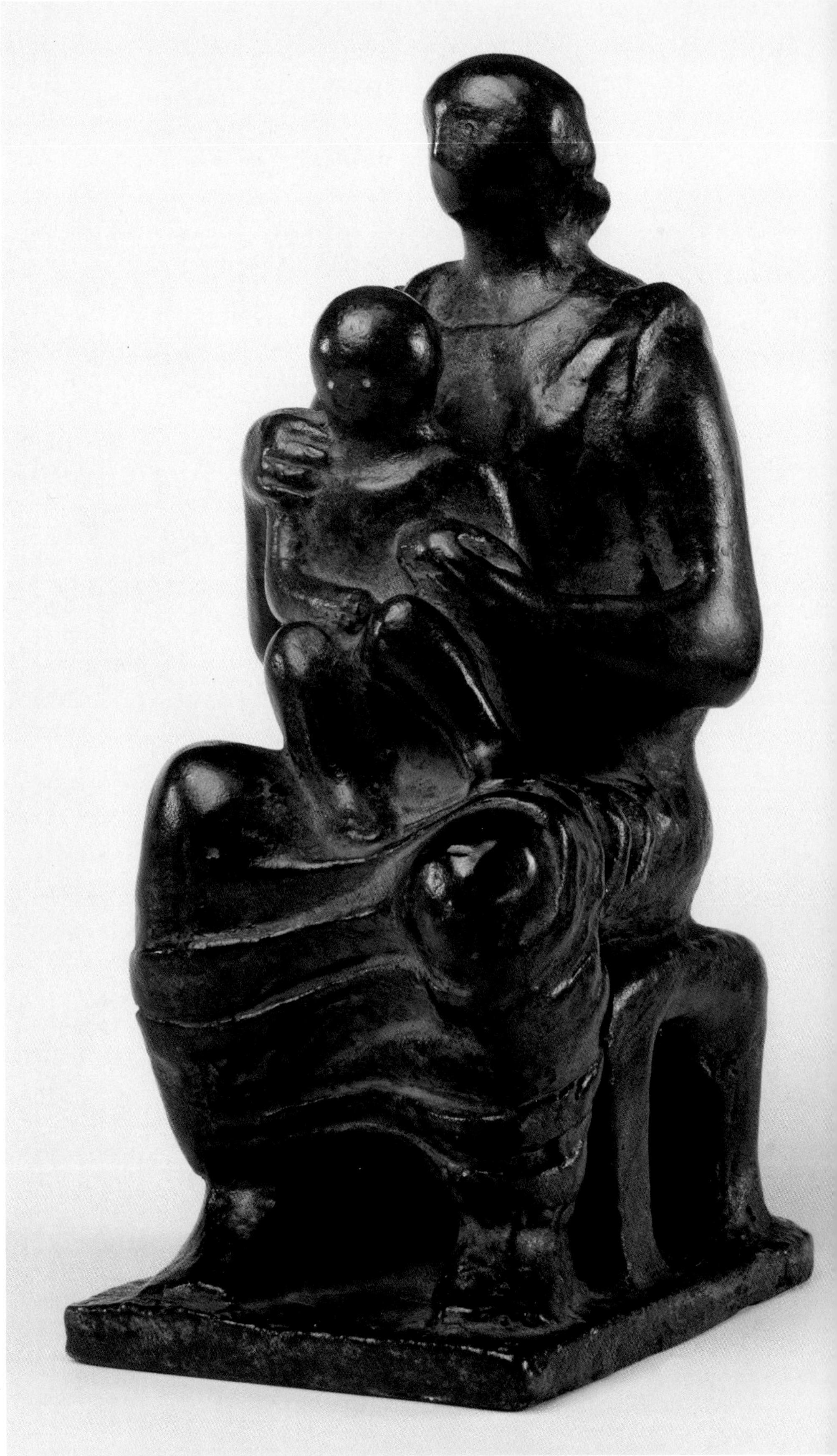

12.
Madonna and Child
1943–4
Bronze
155 x 65 x 85mm
Robert and Lisa Sainsbury
Collection, University of
East Anglia, UEA 84
LH 224

13.
Mother and Child 1943
Pen and ink
170 x 130mm
Signed and dated:
'Moore / 43'
Inscribed lower centre right:
'To David / October 24th / 1953' (date of gift)
David Sainsbury
AG 43.106, HMF 2187

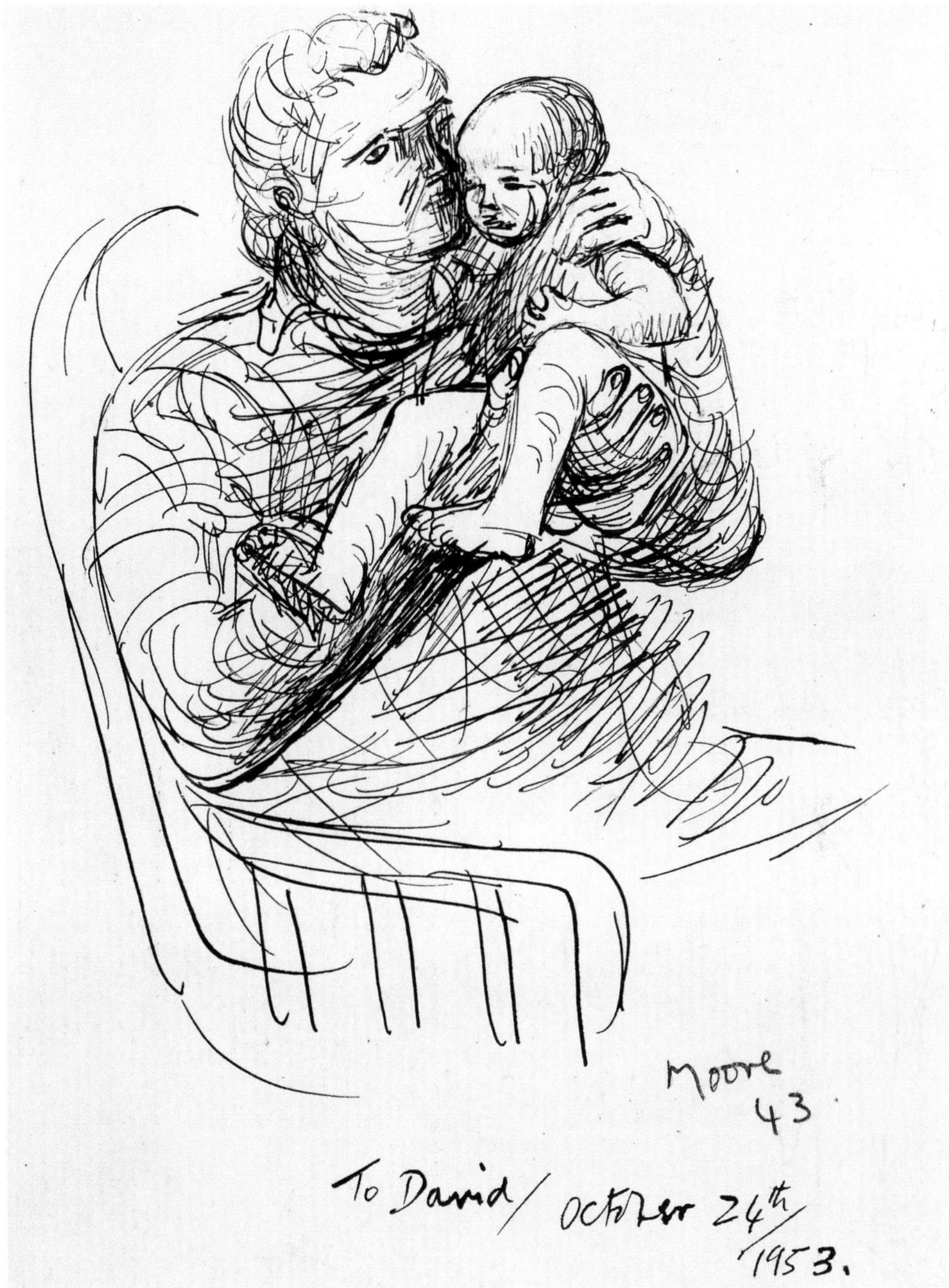

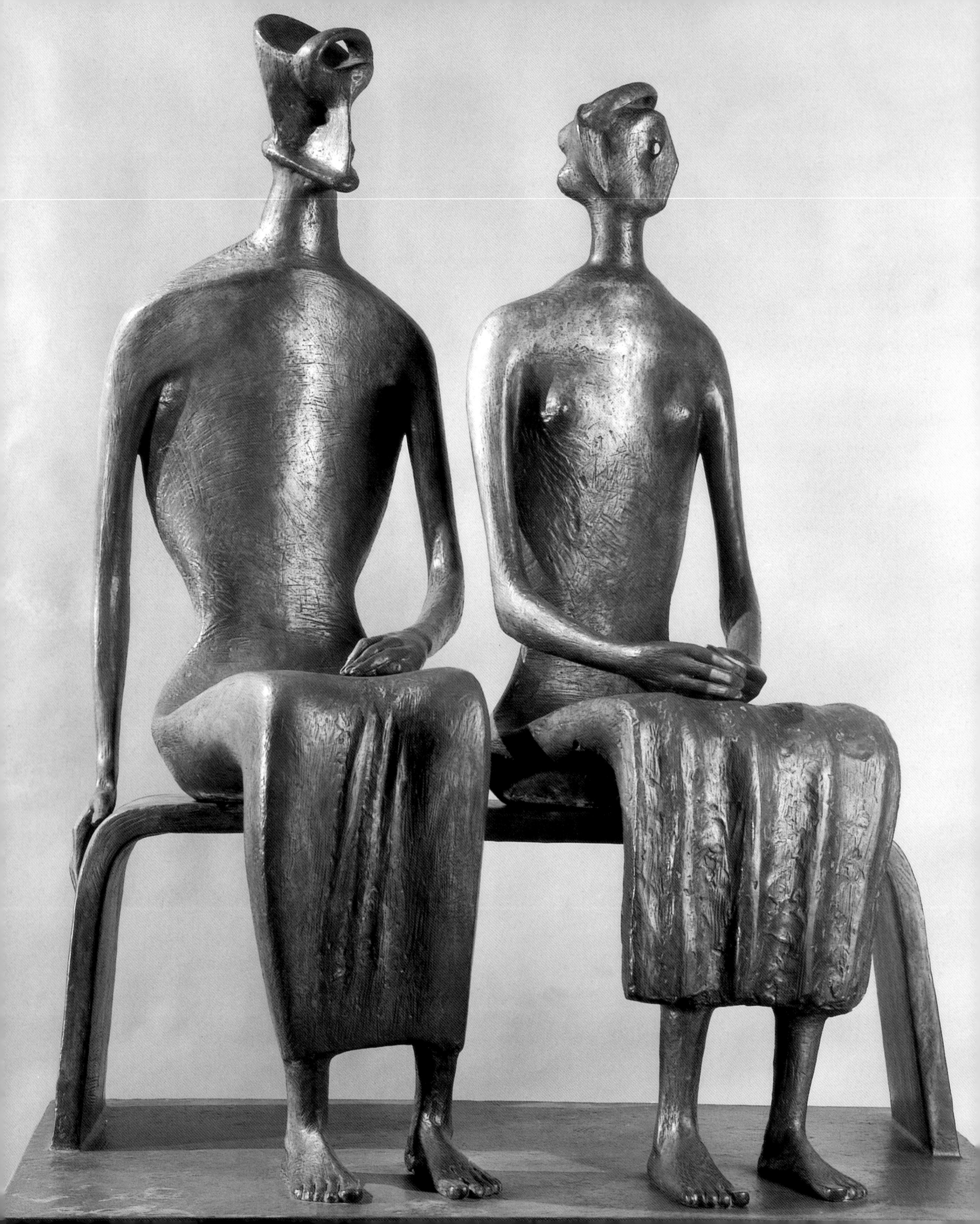

> The family group ideas were all generated by drawings; and that was perhaps because the whole family group idea was so close to one as a person; we were just going to have our first child, Mary, and it was an obsession.[14]

THE MOTHER AND CHILD THEME continued to surface in Moore's work, sometimes less overtly, as in some of the well-known internal/external forms, for example (fig. 33). But the clearest development in the theme followed on from the climax of the Northampton *Madonna* in the family groups (see cats 14–20). Again, as with the mother and child sculptures, the figures are always seated – in general, Moore was at this date unhappy with standing figures, and it was a while before he really tackled upright forms. The weight and stability of the seated figure suited him better. There remains a residual notion of 'the throne' about these simple bench forms, which found its inevitable development in the later *King and Queen* (fig. 32), and the drapery of the female form recalls Moore's *Madonna*. This association definitely adds to the gravitas of the large Tate group (cat. 20), giving it a quasi-moral or allegorical weight – 'the' rather than 'a' family – but another source may well be found in Egyptian or Etruscan sculptures of married couples, which share the hieratic seriousness of the Moore piece.

The genesis of this theme seems to have been partly a matter of patronage, and partly personal. Two profoundly important family events must have informed the theme for Moore. First there was the death of his mother in May 1944, a bitter blow, but one that brought the family together and must have reinforced Moore's grateful memories of his own happy childhood. Secondly, on 7 March 1946, after seventeen years of marriage and in the wake of miscarriages, came the birth of Henry and Irina's only daughter, Mary. Suddenly he was a family man and his so-called 'mother complex' expanded to include himself as father, not child. It was one of the few times in which Henry Moore ever attempted a male figure in his art. While not, of course, a self-portrait, it represents his own joyous self at this happy time.

The other stimulus was a commission from the educationalist Henry Morris, who had developed a 'village college' concept that had attracted some approval. The basic idea was that all education – primary, secondary and adult – should ideally be under one roof, thereby providing a focus for the entire community. Moore had met Morris back in the 1930s, and had liked the idea. In 1944 Morris wanted a major Moore sculpture for the second such college, at Impington in Cambridgeshire, which had been designed by Walter Gropius and Maxwell Fry. A series of maquettes was made, but Morris could not get the backing of the reactionary county council. The deal fell through, though the brisk sale of bronze editions of the maquettes lessened the blow for Moore.

The commission was finally revived by the Hertfordshire County Education Officer, John Newsom, who wanted the sculpture to be sited outside a new secondary school in the new town Stevenage. It was to be Moore's first big public bronze, and there were problems with the casting. It was not installed until September 1950. The usual extreme reactions flared up, both for and against. Sir Alfred Munnings, President of the Royal

Fig. 32
King and Queen, 1952–3 (LH 350), cast in 1957, bronze; Tate.

The Family Groups

Academy and reactionary bull of choice when a newspaper wished to flourish the red rag of modern art, duly obliged the *Daily Dispatch*: 'Distorted figures and knobs instead of heads get a man talked about these foolish days. Anyone can do round balls for heads. Few can chisel the features of a face.'[15] Another favourite barb was fired off by the *Financial Times*: 'One county education authority has recently thought it more worthwhile to buy a lumpish piece of sculpture by Henry Moore than to raise its teachers' salaries.'[16] This one hit a nerve with the education committee; and Moore, in exchange for a reduction of his fee, cannily negotiated a deal by which he could make extra casts and dispose of them himself. No doubt Munnings would have been incredulous that anyone would purchase, but Moore knew better. Casts were made: one (cat. 20) went to the then Tate Gallery; another went to the Museum of Modern Art in New York; and a third ended up in Japan, at the Hakone Open Air Museum, via Nelson Rockefeller's country house. A tidy Yorkshire profit was made.

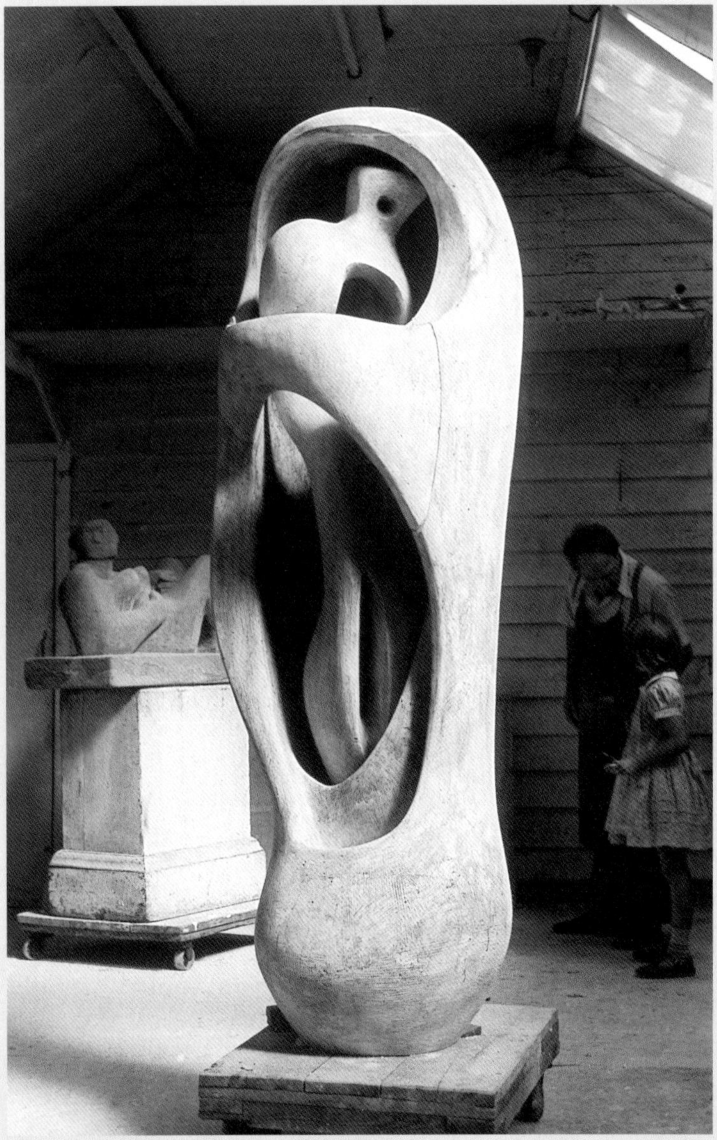

Fig. 33
View of studio showing a working model for *Upright Internal/External Form*, 1951 (LH 296), with Henry and Mary Moore in the background inadvertently (?) posed to illustrate its theme.

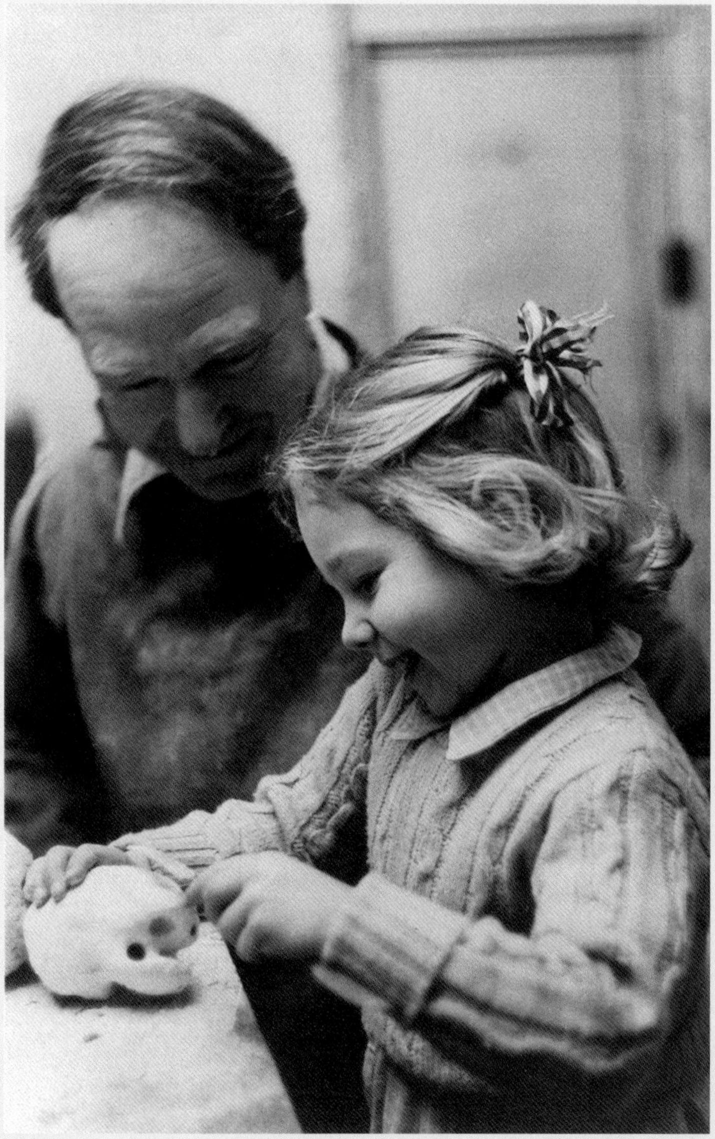

Fig. 34
Henry Moore with his daughter Mary, Perry Green, Easter 1951.

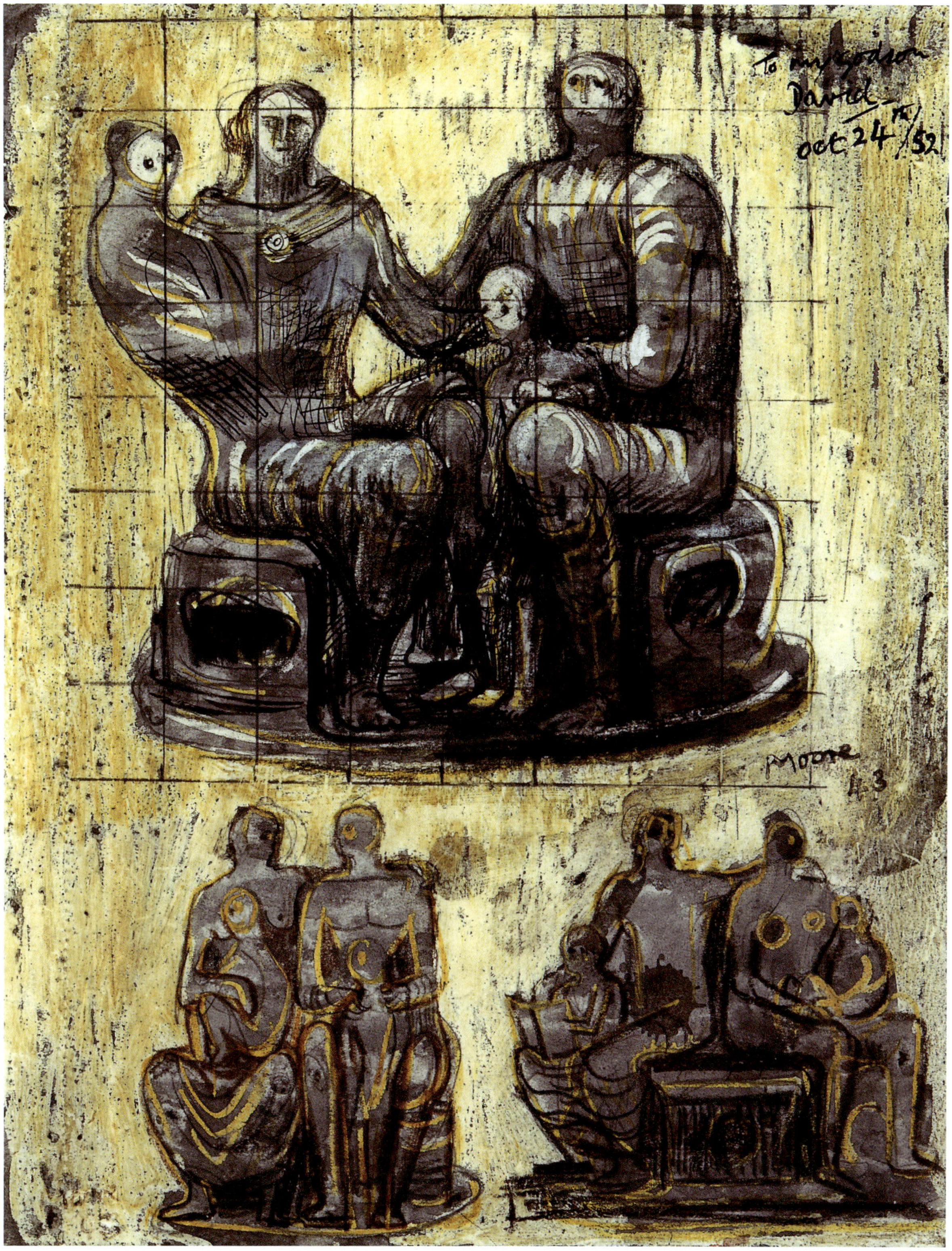

14.
Three Family Groups
*c.*1943–4
Family Group
Notebook, p.30
Pencil, wax crayon,
watercolour wash,
pen and ink
228 x 180mm
Signed and dated in pen
and ink middle right:
'Moore / 43';
lower left (very faint):
'Moore / 45 [written over
43 and misdated]'
Inscribed in pen and ink
upper right: 'To my Godson
/ David / Oct 24th / 52'
David Sainsbury
AG 43-44.1, HMF 2187

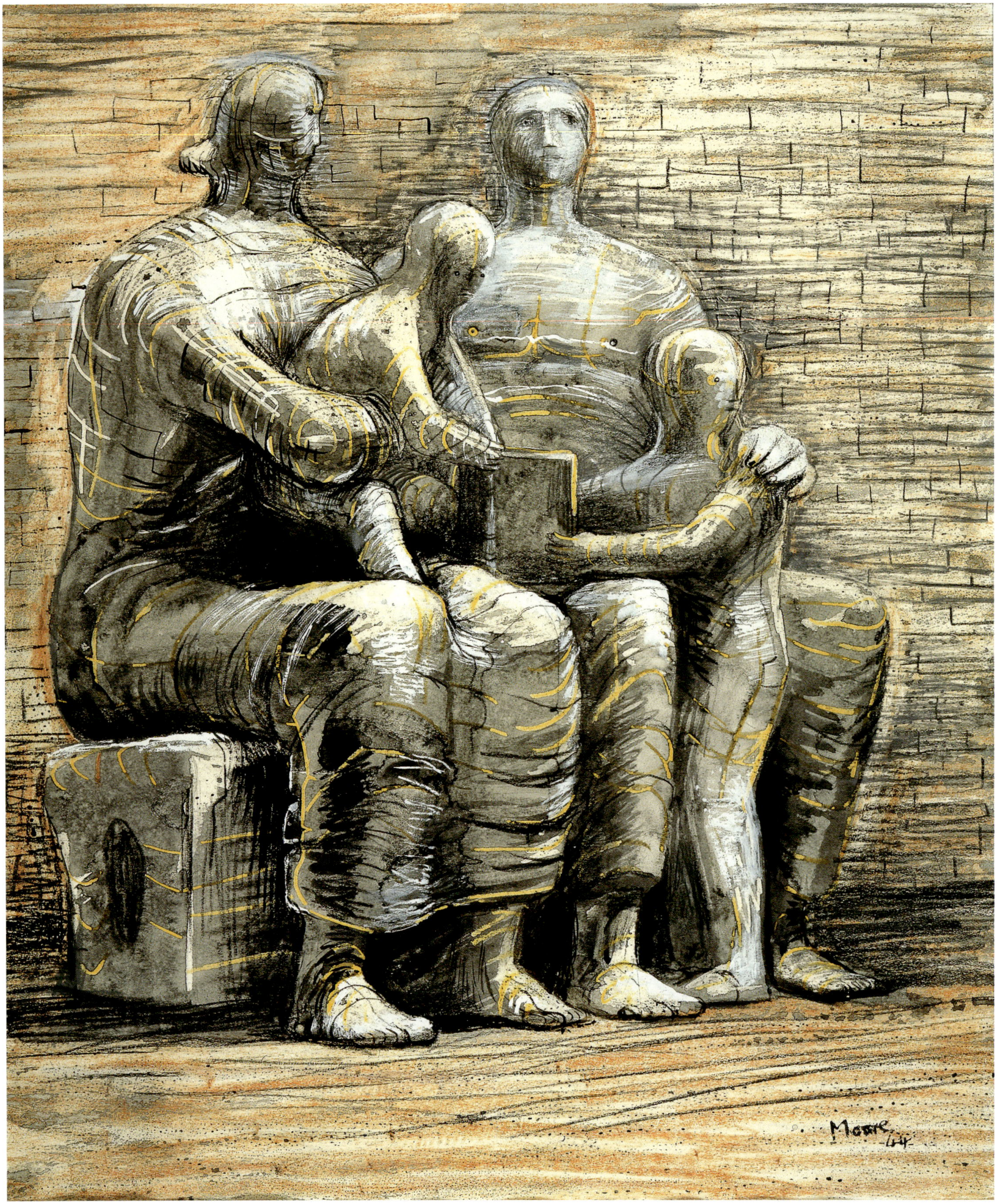

15.
Family Group 1944
Pencil, wax crayon,
coloured crayon,
watercolour wash,
pen and ink
500 x 420mm
Signed and dated lower
right: 'Moore / 44'
Scottish National Gallery of
Modern Art, Edinburgh
AG 44.65, HMF 2237a

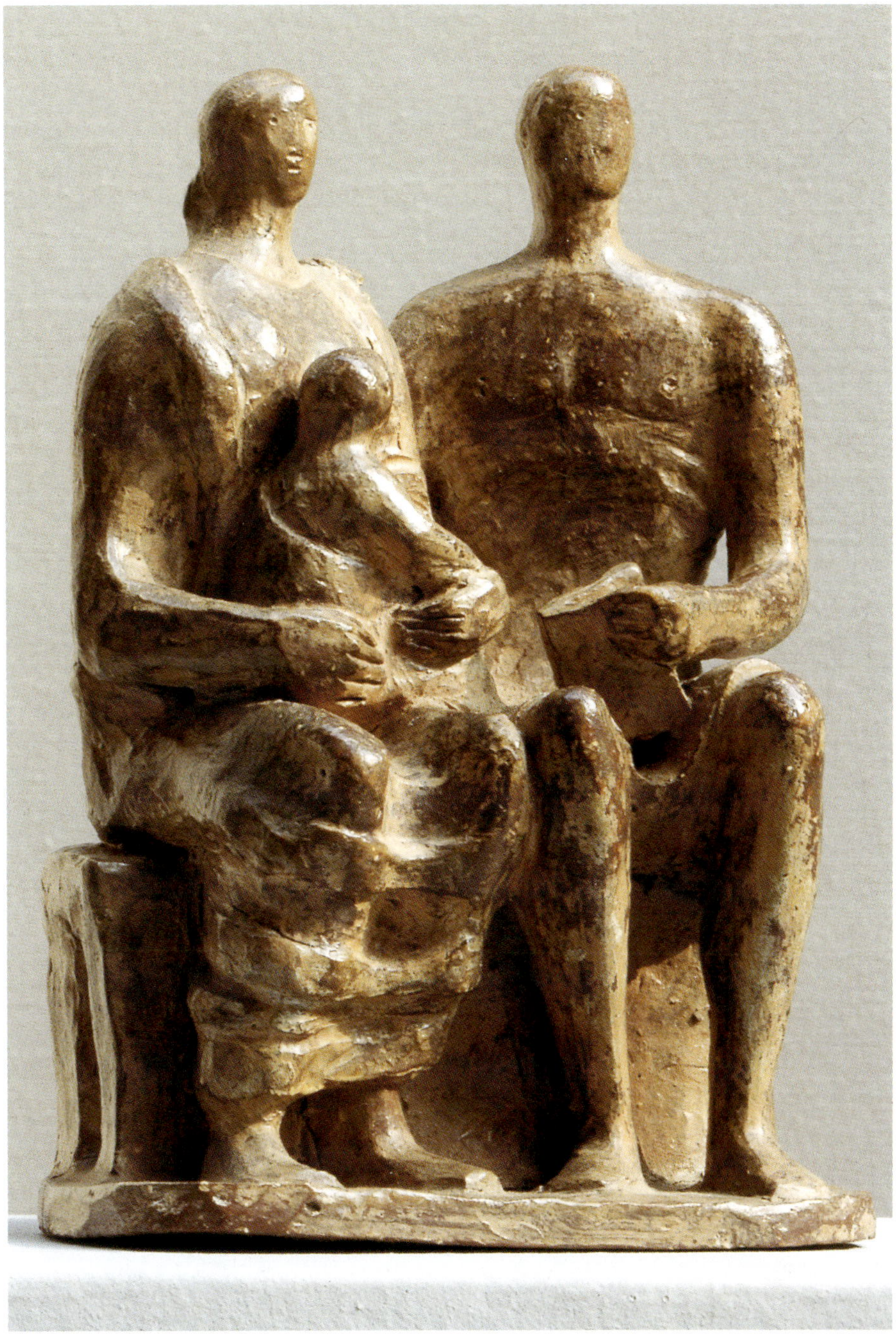

16.
Family Group 1944
Terracotta
h.156mm
The Henry Moore
Foundation: gift of
the artist 1977
LH 231

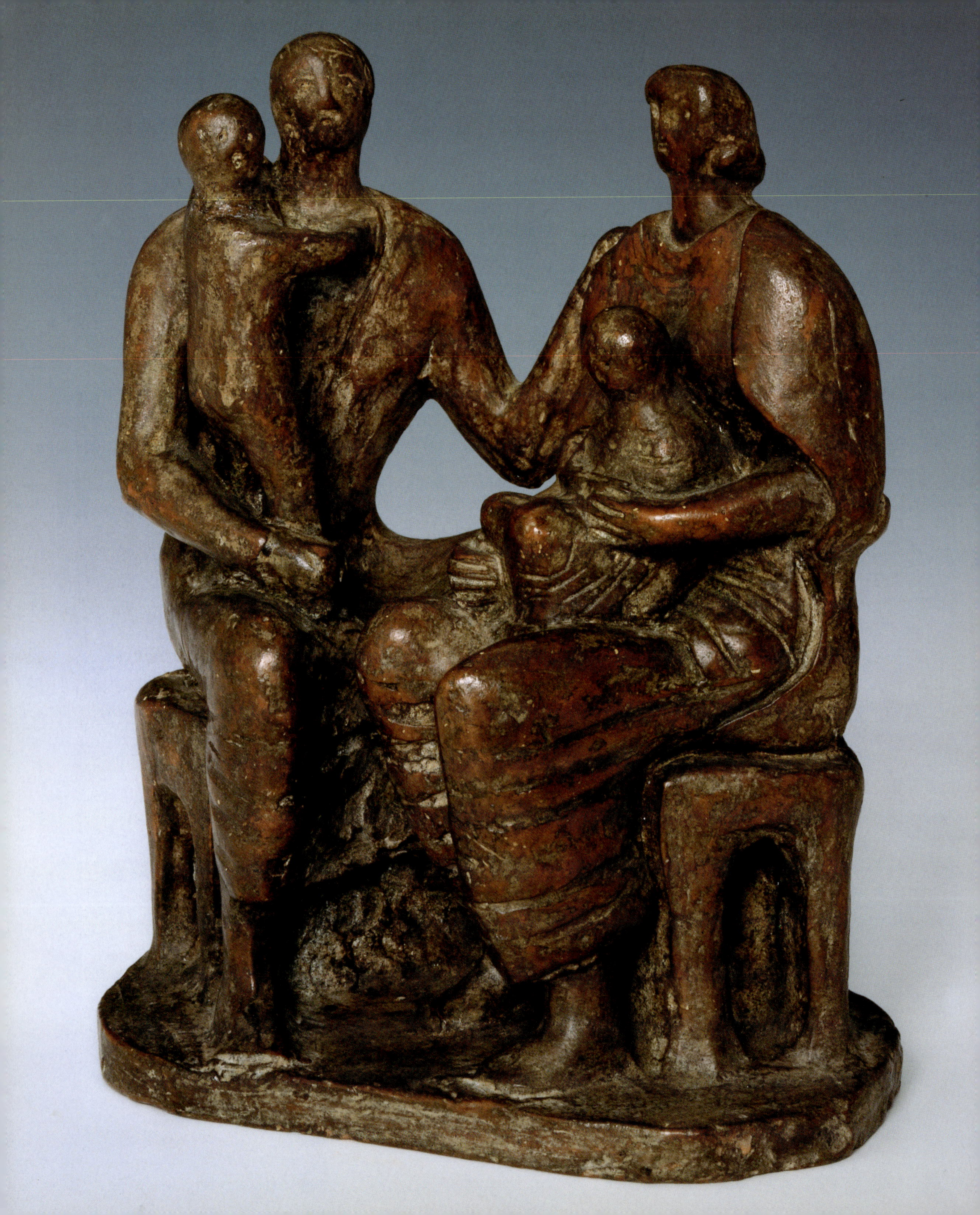

17.
Family Group 1944
Terracotta
150 x 126 x 176mm
Private Collection
LH 233

18.
Family Group 1944
Terracotta
h.162mm
The Henry Moore
Foundation: gift of
the artist 1977
LH 232

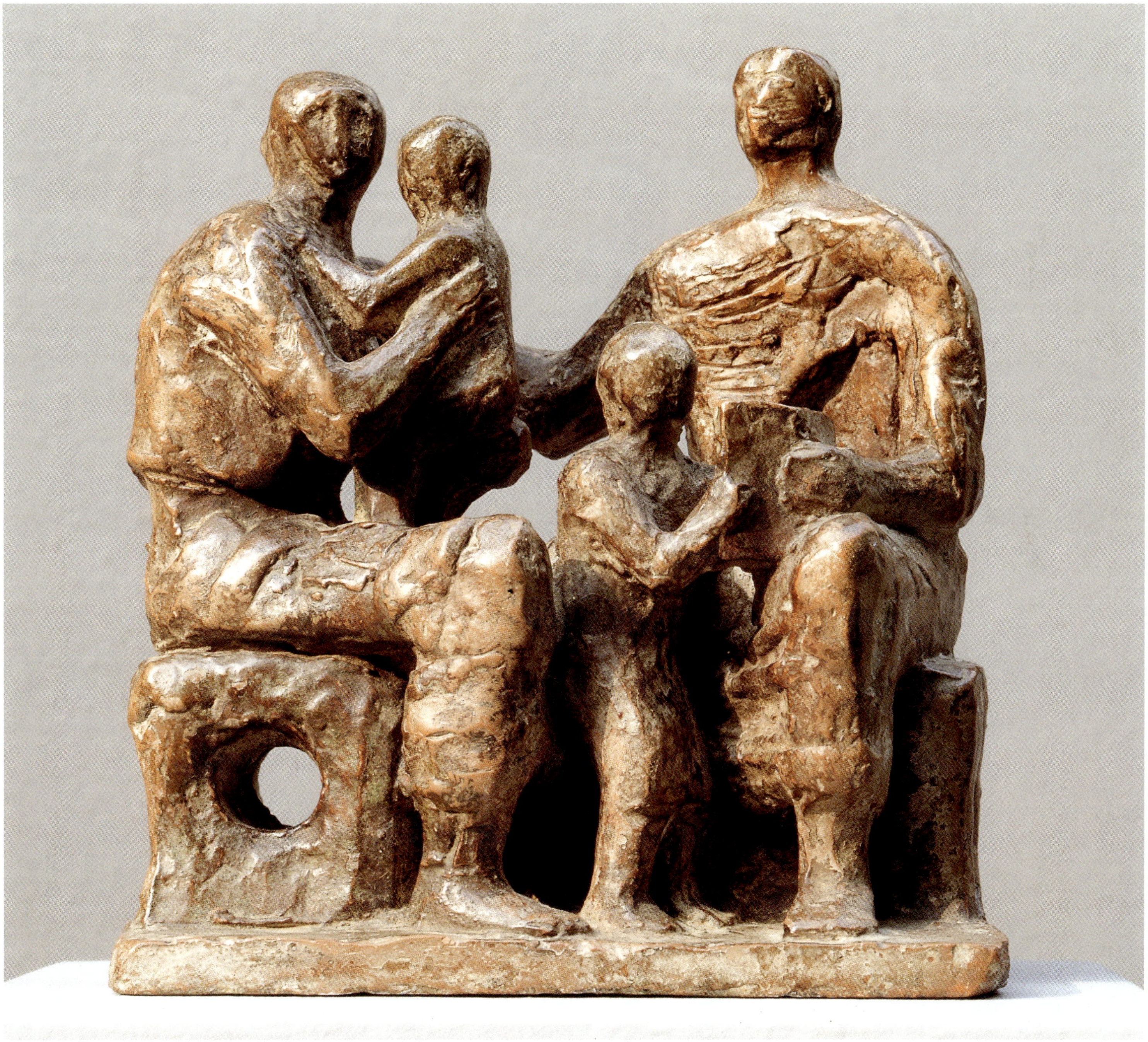

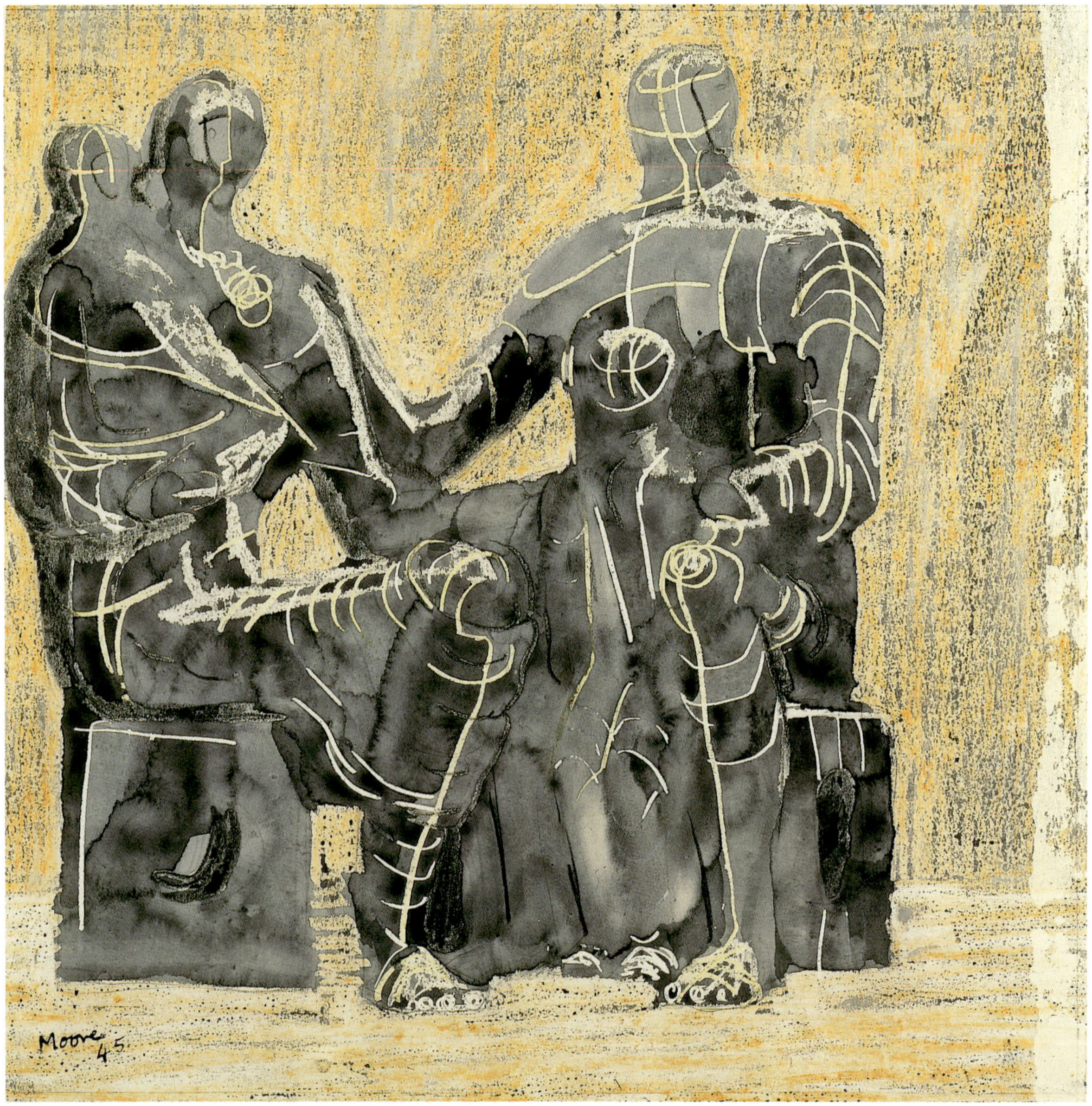

19.

Family Group 1945
Pencil, wax crayon, charcoal, wash
440 x 440mm
Signed and dated in pen and ink lower left: 'Moore / 45'
Robert and Lisa Sainsbury Collection, University of East Anglia, UEA 98
AG 45.6, HMF 2333

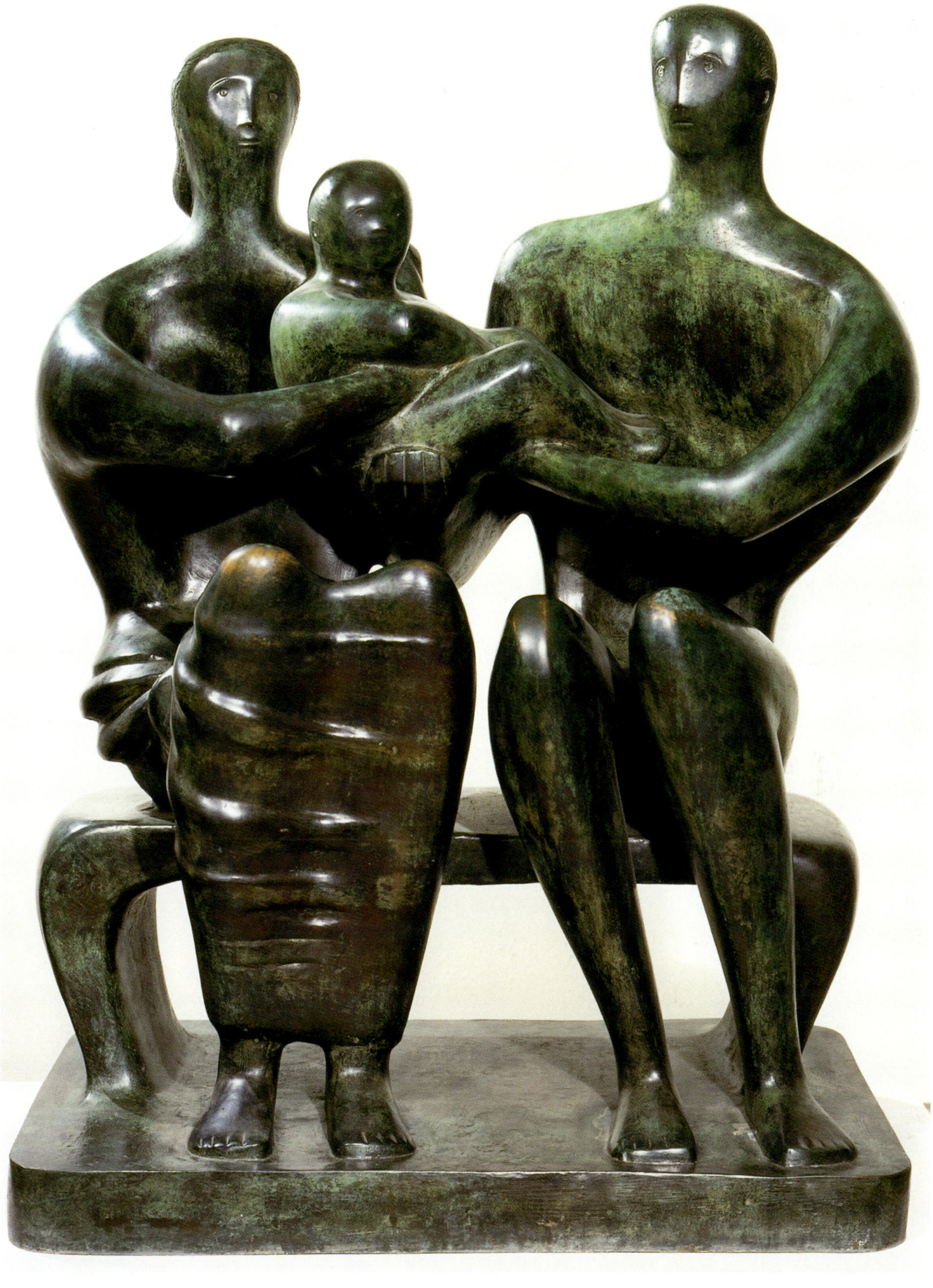

20.
Family Group
1948–9
Bronze
1524 x 1156 x 781mm
Tate, purchased 1950,
NO6004
LH 269

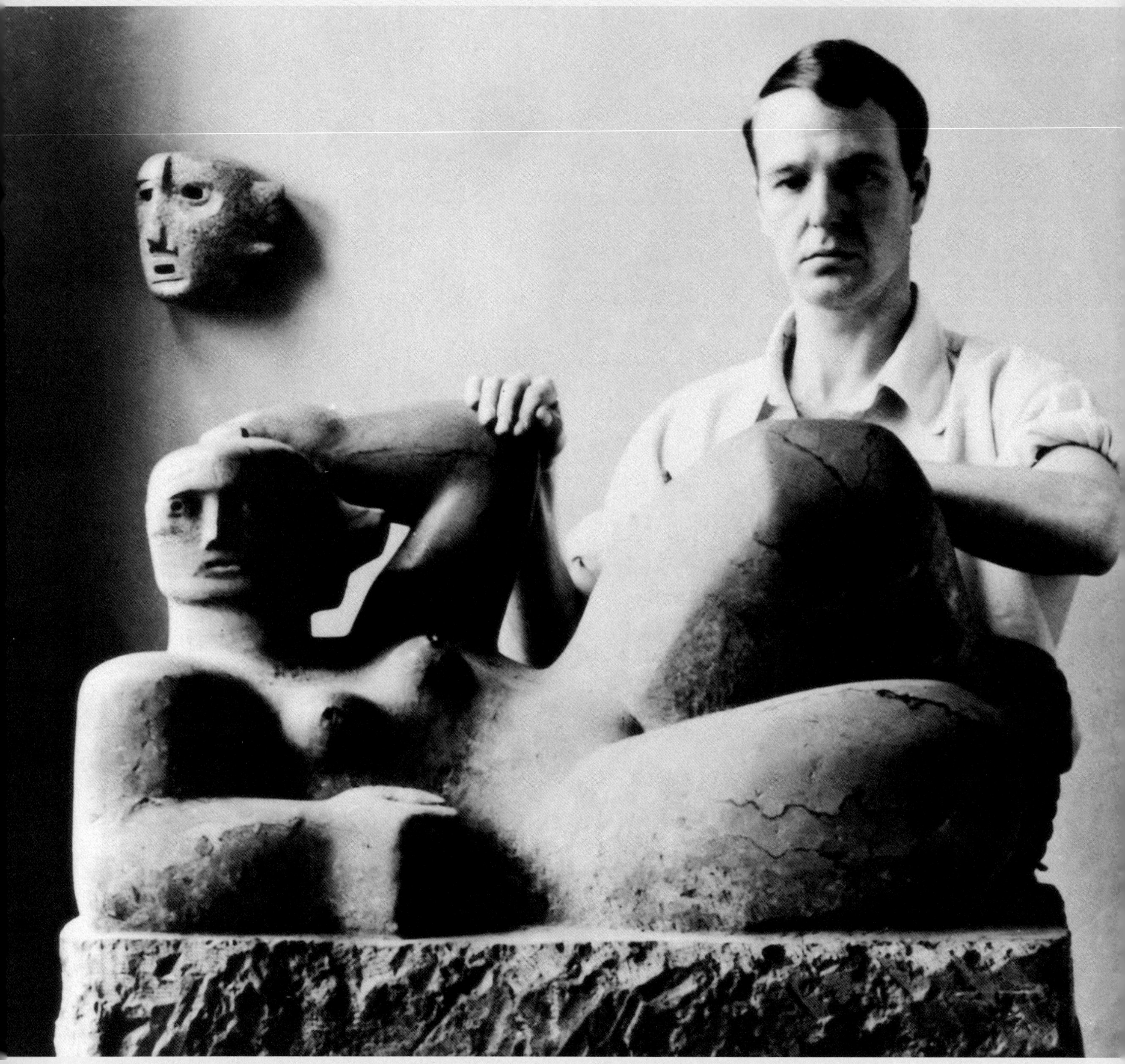

> From the very beginning the reclining figure has been my main theme.[17]

> The vital thing for an artist is to have a subject that allows [him] to try out all kinds of formal ideas – things that he doesn't yet know about for certain but wants to experiment with, as Cézanne did in his 'Bathers' series. In my case the reclining figure provides chances of that sort.[18]

THE RECLINING FIGURE EMERGED as Henry Moore's 'signature theme' not quite from the very beginning but a little later, after his student years, from 1925. The key influence in this development may have been a visit to Paris in that year, where at the Trocadero Museum Moore saw a plaster cast of the Toltec-Mayan sculpture from Chichén Itzá known as the 'Chacmool'.[19] The Chacmool became probably the most influential single sculpture in Henry Moore's life; he hugely admired its mixture of solidity and vivacity, its relationship to the earth and its column-like legs, but there was no shortage of other sources of inspiration for reclining figures, from Etruscan funerary sculpture to Matisse's odalisques. Cézanne's bathers, which shared that block-like sense of three dimensions, no doubt also lent their robust forms to the idea.

Apart from one reclining figure – the earliest recorded, in fact – that was male and has since been destroyed (it was in Mansfield stone, 12in/305mm long), it was the female reclining form that interested Moore. His career was punctuated by masterpieces in this, one of his favourite themes, marking a series of significant leaps forward. The first of these was the great Leeds *Reclining Figure* of 1929 (fig. 35). 'I knew when I had finished it that it was the best sculpture I had done up to then.'[20] The influence of the Chacmool and Mexican sculpture is evident throughout, in the squaring of the limbs, the mask-like stare of the face and the characteristic asymmetrical protruding knob of hair with its suggestion of the headdress of the Chacmool. But the sensuousness of the pose, with raised knee, twisted body and crooked elbow, is new.

The year before had seen Moore working on a related idea, that of his first public commission, a relief representing the *West Wind* on Charles Holden's St James's Underground Building, 55 Broadway. This figure is not, of course, reclining but flying (cat. 21 is a sketch for the final figure). The completed relief can still be seen 80ft (24.4m) above the street. In this difficult situation Moore had to create a body 9ft 6in (2.9m) long, stretched at full horizontal length, but weightless, moving rapidly through air, in relief, and to be seen from below. In the studio the carving was done with a mirror on the floor to replicate the effect of being seen from below, but finishing the carving was a vertiginous experience for Moore:

> I completed the carving on a scaffolding platform where there was only about three feet to stand on, and at first I was alarmed. It was so high up. But when I got down and looked at it from the ground, I realized that the figure's navel couldn't be seen properly. This was terrible, because the umbilical area is absolutely central to me – the cord attaches you to your mother, after all. By this time the scaffolding had been dismantled, so I went up again in a cradle,

Fig. 35
Henry Moore with *Reclining Figure*, 1929 (LH 59, now in Leeds City Art Gallery), and *Mask*, 1930 (LH 77), in the background.

The Reclining Figure

winching it up myself from side to side until I reached the carving. But once there, I found I couldn't carve properly. Every time I struck a blow, the cradle shot back from the figure. So in the end I got out some charcoal and shaded the navel in ... the cradle zigzagged all over the place on the return journey as well. Epstein watched me. After I'd come down he said: 'I wouldn't have done that for all the money in the world.'[21]

This quote seems particularly fascinating in its insight into how Moore's mind worked; his explanation for his concern about the invisibility of the navel – not on purely visual and formal grounds (the position of the navel is, after all, crucial for defining the twist of the pelvic plane) but because of its *psychological* importance (the mother fixation again) – is striking, even if suspiciously 'arty'; and there is a tiny bat-squeak of triumph at a point scored against Epstein.

As a sculptural exercise, there could hardly be a more diametrically opposed experience than this to the sculpting of a piece like the Leeds *Reclining Figure*, but, nonetheless, the careful thought that went into the one no doubt impacted on the other. Physically, the two works are related in type – both Mexican in inspiration, both with squared-off planes defining their heavy limbs, both with similar mask-like features. The weight of the Leeds figure, the way in which it sinks into the stone from which it is sculpted, perhaps owes some of its success to the effort that went into achieving the opposite effect for London Underground. Certainly, the experience may have made up his mind about accepting such commissions again; when Holden later approached Moore to carry out a similar commission high up on London University's Senate House, the offer was (after consideration) declined. There are also very few later attempts to suggest movement. 'It seems to me that it's somehow against the nature of sculpture to be actually moving ... representing movement seems false to me ...'[22] The flying figure came down to earth for good.

Another fascinating contrast with the Leeds figure appeared in 1930, this time on a tiny scale (cat. 22, the Sainsbury *Reclining Figure*). Moore carved it from an ironstone pebble:

we [Ben Nicholson & the Moores] sometimes went on holidays together – I remember there was a summer holiday, maybe the summer of 1930, when a group of us spent a fortnight at Happisburgh on the Norfolk coast [fig. 36] ... I remember it was very good weather, and it was there that we found ironstone pebbles which are hard enough and also soft enough to carve. Some were beautifully simplified shapes.[23]

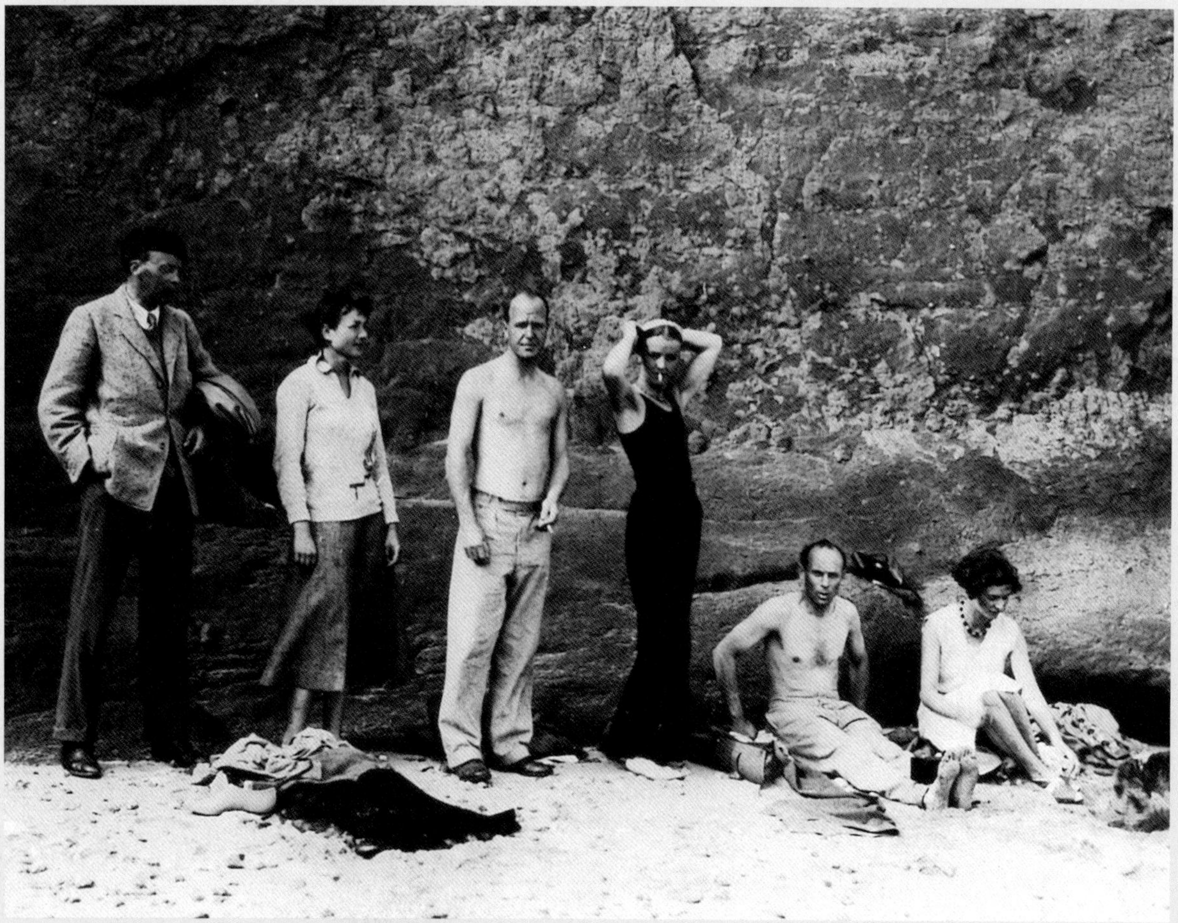

Fig. 36 (left)
On holiday at Happisburgh beach, Norfolk, 1931 (from left to right): Ivon Hitchens, Irina Moore, Henry Moore, Barbara Hepworth, Ben Nicholson and Mary Jenkins.

Fig. 37 (right)
Recumbent Figure, 1938 (LH 191), Green Hornton stone; Tate, presented by the Contemporary Art Society 1939.

This small figure imitates, more or less, the pose of the Leeds figure, but the crucial element of weight is not an issue here, so the figure is sculpted underneath also, and seems light, almost floating. The raised arm also reminds us of the Leeds figure, but here the gesture takes on an emotive power, suggesting either a severe headache or else a sudden ghastly thought. This figure explores the transient, where the Leeds figure suggests permanence; the difference seems almost entirely to be prompted by the different qualities of the stones used – 'truth to material', indeed. The small figure is also significant because of the way Moore has treated the space contained by the raised arm. Unlike with the Leeds figure, the space is not the accidental product of a physical movement by a physical limb. In carving the space, it is as if Moore has decided to make the space itself – or hole – the defining factor. In doing so, the arm is rendered less physically convincing. Although this is not the radical penetration of the body form that was to follow, as in the great Tate *Recumbent Figure* of 1938 (fig. 37), nonetheless it is not impossible to imagine that this tiny sculpture might have provided the 'eureka moment' that led eventually to that.

The mid-1930s saw the issue of Abstraction – seen as a 'pure' form of art – reach its peak. Nicholson was the dogmatic central figure in the debate, and his emphatic influence, not least in his capacity as chair of

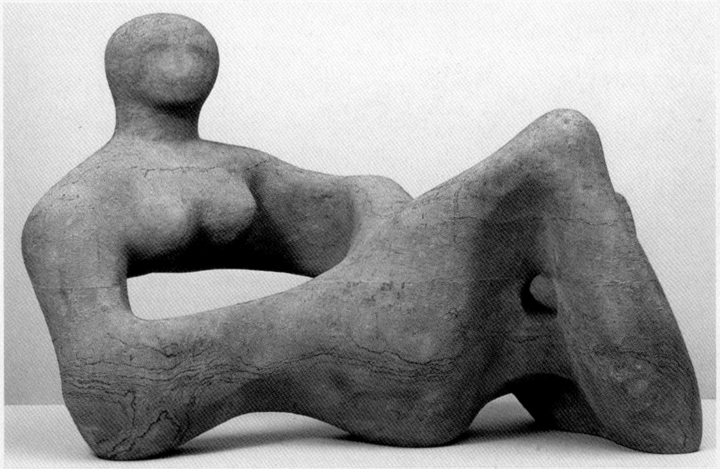

the 7 & 5 Society, turned several figurative artists, such as John Piper, into temporary abstract artists. Moore, too, went through his most abstract phase at this time, producing some reclining figures that are among the most challenging of all his work (see fig. 44 p. 91, *Reclining Figure*, 1937). However, even the most abstract of his work (see cat. 37, *Composition*, 1934) tends to retain the sense of the muscular feel, the balance of weight and tension, of the human form. What seems to disappear from the works of this type is not the human dimension, but rather the sense of landscape that had been a key characteristic of the greatest of Moore's reclining figures so far (and in the future). These are objects resting on earth rather than 'of the earth' themselves.

By 1939, when Moore produced a group of smallish figures in lead and later bronze, including many reclining figures, the biomorphic nature of the figures is back, but even more fluid (cat. 25*, Reclining Figure*), partly as a result of the modelling technique involved in the lost-wax process used. Elsewhere, his brief flirtation with stringed figures produced the odd rather surreal piece also (cat. 26, *Reclining Stringed Figure*). His drawing (cat. 27, *Reclining Figures for Metal Sculpture*, 1940) reveals an ever more skeletal, metallic formal type. It seems in tune with the period: Britain was at war, but personally there was good news, because for the first time Moore was free of teaching. The Chelsea School of Art evacuated in 1940 to Northampton; Moore did not go with it.

The Second World War, in Moore's case, brought the shelter drawings; and it was probably the great popularity and recognition of the suffering and shared experience embodied in those forms that taught many of the public how to relate to Henry Moore's reclining figures. The effect on Moore himself should not be underestimated. Certainly, the small bronze of 1946–7 (cat. 28, *Reclining Figure*) is more overtly expressionist than his pre-war work. Part lethal machine, part corpse, part knife, this figure has a taut, wired quality not seen before.

The alert sinuosity of this new type of reclining figure, though not its more disturbing skeletal quality, finds its way into another important landmark, the *Reclining Figure: Festival,* 1951 (fig. 38), Moore's contribution to the Festival of Britain on the South Bank. He later described it as 'perhaps my first sculpture where the space and form are completely dependent on and inseparable from each other'.[24] The Festival, celebrating the 'brave new world' of post-war optimism, seems to have inspired an uncompromisingly modern sculpture, with a new interest in the surface quality of the bronze. Moore chose to experiment with an effect similar to one that he had developed in his drawings to create the effect of three dimensions without the traditional shading – what he called his 'sectional line' style (see cat. 19). Rather in the spirit of Paul Klee's 'taking a line for a walk', Moore makes his line in these drawings take detours away from the outline, creating an effect almost as if drawing a figure made of plates of metal, the lines marking the joins. In the Festival figure he applied strings to the surface of the model that emphasize the curvature of the forms – the effect is also apparent in the working model on display here (cat. 29).[25] It was not a technique that he was to use often; possibly its decorative quality disturbed him, in much the same way as he reacted against the use of string in his stringed figures.

However, the Festival figure's emphasis on external surface as a means to articulate the surrounding space chimes quite naturally with a development that was to become a new theme in its own right – the internal/external form (cat. 30, *Working Model for Reclining Figure: Internal/External Form*, 1951). This idea – of a related form separate from, but contained within, another – proved to be exceptionally fruitful for Moore (see fig. 26 p. 34, *Upright Internal/External Form*, 1951, or cat. 48, *Helmet Head No. 1*, 1950), applicable to several of his favourite subjects. Deriving

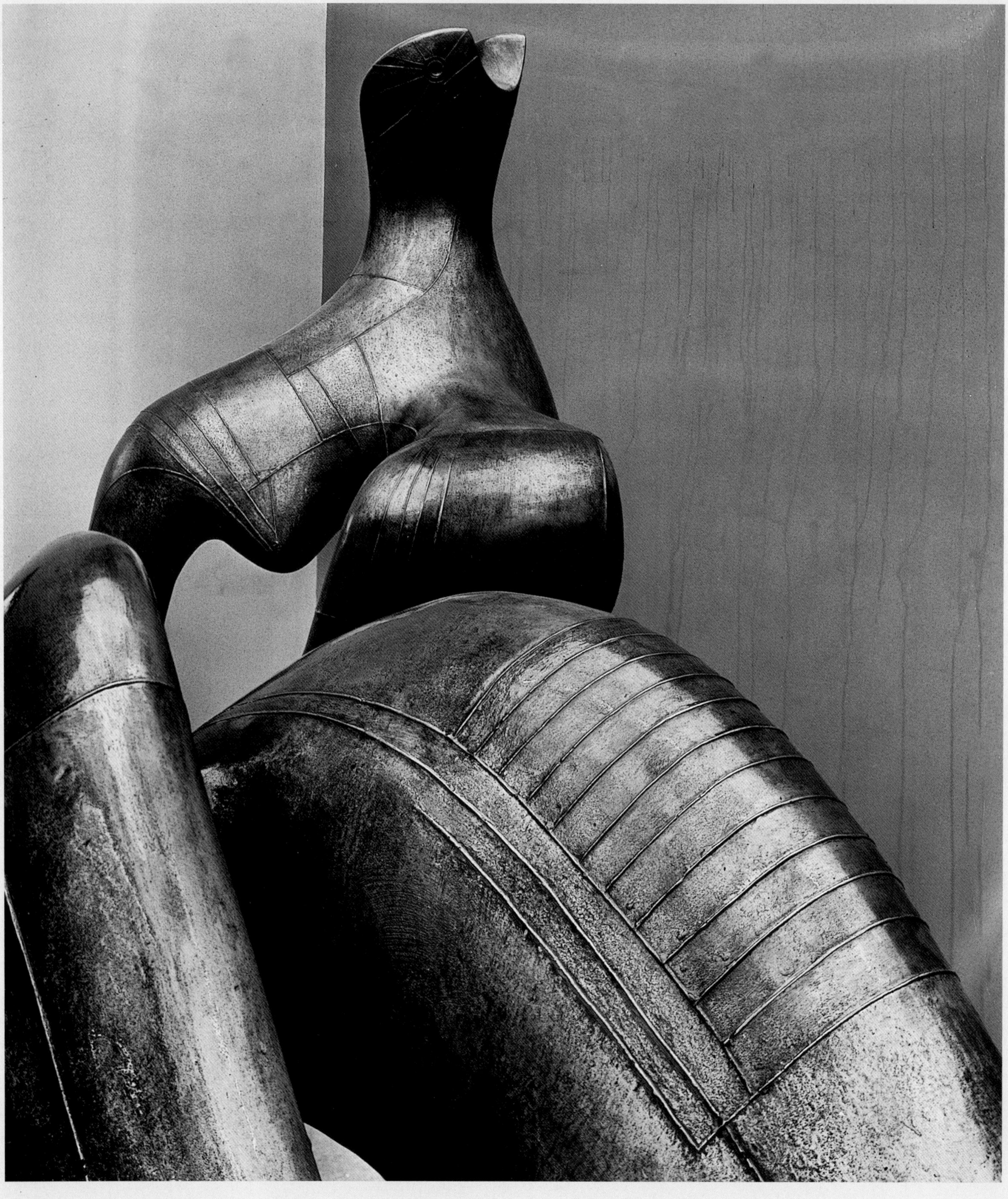

originally from his study of armour in the Wallace Collection, London, the internal/external form provided a perfect metaphor for the human body, making manifest both the outer, visible shell and the internal, hidden mechanism.

> The idea of one form inside another form may owe some of its incipient beginnings to my interest at one stage when I discovered armour. I spent many hours in the Wallace Collection, in London, looking at armour. Now armour is an outside shell like the shell of a snail which is there to protect the more vulnerable forms inside…[26]

Later, Moore was to cast the external form on its own, like an enormous cast-off snail shell. In the *Upright Internal/External Form* of the same year (fig. 33, p. 58) the concept is applied to the mother and child theme, suggesting not only the emotional protectiveness of the larger for the smaller figure, but also literally evoking the foetus within the womb. It was an exceptionally rich vein for Moore to mine.

A perhaps more surprising development of the reclining figure testifies to the continuing influence of the British Museum. In late February 1951 Moore visited Greece for the first time, and as a result faced up to perhaps the most influential reclining figures of all from the ancient world – the goddesses from the Elgin Marbles. In the *Draped Reclining Woman* of 1957–8 (cat. 33) and the *Fragment Figure* (cat. 32) that is a study for it, Moore came up with his own version of the classical. In a natural development of his interest in surface pattern and the carapace of the internal/external forms, he finally came to focus on the force of classical drapery – its rich surface tension – not unlike the effect that some of the stringed figures earlier attempted to achieve in a more abstract way. One can sense a confidence and bravery in Moore in measuring himself unhesitatingly against a tradition that his earlier self would have rejected out of hand – that earlier self that complained of the 'Greek spectacles' that got in the way of 'real' sculpture. Of course, Picasso had been the trail-blazer, but the challenge was still daunting.

The final great innovation represented here lies in Moore's extension of the idea of the 'hole' – this time the actual division of the reclining figure into two or more pieces. The great *Two Piece Reclining Figure No. 3* (cat. 34) brings together the tradition of the Elgin marbles with Moore's own early identification of figure with landscape. More than any other reclining figures, these divided figures suggest the rocky outcrops of Moore's native Yorkshire.

One of the more surprising aspects of Moore's activity within his signature themes is that there is not a rigid chronological order to his work in a more realistic style. In fact, he could, and did, produce more traditional-looking figures at times when the rest of his work was at its most radical and challenging. This was governed by his own sense of the Albertian concept of 'decorum' – he deemed the traditional style more appropriate for certain types of commission. A good example of this is his Northampton Madonna. In the reclining figure category the most obvious example of an 'out of sequence' realistic figure is the Dartington Hall memorial to Christopher Martin, carved in 1945–6 (fig. 39), where Moore obviously felt that the form suited the commemorative nature of the commission. Another example of this tendency in his work can be seen in the *Working Model for the Draped Reclining Figure*, modelled between 1976 and 1979 (cat. 35). Not only does this late work adopt the classical realism of his Elgin marbles-inspired figures, it also – most interestingly – represents another reworking of the Chacmool, the Mexican sculpture that seems to have been the chief inspiration behind this most representative of all Moore's sculptural obsessions.

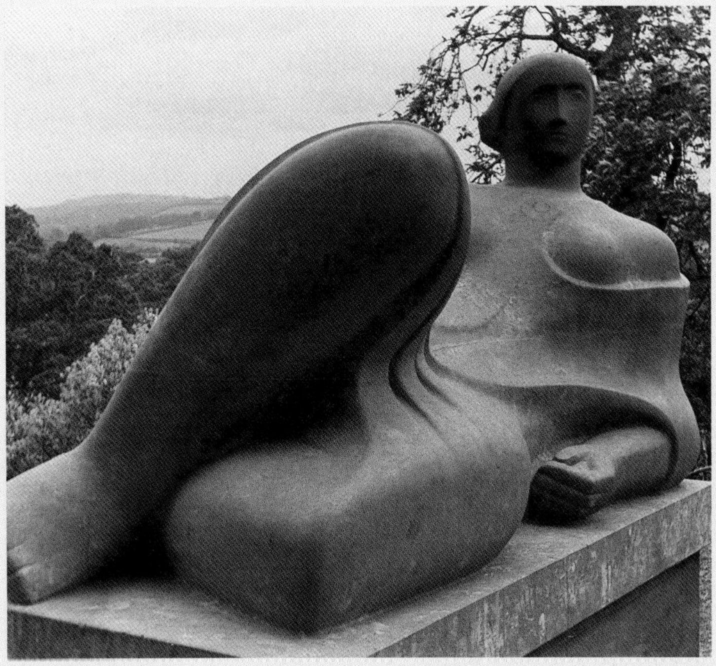

Fig. 39
Memorial Figure, 1945–6 (LH 262), Brown Hornton stone; Dartington Hall, Devon.

Fig. 38
Reclining Figure: Festival, 1951 (LH 293), bronze; The Henry Moore Foundation Archive.

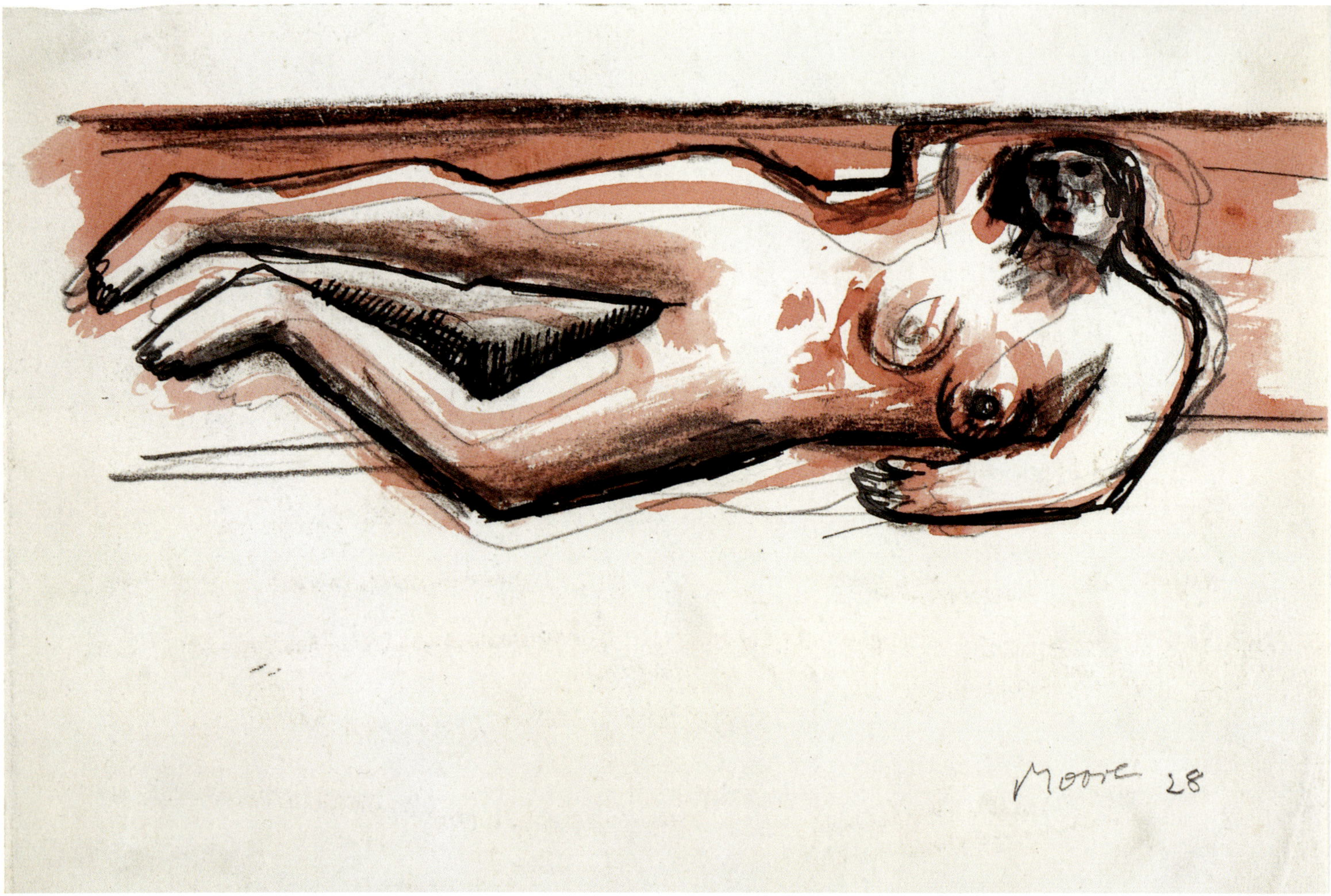

21.
Drawing for Relief on St James's Underground Building 1928
Pencil, watercolour, charcoal, pen and ink
182 x 275mm
Signed and dated in pencil (added later) lower right: 'Moore / 28'
The Henry Moore Foundation: gift of the artist 1977
AG 28.34, HMF 644

22.
Reclining Figure 1930
Ironstone
130 x 163 x 58mm
Robert and Lisa Sainsbury Collection, University of East Anglia, UEA 80
LH 85

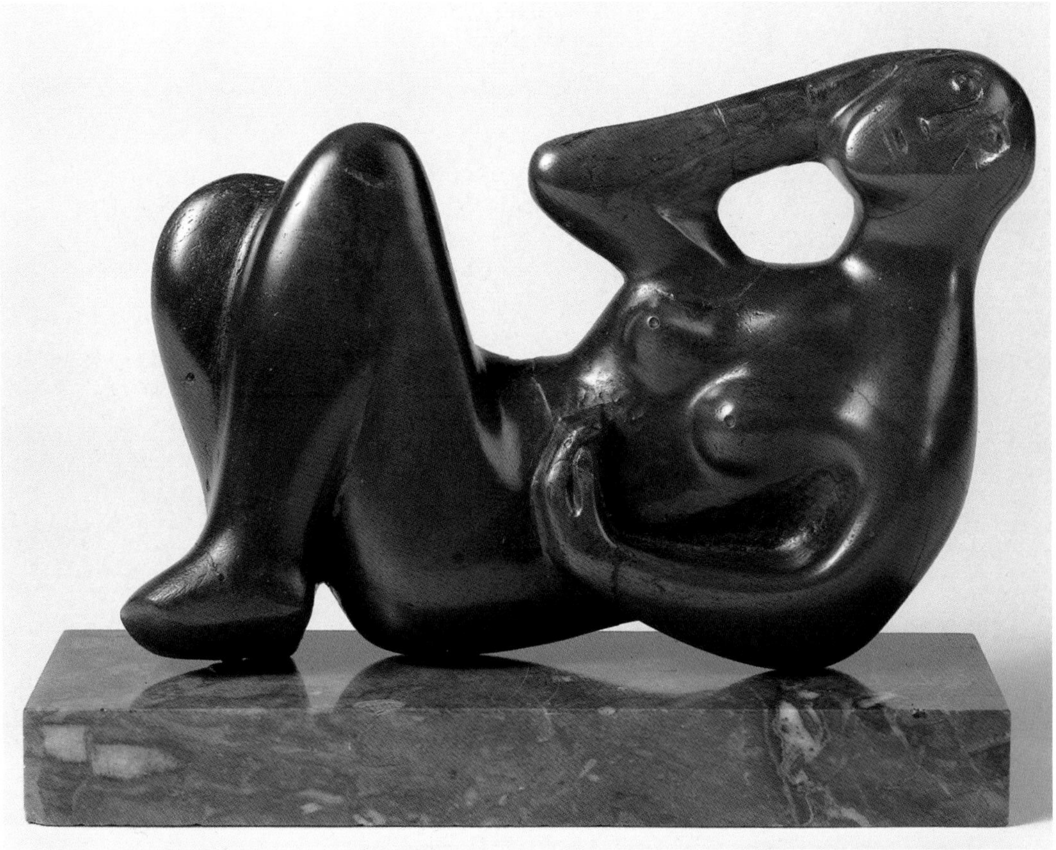

23.
Reclining Figure 1930
Bronze, cast 1962
130 x 163 x 58mm
Robert and Lisa Sainsbury Collection, University of East Anglia, UEA 81
LH 85

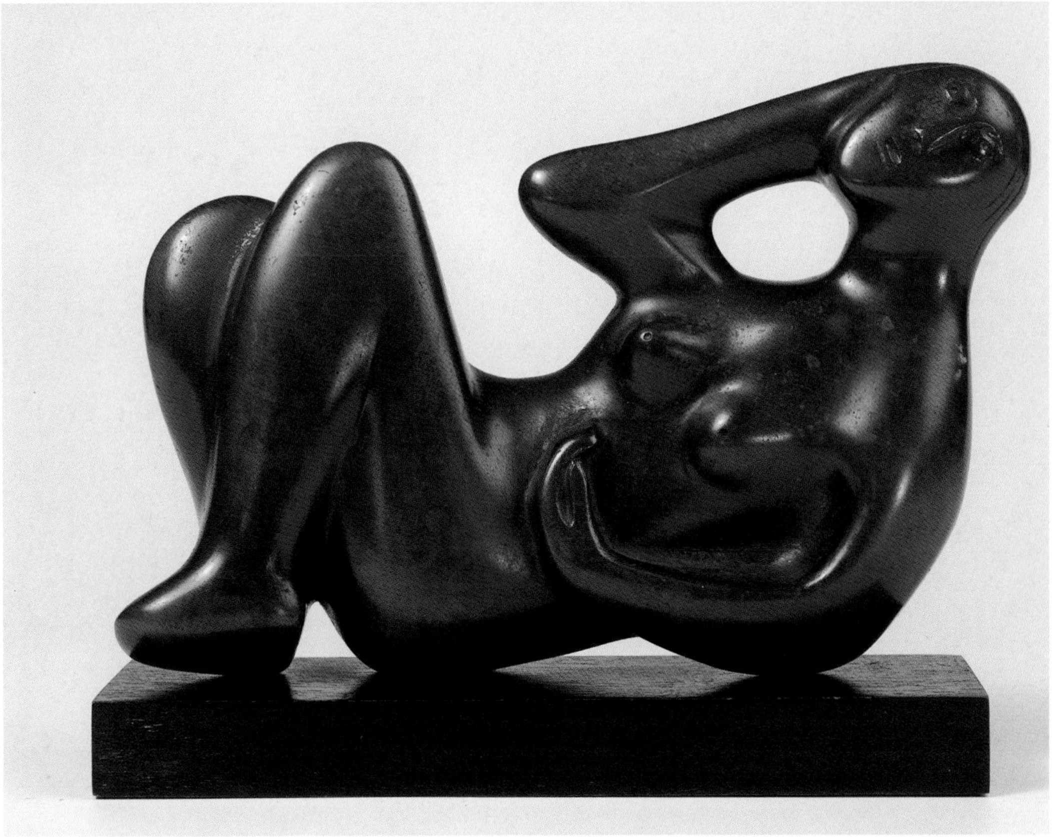

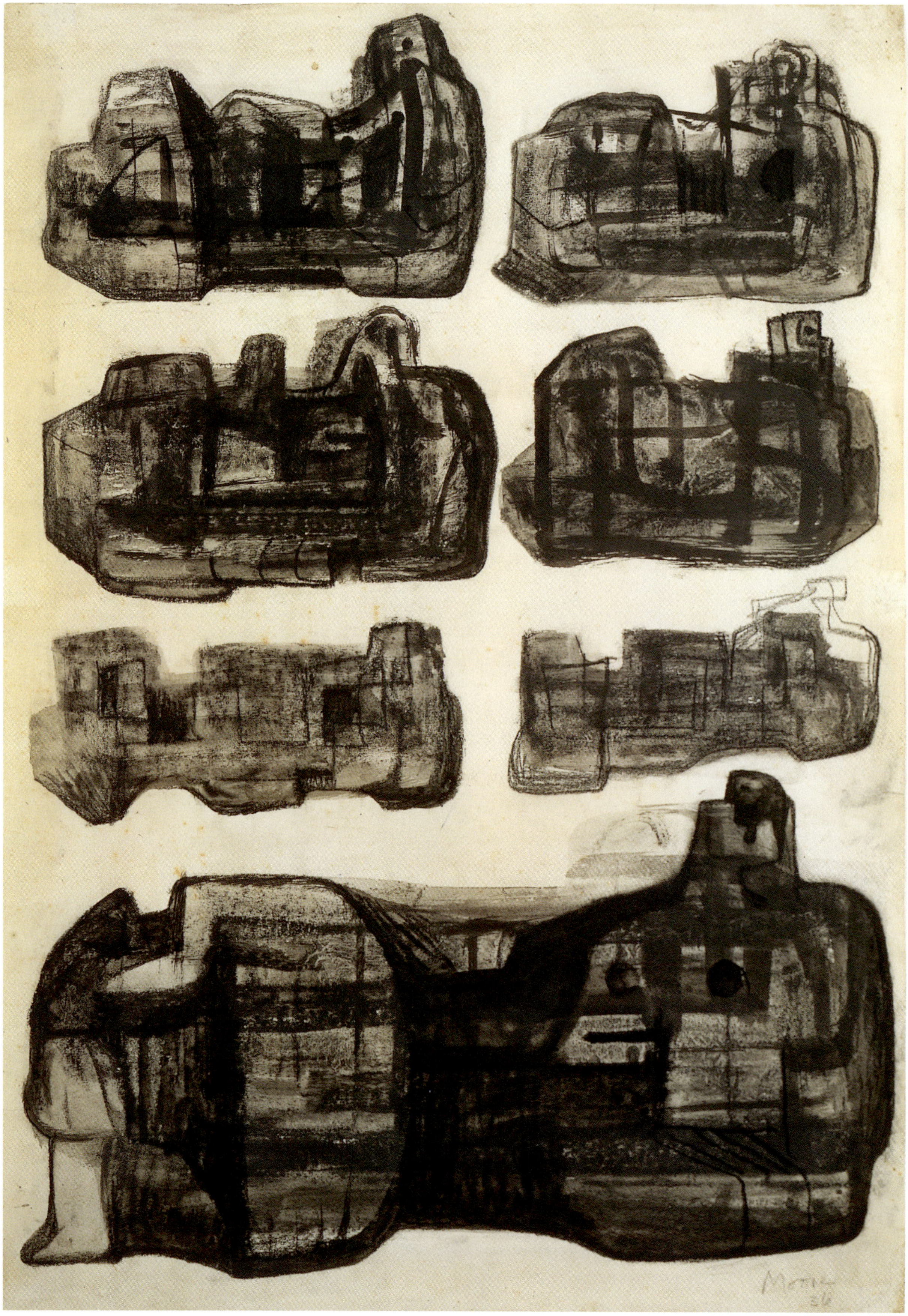

24.
Square Form Reclining Figures 1936
Chalk, brush and ink, wash
555 x 392mm
Signed and dated in pencil (added later) lower right: 'Moore / 36'
The Henry Moore Foundation: gift of the artist 1977
AG 36.5, HMF1242

25.
Reclining Figure 1939
Bronze
l.299mm
British Council
LH 202

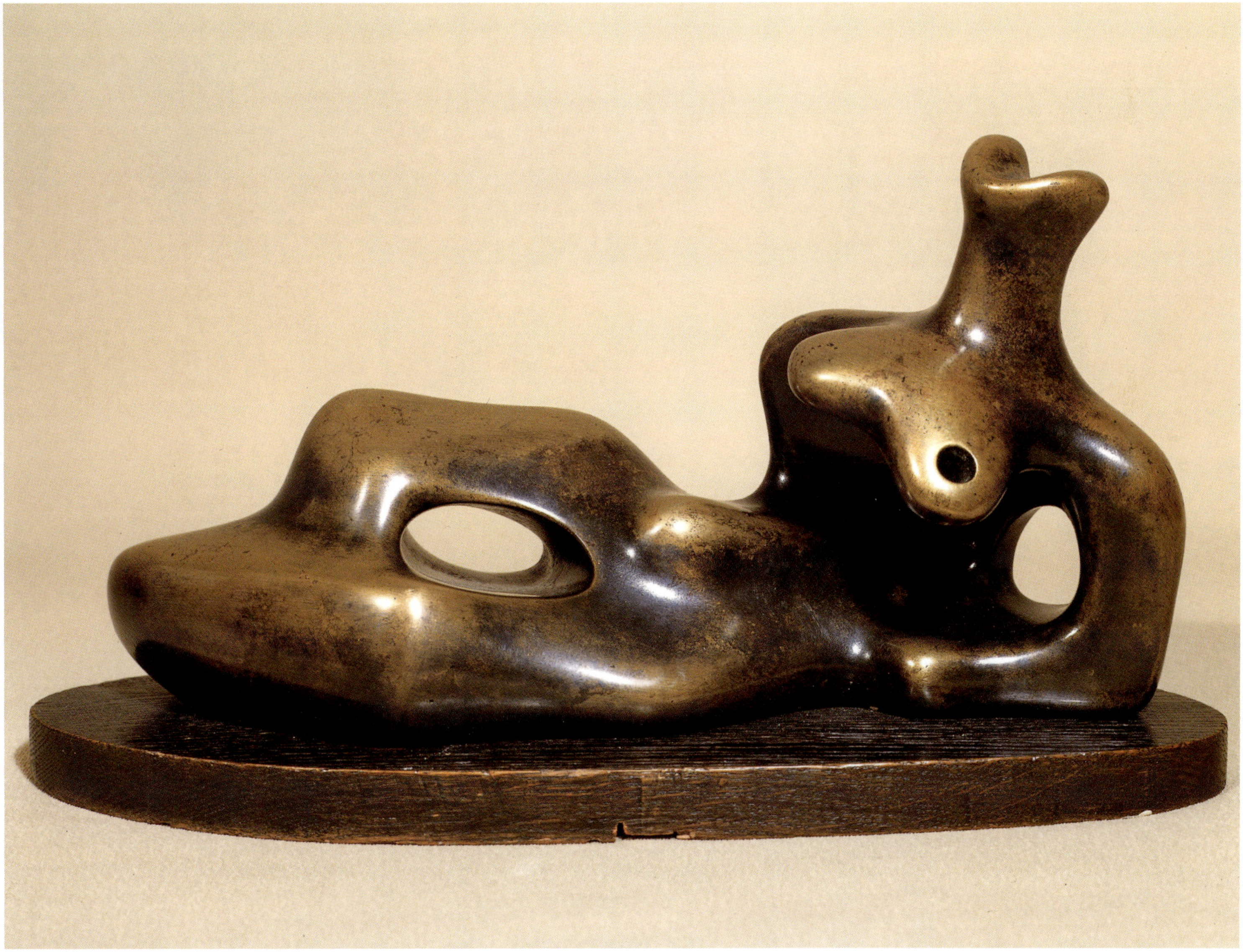

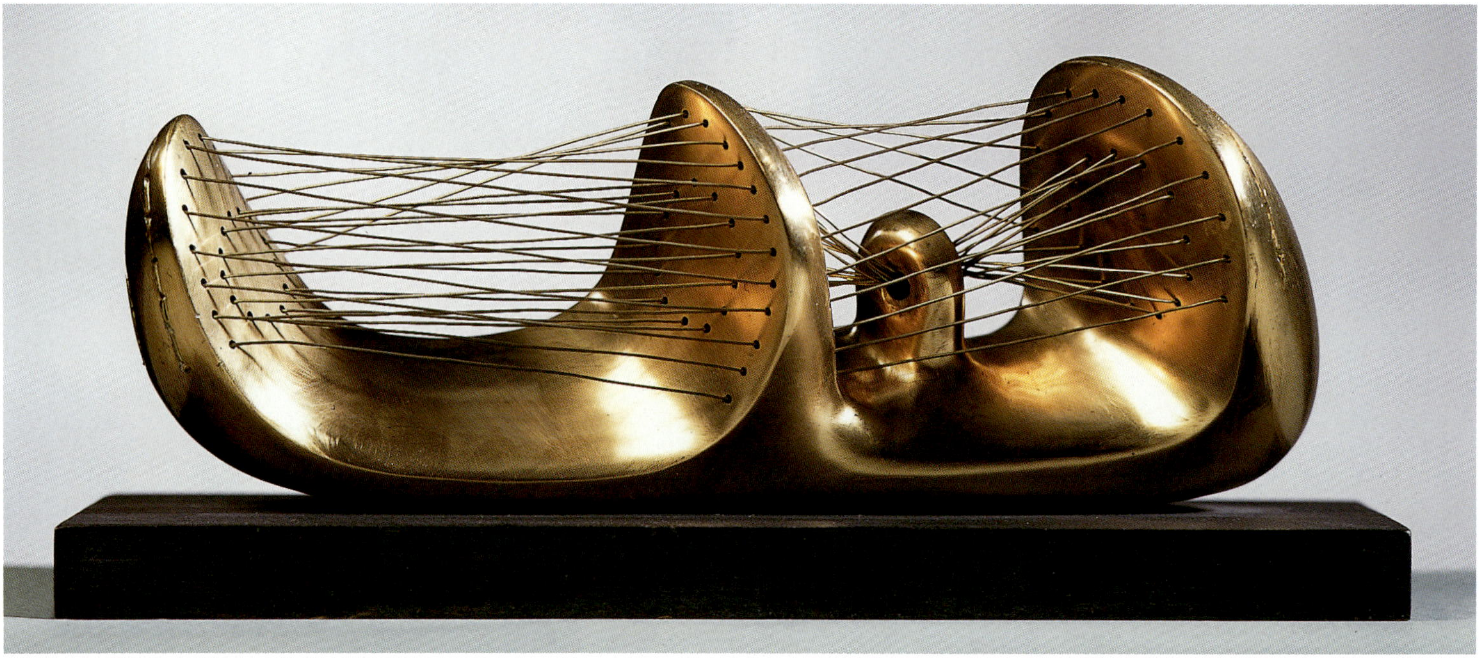

26.
Reclining Stringed Figure 1939
Bronze and brass wire, cast 1982
l.257mm
The Henry Moore Foundation: acquired 1987
LH 199a

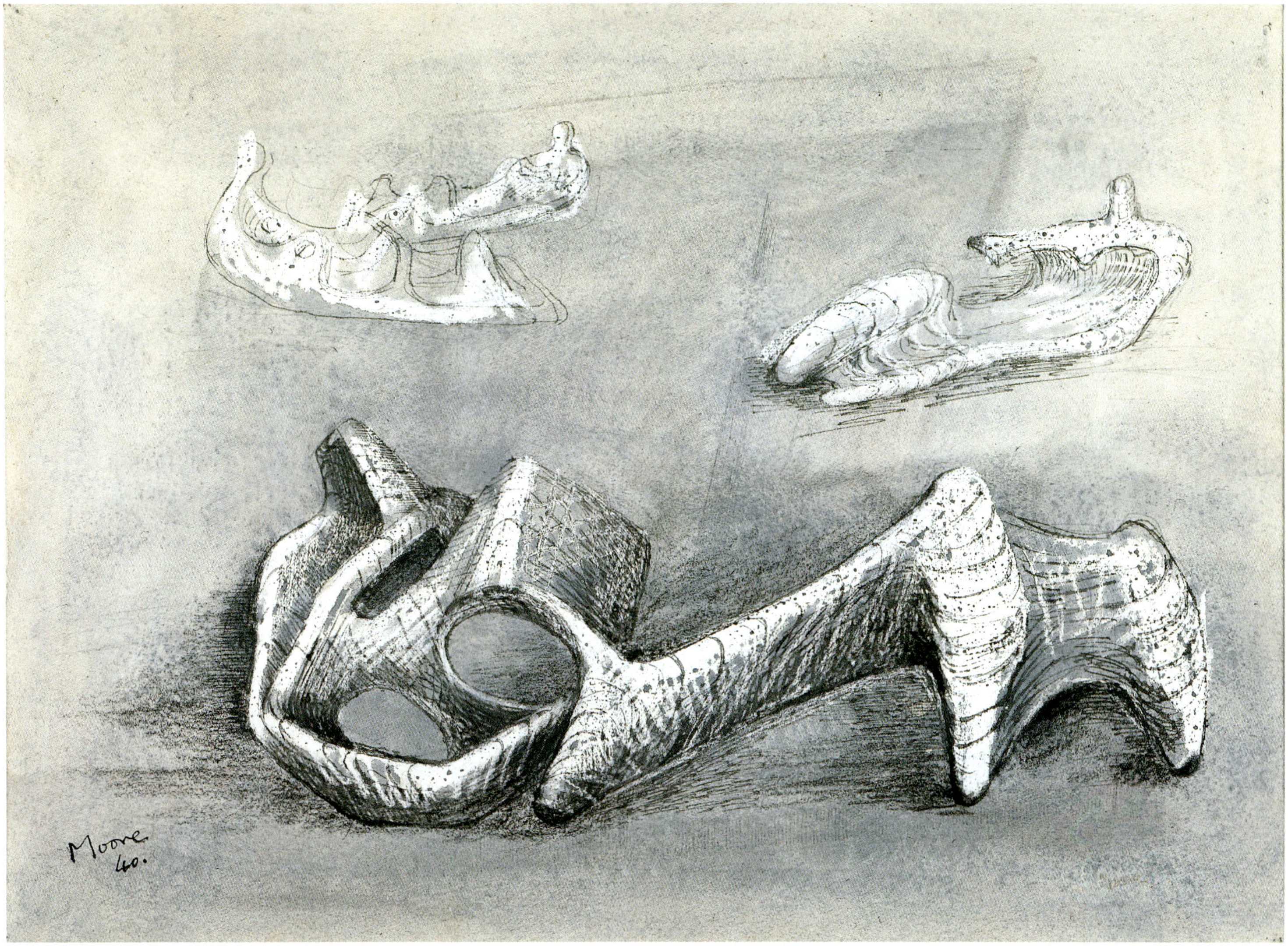

27.
Reclining Figures for Metal Sculpture 1940
Pencil, wax crayon, chalk, watercolour wash, pen and ink
279 x 381mm
Signed and dated in pen and ink lower left: 'Moore / 40'
Robert and Lisa Sainsbury Collection, University of East Anglia, UEA 90
AG 40.20, HMF 1479

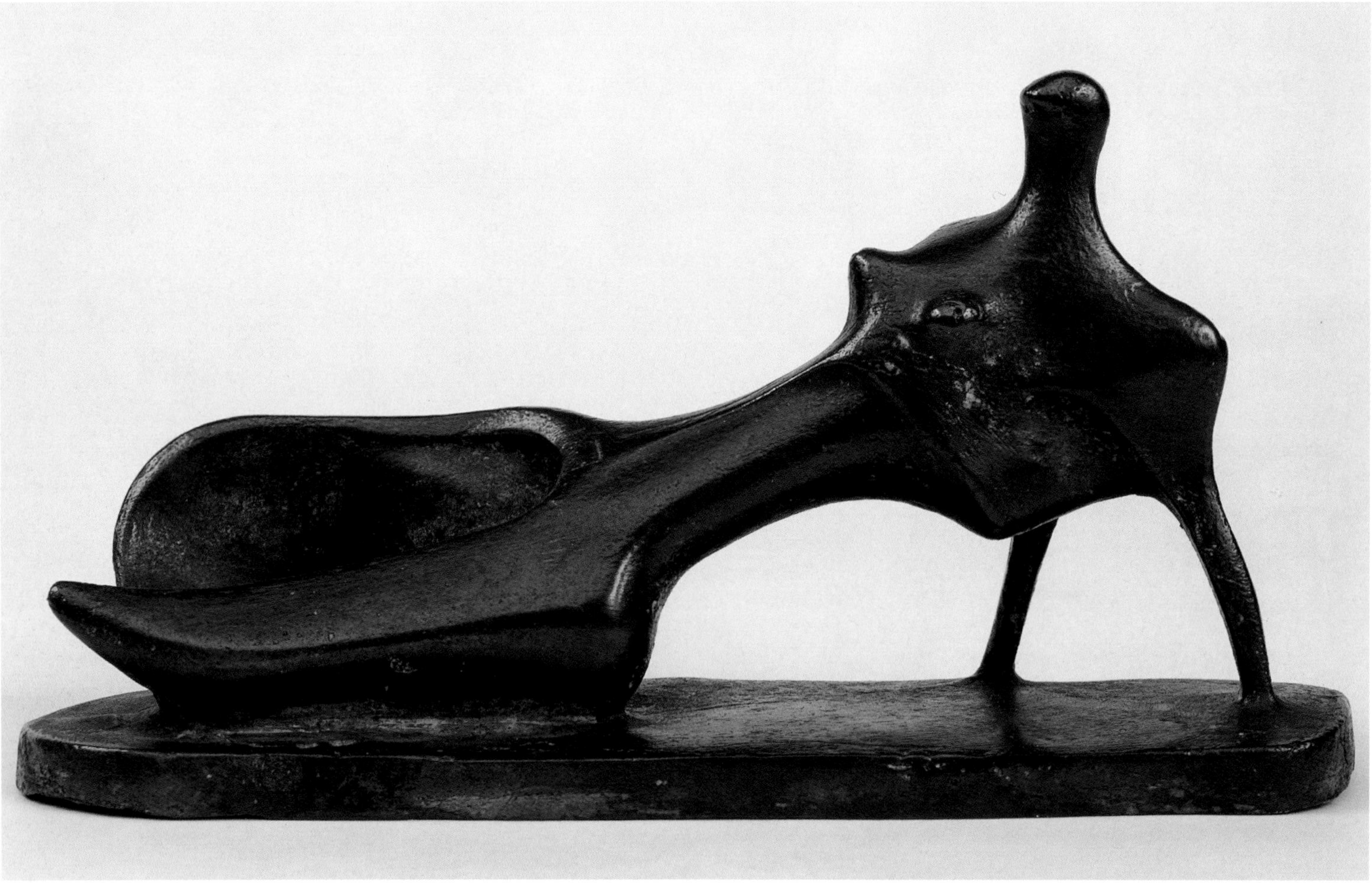

28.
Reclining Figure 1946–7
Bronze
l.178mm
Robert and Lisa Sainsbury Collection, University of East Anglia, UEA 440
LH 252

29.
Working Model for Reclining Figure: Festival 1950
(Photographed in the studio at Hoglands)
Plaster
l.430mm
The Henry Moore Foundation: gift of the artist 1977
LH 292

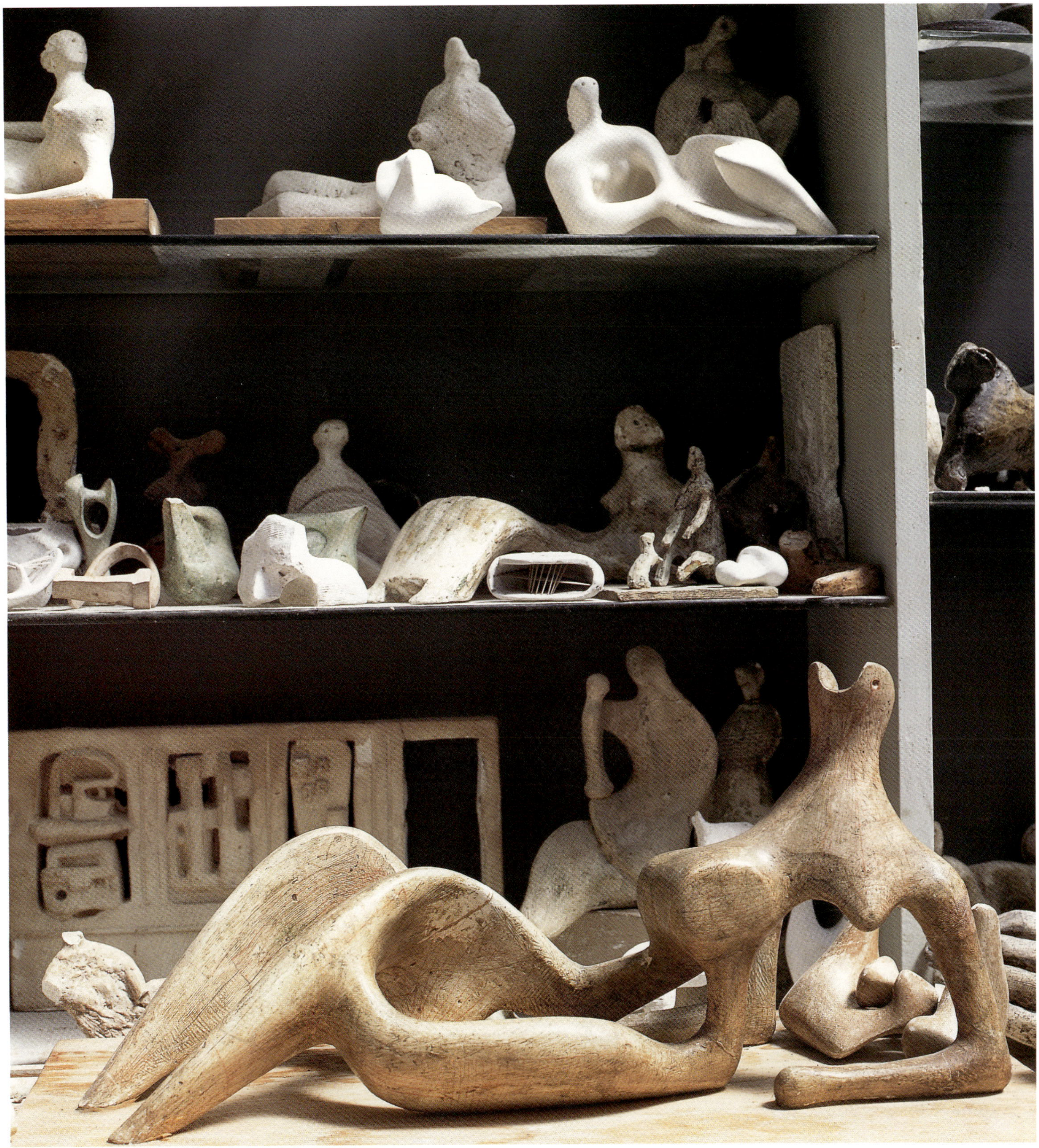

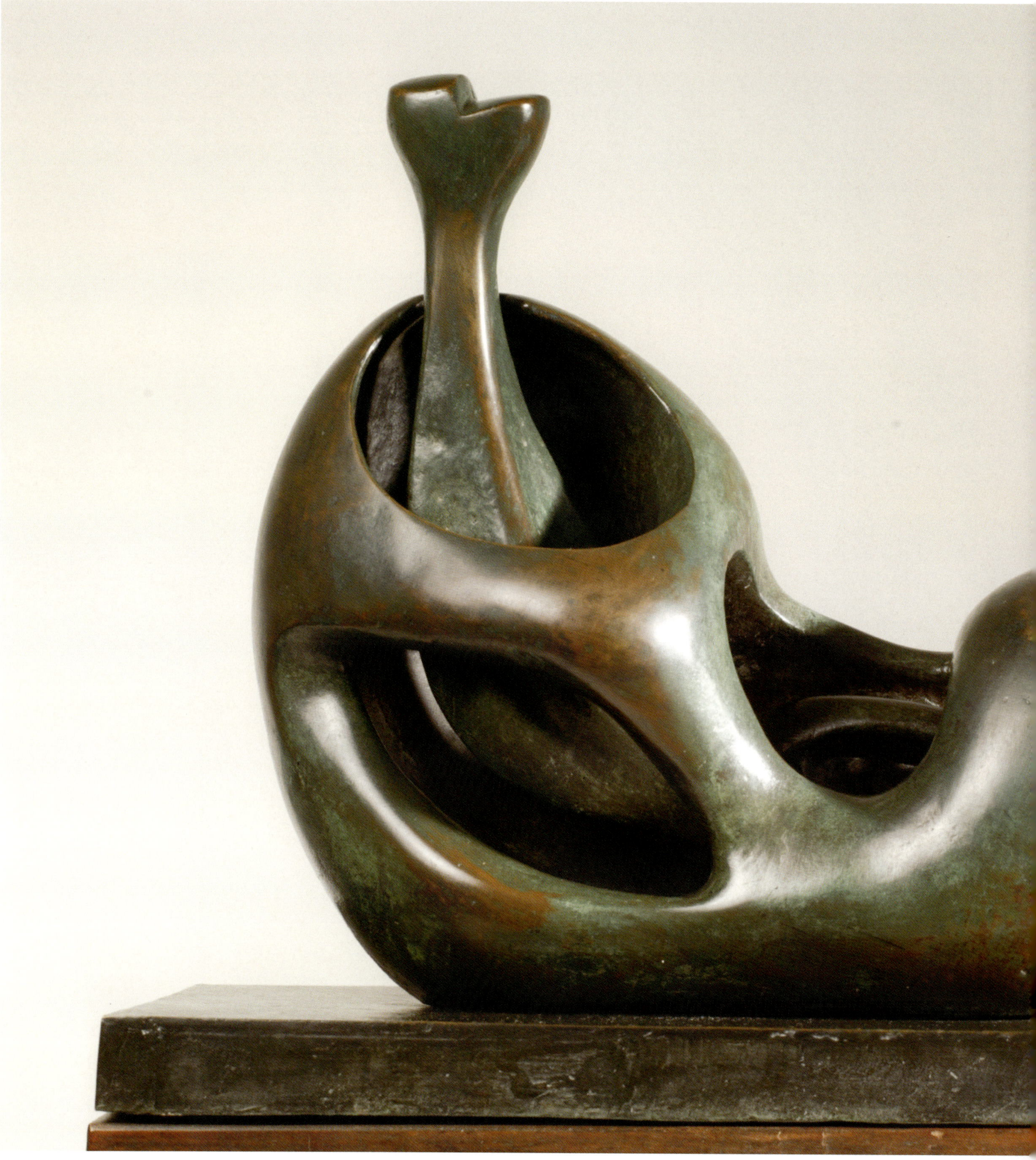

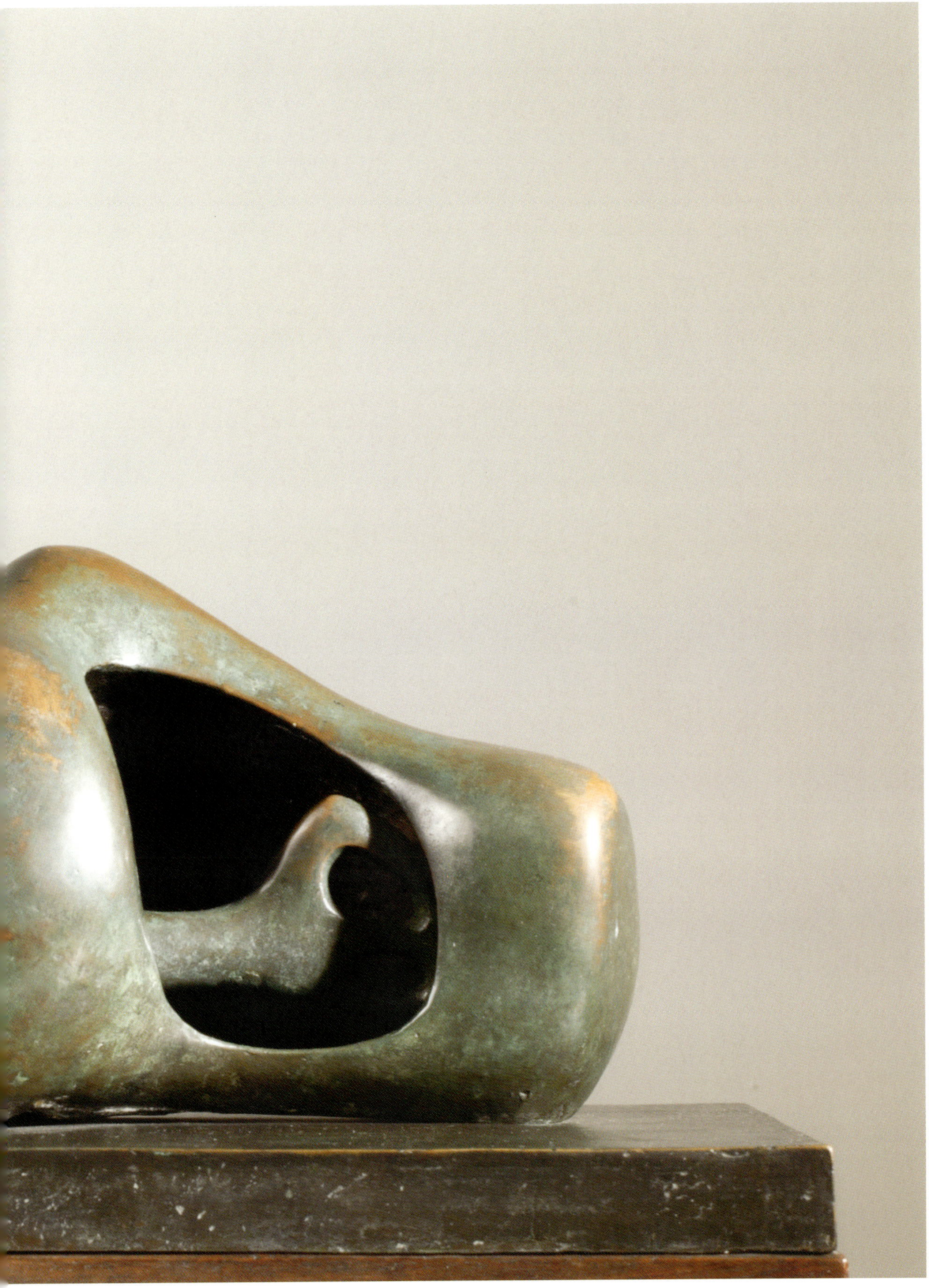

30.
Working Model for Reclining Figure: Internal/External Form 1951
Bronze
330 x 520 x 171mm
Arts Council Collection,
Hayward Gallery, London
LH 298

31.

Reclining Figure

1956–62

Bronze

950 x 2440 x 1015mm

Robert and Lisa Sainsbury Collection, University of East Anglia, UEA 85

LH 402

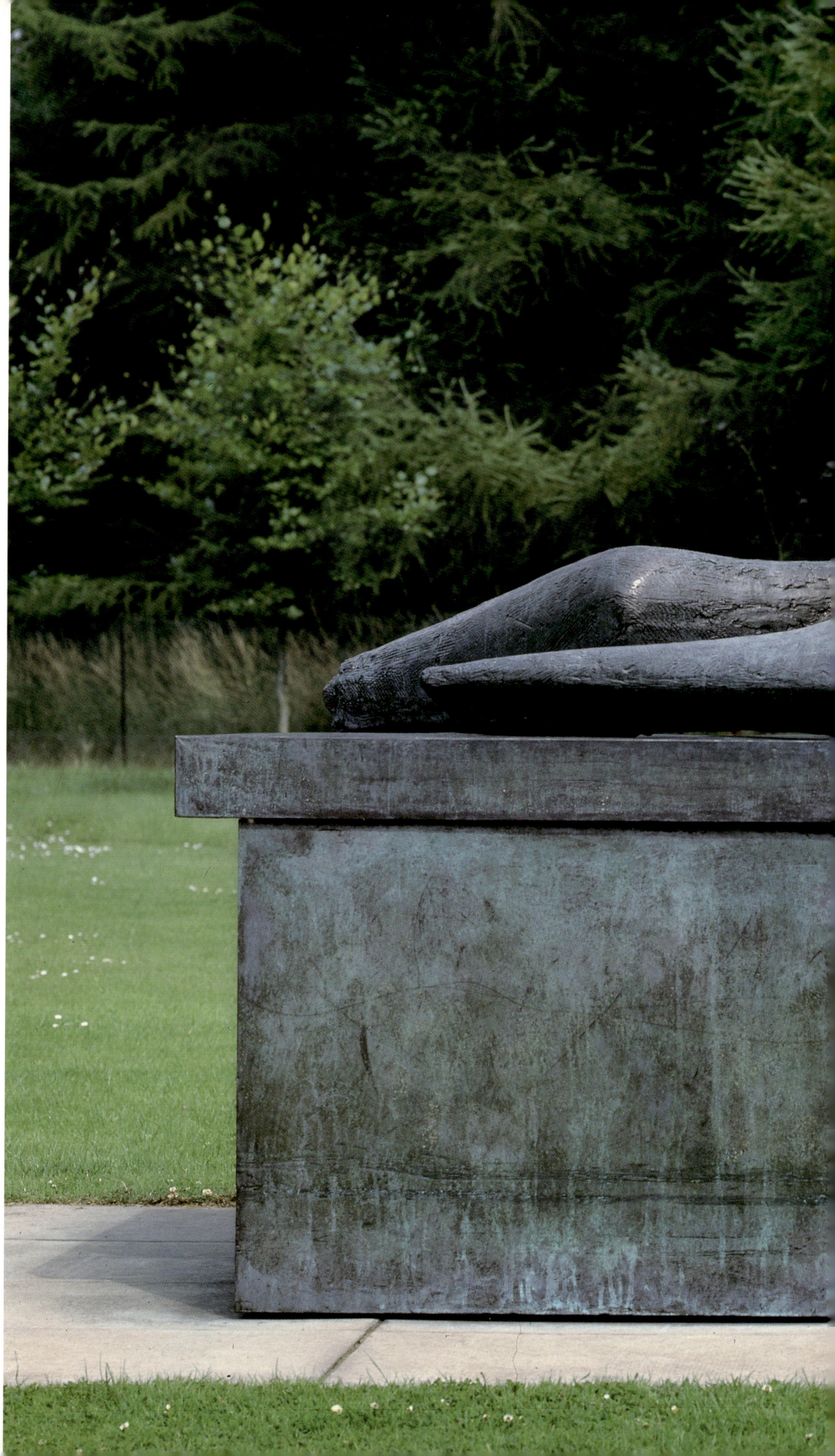

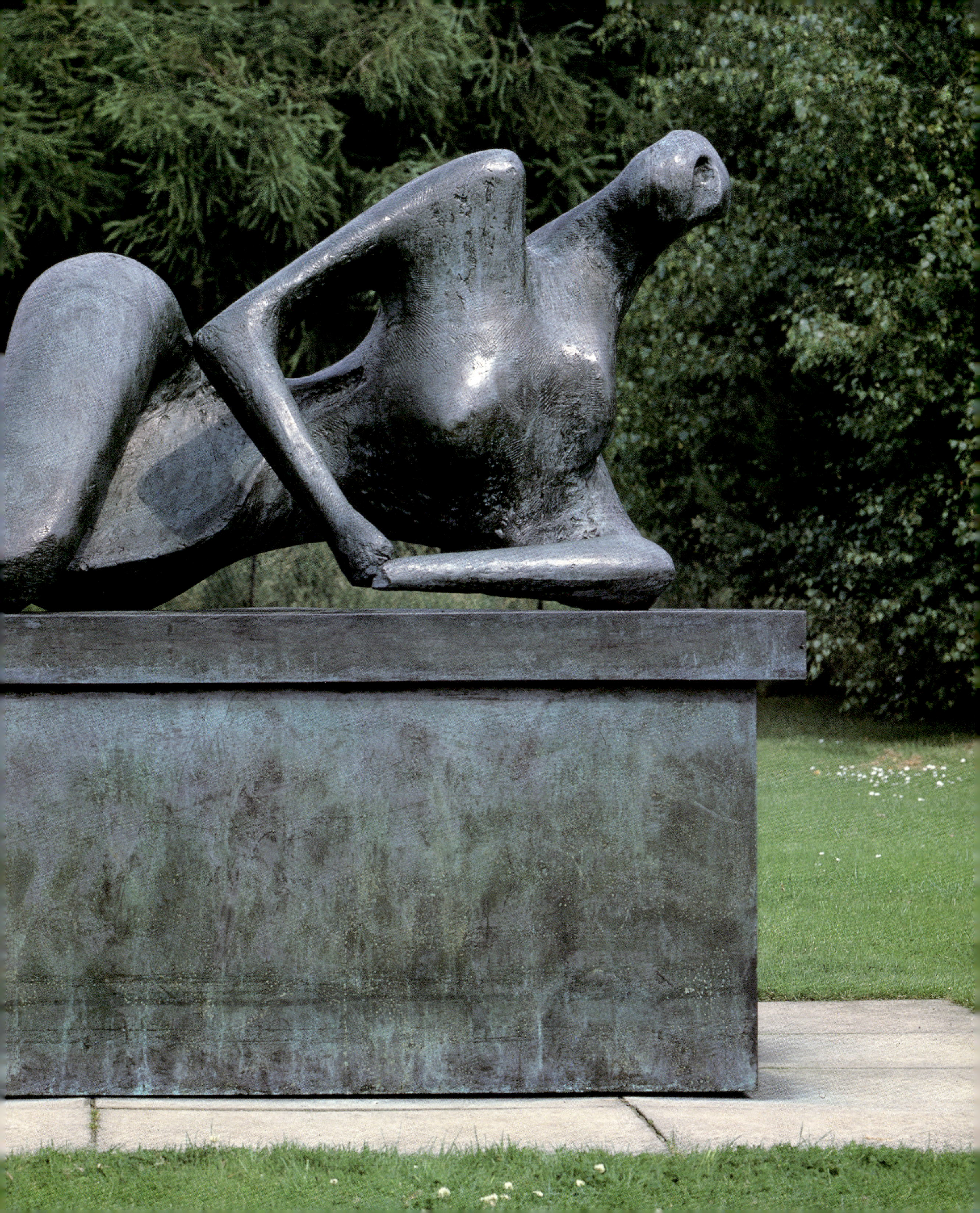

32.
Fragment Figure 1957
Bronze
105 x 200 x 130mm
Private Collection
LH 430
Part of definitive maquette for the Sainsbury Collection's *Draped Reclining Figure* (cat. no. 33)

33.
Draped Reclining Woman 1957–8
Bronze
l.2057mm
Robert and Lisa Sainsbury Collection, University of East Anglia, UEA 86
LH 431

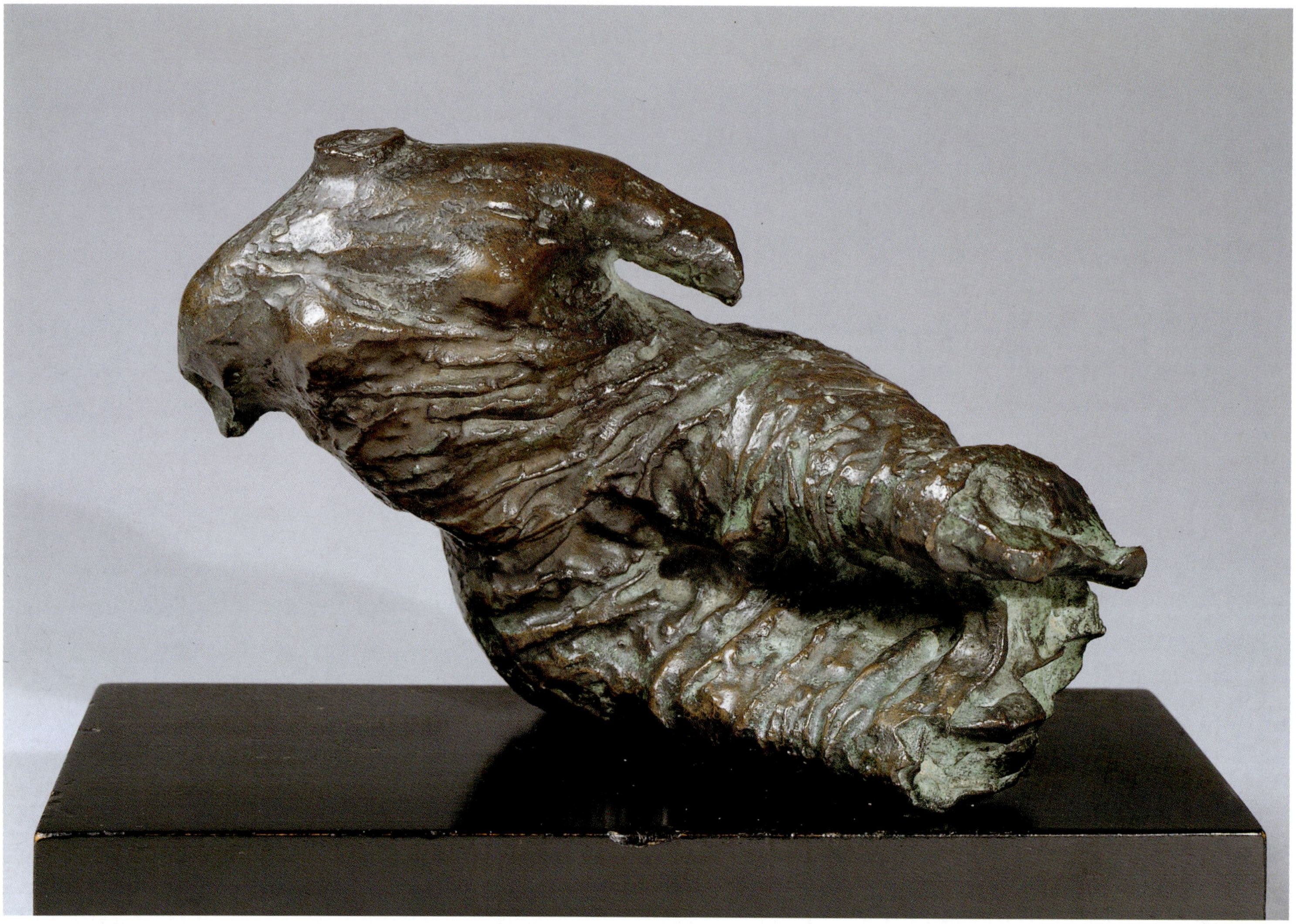

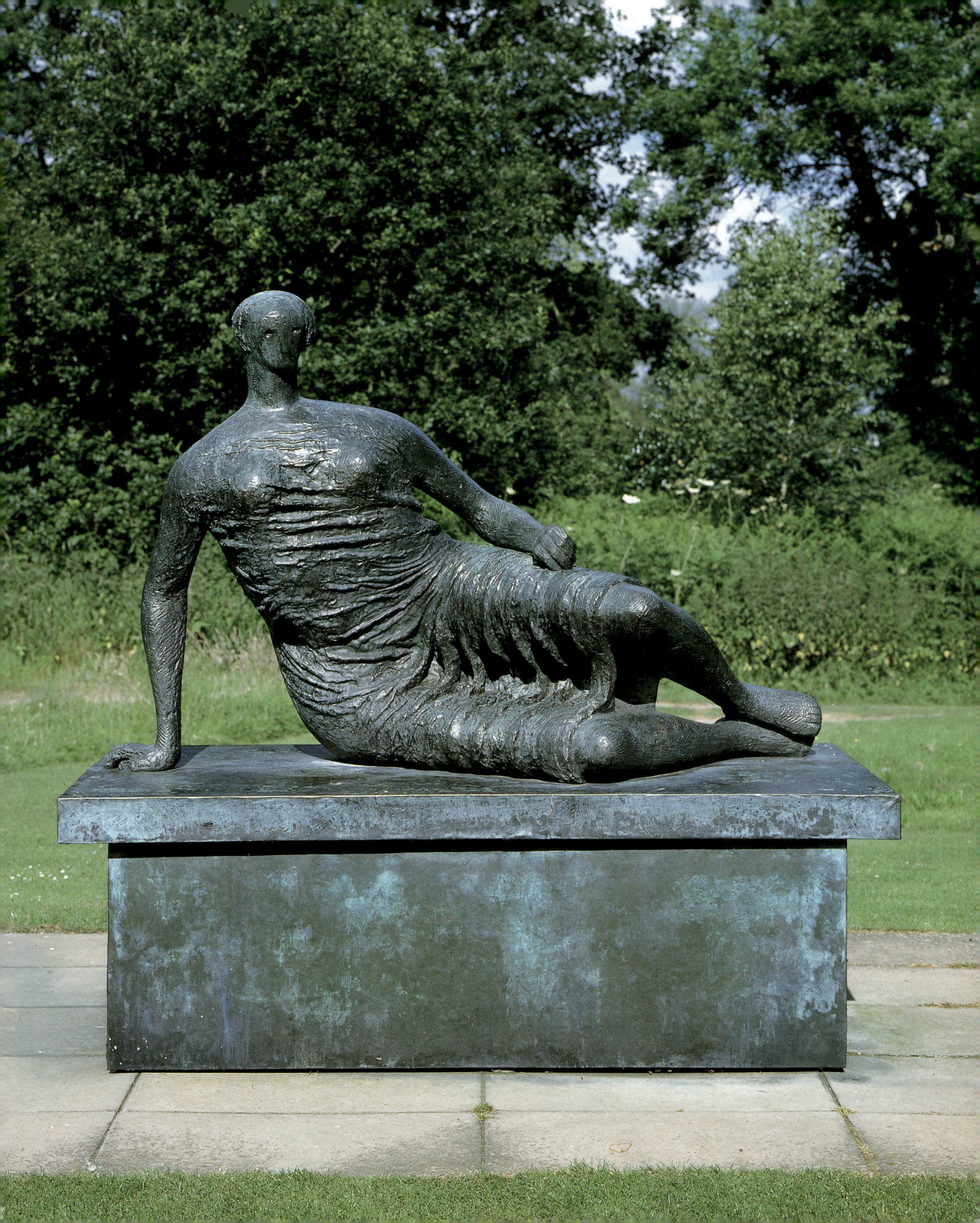

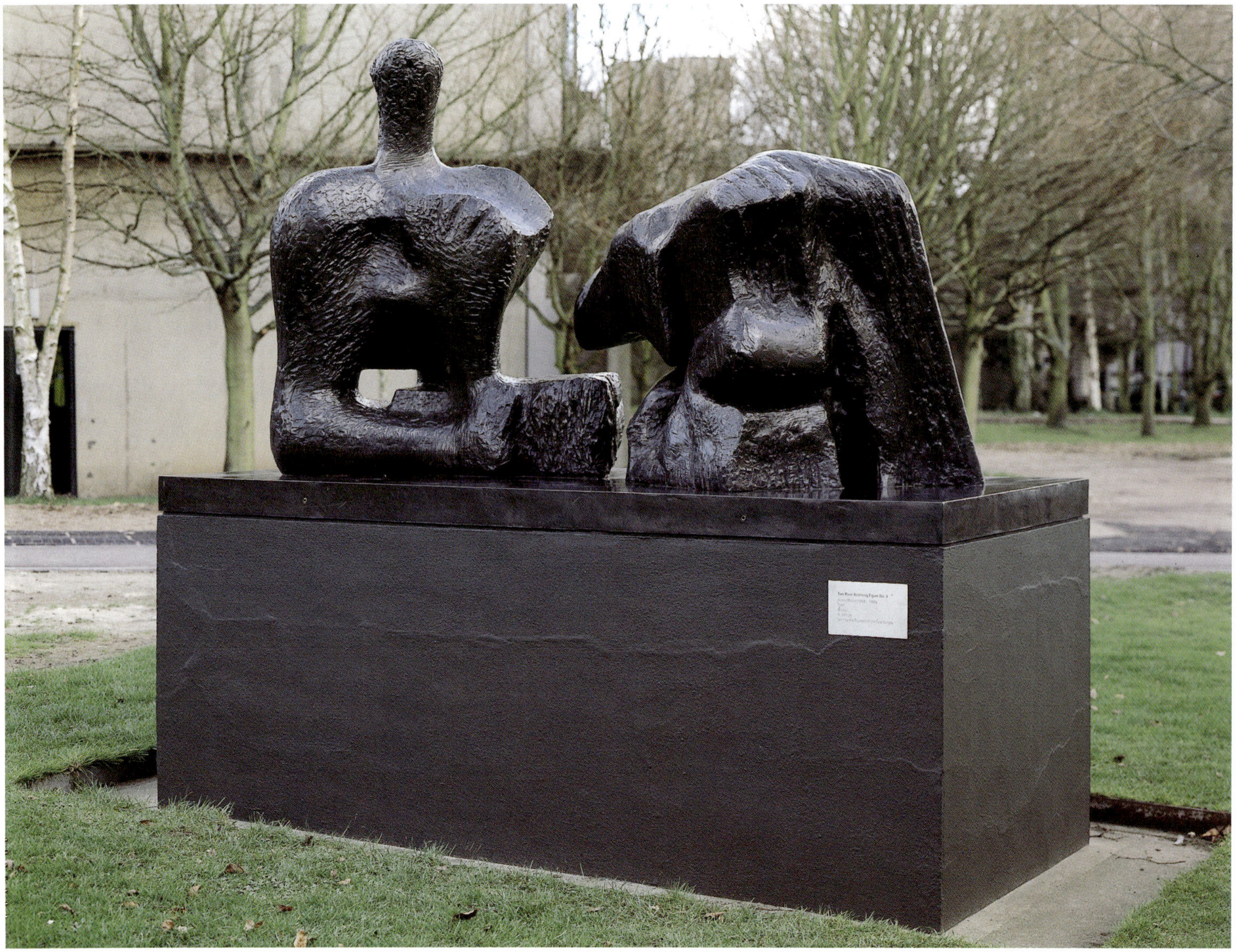

34.
Two Piece Reclining Figure No. 3 1961
Bronze
1473 x 2407 x 1140mm
Tate: presented by the artist 1978
LH 478

35.
Working Model for Draped Reclining Figure 1976–9
Plaster
l.990mm
The Henry Moore Foundation: acquired 1986
LH 705

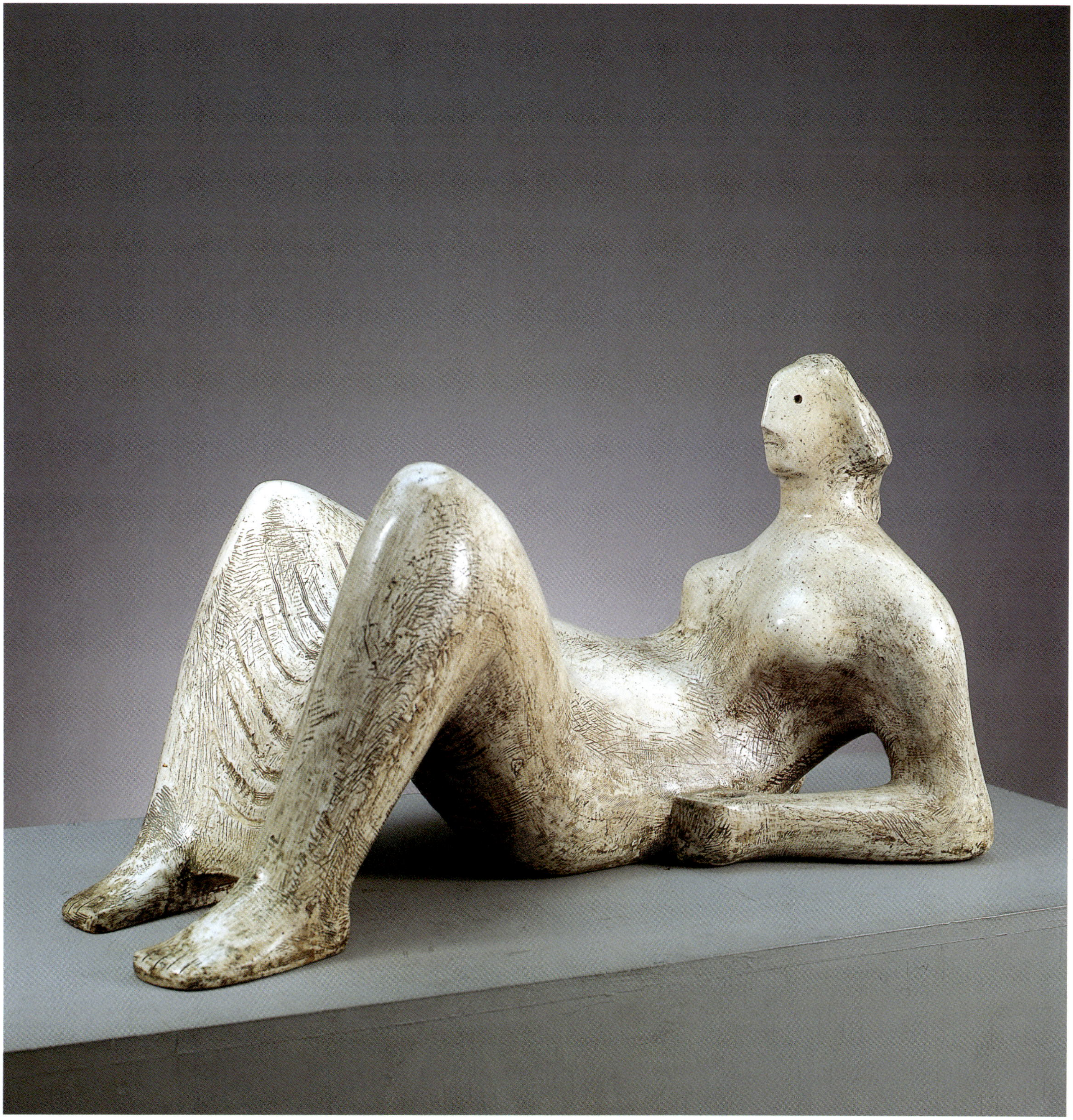

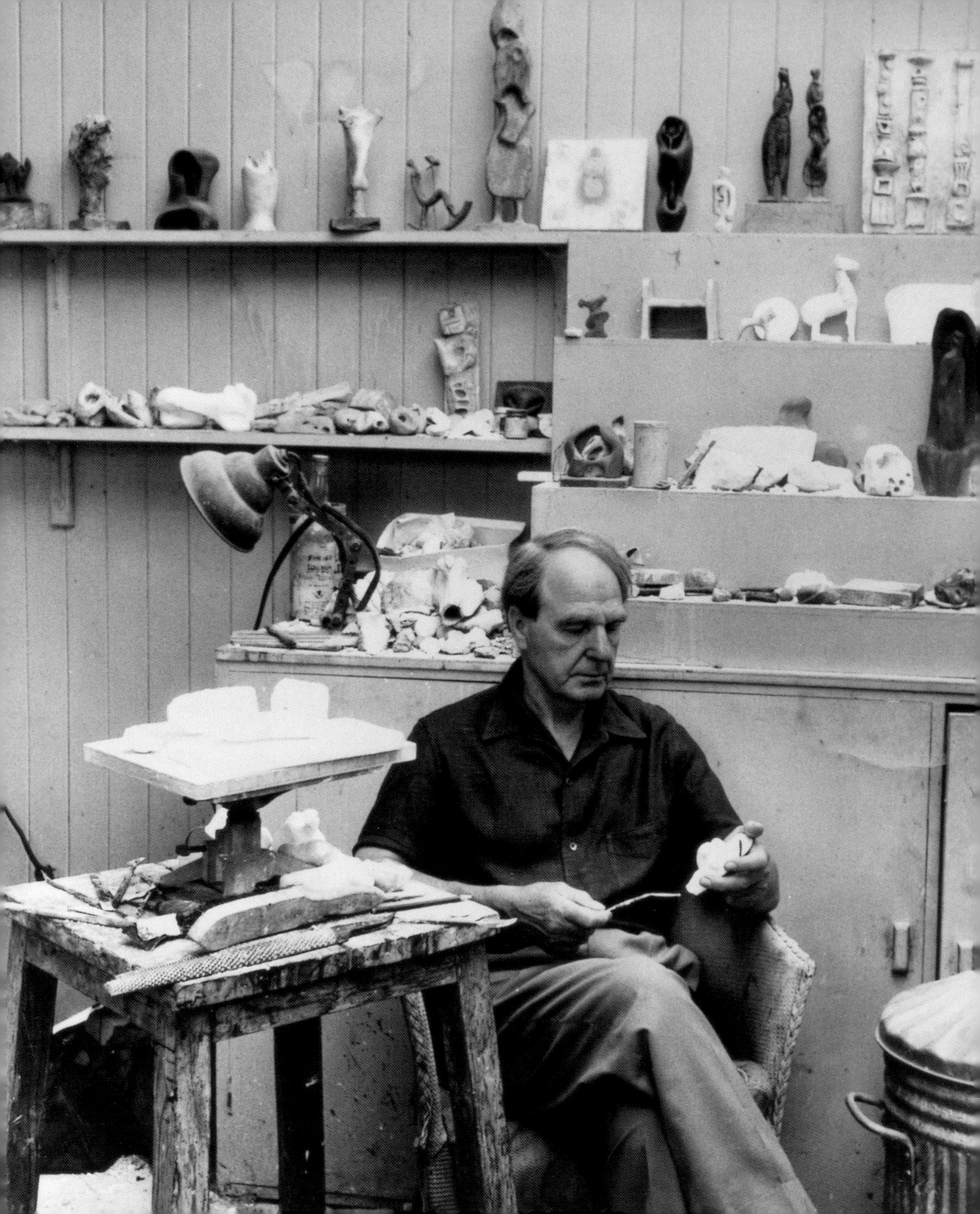

THE IRONSTONE PEBBLES that Henry Moore made use of in his *Reclining Figure* and *Mother and Child* (cats 7, 22) mark only two examples of what was a lifelong habit of looking out for, and collecting for reference, inspiration from the natural world, whether bones, rocks, tree forms, leaves or shells. In 1934, as a member of Paul Nash's short-lived Unit One and of the 7 & 5 Society under the leadership of Ben Nicholson, Moore may be said to have been, briefly, in the vanguard of a movement, rather than simply his own man. Just as John Piper dutifully produced abstract constructions in these years, so Moore responded to the zeitgeist with his most abstract creations. But he can never really be described as fully abstract; he admitted that he was apt to project human attributes onto the most formally abstract creations (see 'Square Forms and Heads', pp. 97ff.). His 1934 *Composition* (cat. 37), at first glance abstract, is, at a second glance, doubly figurative. It is not only a reclining figure, and therefore unavoidably suggestive of humanity, its human qualities are also inspired by organic forms.

Fig. 41 (below)
Standing Figure: Knife Edge, 1961 (LH 482), bronze.

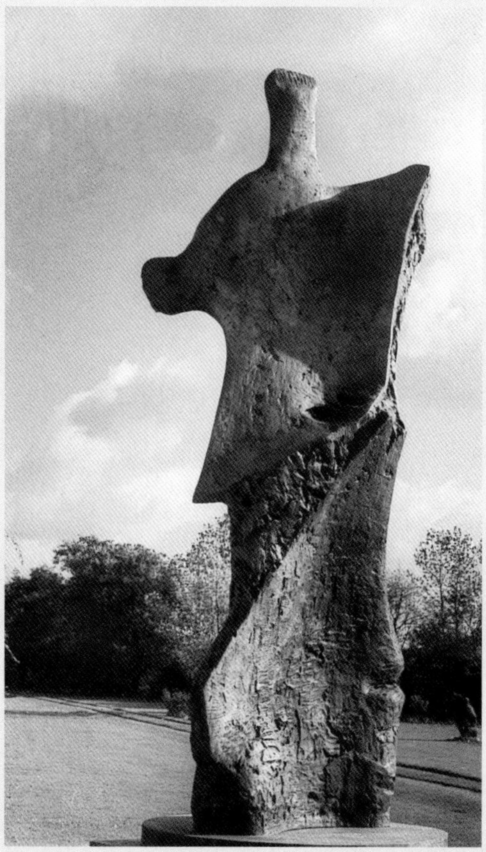

Moore's maquette studio at Hoglands (his final home at Perry Green, Much Hadham, next door to what is now The Henry Moore Foundation) testifies eloquently to the influence of found objects and organic forms on his work. One of the unexpected boons of moving to Hoglands was that its garden turned out to be rich in buried animal bones. The studio (fig. 40) contains everything from tiny birds' skulls to the skull of an elephant, via bones from the Sunday joint and curiously shaped stones or driftwood – anything, indeed, that struck the sculptor as having a natural form that could feed his own formal language. Often, the attraction took the form of a kind of recognition: a sea-eroded pebble could look uncannily like 'a Henry Moore'. Quite often, such objects could become the basis for a maquette; probably the most famous of these is the dramatic *Standing Figure: Knife Edge* of 1961 (fig. 41), where the original model is a piece of bone with plasticine additions. This small scrap was to evolve into a statue over 9ft (2.7m) high, Henry Moore's own *Victory of Samothrace*. By the end of the 1940s the inspiration of these small found objects that could be held in the hand and viewed from every angle, or placed against the sky to simulate a larger scale, was one of the factors leading to a profound change in Henry Moore's *modus operandi*. Before then, drawings had provided the principal creative means of visual experimentation with different forms. Whole sketchbooks were given over, for instance, to studies for the *West Wind* or for the family groups.

The latter sculpture idea was the last for which drawings provided the principal preparatory work; thereafter, Moore preferred to work directly with small models. 'With a small maquette a few inches in size you can turn it over in your hand and treat it almost as though you are a god creating something complete from every point of view.'[27] The difference in approach was fundamental, and several factors brought it about. Firstly, from 1935, when he employed Jack Hepworth, Barbara's cousin, for the summer, Moore had employed assistants to whom was delegated the roughing out of the sculpture – it was therefore important that the ideas in Moore's head had reached a tangible form that

Fig. 40 (left)
Henry Moore in his maquette studio, Perry Green, 1963.

Organic Abstraction

they could work from. Secondly, it is clear that, as Moore entered his post-war maturity, one of his greatest defining skills was his ability to manipulate scale. Some purists criticized the later work for what they saw as a cynical 'production line' approach to sculpture: instead of the truth to materials and direct carving fetishes of the 1920s and 1930s, they saw Moore coming up with a small model in clay or plasticine which was then blown up to skyscraper proportions by a team of assistants – where, they asked, was the artistic integrity in that? Of course, the skill was considerable and hard won, and as much a part of Moore's claims to genius as anything. Firstly, these enlargements were never simply that – this was not a cynical replication of the pointing-machine skills that Moore had rejected at college. Moore always changed detail or surface quality on the finished sculpture, appropriate to its scale. He would also sometimes use full-scale cardboard cut-outs (or, later, models in polystyrene) to ensure that the effect of his finished work suited its setting. But, ultimately, it was his instinctive recognition of the large in the small that stimulated his brilliant eye; when in 1937 several pieces of Hopton-wood stone that he had purchased for carving were arranged in his garden (his assistant, Bernard Meadows, made concrete blocks for them to stand on until used), he typically described the effect as like 'a miniature Stonehenge' (fig. 42). Later, he was to attempt to repeat the effect with an arrangement of bones as a model for what would have been, had it ever been made, a hilltop installation of truly megalithic scale (*Stone Maze*, fig. 43).

Then, again, there was the power of the photograph. One of the first sculptures from the batch of Hopton-wood stone, the remarkable *Reclining Figure*, 1937 (fig. 44), was then photographed by Moore against the sky, filling the entire frame of the photograph. The resulting image makes the sculpture look anything from 9 to 30ft (2.7–9.1m) long; it is in fact less than 3ft (0.9m). Moore had quickly discovered a) that, if he wanted a decent photograph of his work, he had much better do it himself, and b) that such photographs could play remarkable games with scale. It was a very liberating discovery; and it was much cheaper – still a crucial consideration at this time.

It was a discovery that informed his drawings also. The Sainsbury *Sculptural Object in a Landscape* (1939, cat. 38) combines an organic form – the bone-like quasi-reclining figure – with a landscape in such a way as to suggest that the object is vast. Three tiny cows are included to enforce the visual message. In this, as with the photograph of the Hopton-wood *Reclining Figure*, Moore gives a very clear intimation of what the future might hold. In terms of scale, only technical considerations really held him back at this point; visually, he was already there. However, on 3 September that year war was declared, and it was to be some time before Moore would have the opportunity to make that technical leap.

Large Two Forms of 1966 (cat. 39) illustrates very well where the obsession with organic forms and the related sense of scale were to lead. This is one of the grandest of the procession of enormous late Moore bronzes that were to crop up all over the world in the last two decades of Moore's life. The maquette shows two simple bone forms in relation; the end result, 20ft high (6.1m), is a masterpiece of balance and scale. The two forms' relation to each other (much closer than in the maquette) is mysterious but not oppressive; children and adults alike love to inhabit the spaces between. The shapes change endlessly depending on where you are standing. The forms are welcoming and rounded. Views out are framed by huge doughnut-shaped forms, like the 'hole' in the Tate *Recumbent Figure* of 1938. Because it emerges from organic forms, it can look alive, like an enormous elephant that has wandered off to die; but because of its scale it is also architectural, and might even be said to prefigure buildings such as Frank Gehry's Guggenheim Museum in Bilbao. By the same token, Moore once observed that the Parthenon had become, over time, a piece of sculpture and 'much more impressive than when it was first made'.[28]

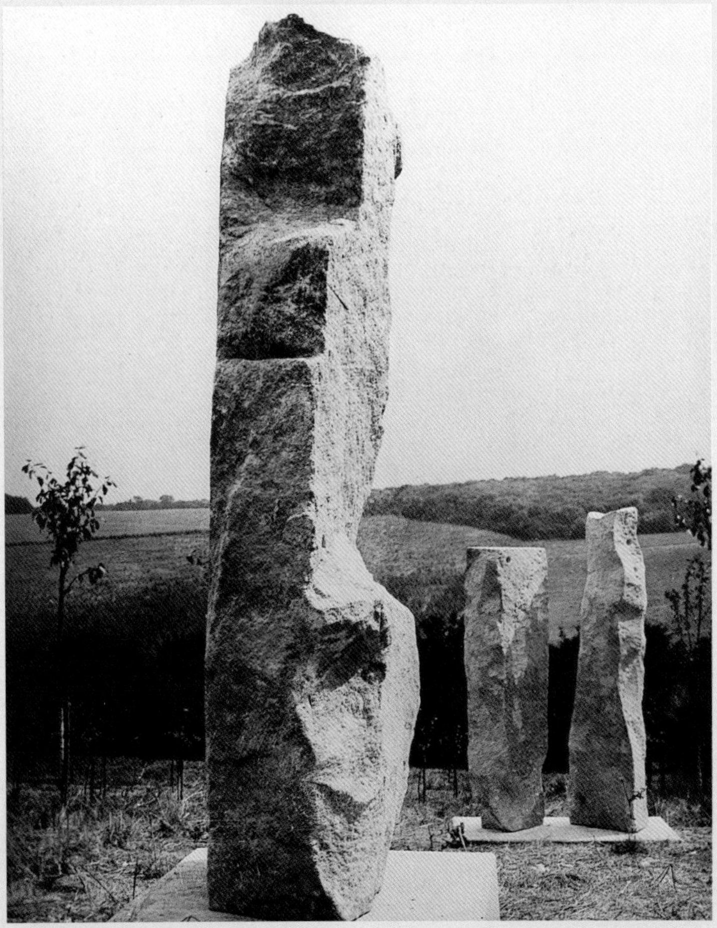

Fig. 42
Blocks of uncut stone at Burcroft, Kent.

Fig. 43 (right)
Stone Maze: Project for Hill Monument (detail), 1977
plaster, photographed in front of a sky backdrop; The Henry Moore Foundation Archive: gift of the artist, 1977.

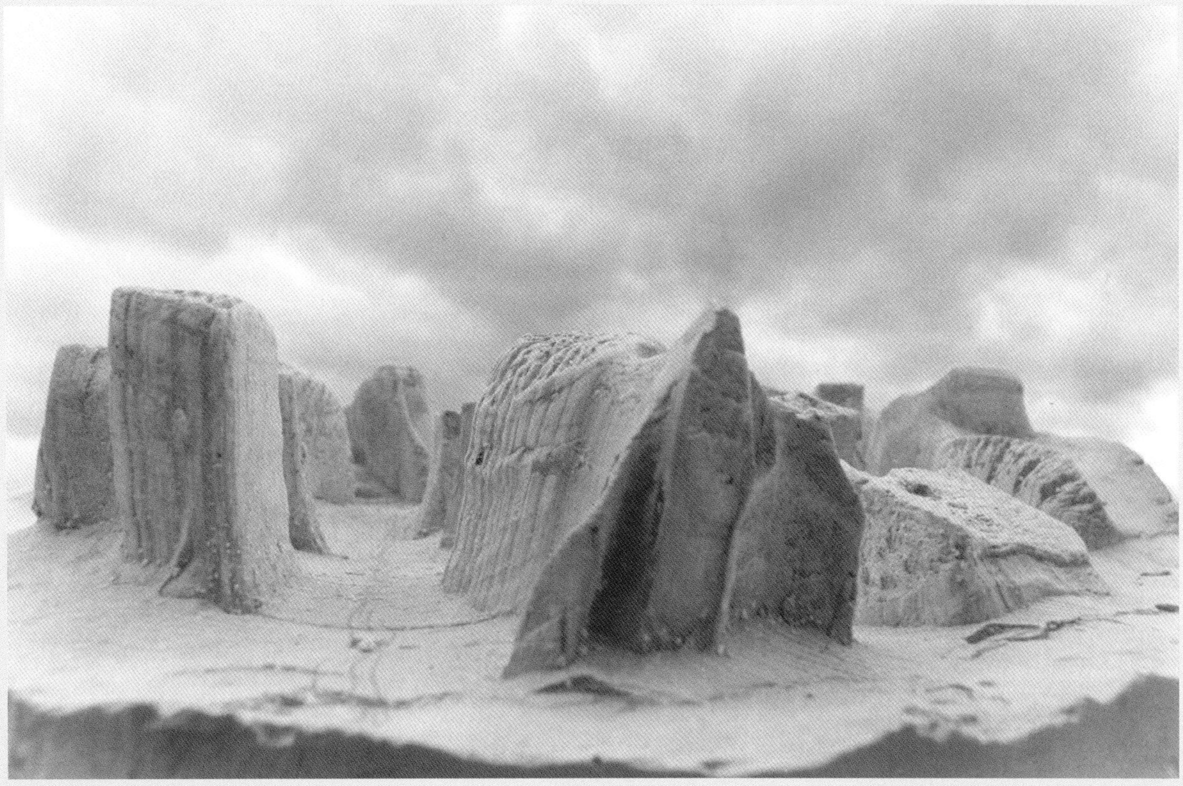

Fig. 44 (below)
Reclining Figure, 1937 (LH 178), Hopton-wood stone; Fogg Art Museum, Harvard University, Cambridge MA.

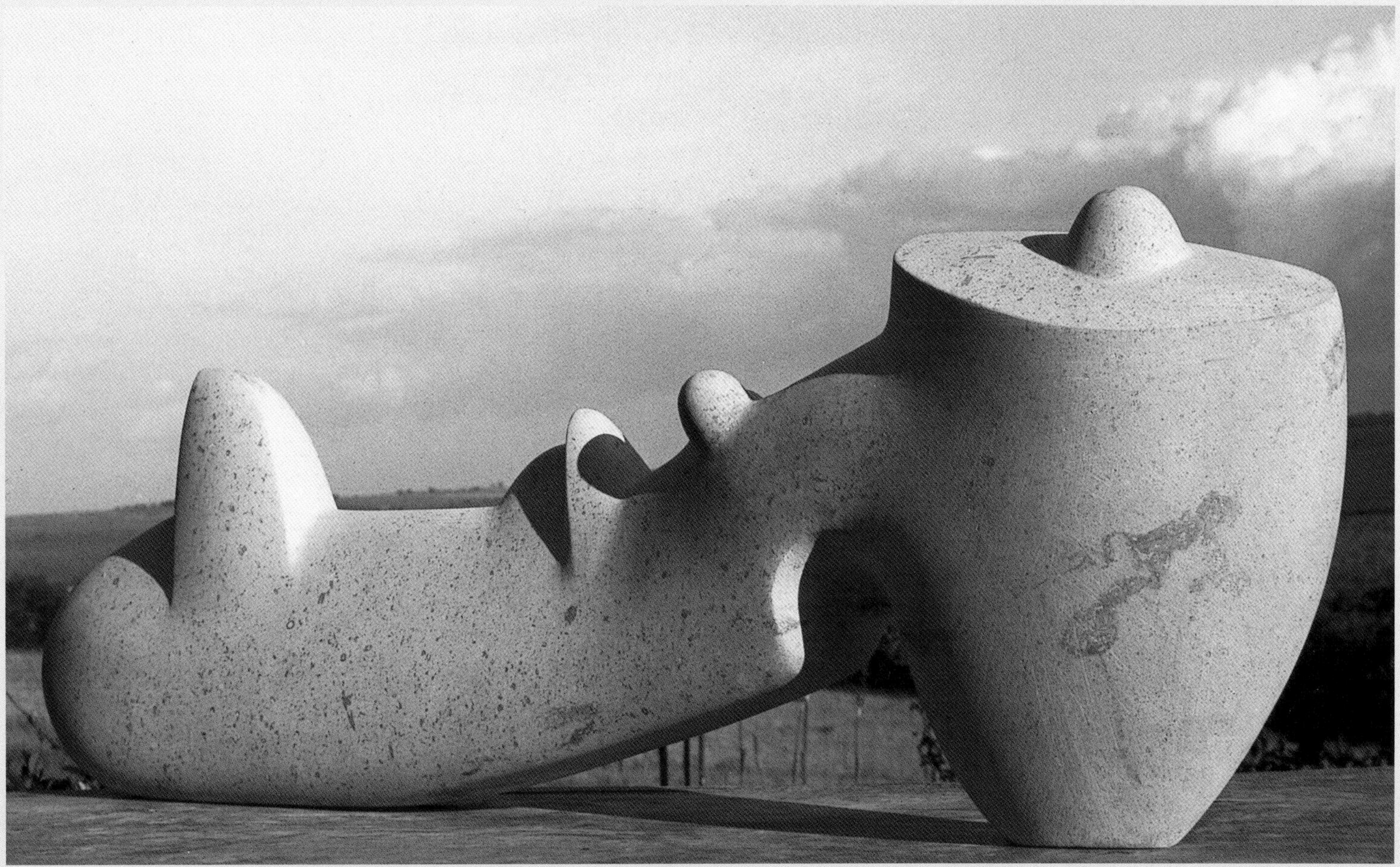

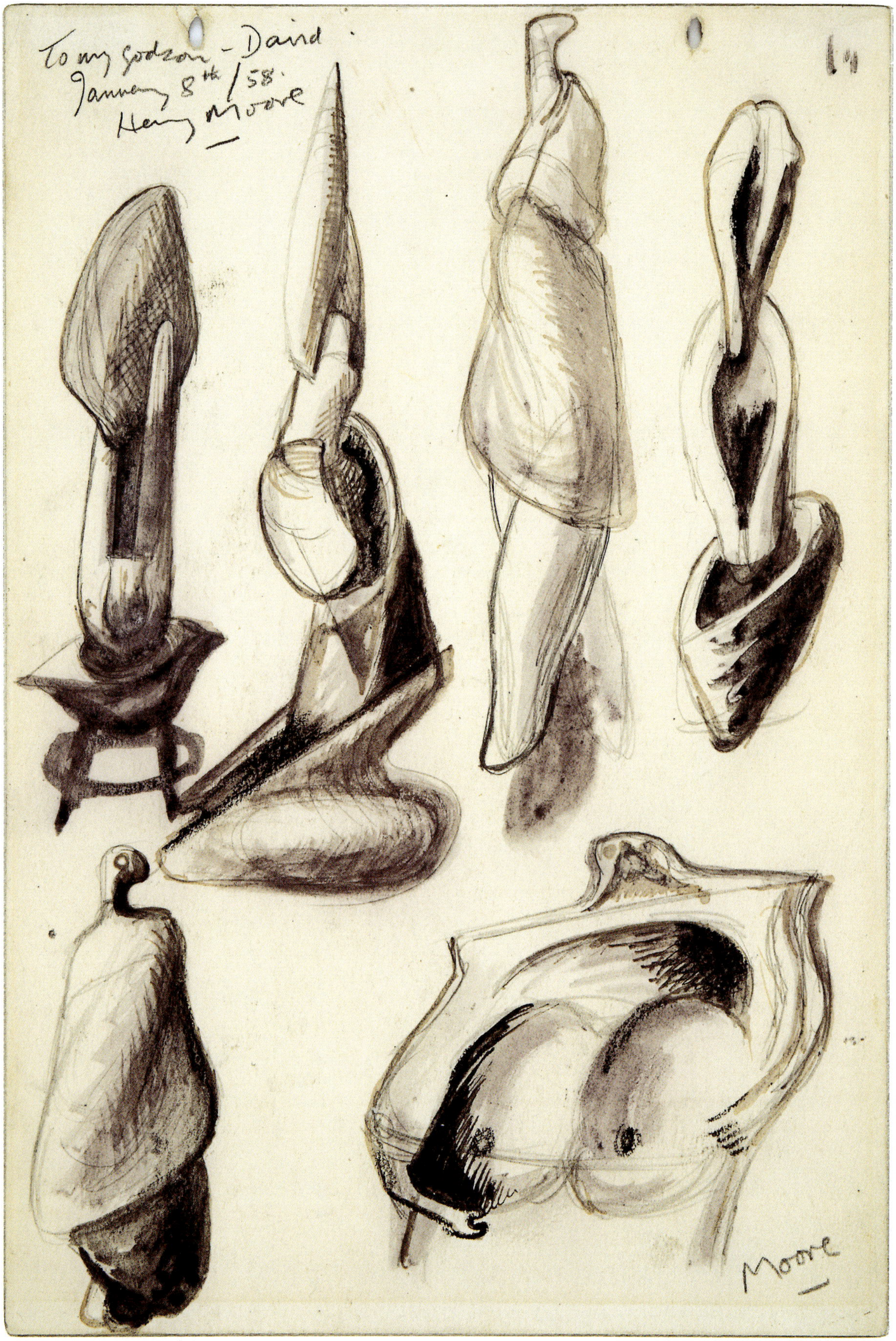
To my godson - David
January 8th /58.
Henry Moore
Moore

36.
Six Studies for Sculpture (left)
1931(recto)

Fourteen Ideas for Sculpture (right)
1931(verso)

From Sizewell Sketchpad 1931
Pencil, chalk, pen and ink, wash
260 x 178mm
Signed on recto (added later) in pencil lower right: 'Moore'
Inscribed in pencil upper left: 'To my godson – David / January 8th / 58 / Henry Moore'
David Sainsbury
AG 31.5, HMF 892

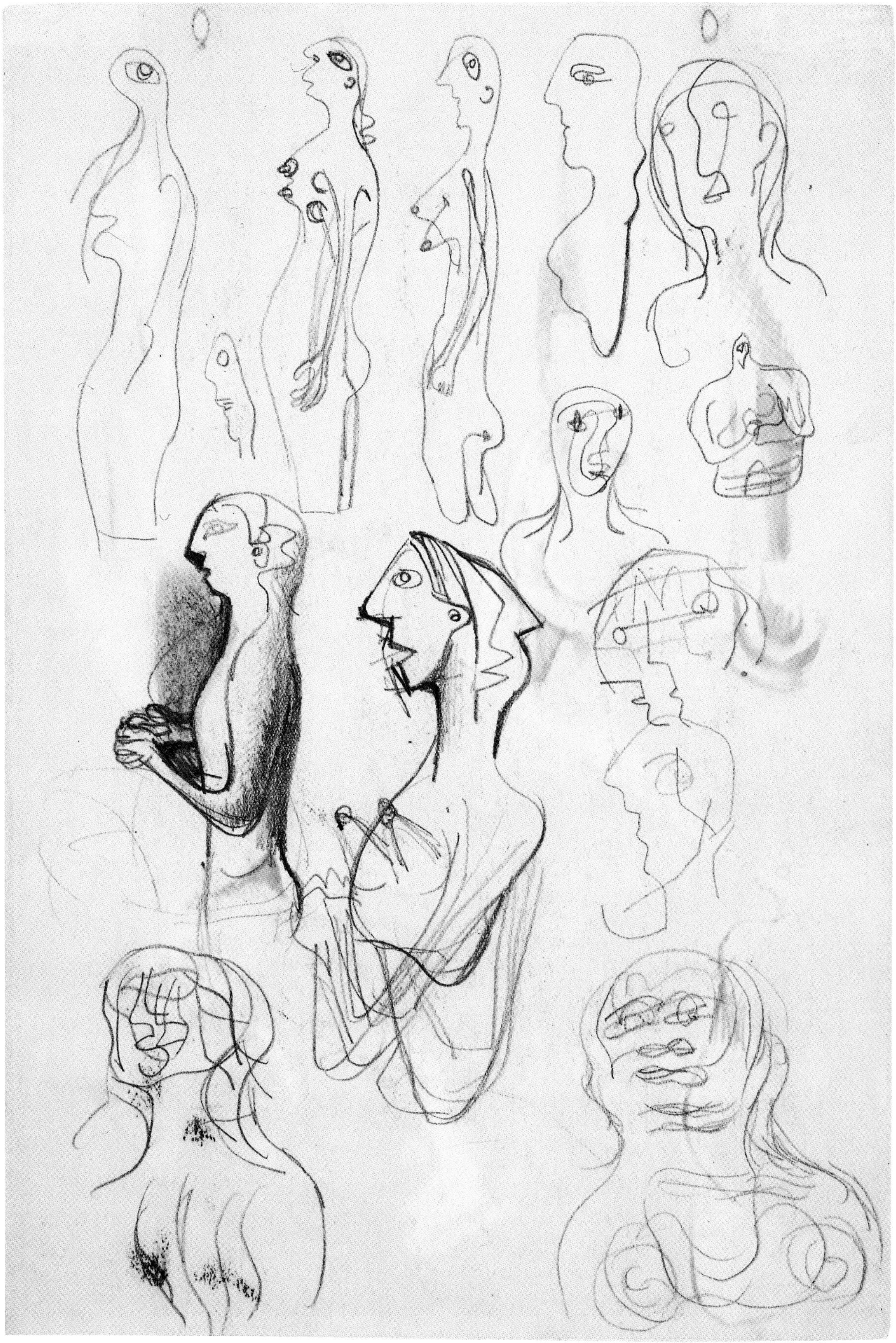

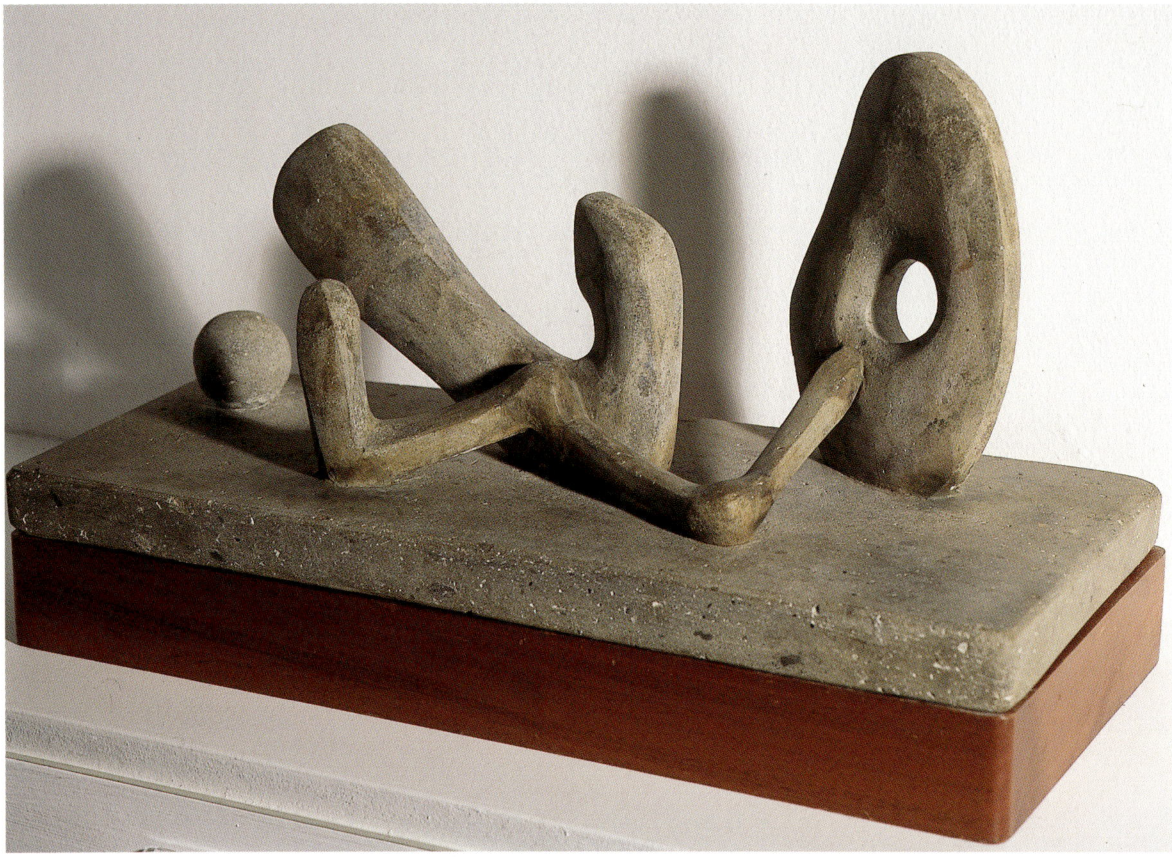

37.
Composition 1934
Cast concrete
l.445mm
The Henry Moore Foundation: gift of the artist 1977
LH 140

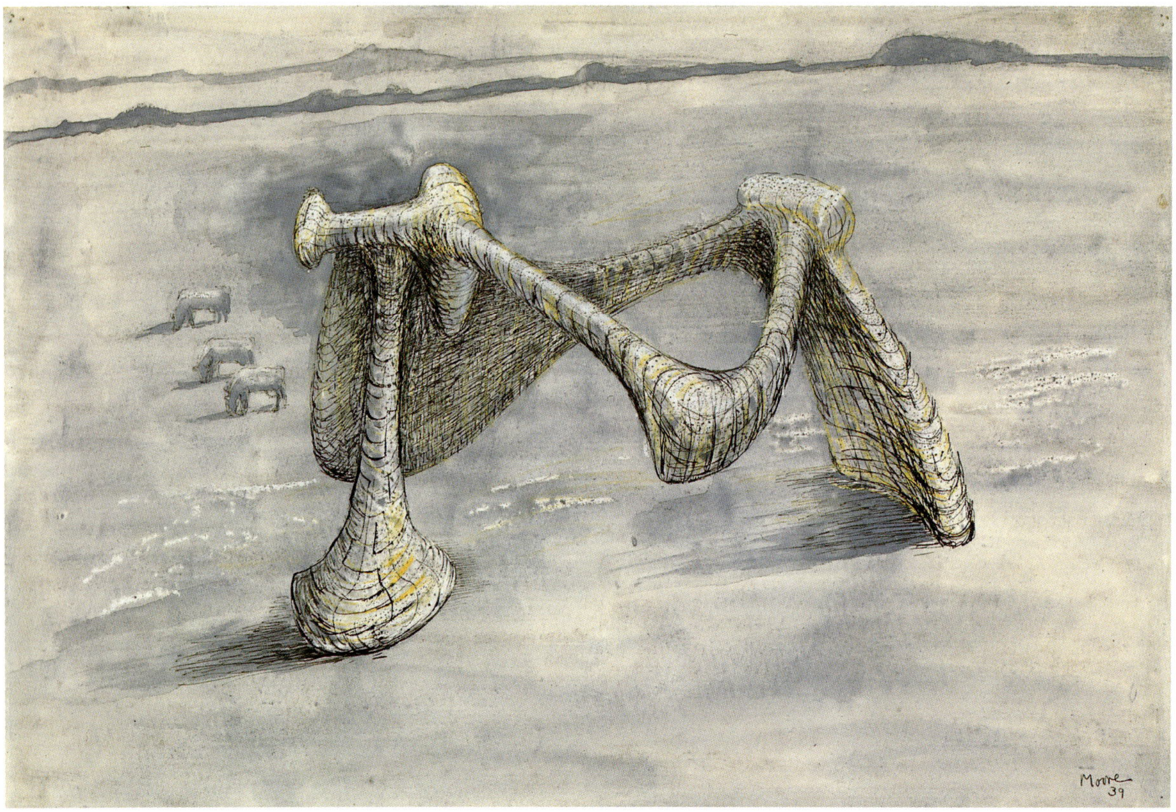

38.
Sculptural Object in a Landscape 1939
Pencil, wax crayon, watercolour wash, pen and ink, coloured crayon
375 x 546mm
Signed and dated lower right in pen and ink: 'Moore / 39'
Robert and Lisa Sainsbury Collection, University of East Anglia, UEA 89
AG 39.2, HMF 1441

39.
Large Two Forms 1966
Bronze
l.6100mm
The Henry Moore Foundation: acquired 1992
LH 556

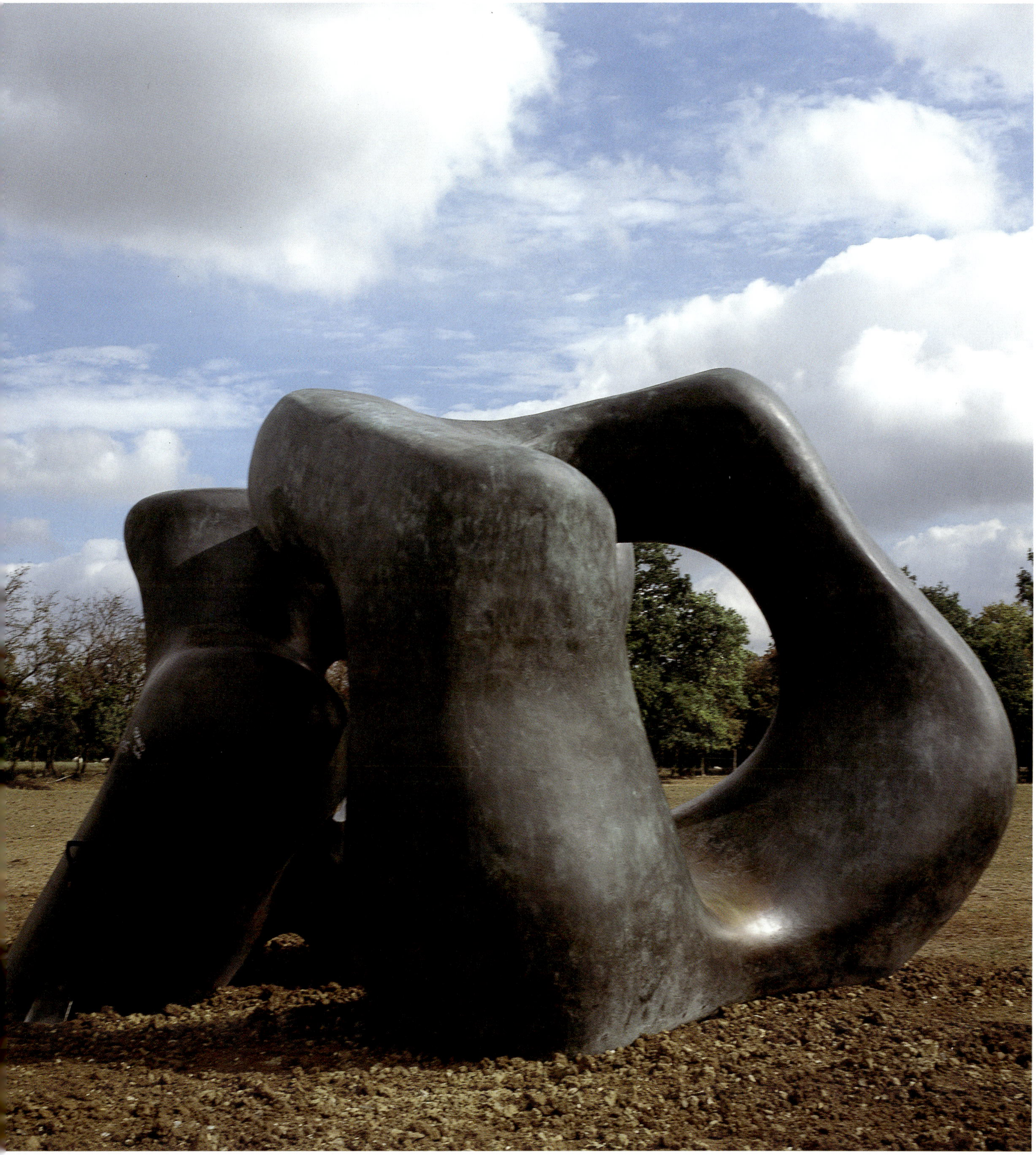

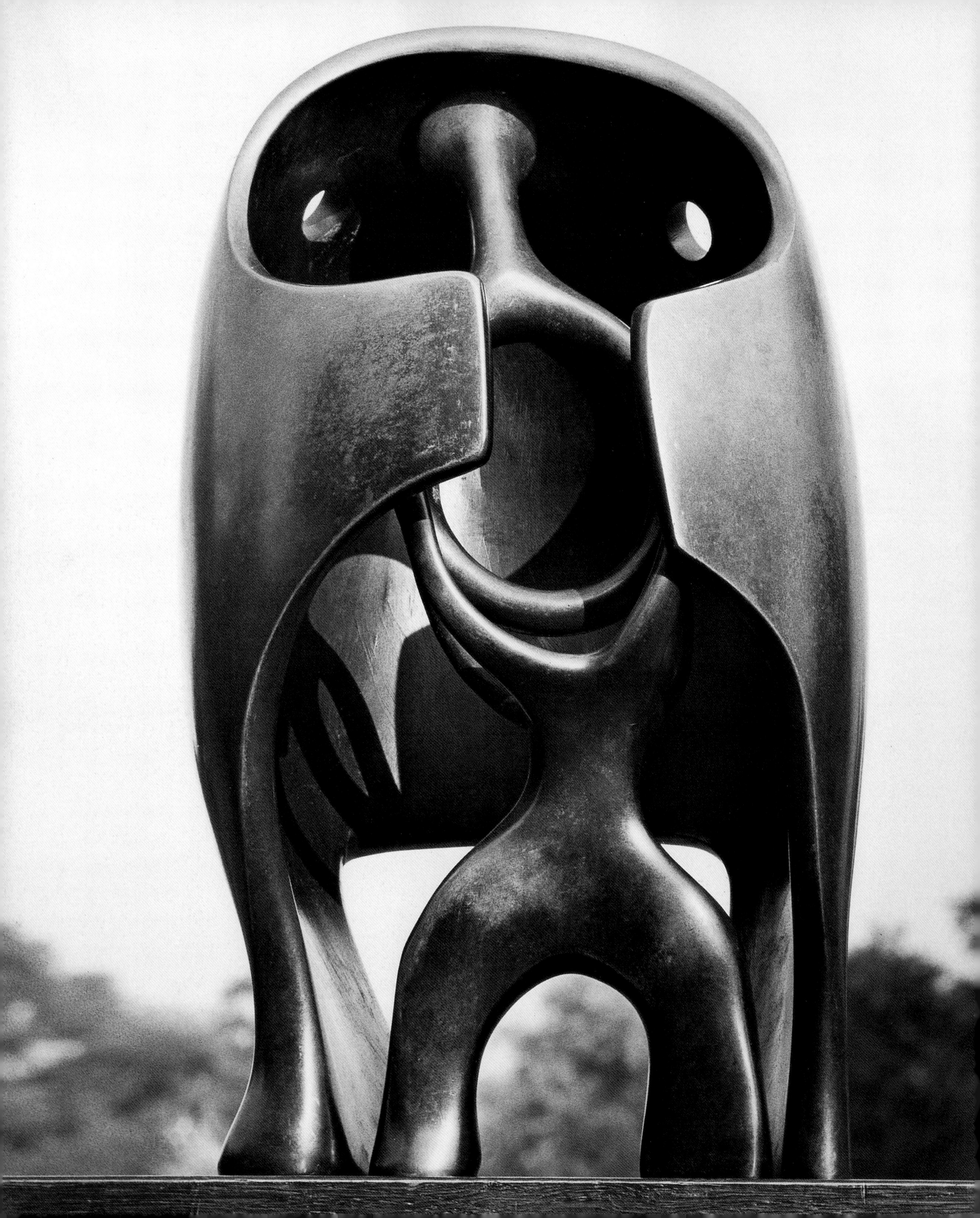

> Beauty, in the later Greek or Renaissance sense, is not the aim in my sculpture. Between beauty of expression and power of expression there is a difference of function. The first aims at pleasing the senses, the second has a spiritual vitality which for me is more moving and goes deeper than the senses. Because a work does not aim at reproducing natural appearances it is not, therefore, an escape from life – but may be a penetration into reality … an expression of the significance of life, a stimulation to greater effort in living.[29]

THE YEARS 1934–5 were not only the high water mark of Abstraction in Britain but also the time when Moore and Irina acquired a small house at Burcroft, Kent, which came with a few acres of land and a good view of the horizon. Into this landscape space Moore could place the lumps of stone that he had bought in Derbyshire and contemplate them. He was still preoccupied with the 'stoniness' of stone; a series of 'square forms' was one product of his search for forms that suited their material. Like all his 'abstract' pieces, the square forms doggedly retain their relation to the human form; and, again, inspiration was to be found in the British Museum. Cat. 40, simply called *Carving*, is carved from African Wonderstone. It is, from the front anyway, clearly a head, although its bold planar forms dissolve into something more abstract from different angles. When the head does emerge, it has a distinctly cubist appearance, with something of a Dan Dare chin. In the *Square Form* of the same year (cat. 41) in Burgundy stone a more extreme abstract form is presented, but it remains a head, with inscribed eyes and grooved mouth.

Fig. 46 (below)
Spanish Prisoner, 1939
(AG 39.34, HMF 1464),
charcoal, wax crayon,
chalk, watercolour
wash on medium to
heavyweight wove;
The Moore Danowski Trust.

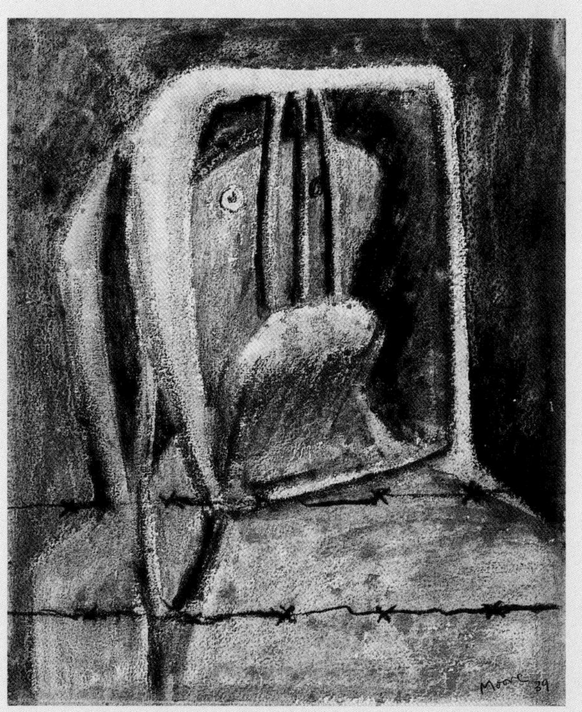

The Sainsbury *Square Form* of 1936 (cat. 42) in Green Hornton stone is reminiscent of Mexican carving in its rounded-off planes. The grooved mouth form reappears, and holes or protrusions suggest eyes or nostrils; but in general, despite its many suggestions of human or animal features, it remains as nearly abstract as anything Moore ever produced. Indeed, it illustrates very clearly his concerns of the time, as expressed in his contribution to the Unit One book published to coincide with the first (and last) Unit One group show at the Mayor Gallery, Cork Street, W1, in April 1934: 'If both abstract and human elements are welded together in a work, it must have a fuller, deeper meaning.'

Carving, also of 1936 (cat. 43, of travertine marble), is more obviously a human face and neck, and its abstract qualities owe most to the simplified forms of Cycladic figures of about 2700–2300 BC. Moore admired such things very much for their sense of inevitability, 'as though the sculptor can't make a mistake, never arrives at a result that was not inevitable from the beginning'.[30]

In May 1937 Moore and Irina visited Picasso's studio in Paris in a party that included Alberto Giacometti, Max Ernst, Paul Eluard, André Breton and Roland Penrose, where they were treated to a preview of the unfinished *Guernica*, a reminder – not that one was needed – of the gathering threat of European war. Moore was deeply troubled by events in Spain and by the rise of Fascism. It is hardly surprising, then, that the *Head* of 1937 (cat. 44, in green serpentine stone, carved in 1968) has shed any relationship with the square forms and become part-helmet, part-spearhead.

Two years later, his study of the armour in the Wallace Collection had married this idea

Fig. 45 (left)
The Helmet, 1939–40
(LH 212), lead;
The Henry Moore
Foundation.

Square Forms and Heads

of the helmet with that of the internal/external form (fig. 45, *The Helmet*. Also in 1939 the idea's expressionist power appeared in the mixed media drawing, *Spanish Prisoner*, where head and prison have become one (fig. 46). Although the onset of war effectively put an end to sculpting for three years, the helmet idea was too powerful not to re-emerge. Two examples from 1950 illustrate the theme: *Openwork Head No. 2* (cat. 47), where the helmet and head have blended with more than a hint of 'the man in the iron mask' about it; and *Helmet Head No. 1* (cat. 48). By an extremely interesting and characteristic extension of ideas – and perhaps the most powerful imaginative leap of his career – the helmet head idea finally climaxed in Moore's huge sculpture *Nuclear Energy* (1964–6; see fig. 47, a cast of the working model), which overlaid on the skull/helmet form one of the most nightmarish shapes spawned by the war – the vast and sinister mushroom cloud of the atomic bomb.

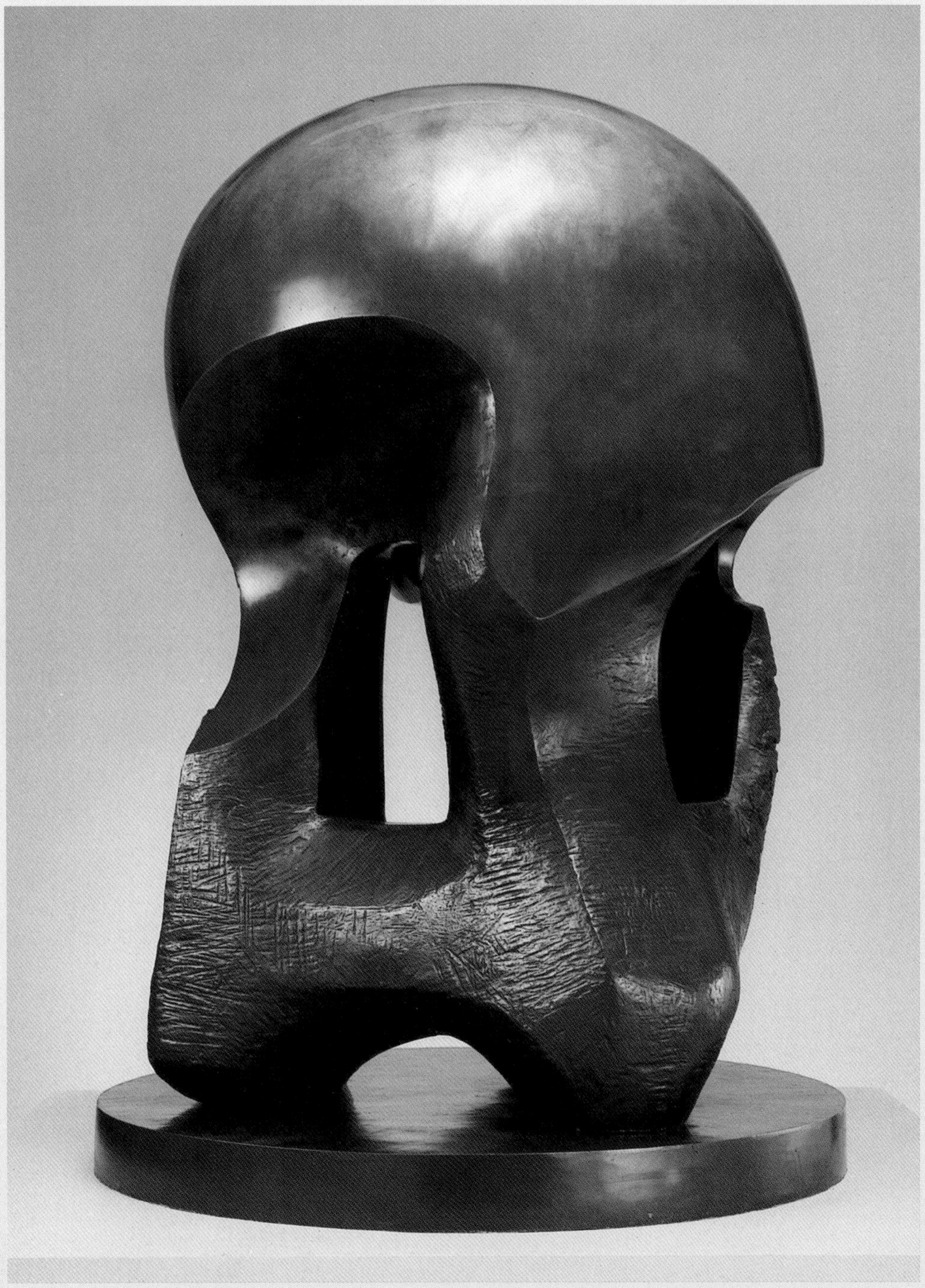

Fig. 47
Atom Piece, cast of a working model for *Nuclear Energy*, 1964–5 (LH 525), bronze; Tate.

40.
Carving 1934
African Wonderstone
h.98mm
The Henry Moore
Foundation: gift of
Irina Moore 1977
LH 142

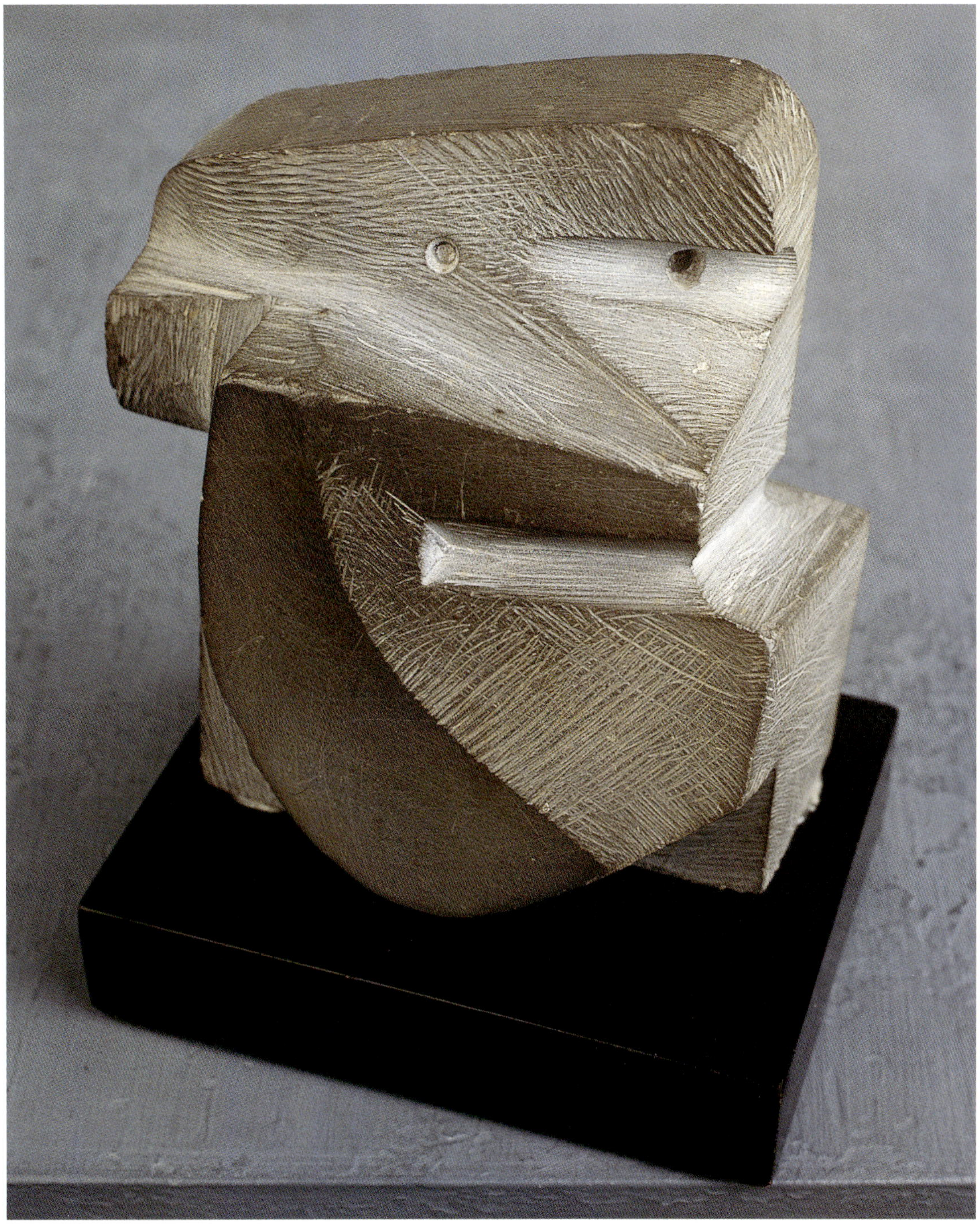

41.
Square Form 1934
Burgundy stone
h.317mm
The Henry Moore
Foundation: gift of Irina
Moore 1979
LH 154b

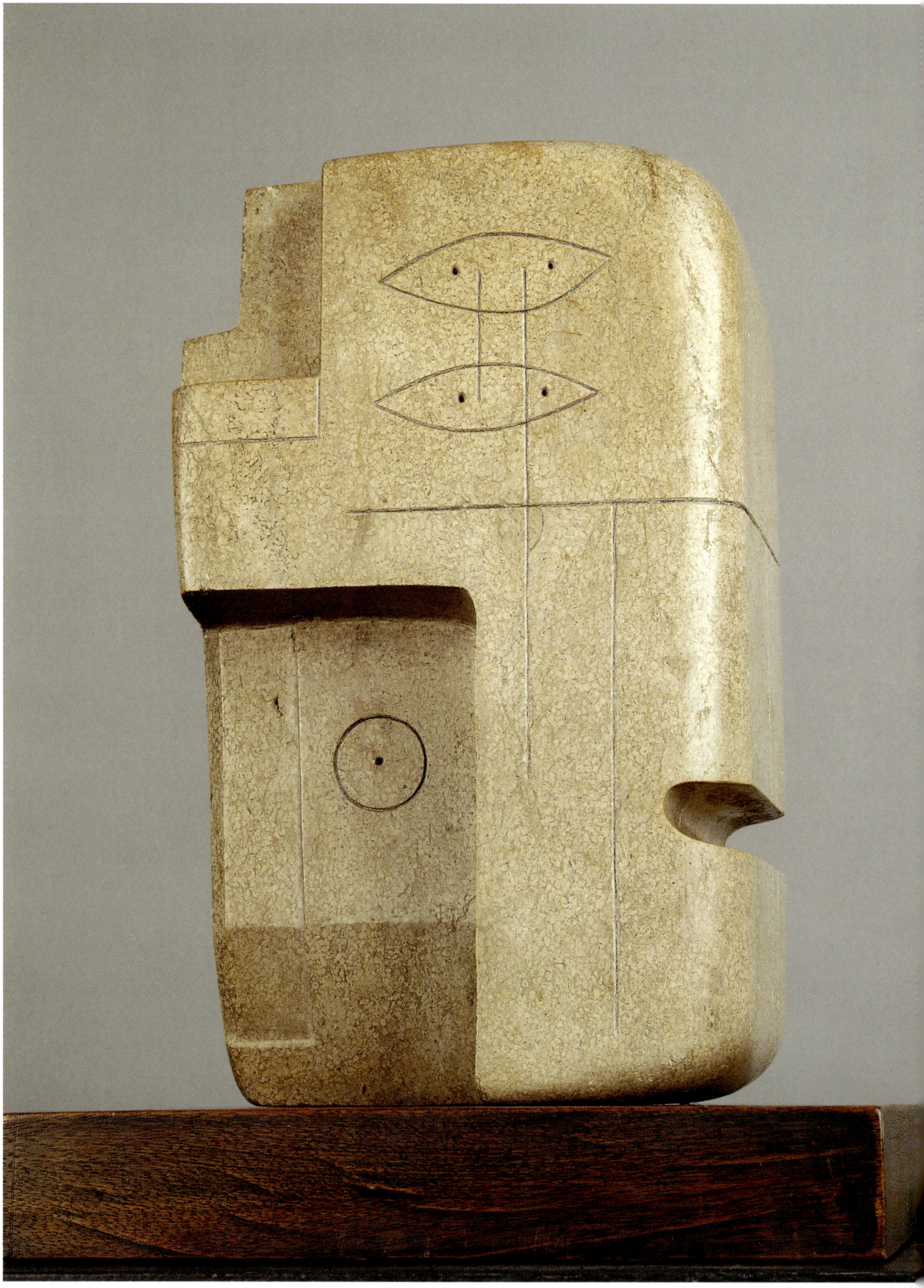

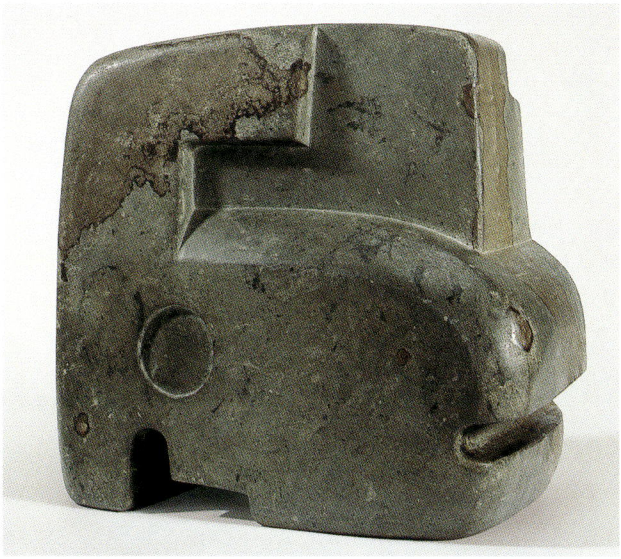

42.
Square Form 1936
(two views)
Green Hornton stone
350 x 235 x 385mm
Robert and Lisa Sainsbury
Collection, University of
East Anglia, UEA 83
LH 167

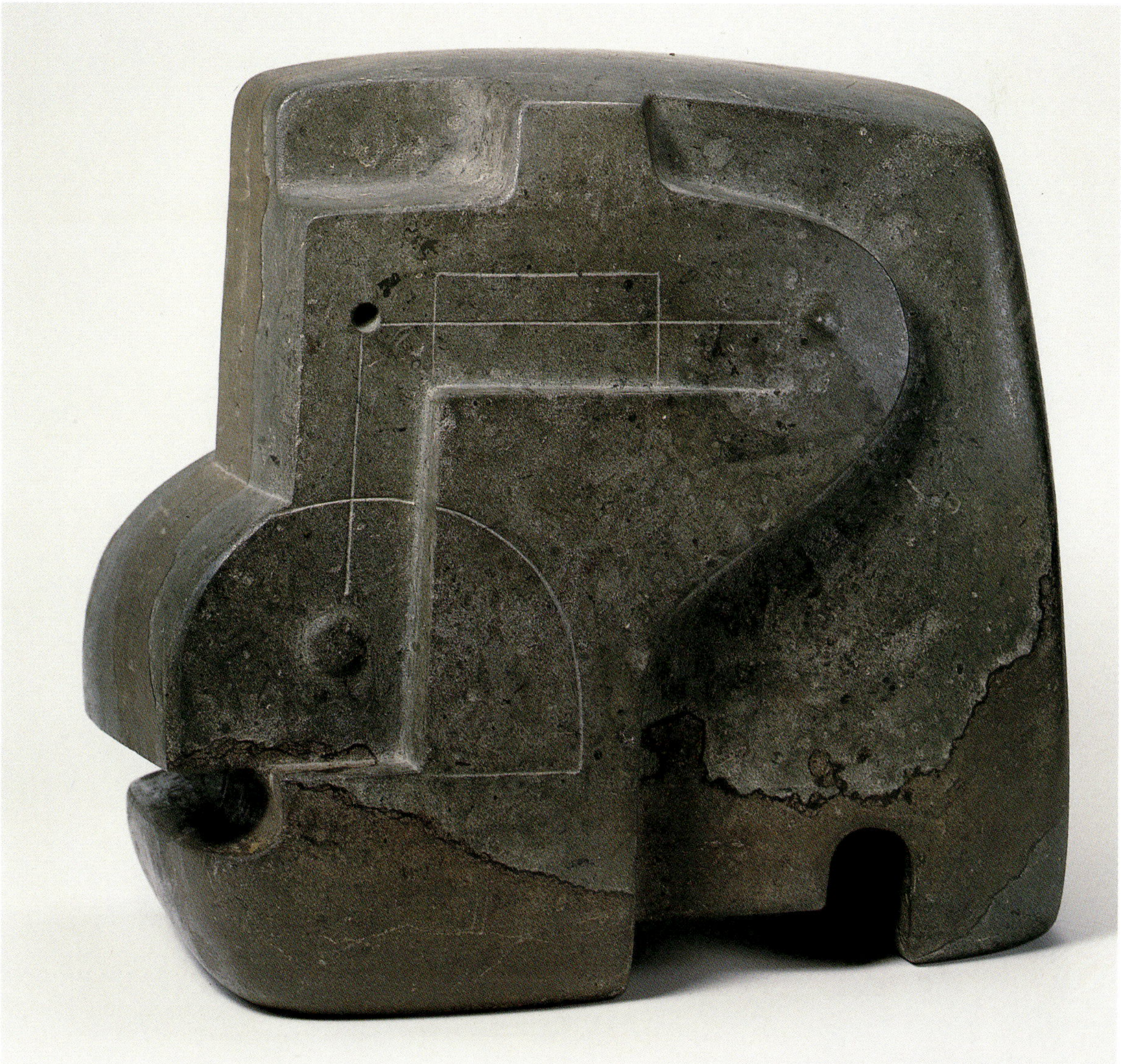

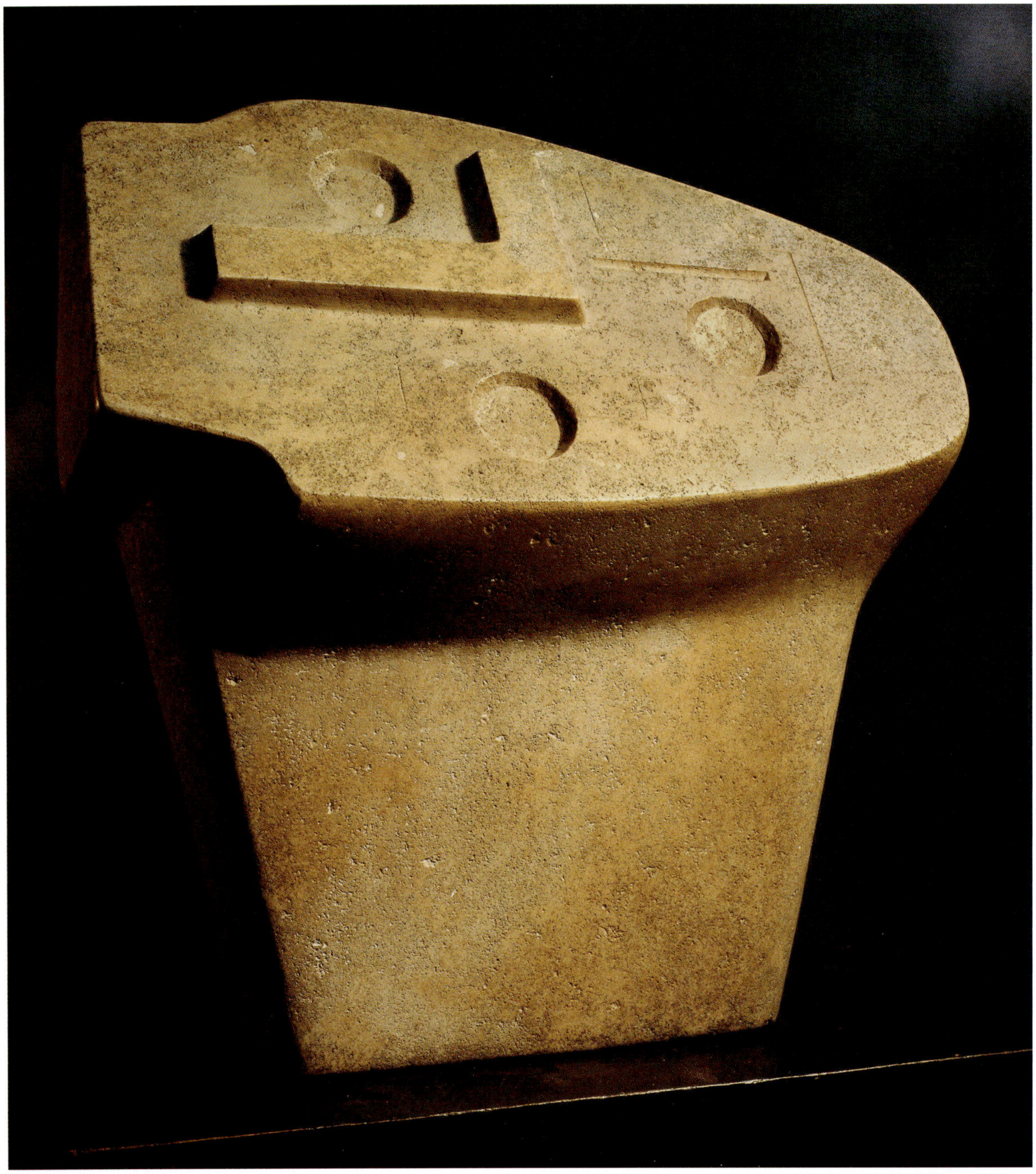

43.
Carving 1936
Travertine marble
h.457mm
The Henry Moore Foundation: gift of Irina Moore 1979
LH 164

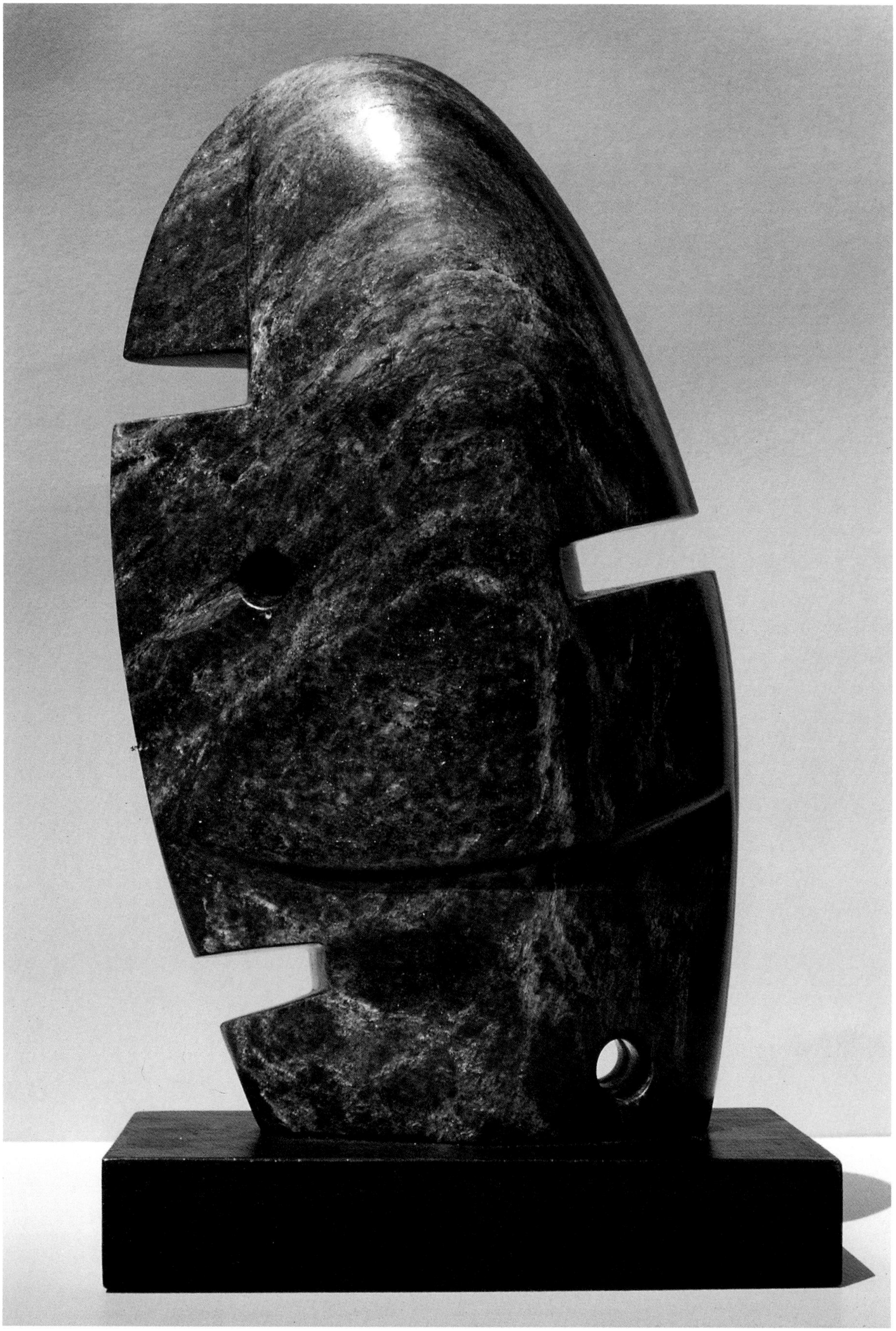

44.
Head 1937, carved 1968
Green serpentine
h.337mm
The Henry Moore
Foundation: gift of the artist
1977
LH 182a

45.
Stringed Figure: Bowl 1938
Bronze and string, cast 1967
h.546mm
The Henry Moore Foundation: gift of the artist 1979
LH 186c

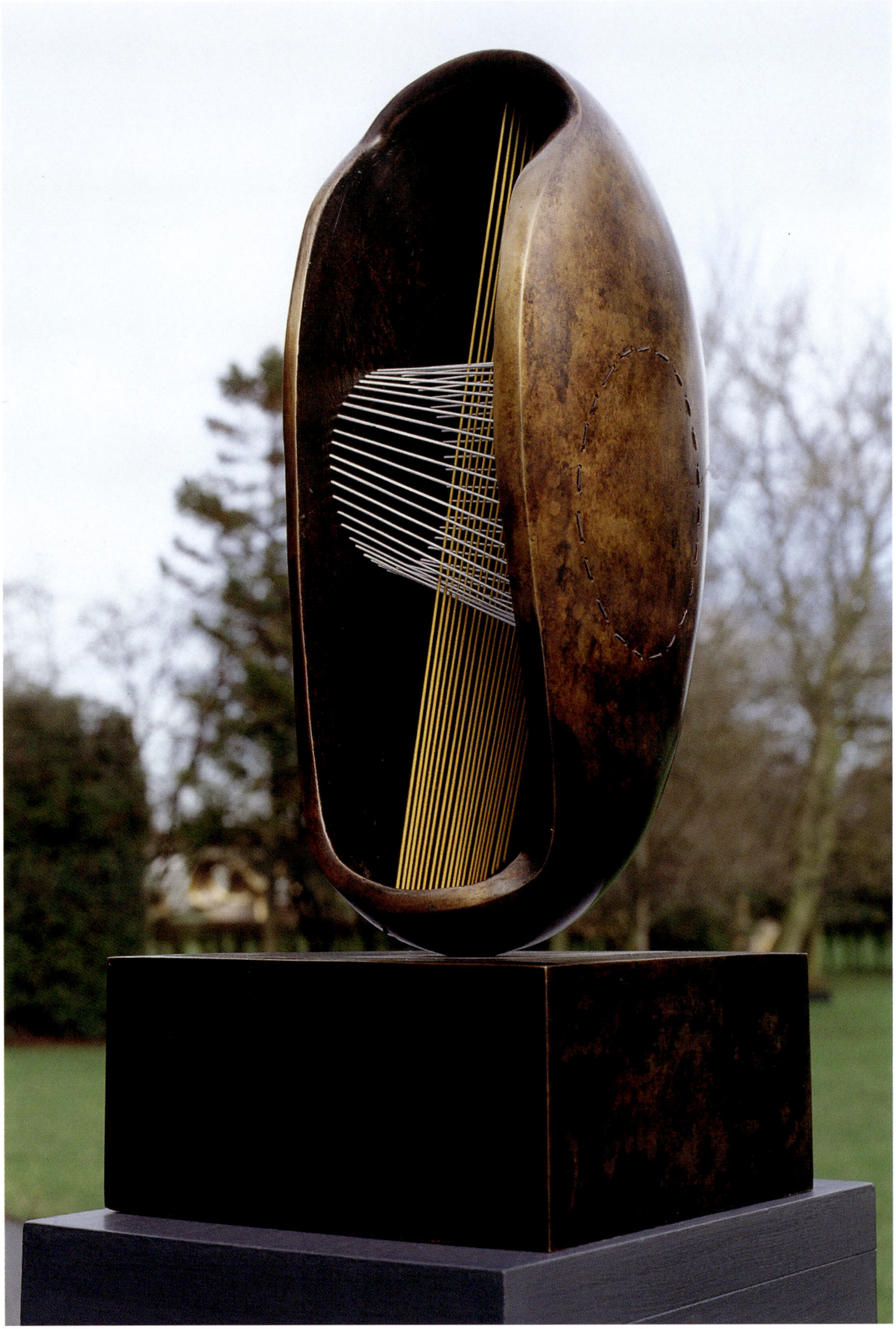

46.
Bird Basket 1939
Lignum vitae and string
l.419mm
The Henry Moore Foundation: accepted by HM government in lieu of inheritance tax and allocated in 2002
LH 205

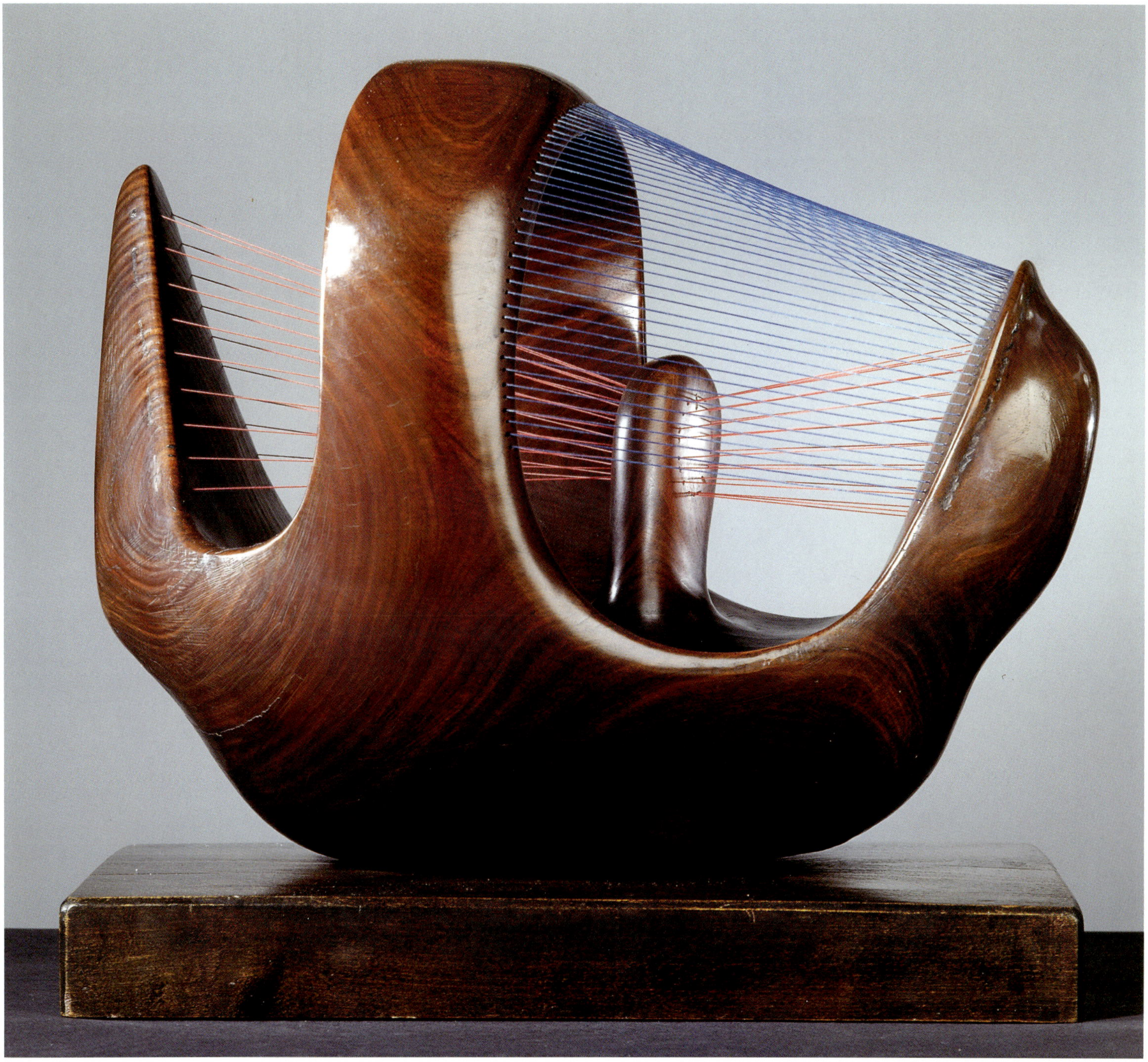

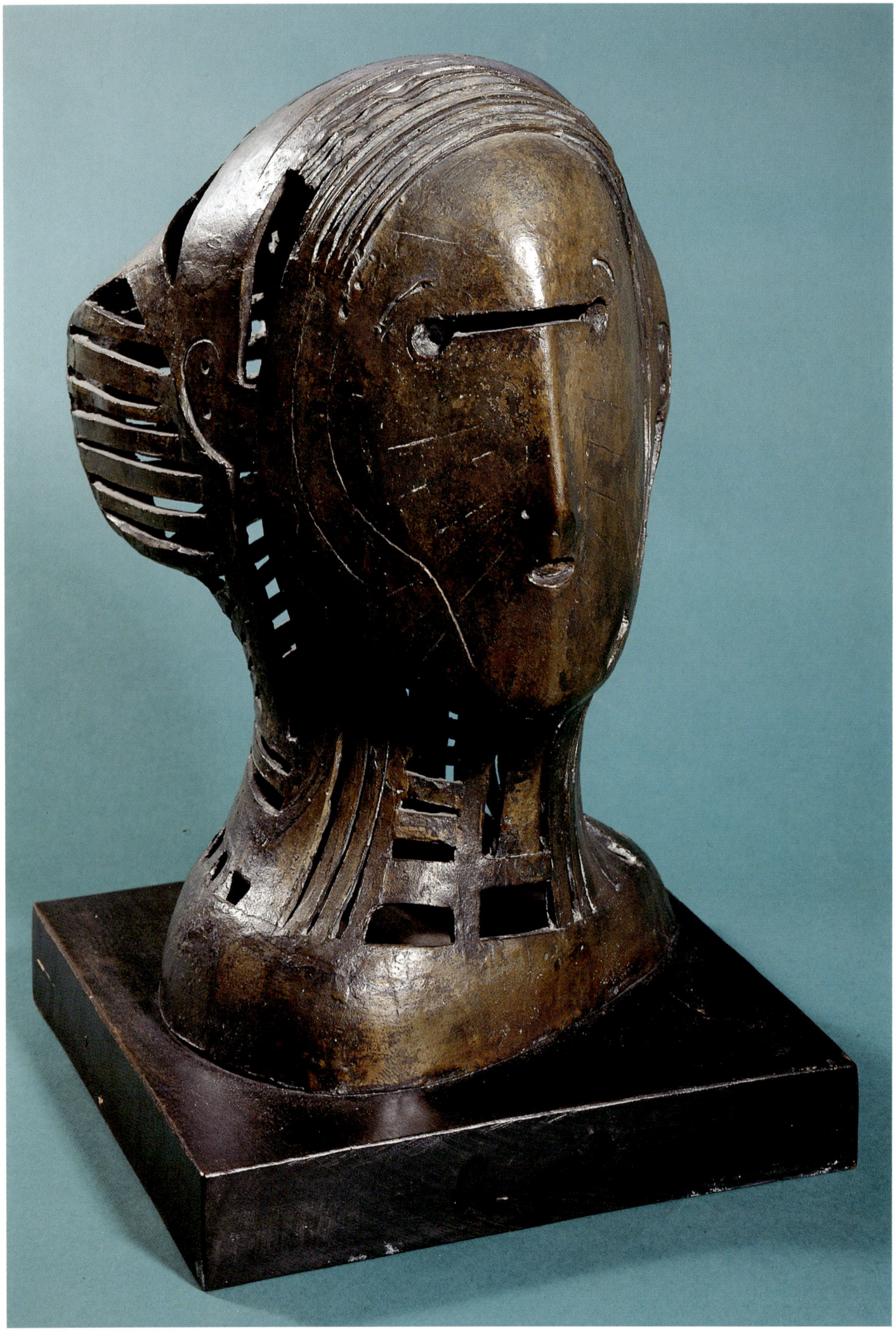

47.
Openwork Head No. 2
1950
Bronze (unique cast)
410 x 245 x 290mm (base size: 285 x 277 x 46mm)
Wakefield Art Gallery, A2.32
LH 289

48.
Helmet Head No. 1 1950
Bronze
400 x 355 x 300mm
Tate, presented by the Friends of the Tate Gallery, 1960, T00388
LH 279

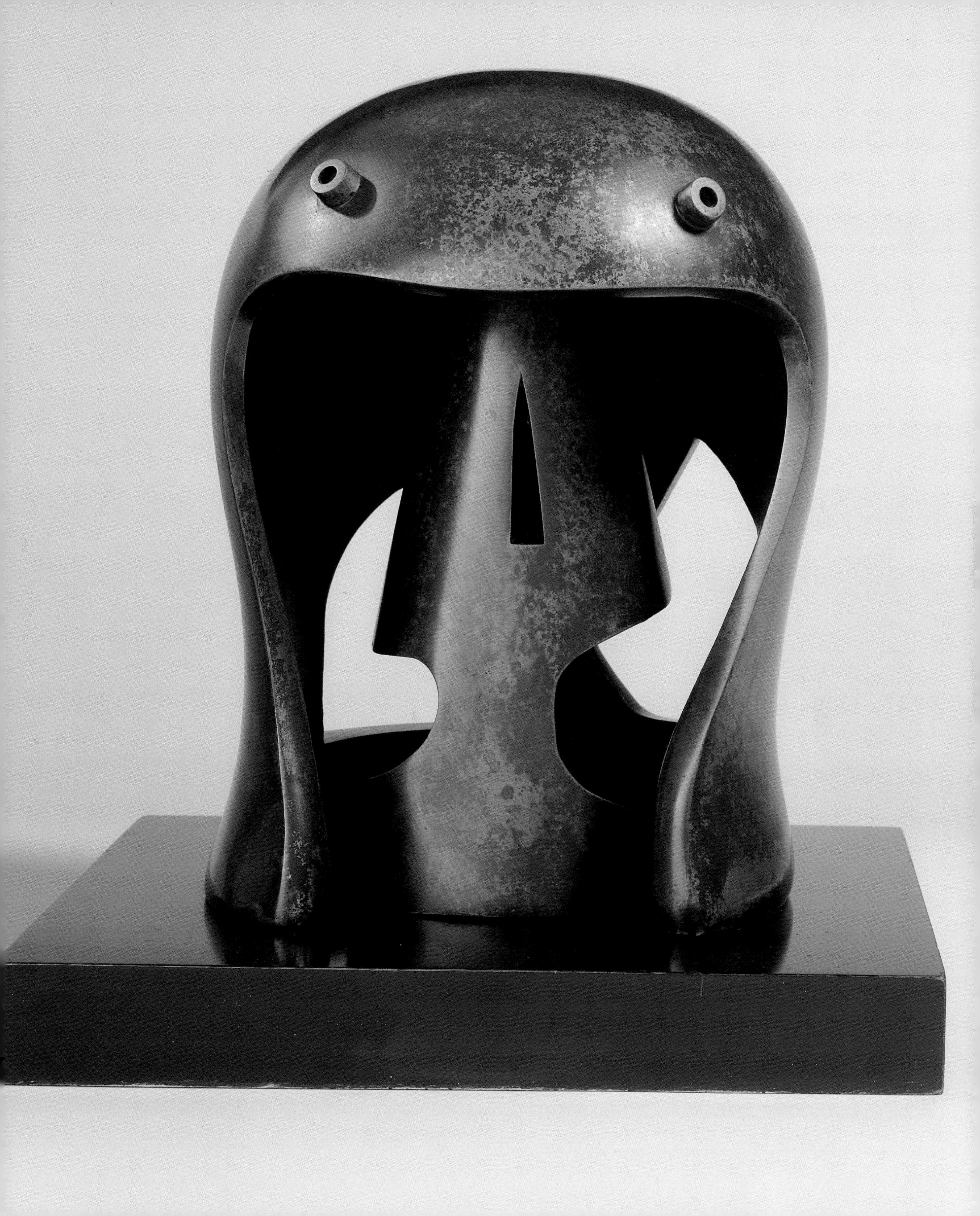

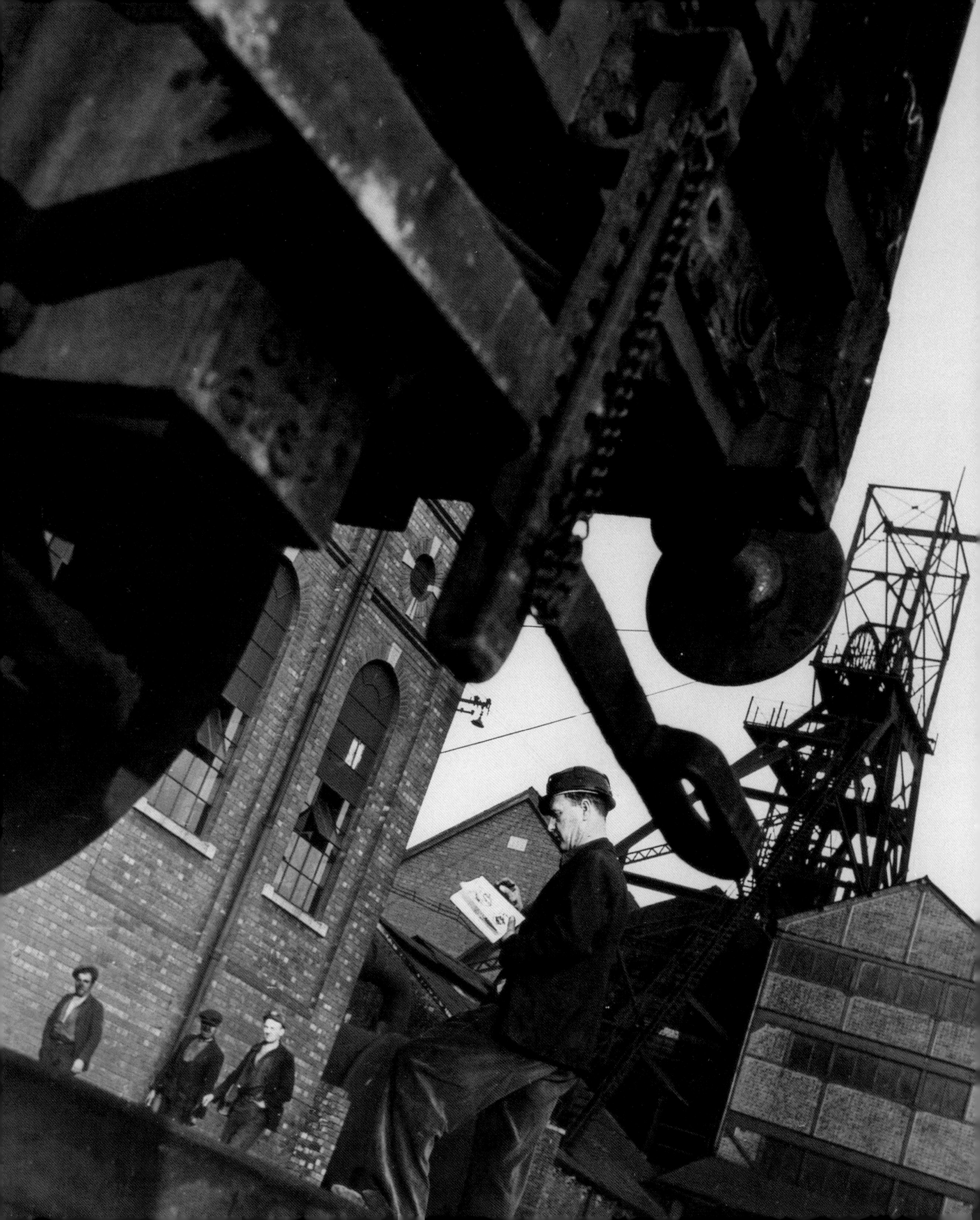

The War Artist

HENRY MOORE'S FIRST SOLO SHOW, at the Warren Gallery, Maddox Street, London, W1, in 1928 contained forty-two sculptures and fifty-one drawings. Right from the start his drawings were seen as an integral part of his output as an artist. That said, they were for the most part related to his sculptures. Until the late 1940s it was in drawing that he worked out his ideas, dashing off variants of forms or working out views from different angles. The latter issue eventually caused him to cease using drawing as his principal preparatory work for sculpture: drawings impose a single viewpoint, models don't.

Presumably it was originally the sheer quantity of ideas that led Moore to cover single pages of his sketchbooks with dozens of related images (see cat. 83, *Ideas for Sculpture: Seated Figures and Heads*, 1930). But, as the 1930s progressed, Moore began, no doubt instinctively at first, to exploit the decorative potential of these multiple images, and to present an individual page containing many images as a single work of art (see cat. 85, *Ideas for Sculpture*, 1931, or cat. 24, *Square Form Reclining Figures*, 1936). The variant figures could be made to relate physically, as if in real space; or they could be linked by technique or – say – by a swirl of wash. His technique developed in tandem with this tendency. In particular, the use of wax crayon, which could then be washed over, causing the original figure to loom out of the surrounding colour in a way that linked the object most satisfyingly to its environment,[31] tended to favour the unifying of individual objects into a single presentation page. The notion of presentation is a crucial factor in all Moore's art; whether it was a drawing on the page or a sculpture in its setting, Moore's sense of completion encompassed the surrounding space (the page, the landscape) as well as the object itself.

The wax-resist technique was of particular importance for Moore, contributing much to his already distinctive drawing vocabulary (it was to become a kind of 'party trick' that he would be asked to perform for cameras or visitors). Psychologically it gave the object drawn a physical identity related to that of a sculptural object. Its existence is not wiped out or flattened by the sweep of watercolour wash laid over it, only enhanced, just as a sculpture resists, but is transformed by, the rain. Even in purely visual terms the wax-resist technique results in forms that have something of the tactile quality of the surface of stone or bronze. For an artist who always thought sculpturally, the technique opened up all sorts of possibilities both of atmosphere and colour.

When the outbreak of war came in September 1939, Moore was consequently already fully equipped with an alternative means of expression to sculpture, which had temporarily no longer become feasible due to wartime restrictions. Approached by his friend Kenneth Clark to become an official war artist, Moore was initially reluctant, largely because he felt his subject matter didn't 'fit the brief'. He was presumably uncomfortably aware that, under the genuine worthiness of the concept, Sir Kenneth's not-so-hidden agenda was to try and keep great artists alive if at all possible, without loss of self-respect. To a veteran of the First World War, such an idea must have been hard to swallow – how could he adapt any of his favourite themes as images of war in such a way as to justify his status (and pay, however small) as war artist? Drawings exist showing how hard Moore struggled to find conducive subject matter. His *Eighteen Ideas for War Drawings* of 1940

Fig. 48
Henry Moore sketching at the pithead of Wheldale Colliery, Castleford, 7 January 1942.

(cat. 49) presents a visual catalogue of potential solutions: his pencil headings include 'searchlights; Flashes from ground; gunshells bursting like stars; Night & day – contrast; devastated houses; bomb crater; contrast of opposites [dark tortured figure on left, peaceful seated figure on right]; contrast of peaceful normal with sudden devastation; disintegration of farm machine; fire at night; Haystack & airplane; Nightmare [a sculptural abstract]; contrast of opposites [another abstract form divided between light and dark]; Burning cows; spotters on buildings; barbed wire; Cows & Bombers; Bombs bursting at sea.' Many of these are fascinating and dramatic, and no doubt witnessed during his night-time patrols for the Home Guard; some are sculpturally interesting; some unintentionally funny – but none look quite 'like a Henry Moore'.

The Blitz, however, indirectly brought Moore the inspiration he needed. The bombing of London began on 7 September 1940, intensive at first. Travelling by Tube during this early period (something he and Irina rarely did, but on this occasion their car was out of action), he encountered for the first time the hundreds of thousands of people who had taken to sheltering in the Tube stations. Held up at Belsize Park for an hour, he was able to study and make notes (he was always careful not to be obvious about his activity: clearly these people were suffering enough without being exploited by an artist; Moore made most of his sketches back at the studio from memory, sometimes roping in members of his family as models, see cats 51, 53 [32]). The eureka moment had come: 'When I first saw it ... I saw hundreds of Henry Moore reclining figures stretched along the platform'; [33] 'even the train tunnels seemed to be like the holes in my sculpture.'[34]

Despite Moore's apparently entirely formal response to the spectacle of suffering humanity laid out before him, the particular value of the shelter drawings was precisely the humanizing effect they brought to his formal language, both from his own point of view and that of the public. Suddenly his formal interests were presentable in a way that spoke directly to his audience. His technique, particularly his use of wax crayon, seemed made to evoke the sculptural effect of 'hundreds of Henry Moore reclining figures' looming out of the darkness. And the experience led to other formal discoveries, most notably the expressive power of drapery:

> ... drapery can reveal the form more effectively than if the figure were nude because it can emphasise the prominent part of the body, and falls slackly in the hollows. This is something I learned when I came to do the Shelter drawings, in which all the figures are draped. Before then I avoided using drapery because I wanted to be absolutely explicit about shapes and forms.[35]

The shelter drawings come in different forms. Firstly, there are two sketchbooks; the first was given to Jane Clark (wife of Sir Kenneth), and then bequeathed by her to the British Museum; the second Moore gave to Irina, from whom it went to The Henry Moore Foundation. From these two resources packed with material, Moore worked up completed drawings, which were exhibited alongside other war artists' work at the National Gallery and elsewhere around the country.

By autumn 1941 Moore felt the idea had reached the end of its interest for him. Herbert Read came up with his next subject as a war artist, which had the additional value of a personal connection. In going down the Wheldale Colliery (fig. 48) to record the underground army of miners at work, Moore was revisiting his father's old workplace as well as drawing attention to the heroism of the miners and the conditions they had to endure to provide the fuel essential to the war effort. A return to the scenes of his childhood was no doubt moving for Moore (his family's focus had shifted to Norfolk in July 1922, soon after he left for London), and he responded with customary grit to the difficulty of working by artificial light, crouched in unbearable heat a mile underground. The drawings are dark and powerful, somewhat reminiscent of Seurat's remarkable technique where forms emerge from darkness (which Moore admired enormously). That they were not as critically successful as the shelter drawings is perhaps not surprising, in that they necessarily feature the male body in concentrated action – the very opposite of Moore's usual preference for the female body in repose.

Another indirect by-product of the shelter drawings came with Moore's illustrations to accompany a publication of *The Rescue*, a melodrama in verse for the radio by Edward Sackville-West based on Homer's *Odyssey* (published by Secker and Warburg, London, 1945). Both drawings shown here relate quite clearly to the shelter drawings. In *Odysseus in the Cave of the Naiads* (cat. 72) the hero reclines in front of what is to all intents and purposes a Tube tunnel, while the *Death of the Suitors* (cat. 73) takes place in an interior strongly reminiscent of the largest public shelter in London, at Tilbury (see cat. 54). Both exploit Moore's new-found sense of empathy for human suffering in a claustrophobic atmosphere. It is as if, along with the discovery of the expressive power of drapery, Moore recognized in the tunnels of the London Tube a scale of human experience that matched the sweep of Greek myth, and a language in which to express it.

The shelter drawings were a great success, both absolutely and in their particular impact on the public. For the first time, the general public seem to have 'got it', where Moore was concerned. His reputation had been high in certain circles more or less from the start; to an extent the public were used to the idea that – whatever they thought – Moore was a great artist, even a 'genius' because Kenneth Clark and Herbert Read (and others of similar standing) said so. But it was the shelter drawings that really made his quality perceptible to the public at large. From Moore's point of view, the formal and expressive lessons learned from the experience fed directly and indirectly into his post-war sculpture.

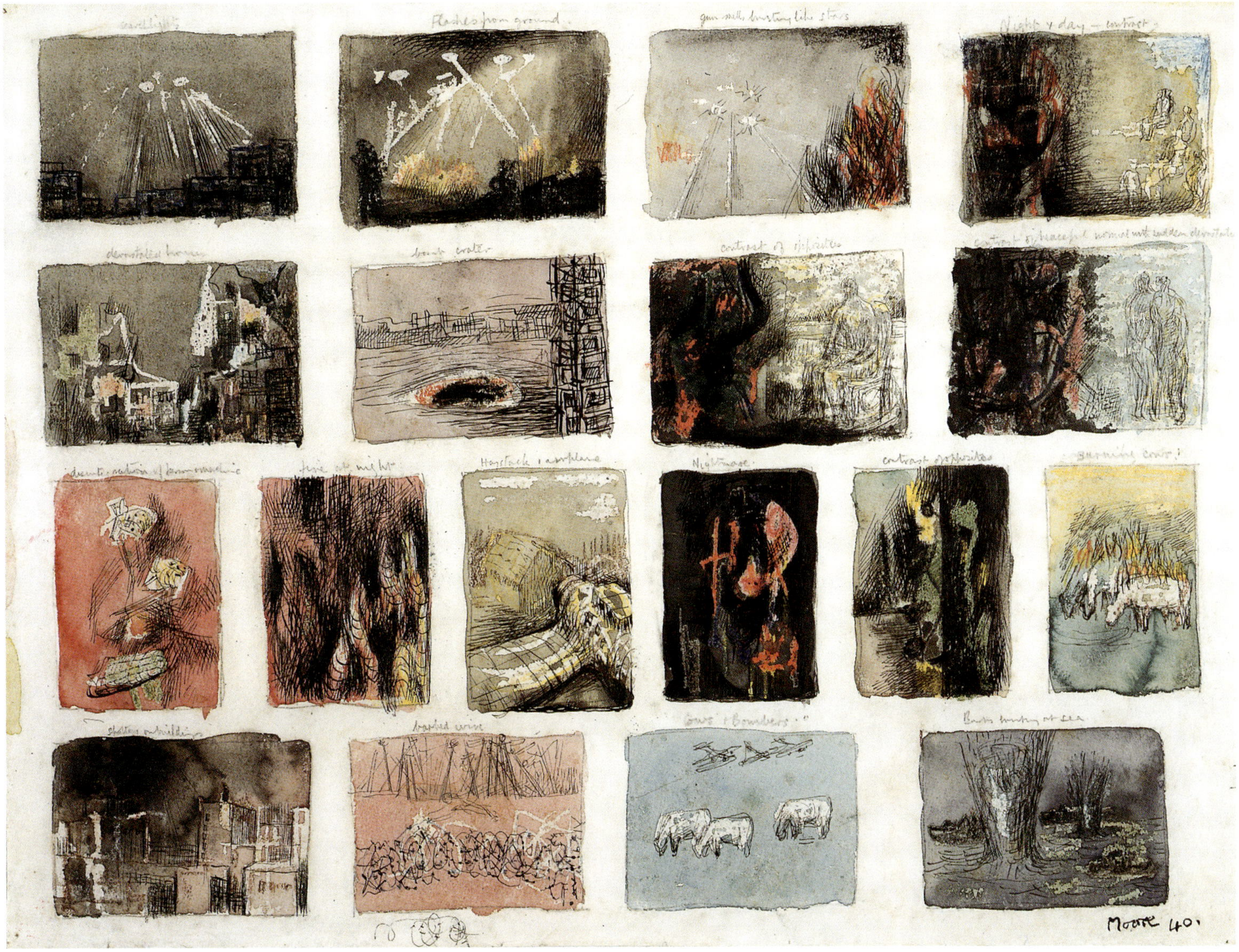

49.
Eighteen Ideas for War Drawings 1940
Pencil, wax crayon, coloured crayon, watercolour wash, pen and ink
274 x 376mm
Signed and dated in pen and ink lower right: 'Moore / 40'

Inscribed in pencil from top to bottom and from left to right: 'searchlights; Flashes from ground; gunshells bursting like stars; Night & day – contrast; devastated houses; bomb crater; contrast of opposites; contrast of peaceful normal with sudden devastation; disintegration of farm machine; fire at night; Haystack & airplane; Nightmare; contrast of opposites; Burning cows; spotters on buildings; barbed wire; Cows & Bombers; Bombs bursting at sea'
The Henry Moore Foundation: gift of the artist 1977
AG 40.67, HMF1553

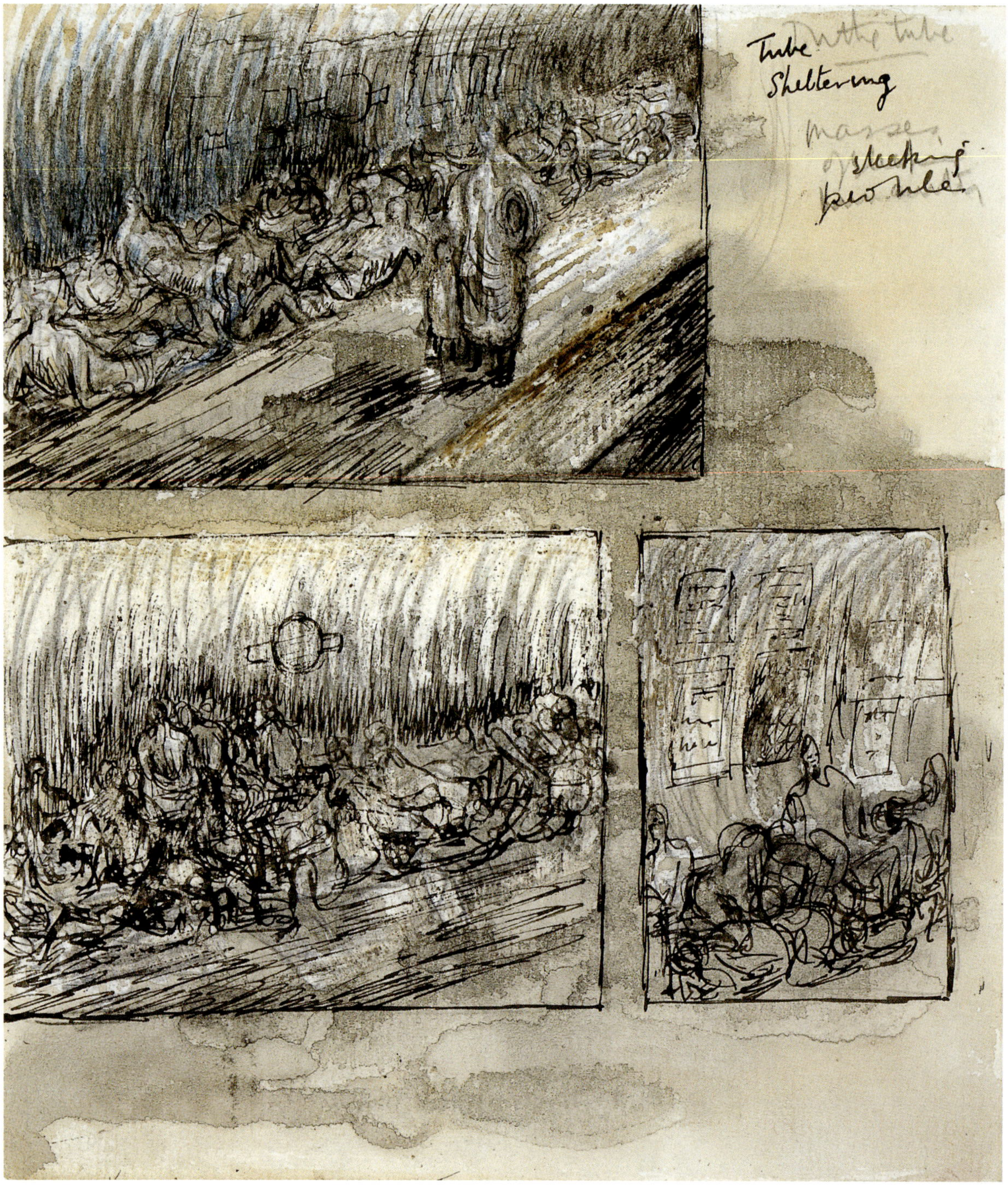

50.
Tube Sheltering Sleeping People
1940–41
First Shelter Sketchbook, p. 5
Pencil, wax crayon, coloured crayon, watercolour wash, pen and ink
186 x 162mm
The British Museum, London: bequest of Jane Clark 1977, 1977-4-2-13(5)
AG 40-41.5, HMF 1563

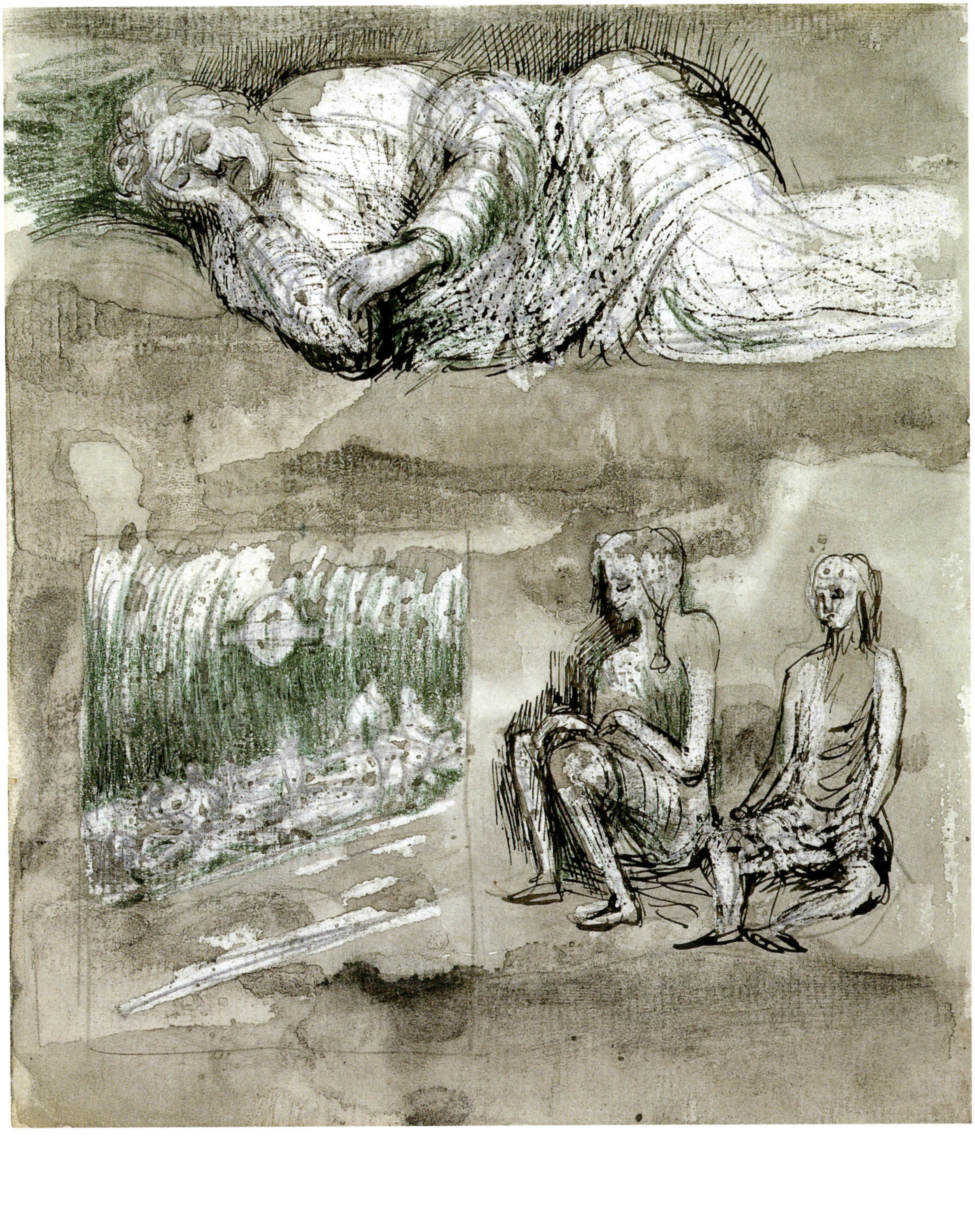

51.
Seated and Sleeping Figures 1940–41
First Shelter Sketchbook, p. 8
Pencil, wax crayon, coloured crayon, watercolour wash, pen and ink
186 x 162mm
The British Museum, London: bequest of Jane Clark 1977, 1977-4-2-13(8)
AG 40-41.8, HMF 1566

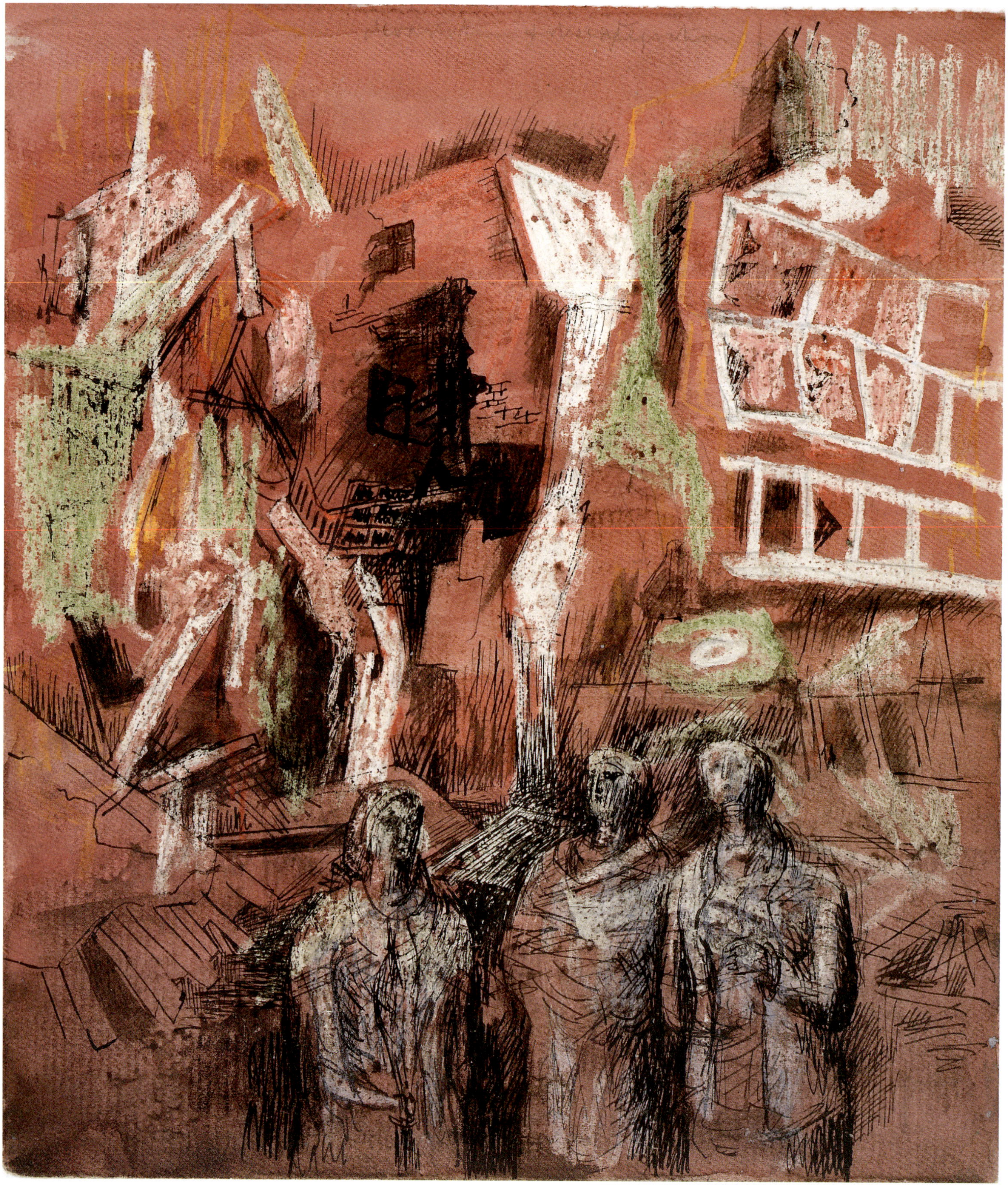

52.
Three Women in Front of Devastated Buildings
1940–41
First Shelter Sketchbook, p. 14
Pencil, wax crayon, coloured crayon, watercolour wash, pen and ink
186 x 162mm
The British Museum, London: bequest of Jane Clark 1977,
1977-4-2-13(14)
AG 40-41.14, HMF 1572

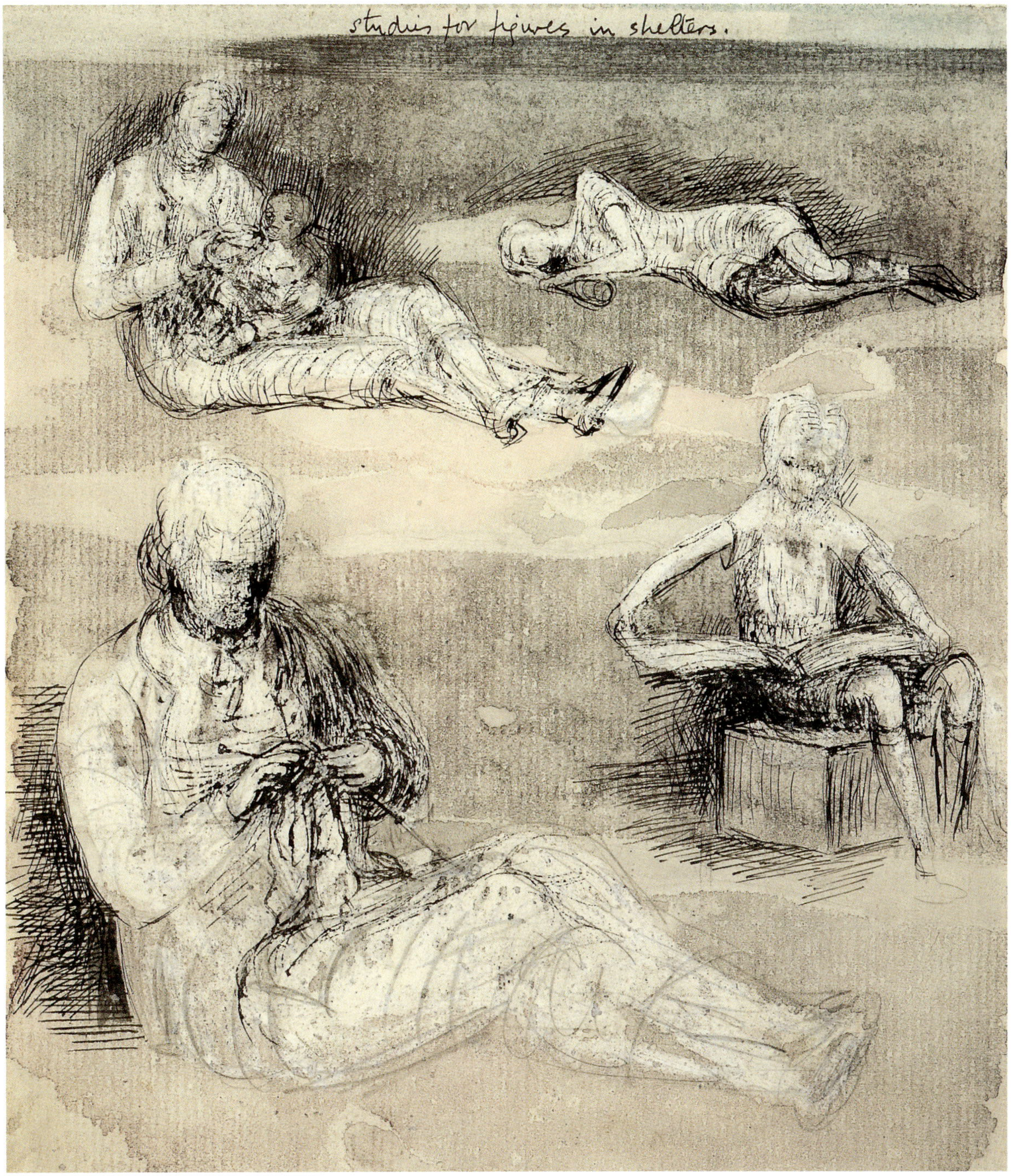

53.
Positions of Shelterers
1940–41
First Shelter Sketchbook, p. 24
Pencil, wax crayon, watercolour wash, pen and ink
186 x 162mm
The British Museum, London: bequest of Jane Clark 1977,
1977-4-2-13(24)
AG 40-41.24, HMF 1582

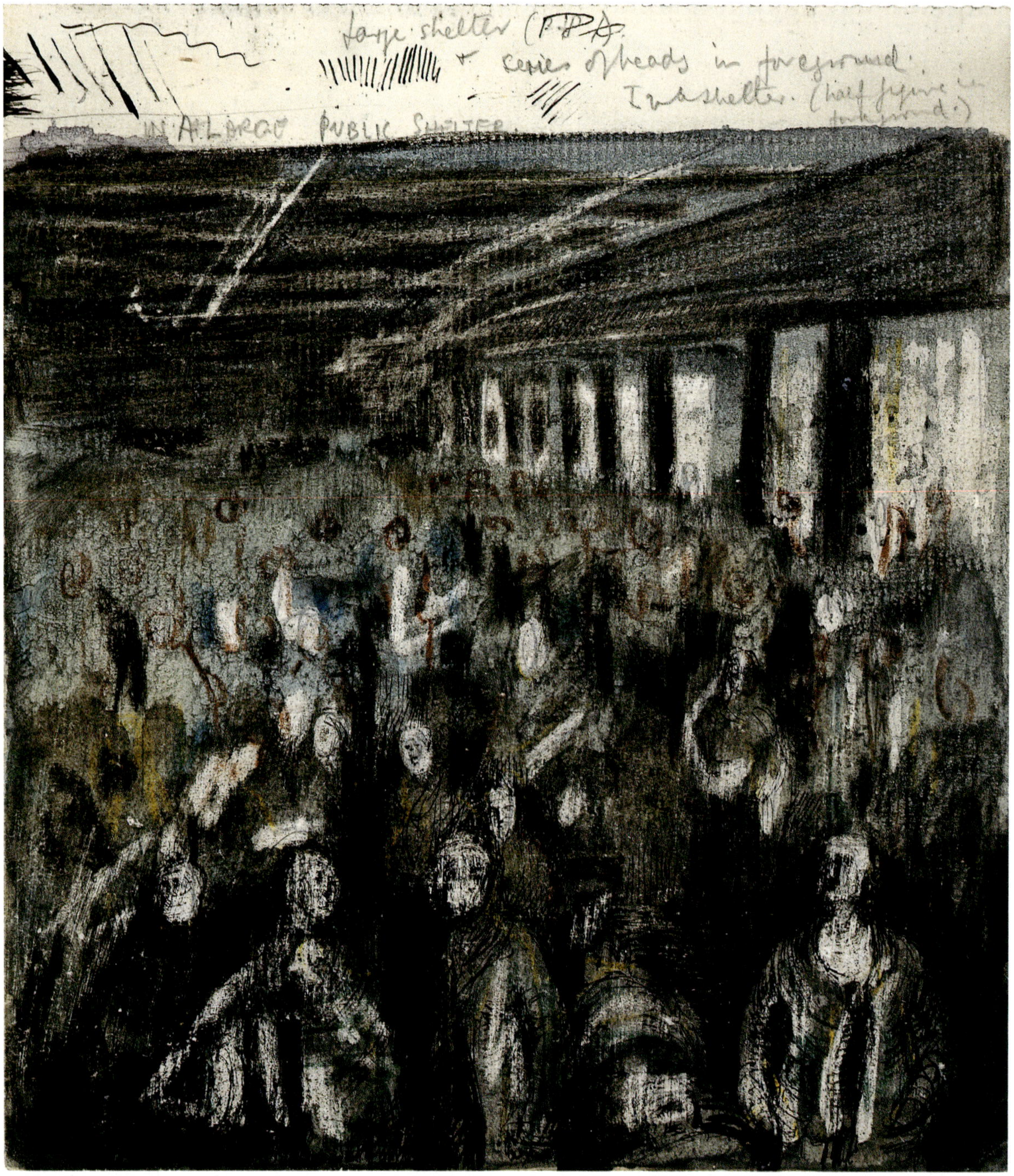

54.
In a Large Public Shelter 1940–41
First Shelter Sketchbook, p. 34
Pencil, wax crayon, coloured crayon, watercolour wash, pen and ink
186 x 162
The British Museum, London: bequest of Jane Clark 1977, 1977-4-2-13(34)
AG 40-41.34, HMF 1592

55.
Woman Seated with Hands in Lap 1940–41
First Shelter Sketchbook, p. 44
Pencil, wax crayon, coloured crayon, watercolour wash, pen and ink
186 x 162
The British Museum, London: bequest of Jane Clark 1977, 1977-4-2-13(44)
AG 40-41.44, HMF 1602

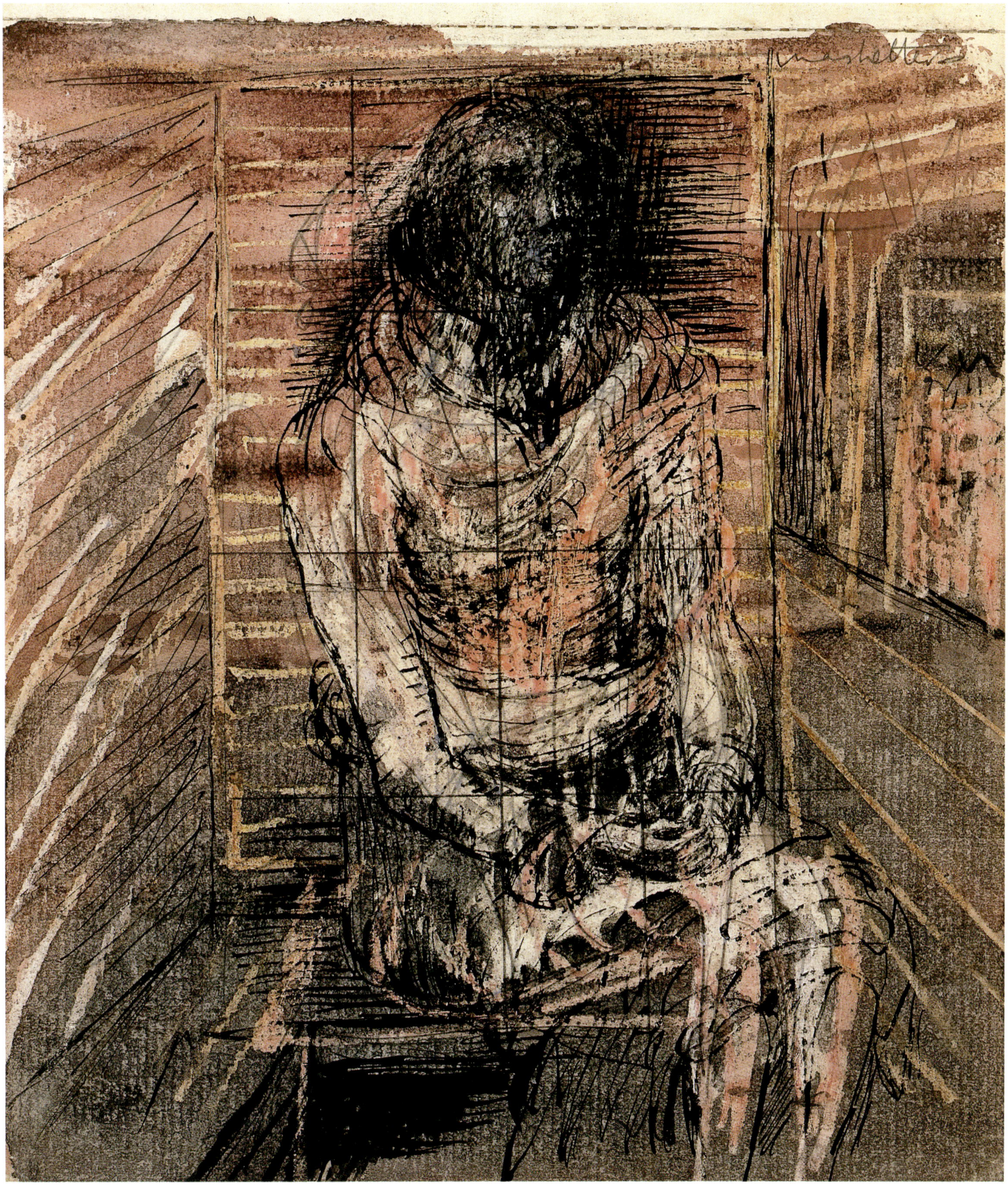

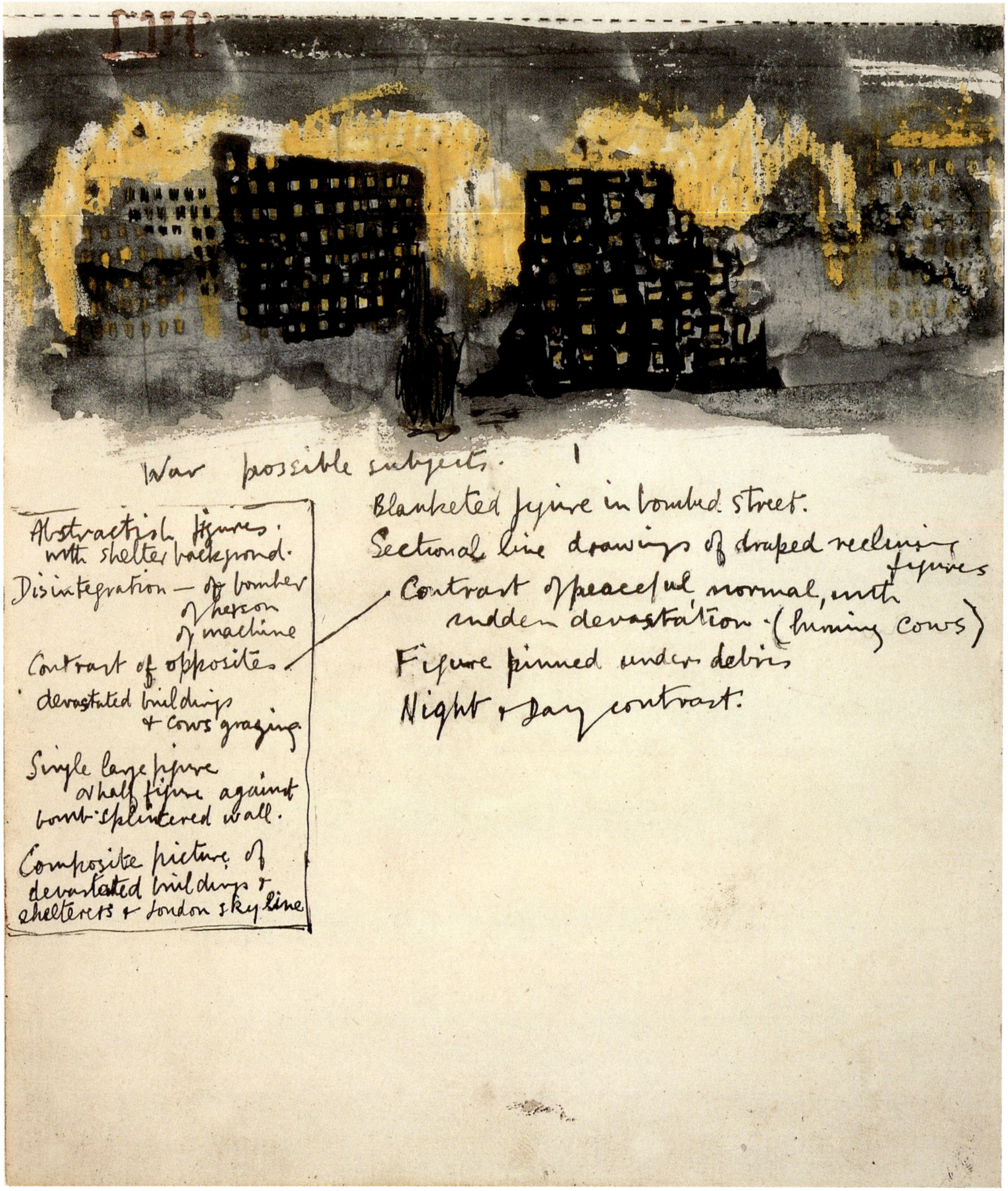

56.
War: Possible Subjects
1940–41
First Shelter Sketchbook, p. 45
Pencil, wax crayon, watercolour wash, pen and ink
186 x 162mm
The British Museum, London: bequest of Jane Clark 1977, 1977-4-2-13(45)
AG 40-41.45, HMF 1605

57.
Two Women Seated in an Empty Building
1940–41
First Shelter Sketchbook, p. 48
Pencil, wax crayon, coloured crayon, watercolour wash, pen and ink, gouache
186 x 162mm
The British Museum, London: bequest of Jane Clark 1977, 1977-4-2-13(48)
AG 40-41.48, HMF 1606

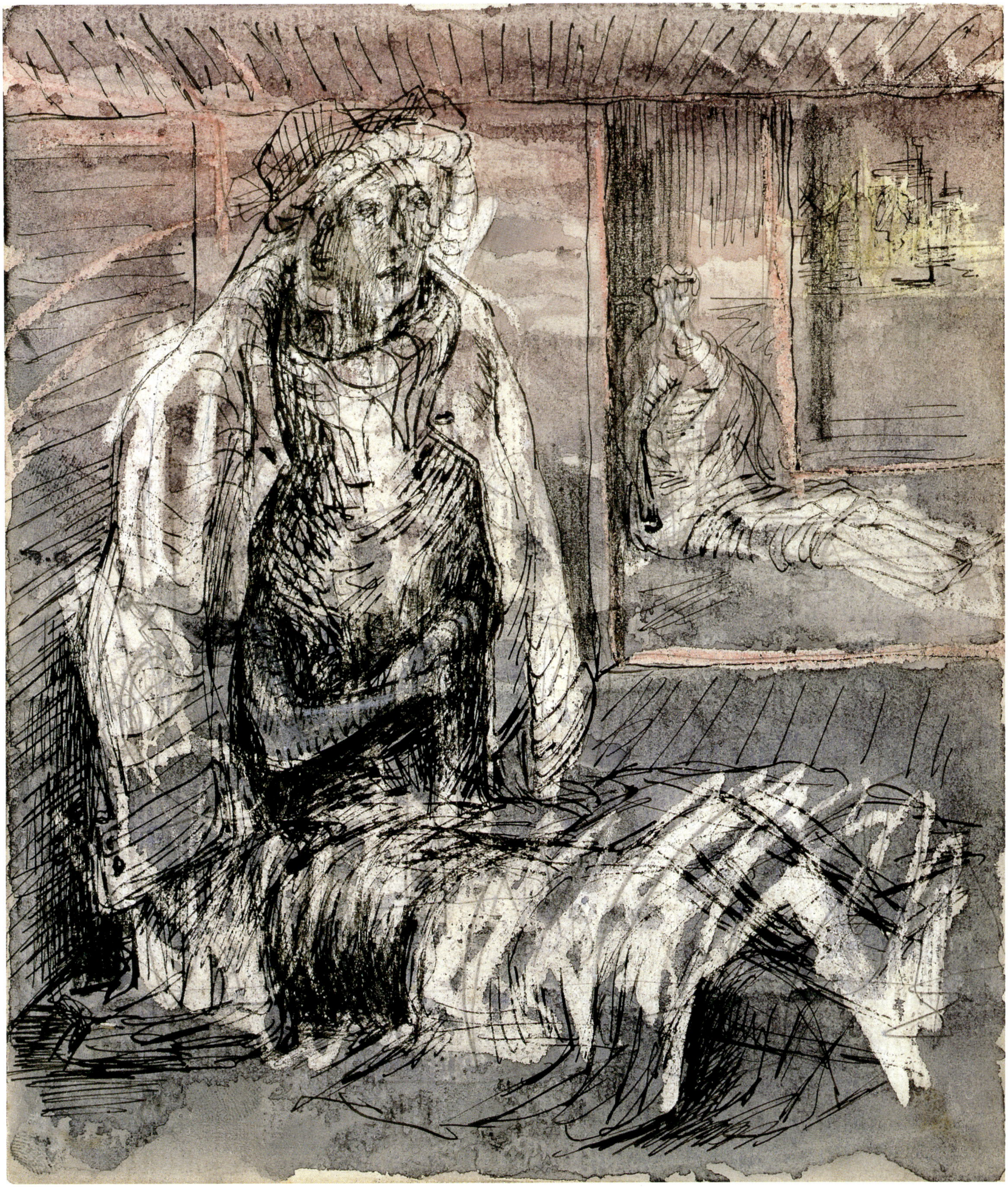

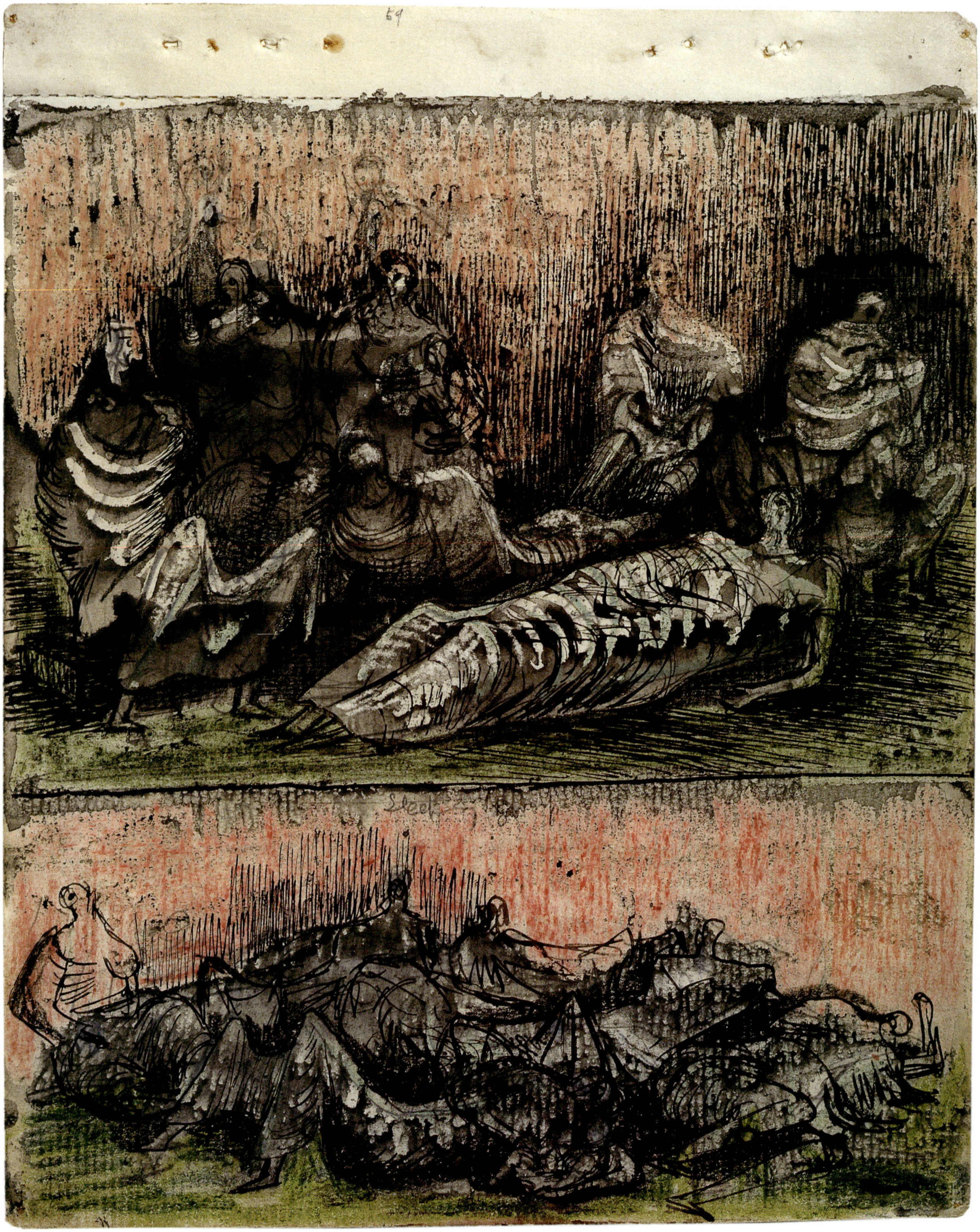

58.
Group of Shelterers
1940–41
Second Shelter Sketchbook, p. 48
Pencil, wax crayon, coloured crayon, watercolour, wash, pen and ink
204 x 165mm
Inscribed in pencil lower centre: 'Sleeping figures'
The Henry Moore Foundation: gift of Irina Moore 1977
AG 40-41.116, HMF 1673

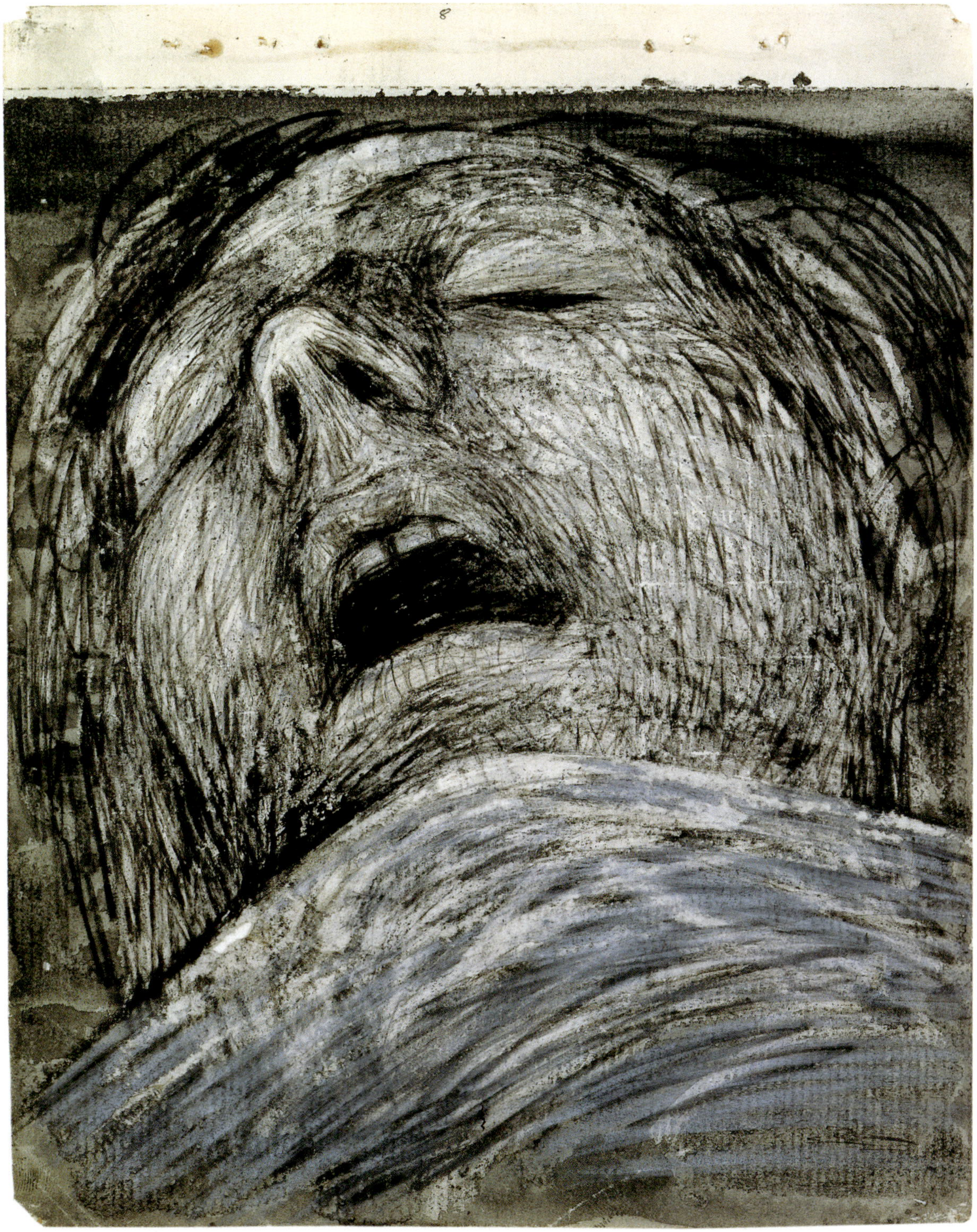

59.
Sleeping Shelterer
1940–41
Second Shelter Sketchbook, p. 69
Pencil, wax crayon, coloured crayon, watercolour wash, gouache
204 x 165mm
The Henry Moore Foundation: gift of Irina Moore 1977
AG 40-41.137, HMF 1694

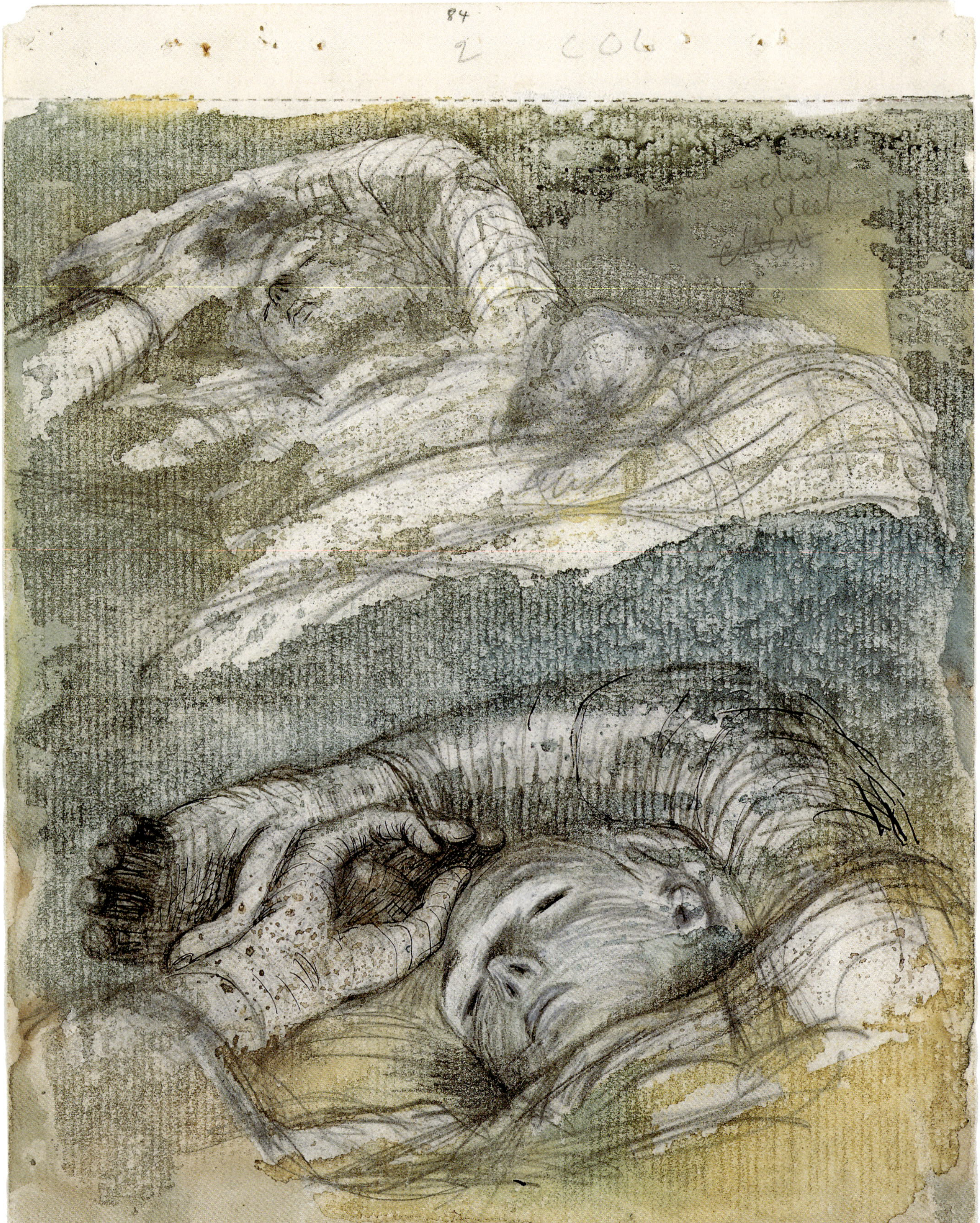

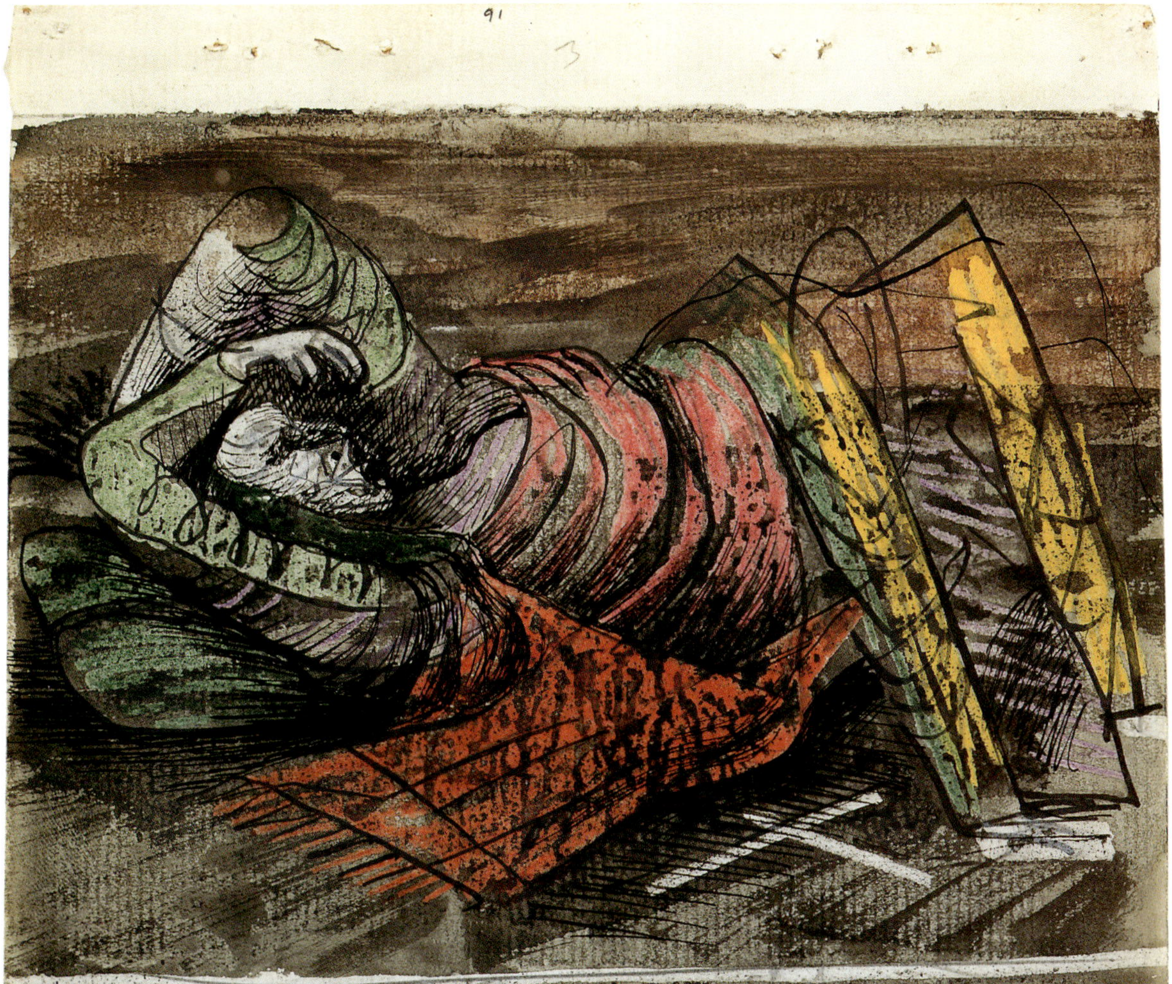

60.
Study for 'Shelter Sleepers' 1940–41
Second Shelter Sketchbook, p. 84
Pencil, wax crayon, coloured crayon, pastel, watercolour wash, pen and ink
204 x 165mm
Inscribed in pencil lower upper right: 'Mother & child / sleeping / child [crossed out]'
The Henry Moore Foundation: gift of Irina Moore 1977
AG 40-41.152, HMF 1709

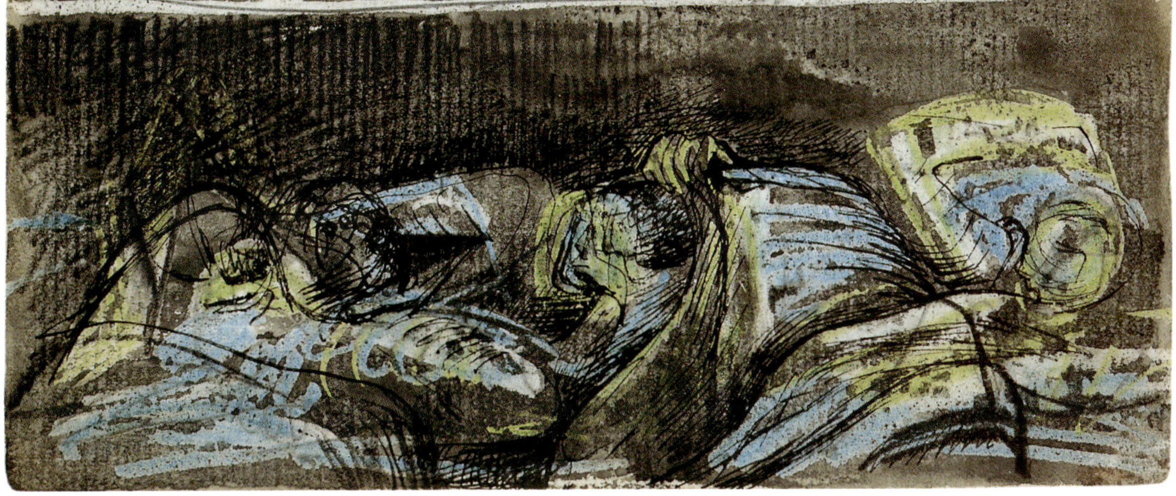

61.
Restless Sleepers
1940–41
Second Shelter Sketchbook, p. 91
Pencil, wax crayon, coloured crayon, watercolour wash, pen and ink
204 x 165mm
The Henry Moore Foundation: gift of Irina Moore 1977
AG 40-41.159, HMF 1716

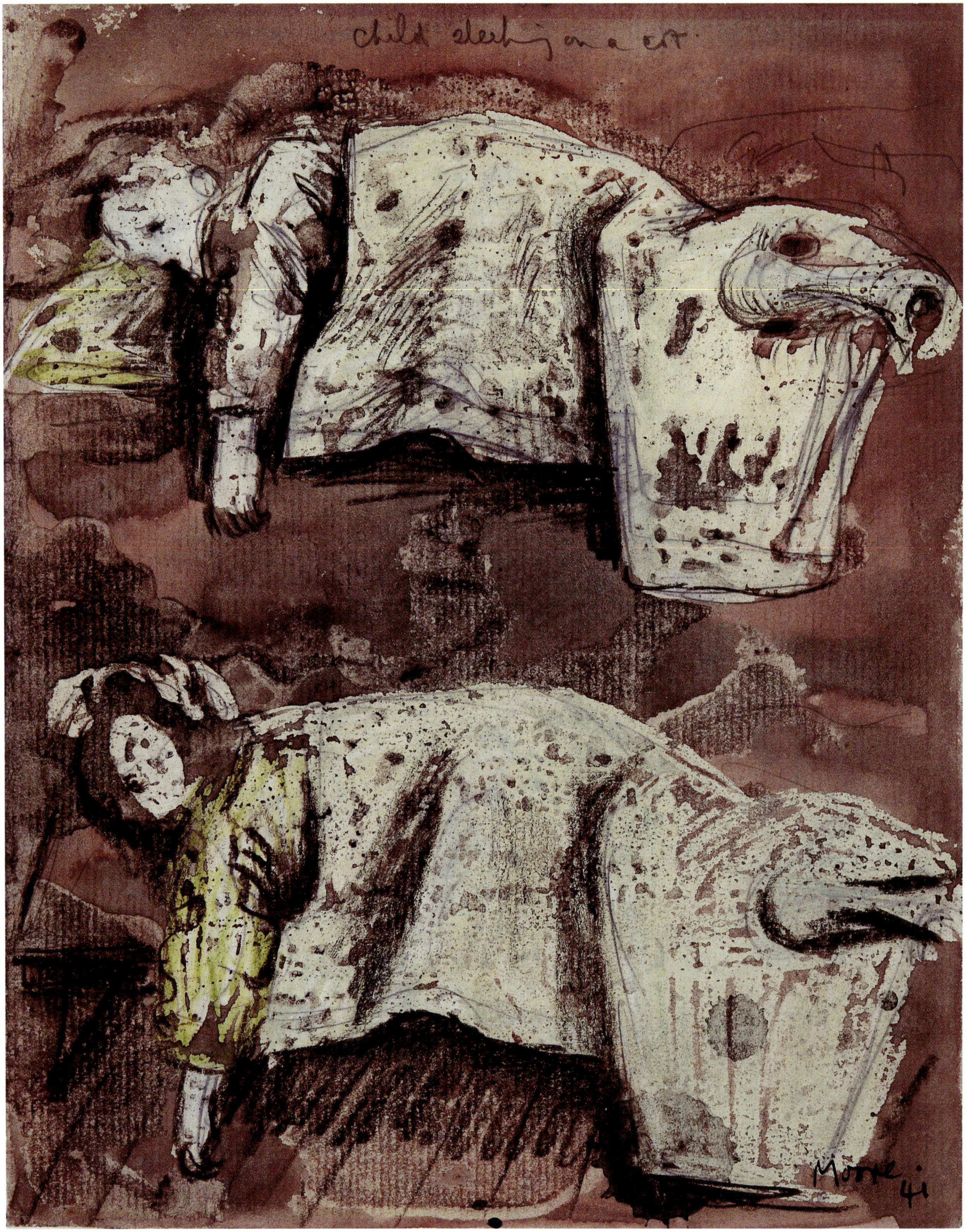
child sleeping on a cot
Moore 41

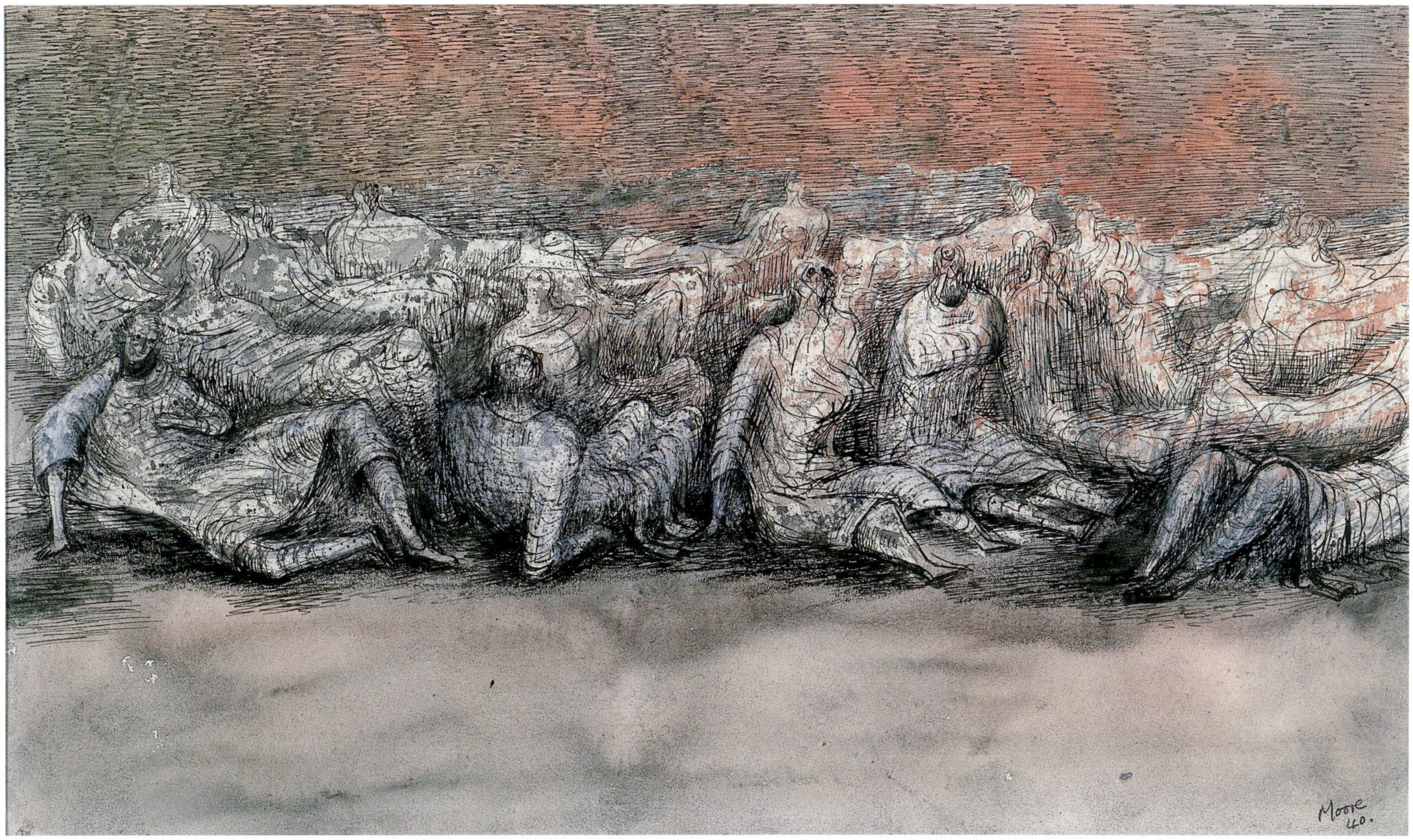

62.
Child Sleeping on a Cot
1940–41
Shelter Sketchbook 1940–41
Pencil, wax crayon,
coloured crayon,
watercolour wash, chalk.
200 x 160mm
Signed and dated in
pen and ink lower right:
'Moore / 41'
Inscribed in pencil
upper centre:
'child sleeping on a cot'
David Sainsbury
AG 40-41.176; HMF 1752

63.
Group of Shelterers
1940
Pencil, wax crayon,
watercolour wash,
pen and ink
254 x 432mm
Signed and dated in pen
and ink lower right:
'Moore / 40'
Robert and Lisa Sainsbury
Collection, University of
East Anglia, UEA 91
AG 40.89, HMF 1736

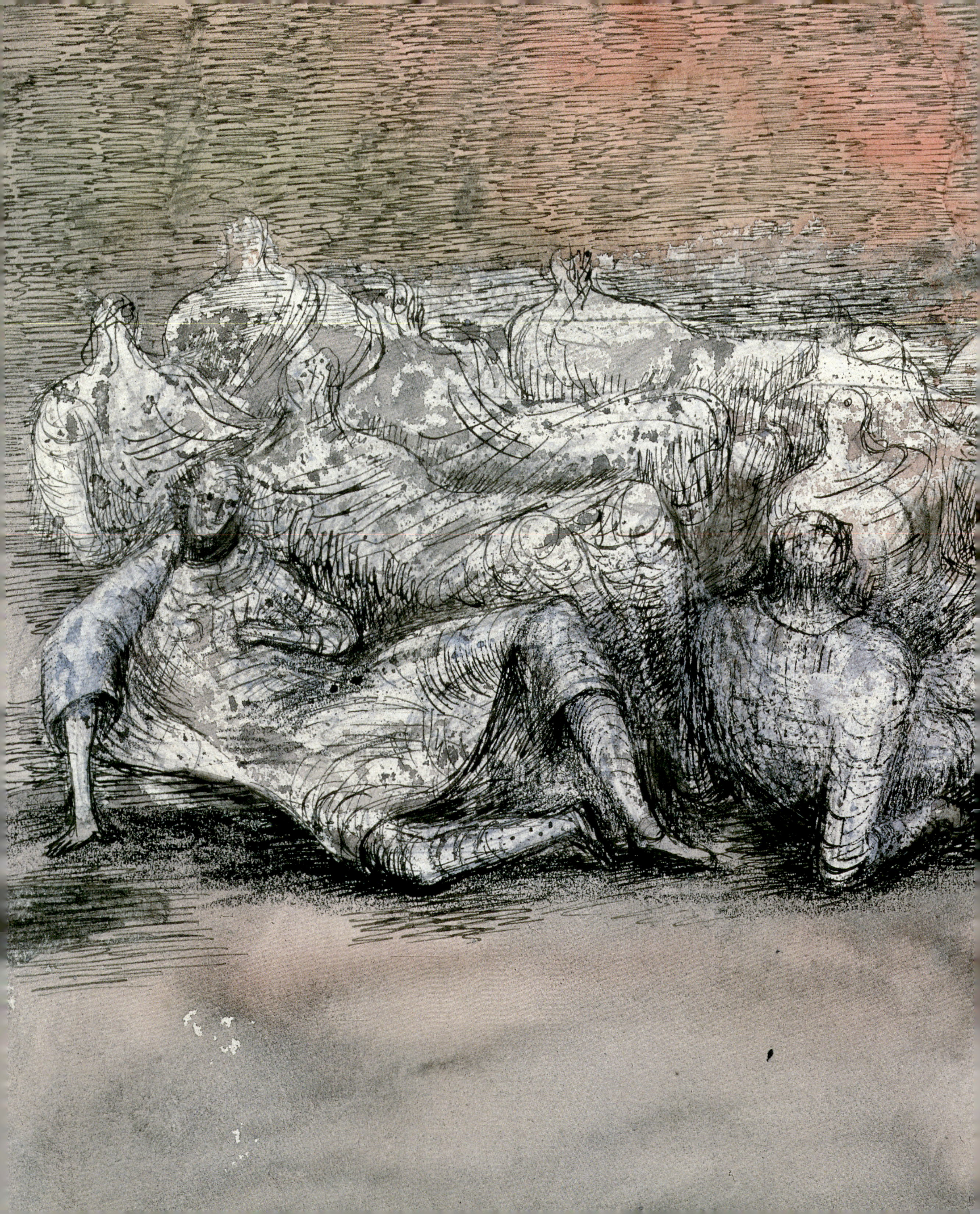

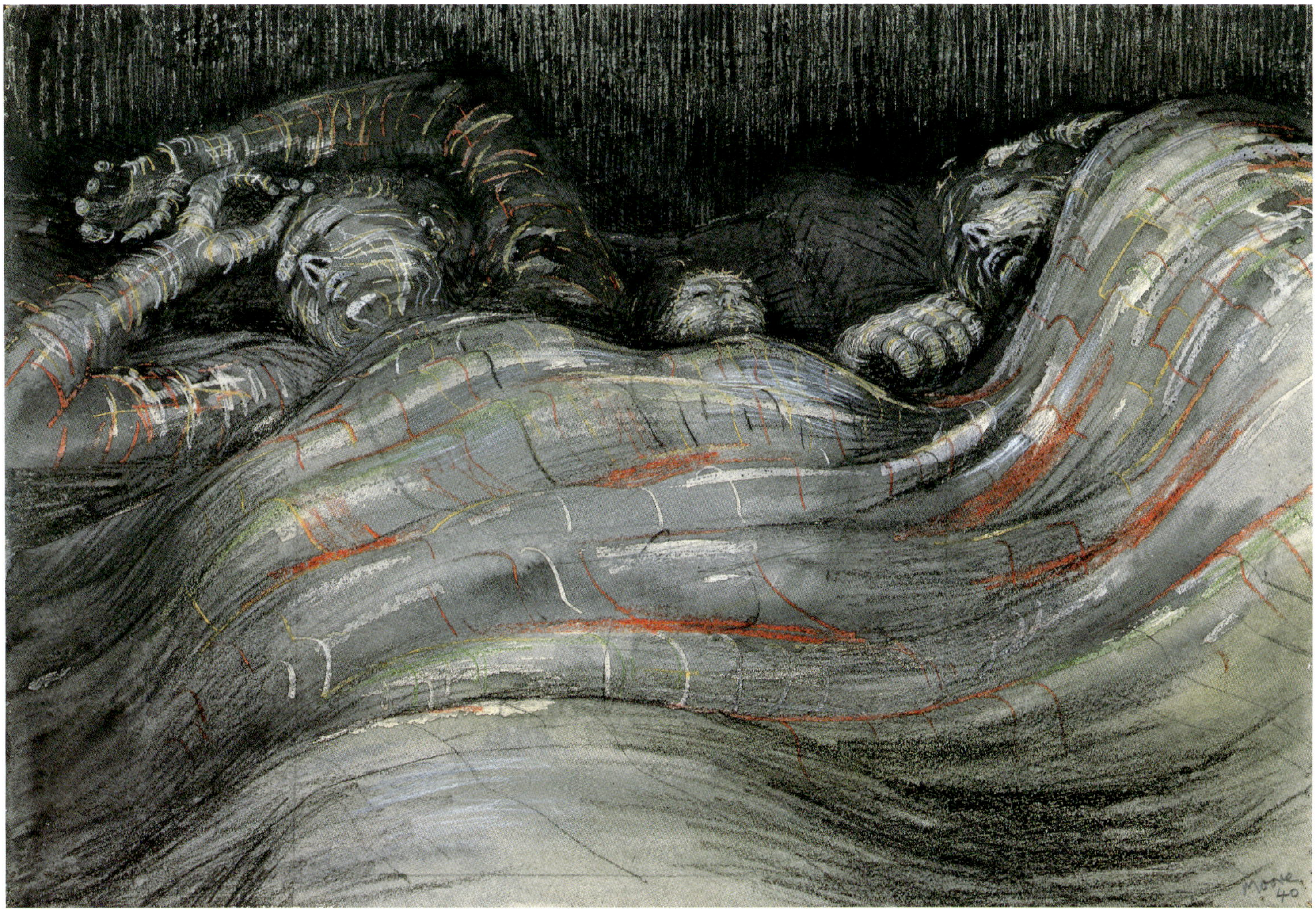

63.
Group of Shelterers
(detail) 1940

64.
Sleeping Shelterers: Two Women and a Child/Shelter Sleepers
1940
Pencil, wax crayon, chalk, watercolour wash, pen and ink
373 x 550mm
Signed and dated lower right: 'Moore / 40'
Robert and Lisa Sainsbury Collection, University of East Anglia, UEA 93
AG 40.91, HMF 1738

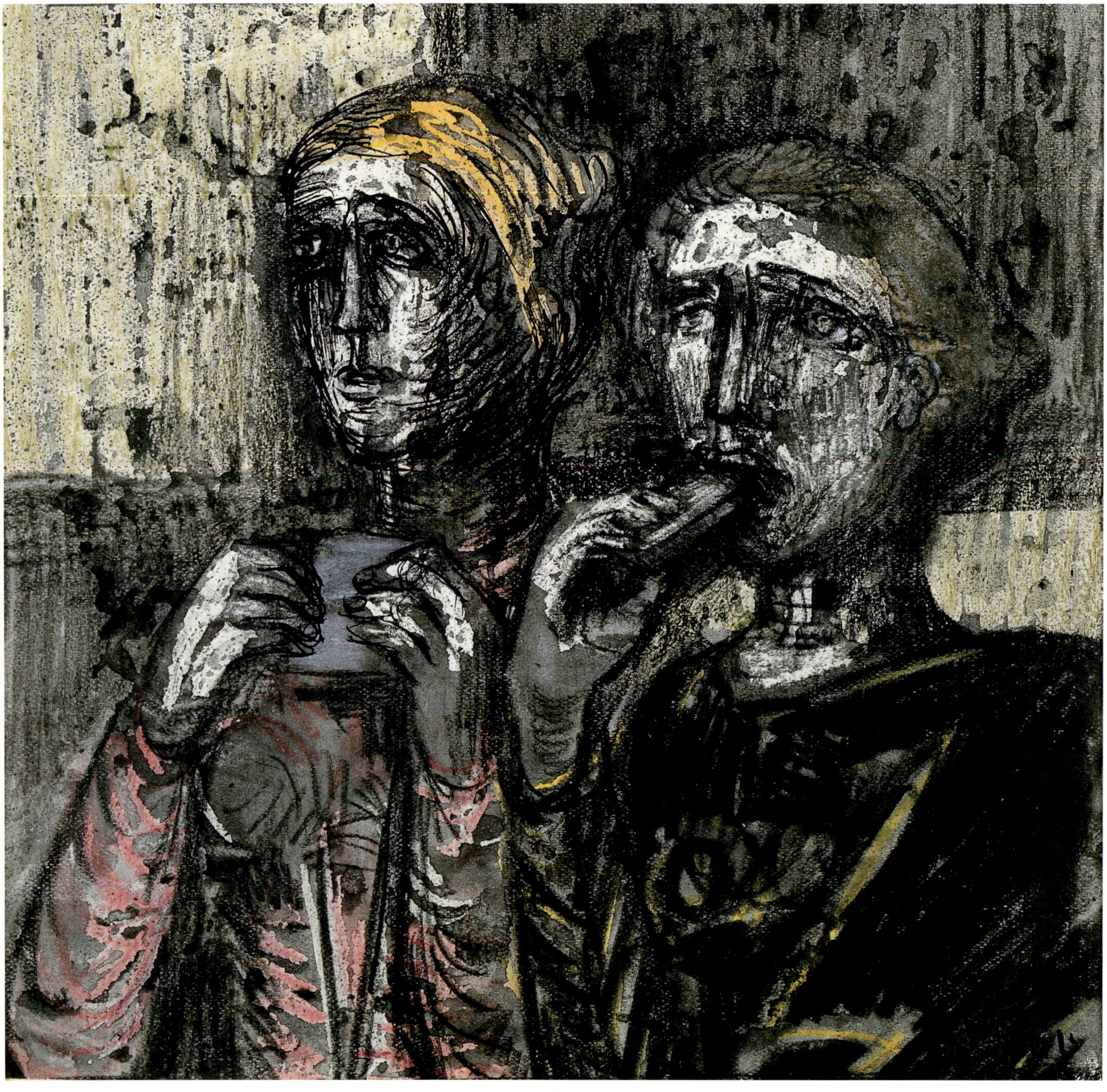

65.
Two Shelterers Eating/ Two Figures Taking a Snack in a Shelter 1941
Pencil, wax crayon, coloured crayon, watercolour wash, pen and ink
156 x 165mm
Signed and dated in pen and ink lower right: 'Moore / 41'
Robert and Lisa Sainsbury Collection, University of East Anglia, UEA 94
AG 41.87, HMF 1839

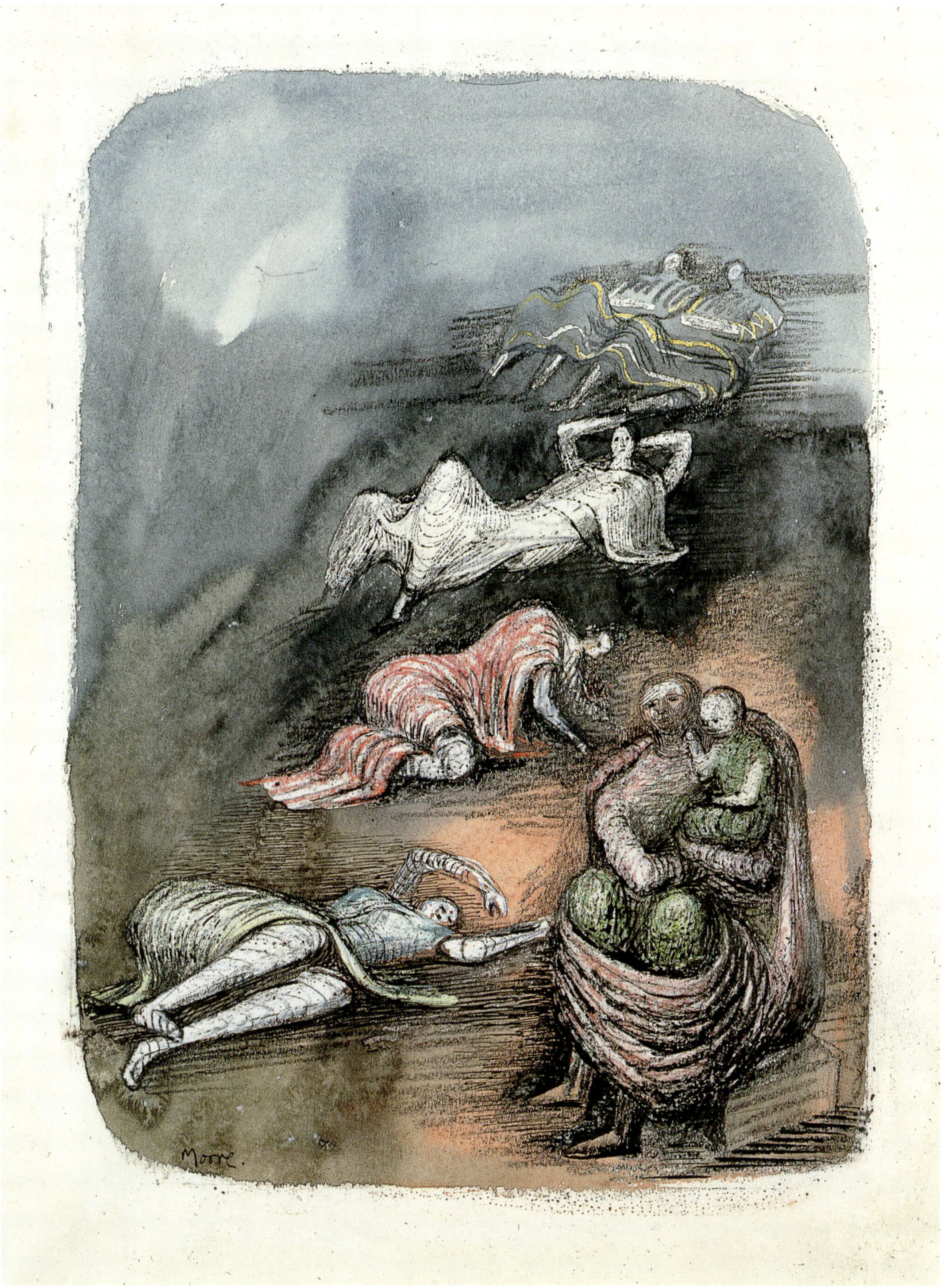

66.
Shelter Drawing/ Mother and Child with Reclining Figures 1942
Pencil, wax crayon, chalk, watercolour wash, pen and ink
317 x 248mm
Signed in pen and ink lower left: 'Moore'
Robert and Lisa Sainsbury Collection, University of East Anglia, UEA 96
AG 42.7, HMF 1822

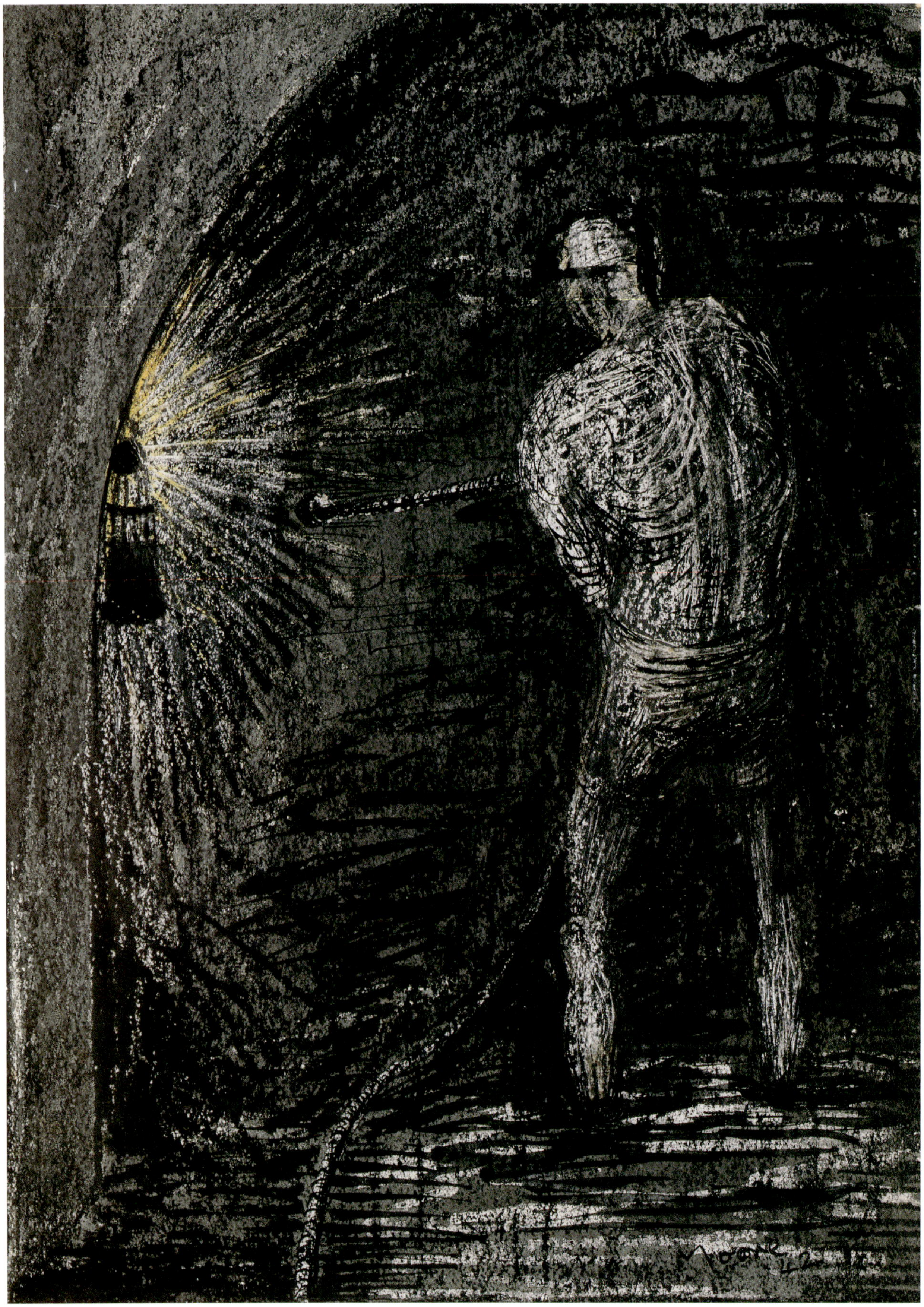

67.
Miner Drilling (Miner with Lamp)/Miner Drilling in Drift 1942
Pencil, wax crayon, coloured crayon, watercolour wash, pen and ink
292 x 216mm
Signed and dated in pen and ink lower right: 'Moore / 42'
Robert and Lisa Sainsbury Collection, University of East Anglia, UEA 95
AG 42.106, HMF 2005

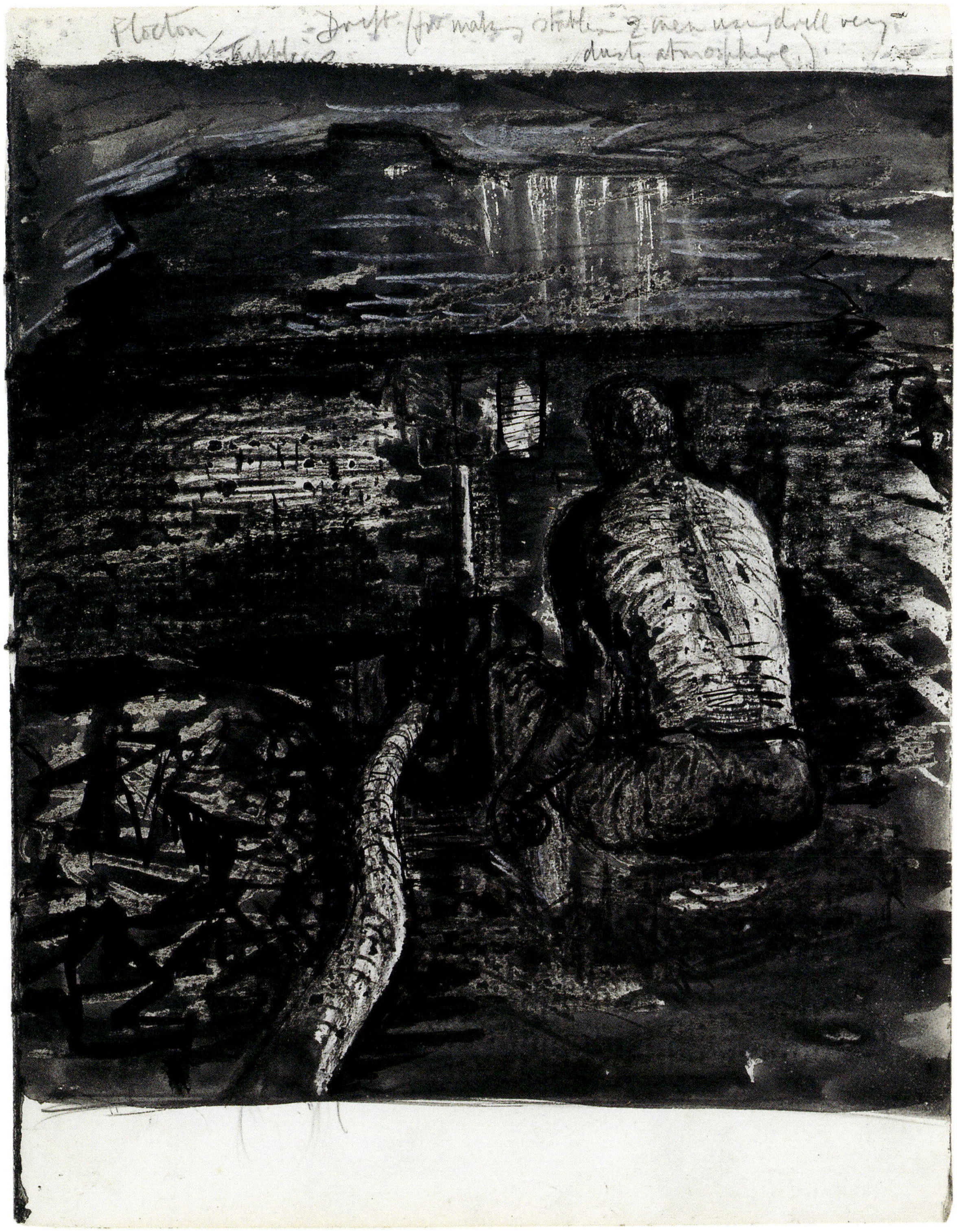

68.
Miner with Tupping Machine in Flocton Colliery 1942
Coalmining Subjects Sketchbook, p. 41
Pencil, wax crayon, watercolour, wash, pen and ink
203 x 162mm
Inscribed in pencil upper centre: 'Flocton / Tupping Drift (for making stable 2 men using drill / very dusty atmosphere)'
The Henry Moore Foundation: gift of the artist 1977
AG 42.40, HMF 1944

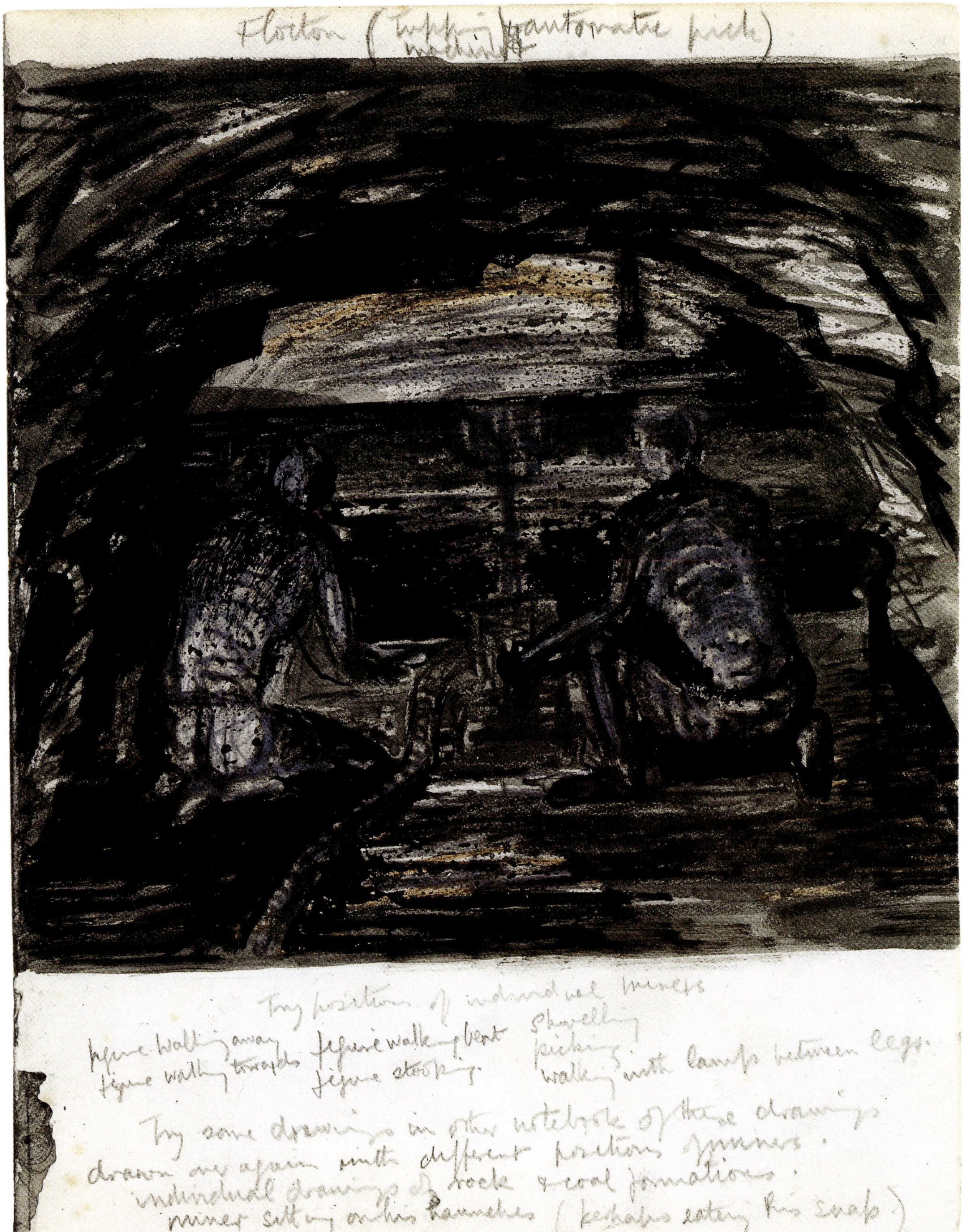
Try positions of individual miners
figure walking away
figure walking towards
figure walking bent
figure stooping
shovelling
picking
walking with lamps between legs.
Try some drawings in other notebook of these drawings
drawn over again with different positions of miners.
individual drawings of rock & coal formations.
miner sitting on his haunches (perhaps eating his snap)

69.
Two Miners with Tupping Machine in Flocton Colliery 1942
Coalmining Subjects Sketchbook, p. 21
Pencil, wax crayon, coloured crayon, watercolour, wash, pen and ink
203 x 162mm
Inscribed in pencil upper centre: 'Flocton (tupping / machine & automatic pick)'; lower centre: 'Try positions of individual miners; figure walking away / figure walking towards; figure walking bent / figure stooping; shovelling / picking / walking with lamp between legs / Try some drawings in other notebook of these drawings / drawn over again with different positions of miners / individual drawings of rock & coal formations / miner sitting on his haunches (perhaps eating his snap)'
The Henry Moore Foundation: gift of the artist 1977
AG 42.30, HMF 1934

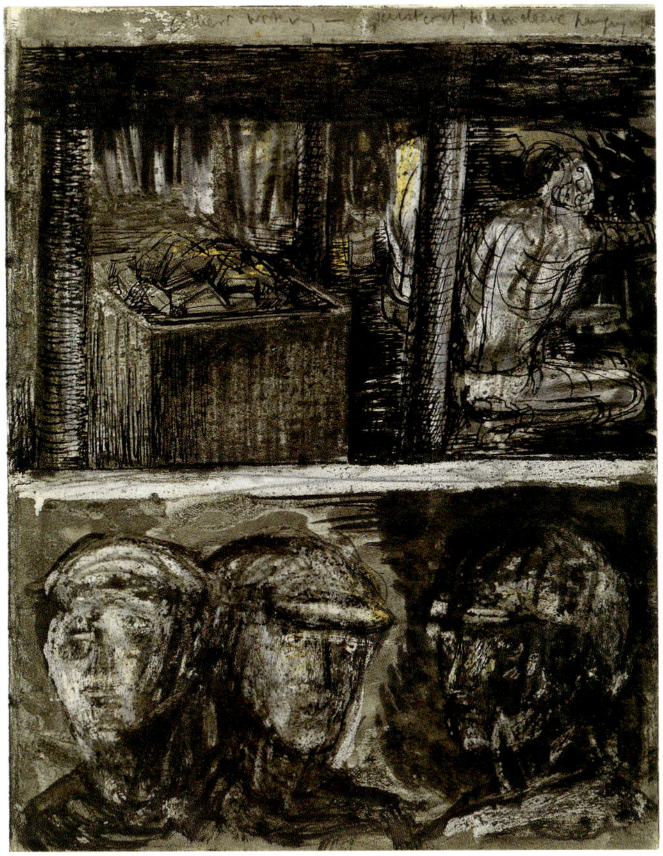

70.
Miners' Heads 1942
Coalmining Subjects Sketchbook, p. 7
Pencil, wax crayon, coloured crayon, watercolour, wash, pen and ink
203 x 162mm
Inscribed in pencil upper centre: 'Collier working – waistcoat, [...] in sleeve hanging'
The Henry Moore Foundation: gift of the artist 1977
AG 42.23, HMF 1927

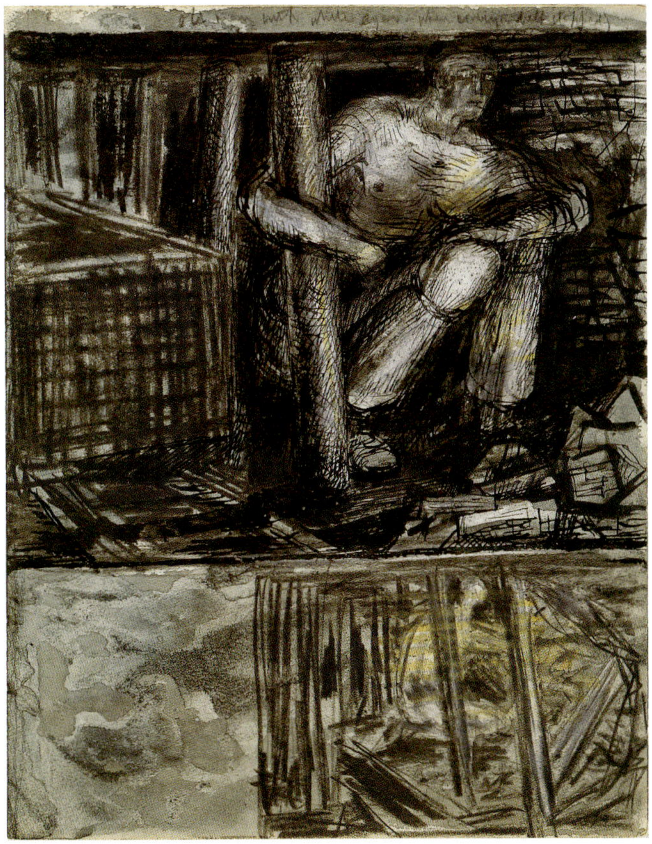

71.
Miner with Truck 1942
Coalmining Subjects Sketchbook, p. 9
Pencil, wax crayon, coloured crayon, watercolour, wash, pen and ink
203 x 162mm
Inscribed in pencil upper centre: 'old man with white eyes – when conveyor belt stopped)'
The Henry Moore Foundation: gift of the artist 1977
AG 42.24, HMF 1928

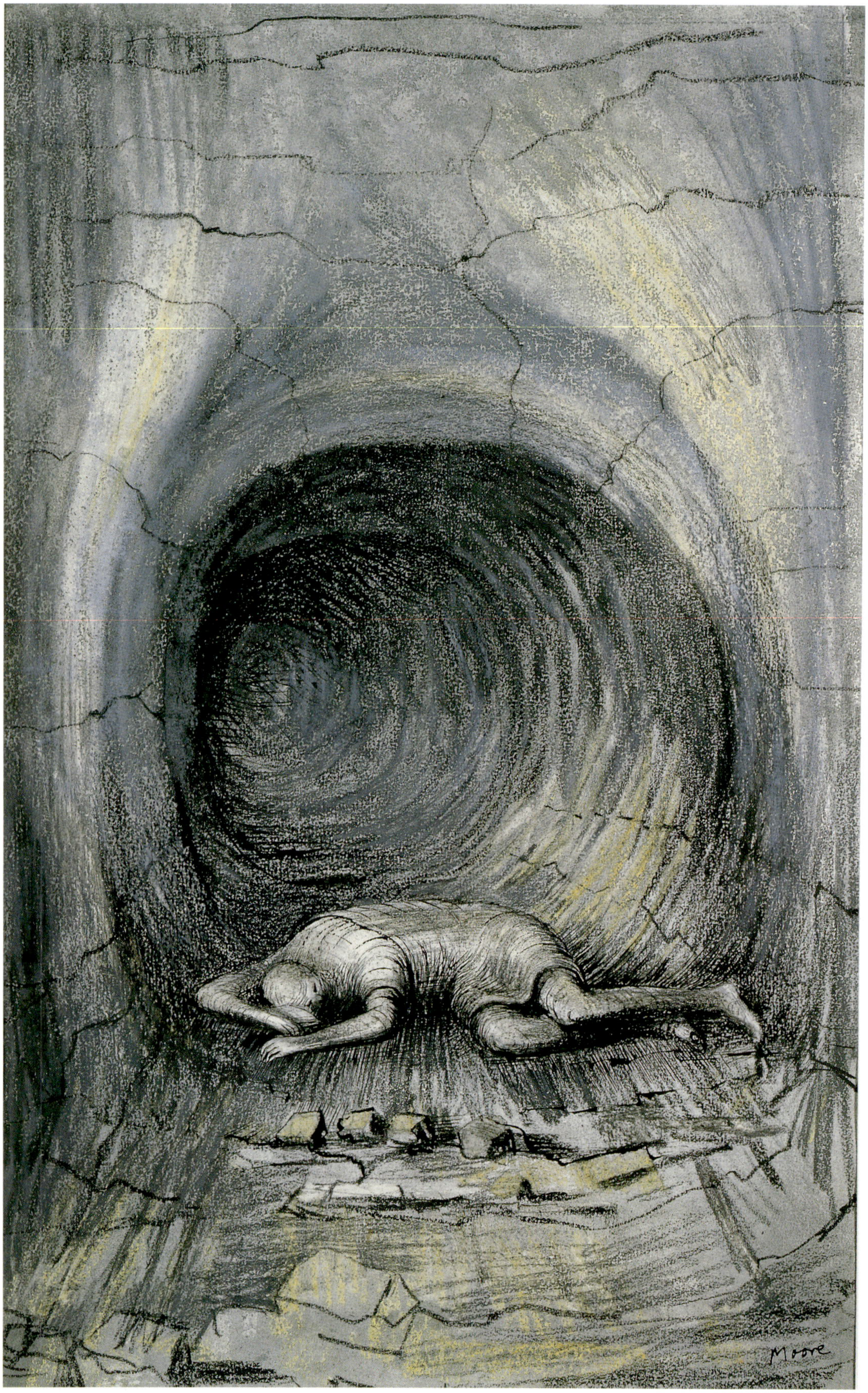

72.
Odysseus in the Cave of the Naiads 1944
Pencil, wax crayon, charcoal, coloured crayon, wash, pen and ink
445 x 292mm
Signed in pen and ink lower right: 'Moore'
Robert and Lisa Sainsbury Collection, University of East Anglia, UEA 97
AG 44.39, HMF 2297

73.
The Death of the Suitors 1944
Pencil, wax crayon,
coloured crayon,
watercolour wash,
pen and ink, brush and ink
445 x 289mm
Signed and dated lower left:
'Moore / 44'
Trustees, Cecil Higgins Art
Gallery, Bedford, England
AG 44.47, HMF 2305

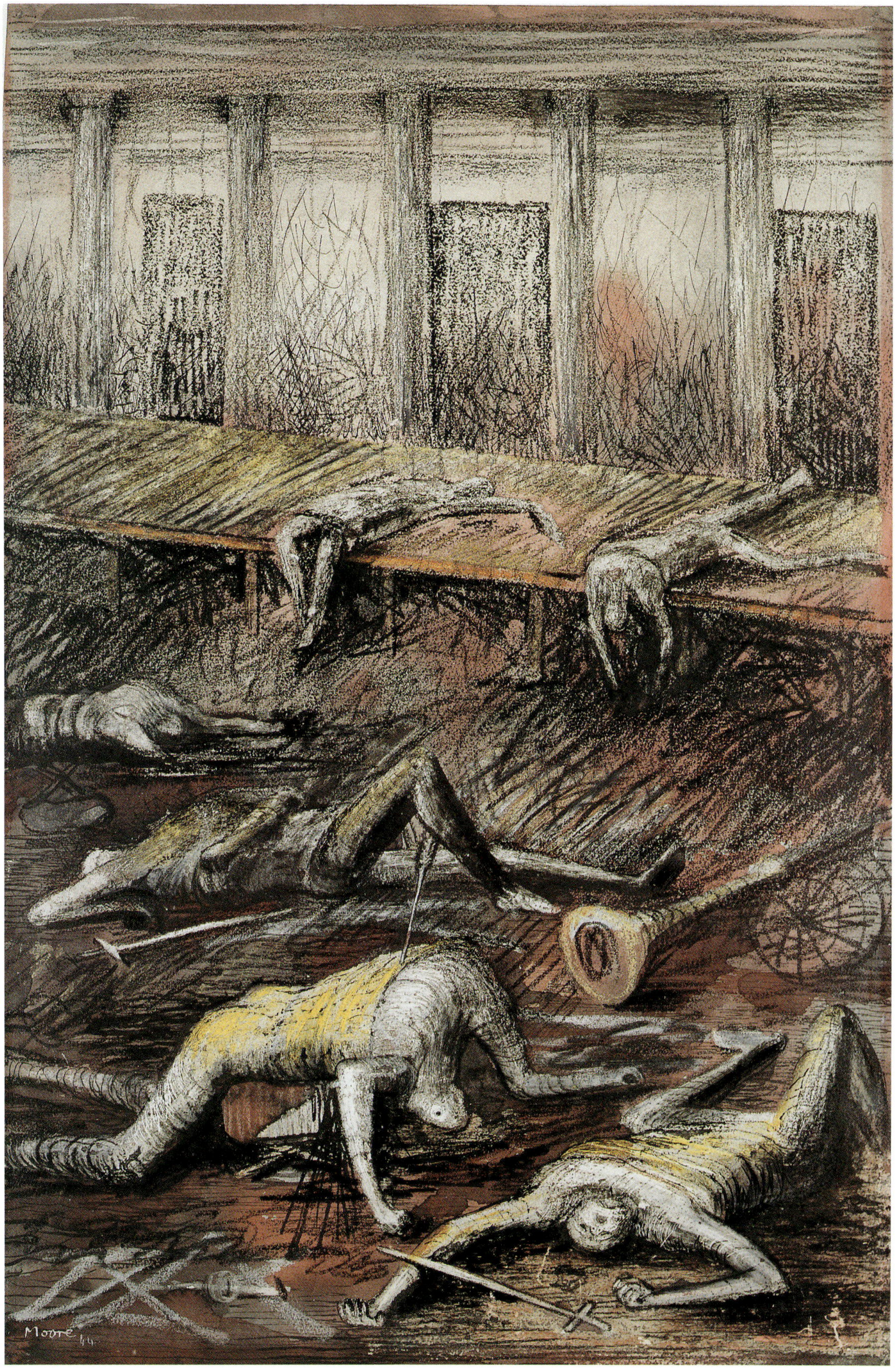

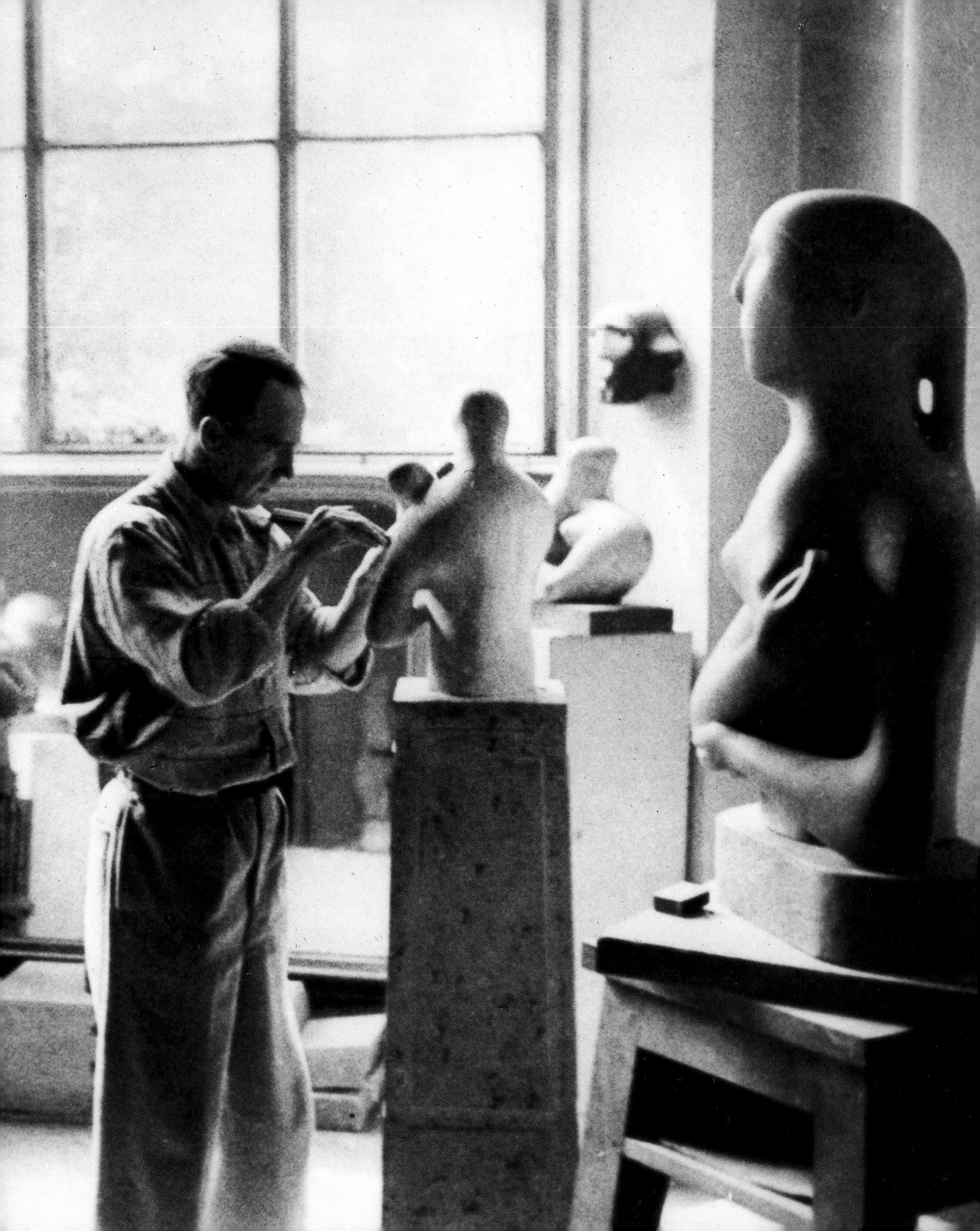

> I was always attracted to seated figures because, being immobile, they seemed essentially right for stone carving, which I thought should not try to represent actual movement. To make a running figure out of stone seemed to me to be a contradiction of reality.[36]

MOORE'S ATTRACTION to seated and half figures ultimately derives from the old 'truth to materials' issue. If a figure was to be carved from stone, then it should partake of the stone's inertia and weight. The 'figures' involved were almost invariably female; and so a Rubensian quality to many of his figure studies is the inevitable result. But theory clearly followed inclination. Moore liked what he once, in his twenties, described with multi-adjectival relish as 'those richly formed, big-limbed, fresh faced, full blooded country wenches, built for breeding, honest, simple minded, practical, common sensed, healthily sexed lasses'.[37] The early *Seated Nude with Mirror* of 1924 (cat. 74) answers the description of the buxom Venus admirably, with a formal nod to Picasso. When he was simply drawing from life, the same qualities emerged – and, surely not coincidentally, Moore's mother seems to have embodied the type (fig. 4, p. 10). Even the elegant Irina would be tailored to fit the image (cat. 78, *Seated Girl in a Petticoat*, 1929).

The *Seated Figure* of 1924 (cat. 75) has a Buddha-like quality to it, and is more finished in the back view – the carving certainly bears witness to the hardness of Hopton-wood stone. In the context of two seated figures in the British Museum – one Aztec and one Egyptian – Moore was later to say: 'Often people forget to look at the back of a sculpture, and sometimes pieces are so displayed that this is impossible. But a back can be very expressive.'[38] This back view relates more to the relaxed, Aztec example, but with a deliberate imbalance.

But the influence of Picasso as catalyst was almost as strong at this time as that of the British Museum. Moore's *Half Figure* of 1928 (cat. 77) may have been one of those 'lumpy masses bound by clumsy contours … revolting' that the reviewer of the *Morning Post* so objected to in Moore's first solo show at the Warren Gallery. Epstein, Augustus John and Henry Lamb begged to differ – all three fellow artists bought works from that first show.

The germ of the idea contained in that drawing bore several sculptural fruits. A series of half figures were made in cast concrete, all sharing the interlocked hands that offered Moore a means of keeping the arms close to the body, while providing a continuous linked form adding interest, tension and strength to the middle area. The Sainsbury *Half Figure No. 2* (cat. 81) is a particularly elegant and attractive piece, not of the usual Rubensian mould at all, a reminder possibly that it was in July 1929 that Moore married his beautiful, aristocratic (and slim) Russian wife Irina. Their first married home was in Belsize Park, at 11a Parkhill Road, just round the corner from Barbara Hepworth and her first husband John Skeaping. The area was to be a hive of interactive inspiration and exchange of ideas until the war. Another *Seated Figure* of that year (cat. 82), also in cast concrete, is a full-length version of the idea, which, for all its schematic

Fig. 49
Henry Moore at work in his Parkhill Road studio with *Half Figure*, 1932 (LH 117; now in the Tate collection), in the foreground.

The Human Form – Seated Figures and Half Figures

face and squared-off forms, remains basically realistic, enlivened by a rather tense sideways glance.

Another drawing (cat. 79, *Drawing for Figure in Concrete*, 1929) precedes another concrete figure (cat. 80, *Half Figure*, 1929), but Moore has evolved the figure in two main ways – firstly, he has unclasped the hands, laying them palm to palm to create a more continuous point of interest in the linked arms. He has also carved out a keyhole shape between the breasts and down to the stomach that anticipates the 'hole' that would emerge as such a defining characteristic five years later.

In January 1931 Moore resigned his teaching post at the Royal College after a long history of disagreement with his professors, Derwent Wood, Richard Garbe and Gilbert Ledward, traditionalists all, and an insidious and disgraceful campaign by certain critics who felt Moore was a bad influence (stylistically) on his students. However, by the autumn he was more happily ensconced in a new teaching position at Chelsea School of Art, which suited him better; and in the meantime he had had his second one-man show, at the Leicester Galleries in Leicester Square. The reaction had been the usual mixture of hysterical abuse and extravagant encomium. Of the latter tendency, Herbert Read, in a review in *The Listener*, established himself as the chief praise-singer, going on to become a great friend and champion (he was a fellow Yorkshireman). Part of the problem in this polarized reaction was that supporters, in their enthusiasm and loyalty, seemed all too prone to patronize those who, for whatever reason, did not like the work. Epstein, on this occasion, wrote the foreword to the catalogue, saying 'Here is something to startle the unthinking out of their complacency', thus at a stroke alienating anyone who dared to disagree with his own appreciation of the work's quality. (Oddly, the silver-tongued Kenneth Clark was to make the same mistake years later, at the unveiling of the Northampton Madonna, sweepingly and from a great height suggesting that the figure 'may worry some simple people, it may raise indignation in the minds of self-centred people, and it may lead arrogant people to protest', thus no doubt defining and offending simultaneously most of the congregation.)

Also in 1931 Moore produced the charming *Girl* (cat. 84, Tate), in which the form has become even more attenuated. It is perhaps the most traditional of the half figures, if only in the sense that considerable effort has gone into the shy and tentative expression of the face, and into the delicate carving of the hands – another essay in interlocking, but here with the thumb of the lower hand linking with little finger of the upper hand, powerfully suggesting a certain nervous anticipation.

In 1933 Moore produced a half figure that he felt moved to describe, in the new anti-figurative parlance of his fellow members of Unit One and the 7 & 5 Society, as *Composition* (1933, cat. 87). A half figure it remains, however, fully recognizable as a sister to the Tate *Girl*, except that the arms have gone. Breasts, shoulders and head remain, but the face has become a scratched scribble, surrounded by a cowl-like form suggesting hair. It looks like a pebble found on the beach – and such may well have been its inspiration.

Two drawings, both from 1948, show two women interacting in the manner learned from the shelter drawings (like the *Three Standing Figures* of the same year, cat. 97). The Sainsbury *Two Women in an Interior*[39] (cat. 89) is a rather fascinating reference to Cézanne's *Card Players*, while the *Women Winding Wool* (cat. 90) inevitably suggests the idea of the Fates (a theme that he certainly attempted elsewhere around this time).

Finally, the *Warrior with Shield* (on display here is the plaster model, cat. 92, which does not have the shield) comes with a very complete explanation from the artist:

> The idea for *The Warrior* came to me at the end of 1952 or very early in 1953. It was evolved from a pebble I found on the seashore in the summer of 1952, and which reminded me of the stump of a leg, amputated at the hip. Just as Leonardo says somewhere in his notebooks that a painter can find a battle scene in the lichen marks on a wall, so this gave me the start of The Warrior idea ... The head has a blunted and bull-like power but also a sort of dumb animal acceptance and forbearance of pain ... I think The Warrior has some Greek influence, not consciously wished for but perhaps the result of my visit to Athens and other parts of Greece in 1951.[40]

A better illustration of the diversity of reference that informed Moore's sculpture, starting from that recognition of pure form on the seashore, could hardly be found.

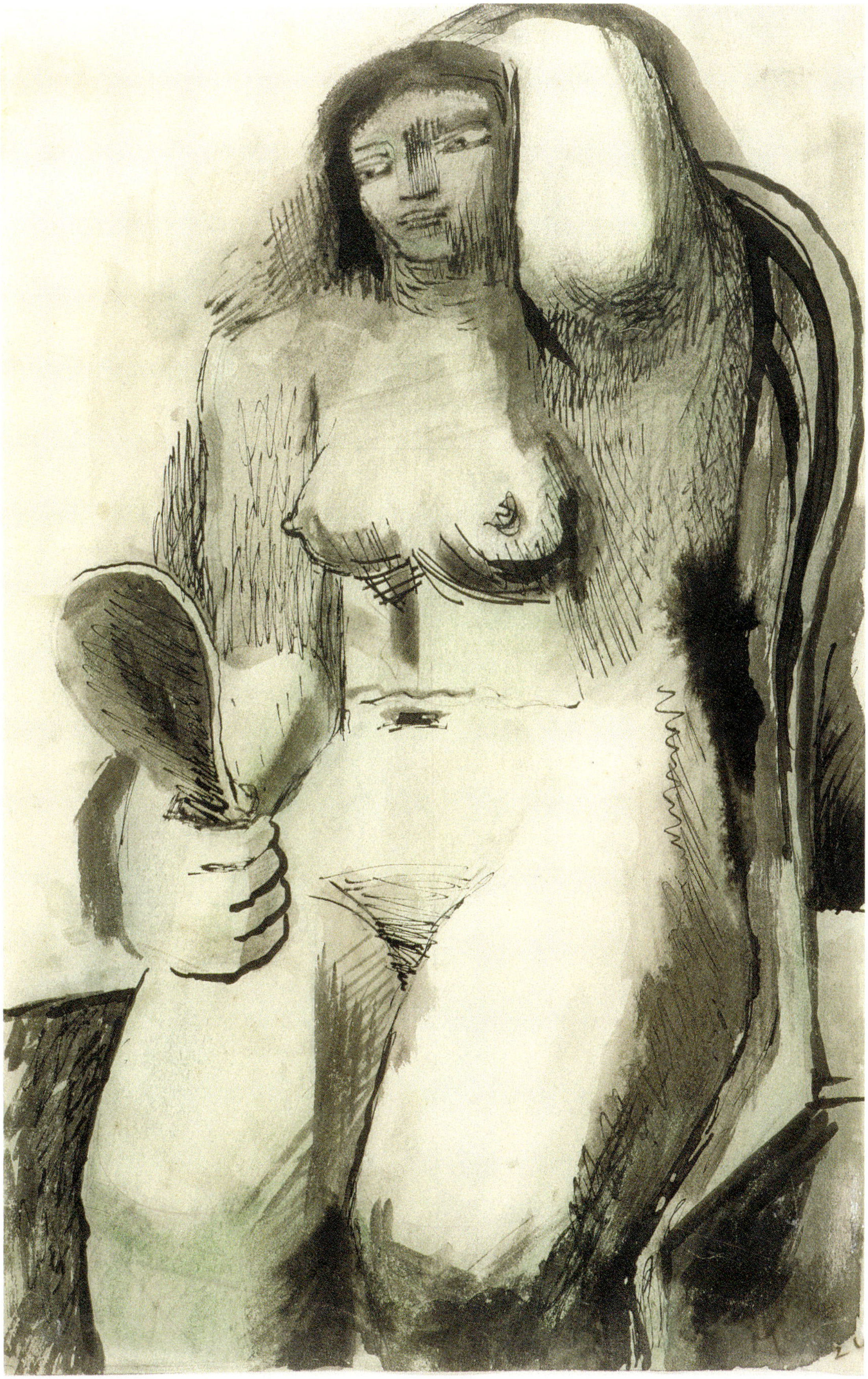

74.
Seated Nude with Mirror 1924
Pencil, charcoal, chalk, watercolour wash, brush and ink, pen and ink
339 x 222mm
Signed and dated lower right: 'Moore / 24'
Private Collection, Switzerland
AG 24.54, HMF 261

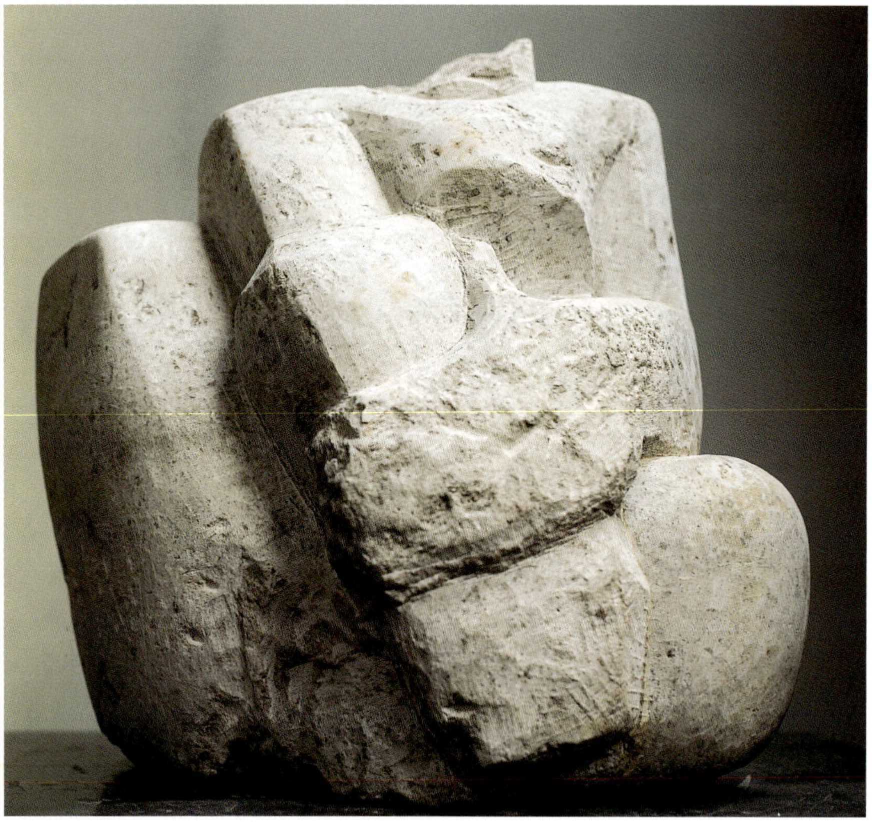

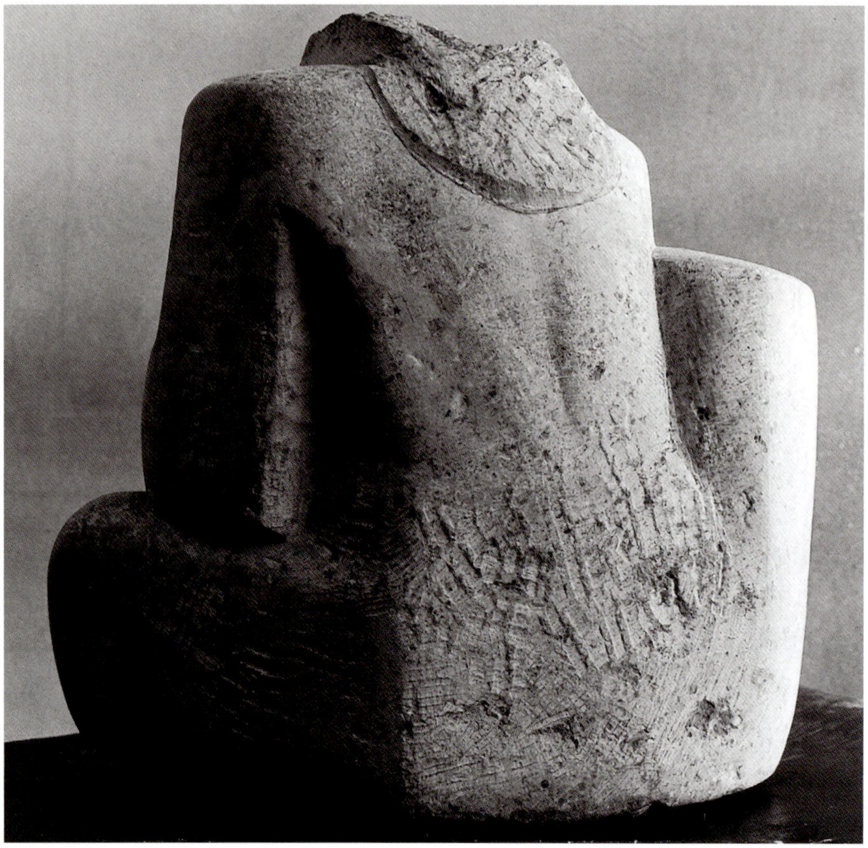

75.
Seated Figure 1924
(front and back)
Hopton–wood stone
h.254mm
The Henry Moore
Foundation: gift of
the artist 1977
LH 19

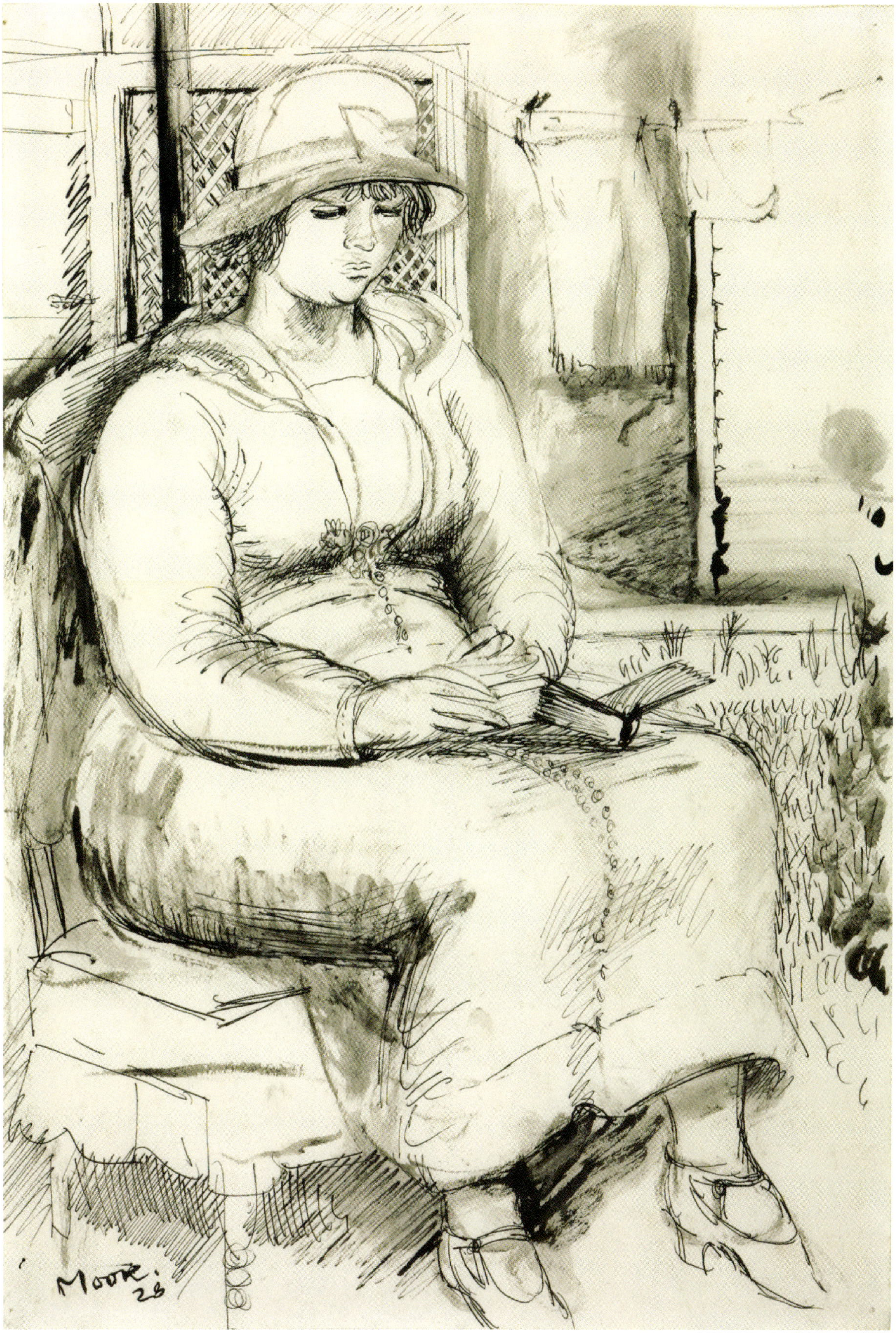

76.
The Artist's Sister Mary
1926
Pen and ink, wash
349 x 240mm
Signed and dated lower left:
'Moore / 28' (added in 1950
and misdated)
Private Collection
AG 26.52, HMF 476

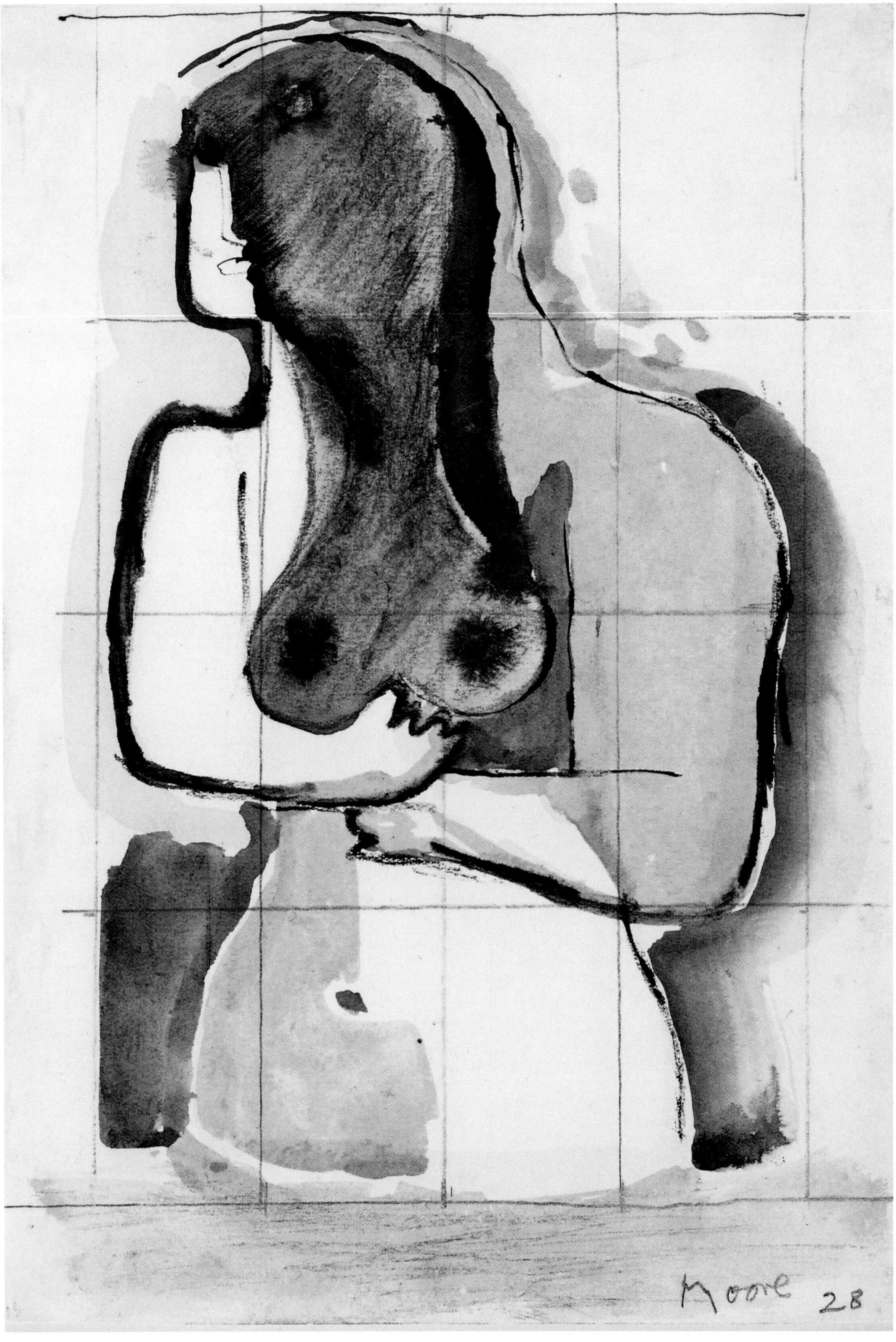

77.
Half Figure 1928
Pen and ink, chalk, wash
232 x 165mm
Signed and dated in pencil
lower right: 'Moore / 28'
The Henry Moore
Foundation: gift of
the artist 1977
AG 28.144, HMF 661

78.
Seated Girl in a Petticoat 1929
Pen and ink, chalk, wash
419 x 298mm
Signed and dated in chalk upper right: ‘Moore / 29’
Robert and Lisa Sainsbury Collection, University of East Anglia, UEA 87
AG 29.10, HMF 697

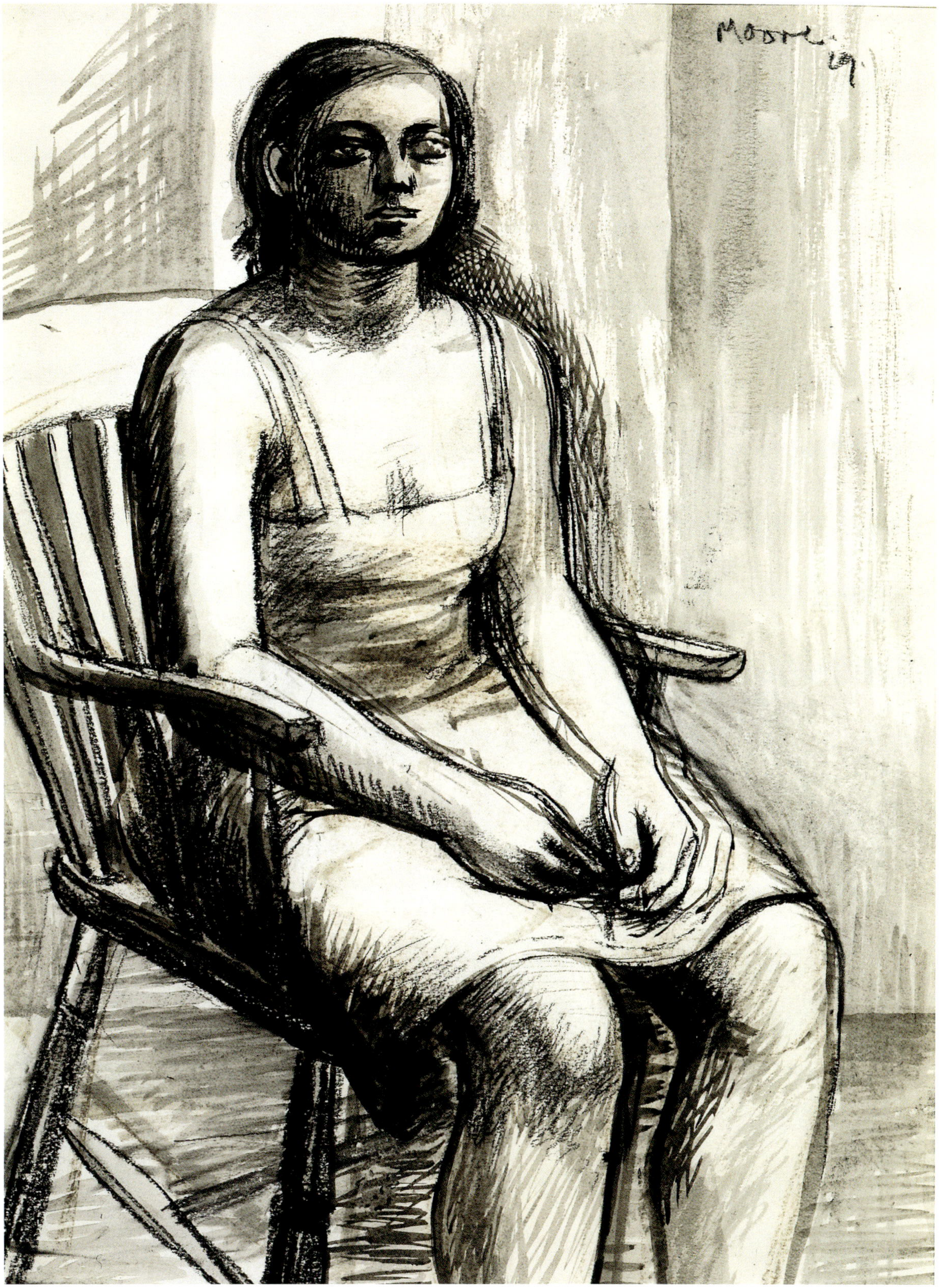

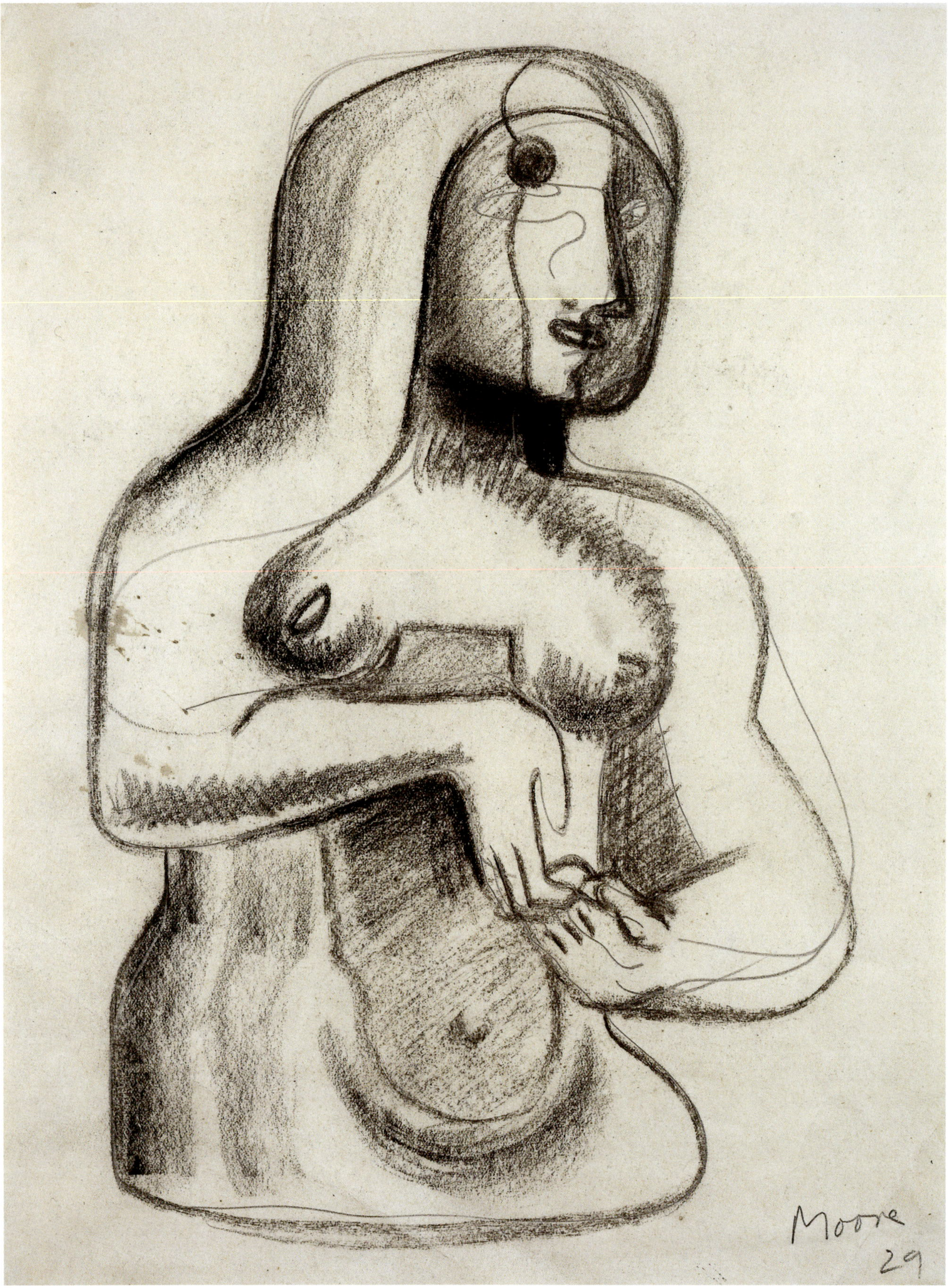
Moore
29

79.
Drawing for Figure in Concrete 1929
Pencil, crayon, charcoal
305 x 229mm
Signed and dated in pencil lower right: 'Moore / 29'
Arts Council Collection, Hayward Gallery, London, ACC8/1963
AG 29.47, HMF 724

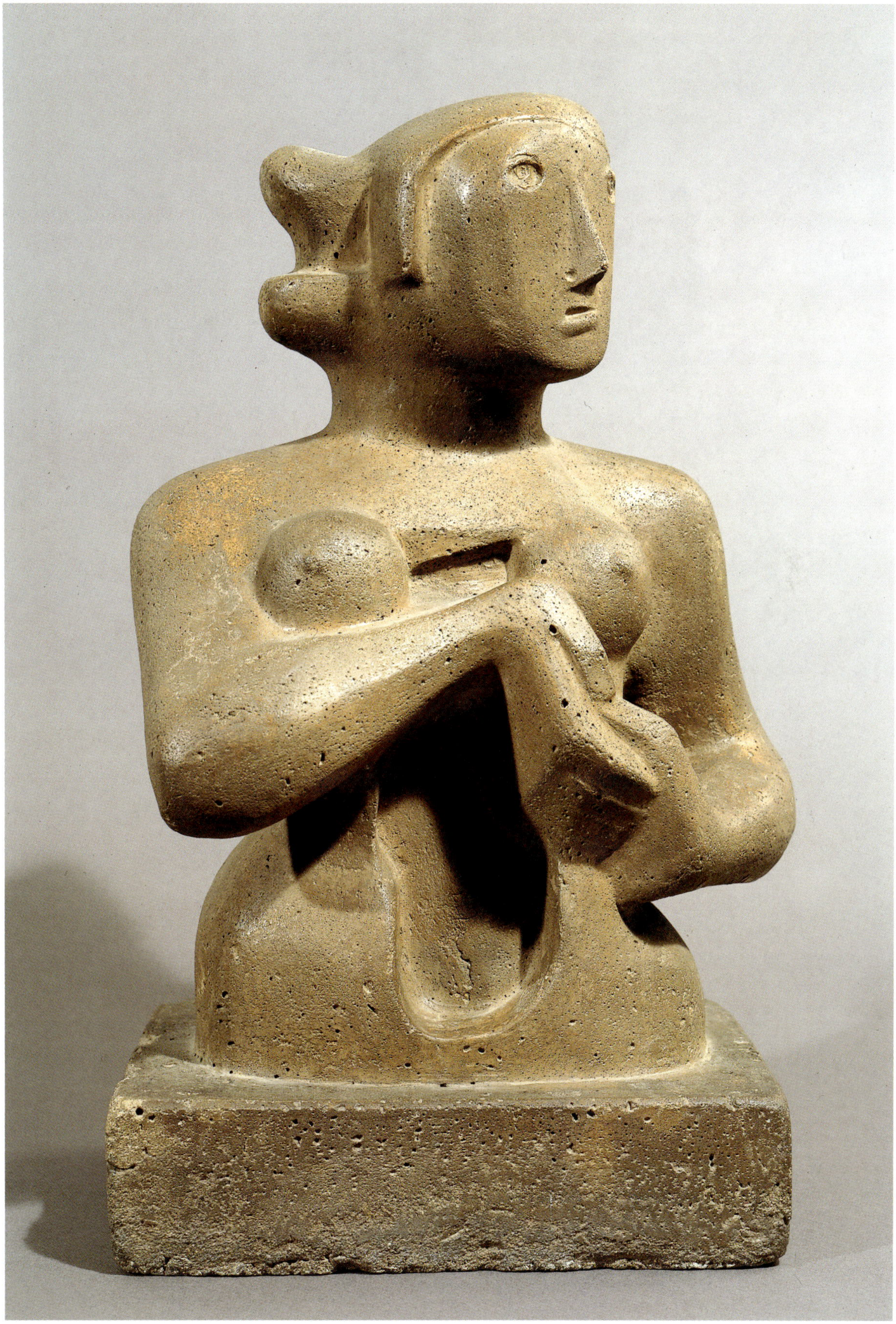

80.
Half Figure 1929
Cast concrete
h.370mm
British Council
LH 67

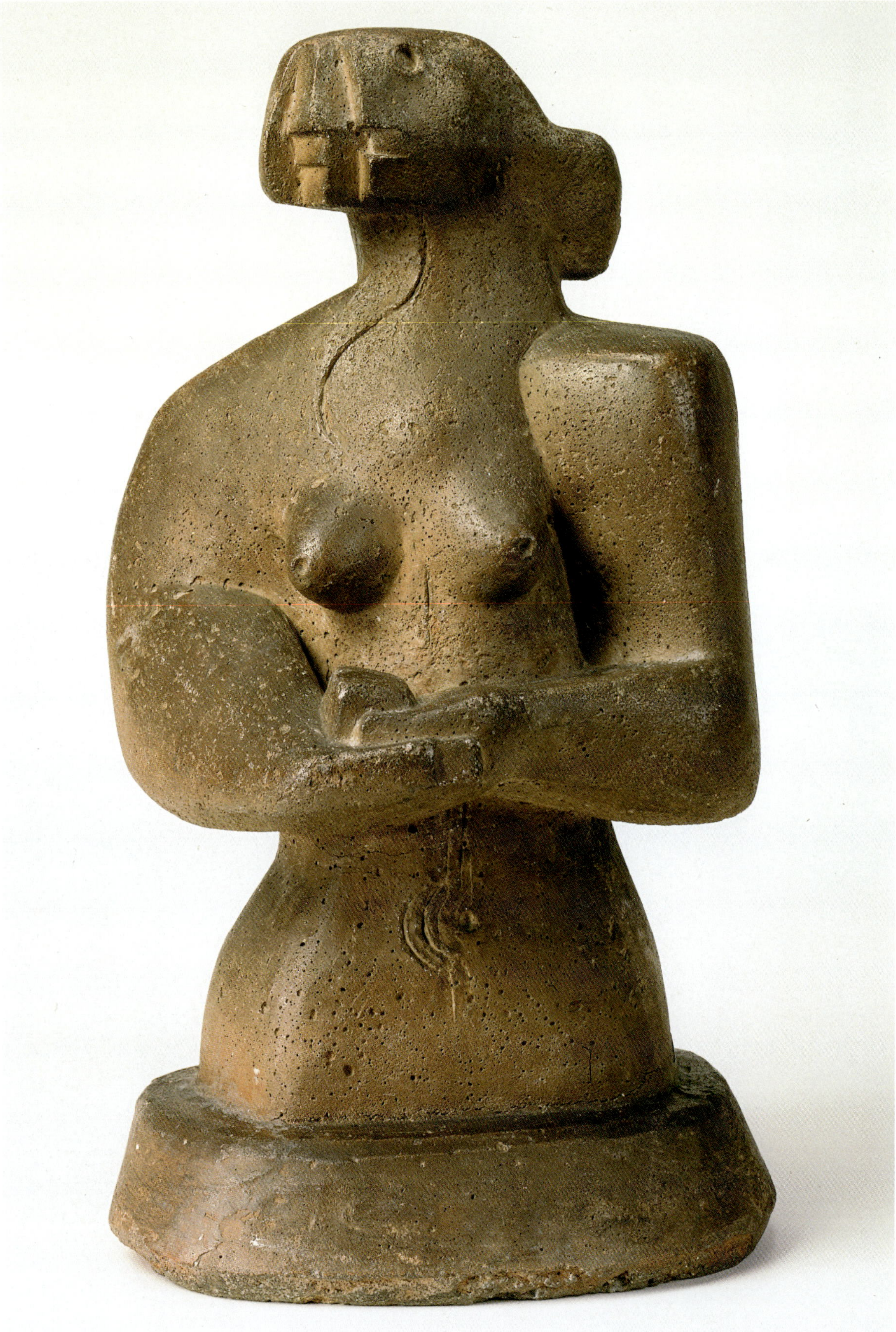

81.
Half Figure No. 2 1929
Concrete
396 x 230 x 170mm
Robert and Lisa Sainsbury Collection, University of East Anglia, UEA 79
LH 66

82.
Seated Figure 1929
Cast concrete
h.445mm
The Henry Moore Foundation: gift of Irina Moore 1979
LH 65

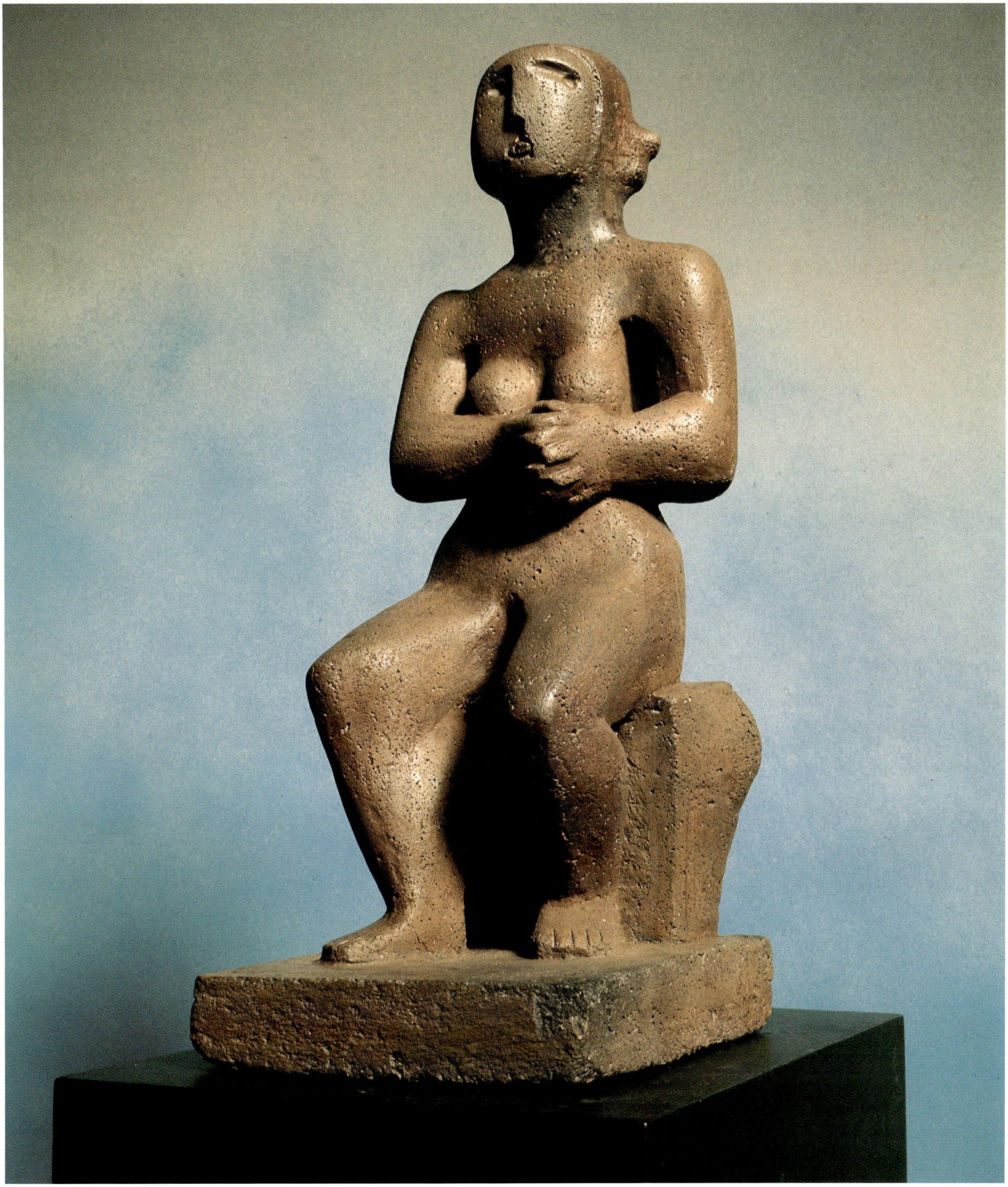

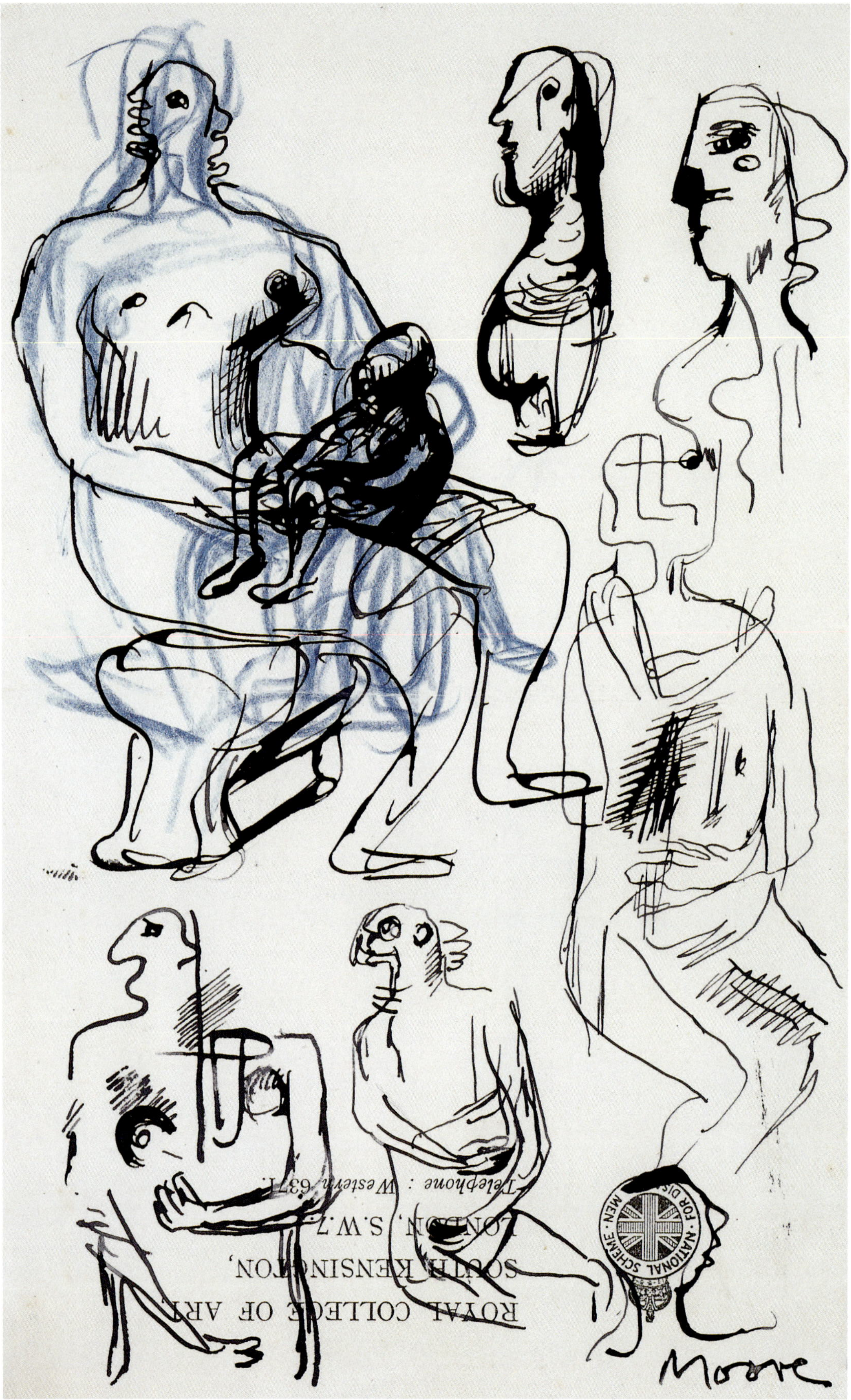

83.
Ideas for Sculpture: Seated Figures and Heads 1930
Pen and ink, crayon
182 x 112mm
Signed in pen and ink (added later) lower right: 'Moore' (undated)
The Henry Moore Foundation: gift of the artist 1977
AG 30.70, HMF 803

84.
Girl 1931
Ancaster stone
737 x 368 x 273mm
Tate, purchased 1952,
N06078
LH 109

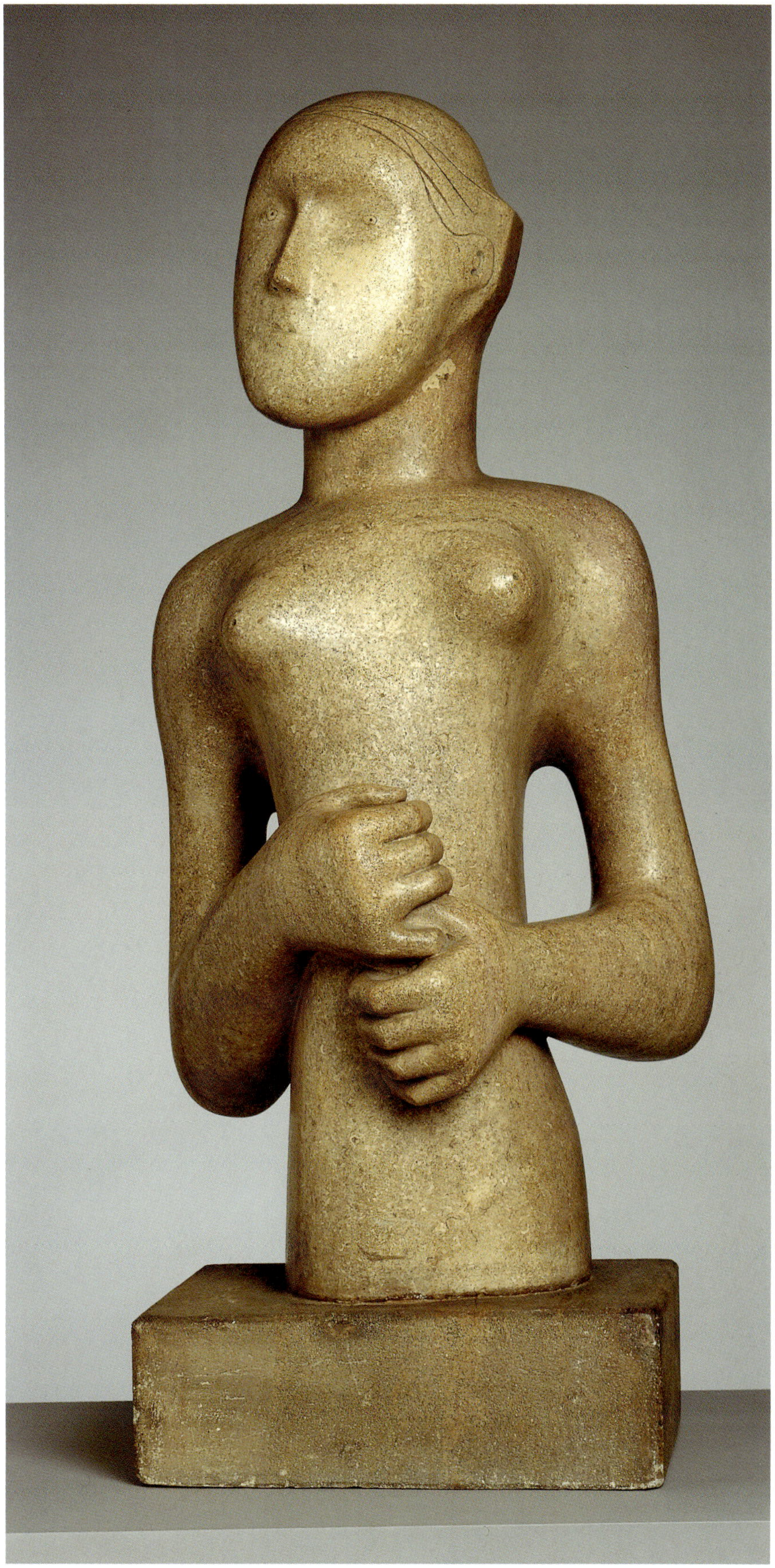

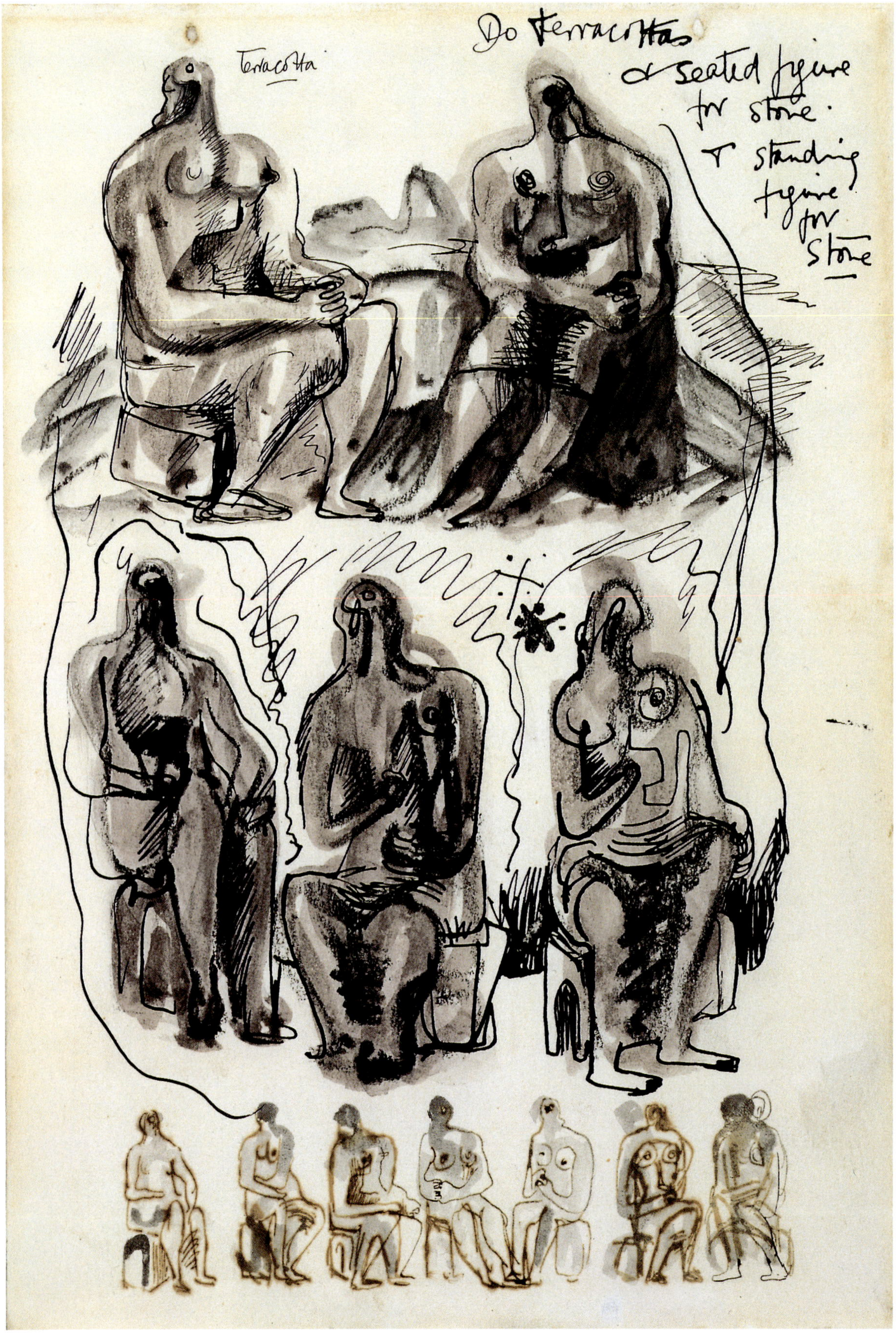

85.
Ideas for Sculpture 1931
Sizewell Sketchbook, 1931
Pencil, chalk, wash, pen and ink
260 x 178mm
Inscribed in pen and ink upper left: 'terracotta'; upper right:'Do terracottas / & seated figure / for stone. / & standing / figure / for / stone'
The Henry Moore Foundation: purchased 1980
AG 31.6, HMF 893

86.
Drawing for Boxwood Figure *c.*1931
Pencil, brush and ink, ink wash
367 x 273mm
Signed in ballpoint pen (added later) lower left: 'Moore'
The Henry Moore Foundation: gift of the artist 1977
AG 31.37, HMF 870

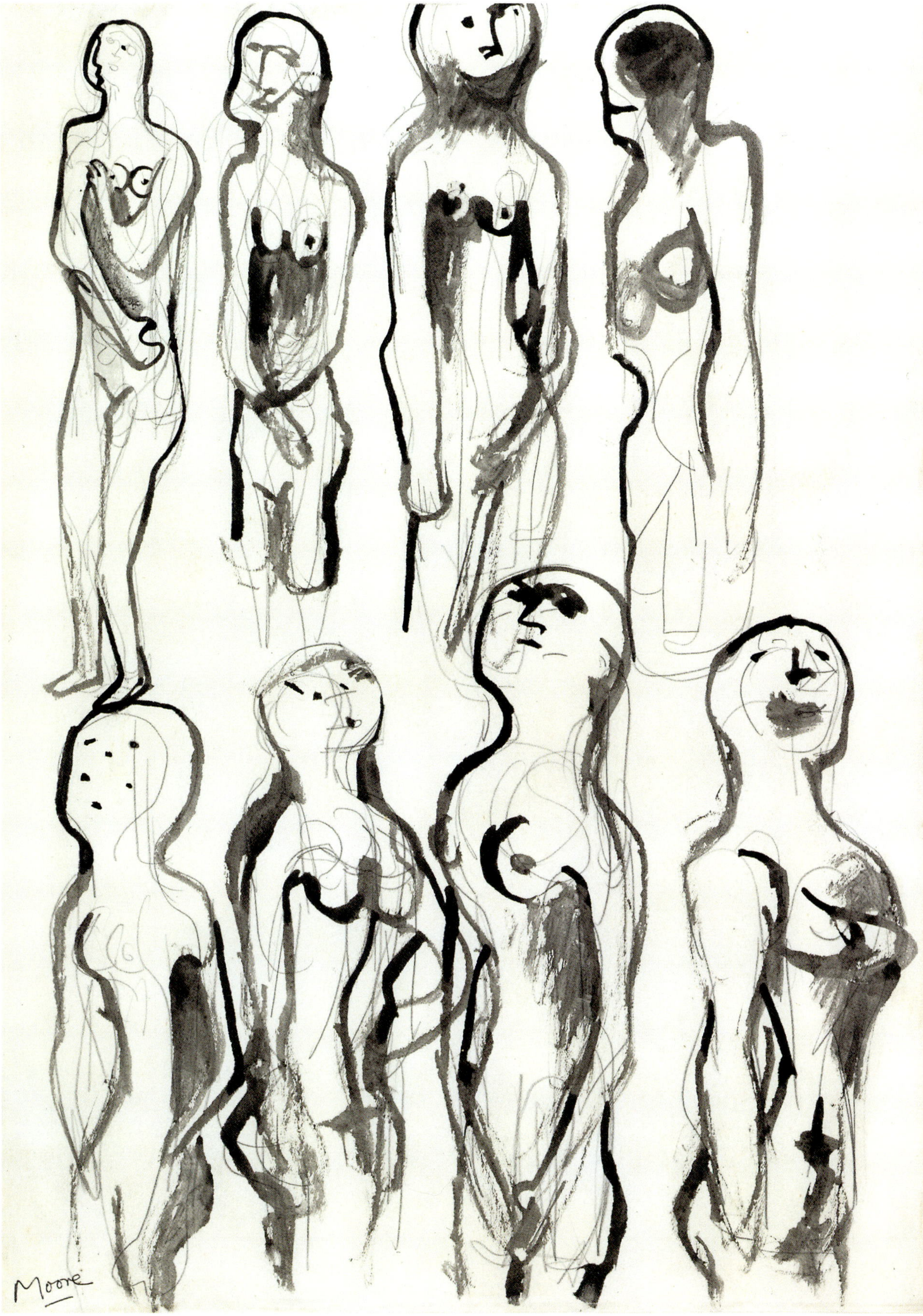
Moore

87.
Composition 1933
Carved concrete
h.584mm
British Council
LH 133

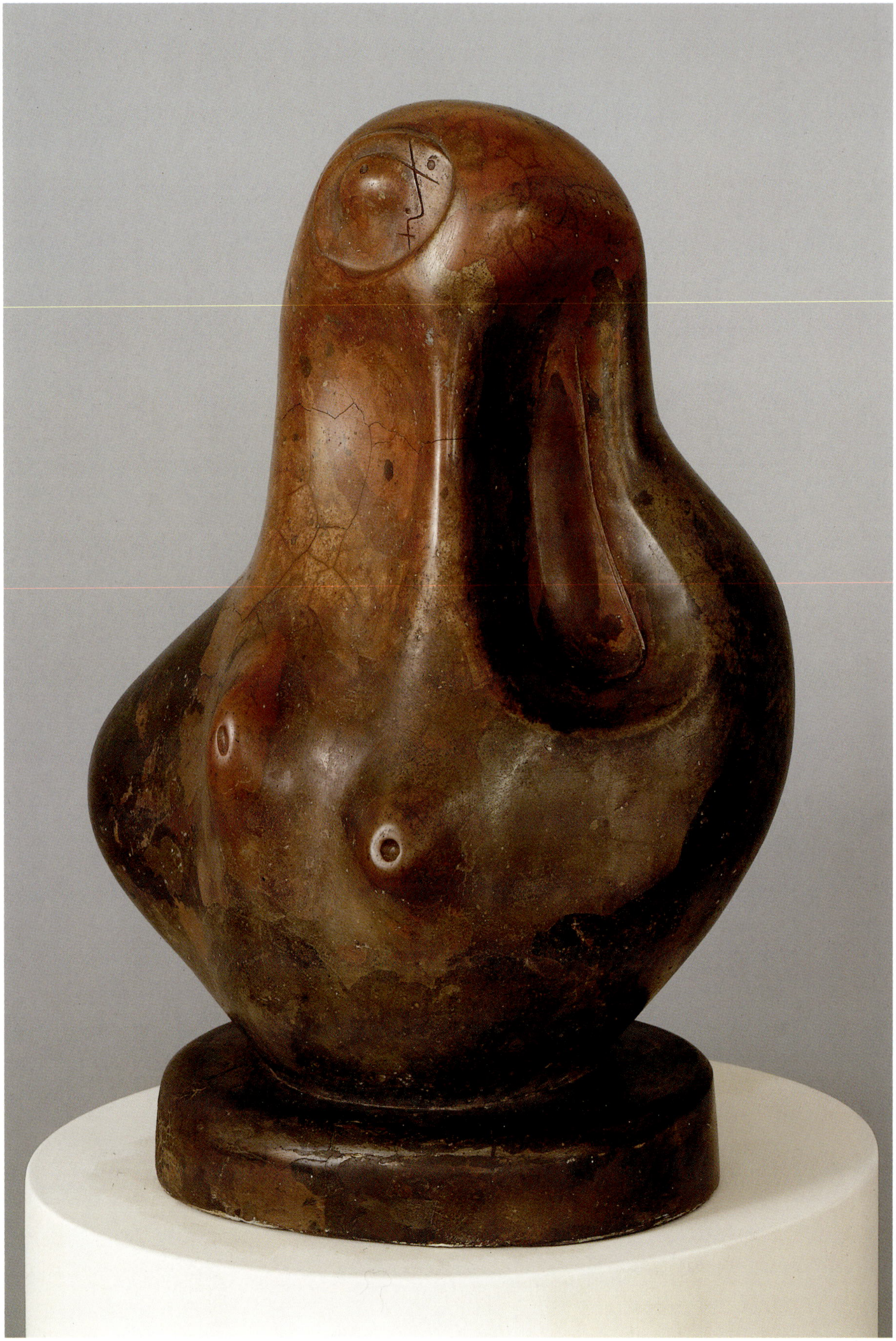

88.
Study of Seated Nude
1935
Pencil, pen and ink,
charcoal (washed), wash
568 x 387mm
Signed and dated in pen
and ink lower right:
'Moore / 35'
Robert and Lisa Sainsbury
Collection, University of
East Anglia, UEA 88
AG 35.50, HMF 1142

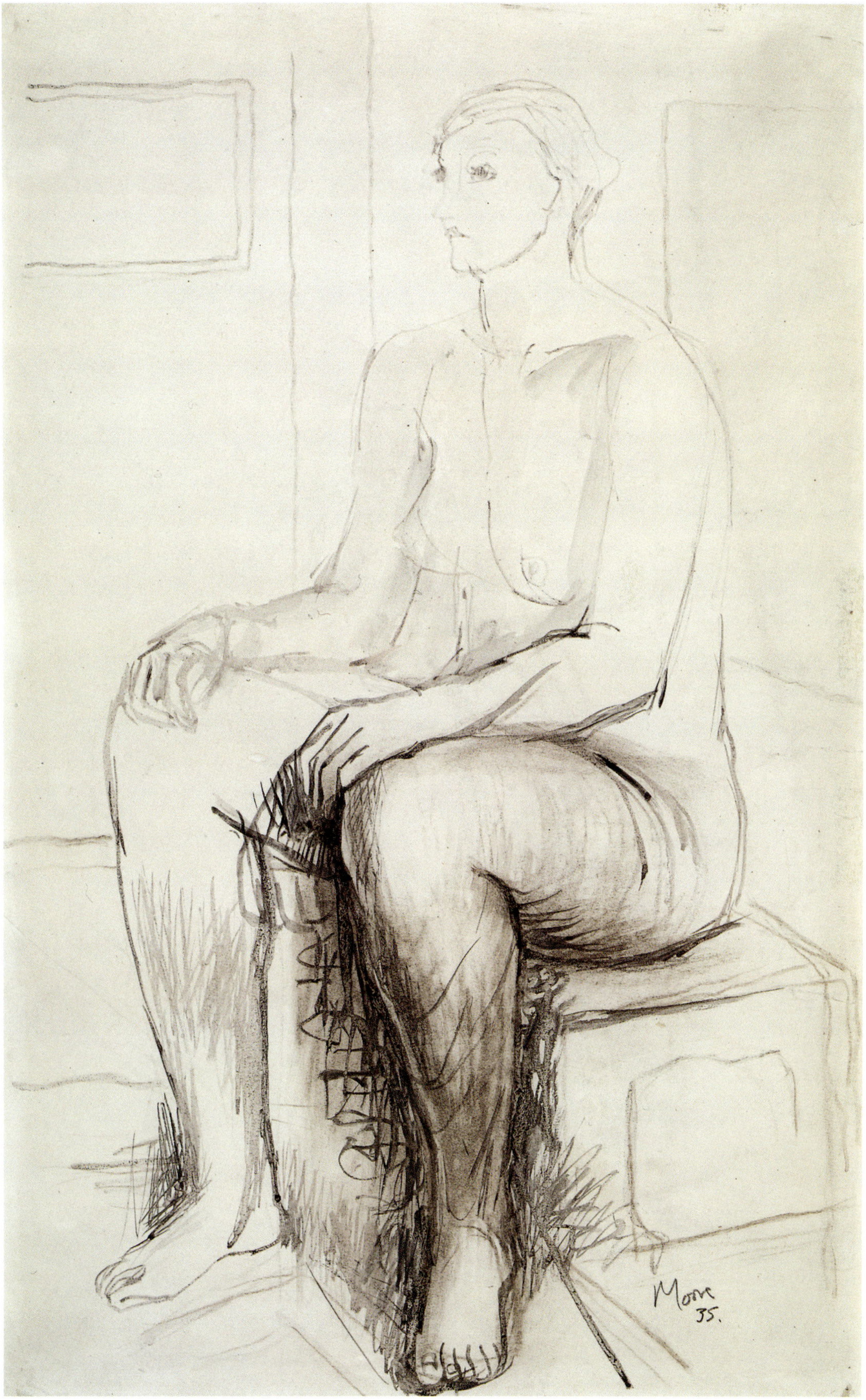

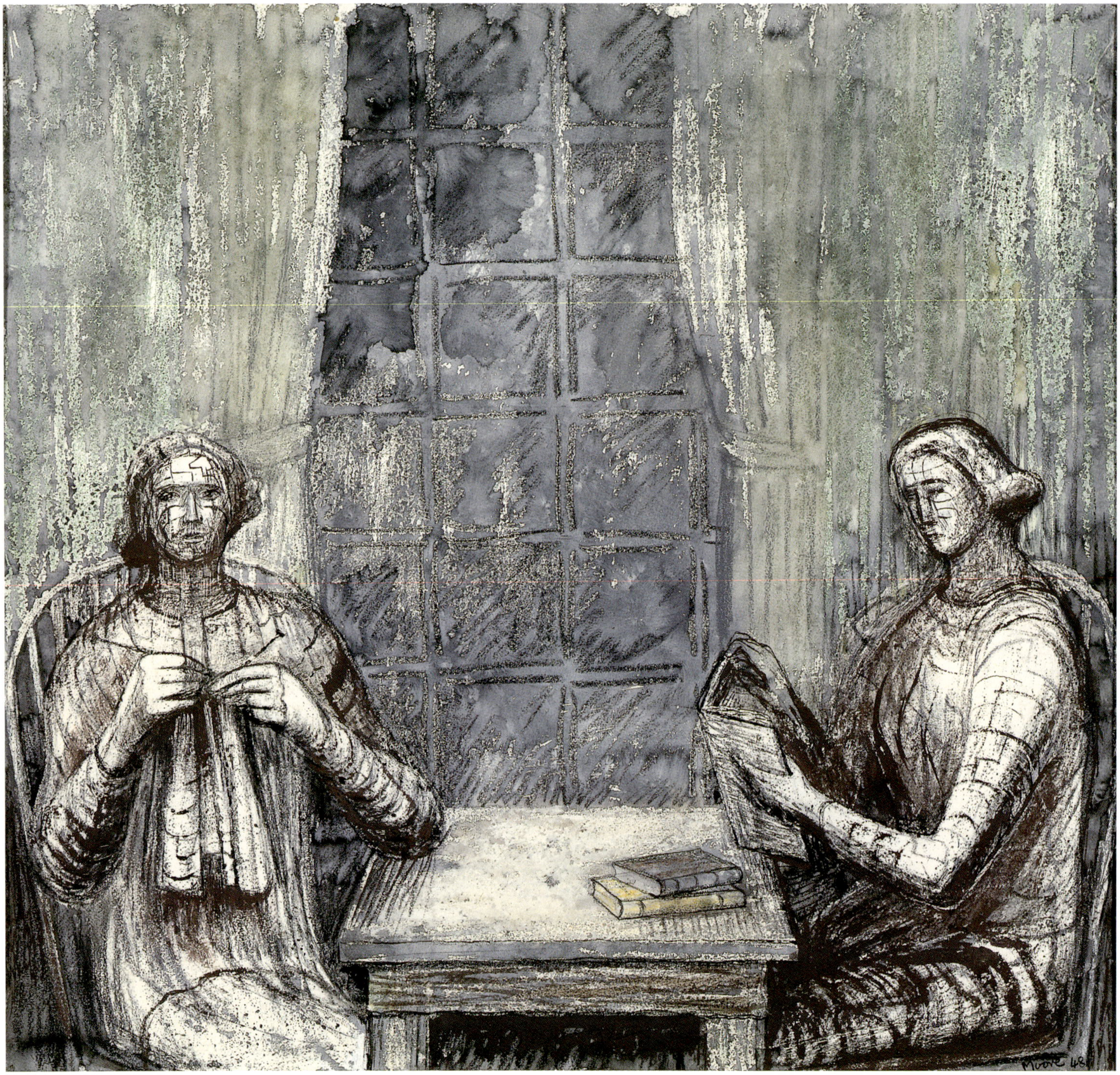

89.
Two Women in an Interior/Two Women Seated at a Table 1948
Pencil, wax crayon, coloured crayon, watercolour wash, pen and ink, brush and ink
520 x 570mm

Signed and dated in pen and ink lower right: 'Moore / 48'
Robert and Lisa Sainsbury Collection, University of East Anglia, UEA 99
AG 48.28, HMF 2499

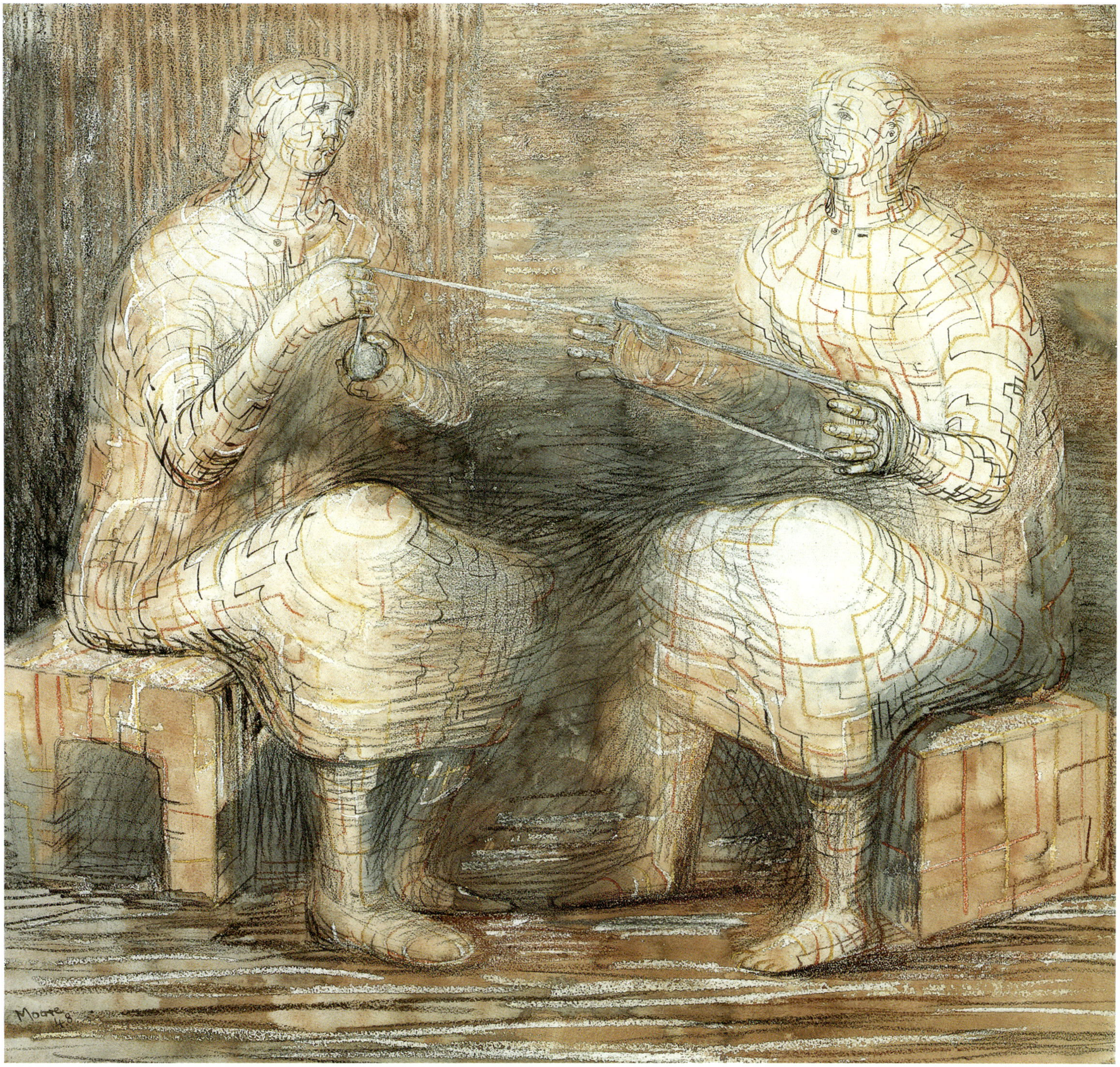

90.

Women Winding Wool

1948

Pencil, wax crayon, coloured crayon, rubbed charcoal, watercolour wash, pen and ink

545 x 560mm

Signed and dated in pen and ink lower left: 'Moore / 48'

Arts Council Collection, Hayward Gallery, London, AC 24

AG 48.25, HMF 2497

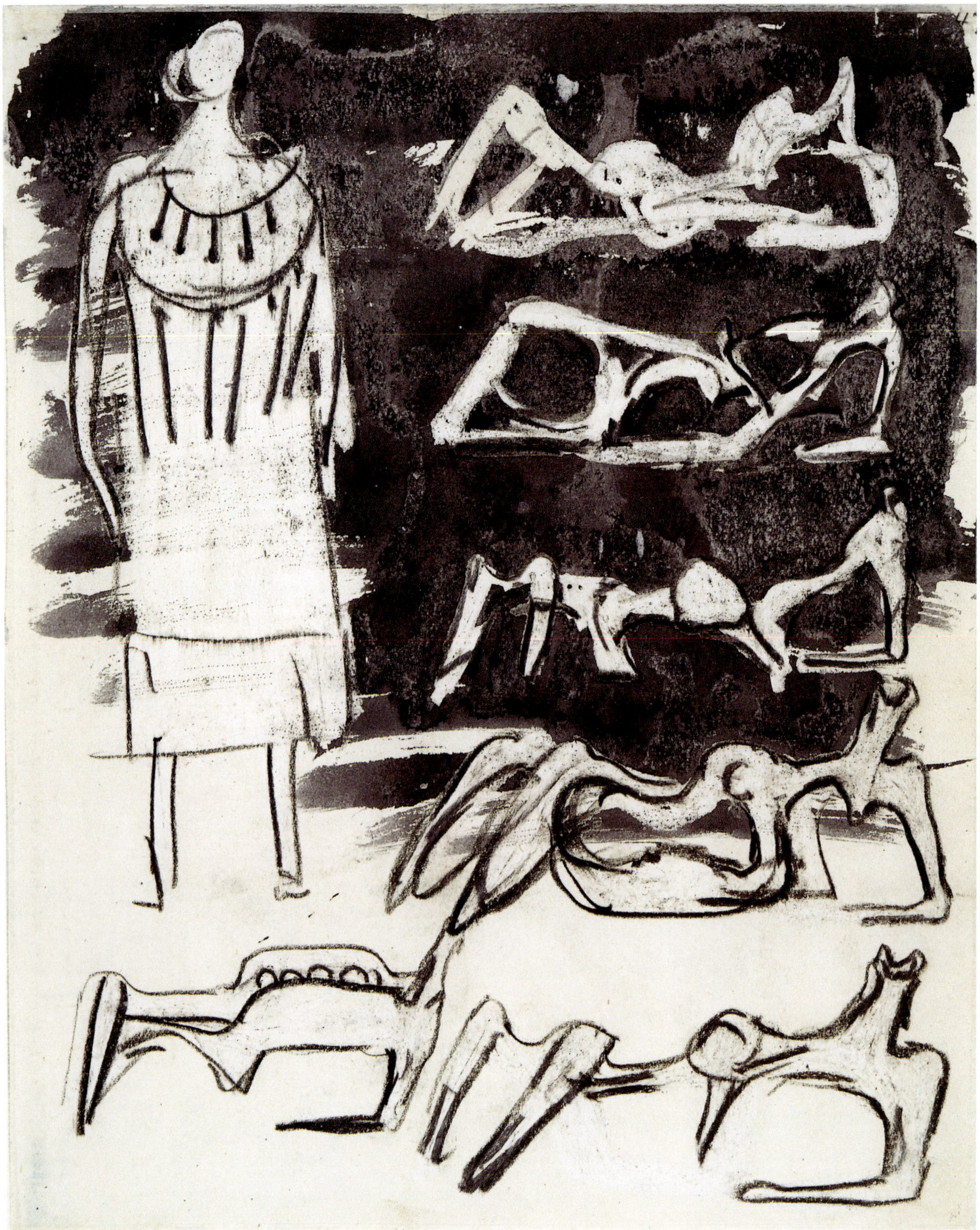

91.
Standing Figure and Six Reclining Figures (left)
*c.*1950–51 (recto, p. 47)
Pencil, wax crayon, coloured crayon, watercolour wash

Two Figures in a Landscape (right)
*c.*1950–51 (verso, p. 48)
Pencil, wax crayon, coloured crayon, watercolour wash, gouache
Signed in pencil lower centre: 'Henry Moore / 51'
Inscribed in pencil lower left: 'For my godson David / Christmas 1951'

Possibly from Sketchbook 1950–51
290 x 235mm
David Sainsbury
AG 50-51.71, HMF 2646

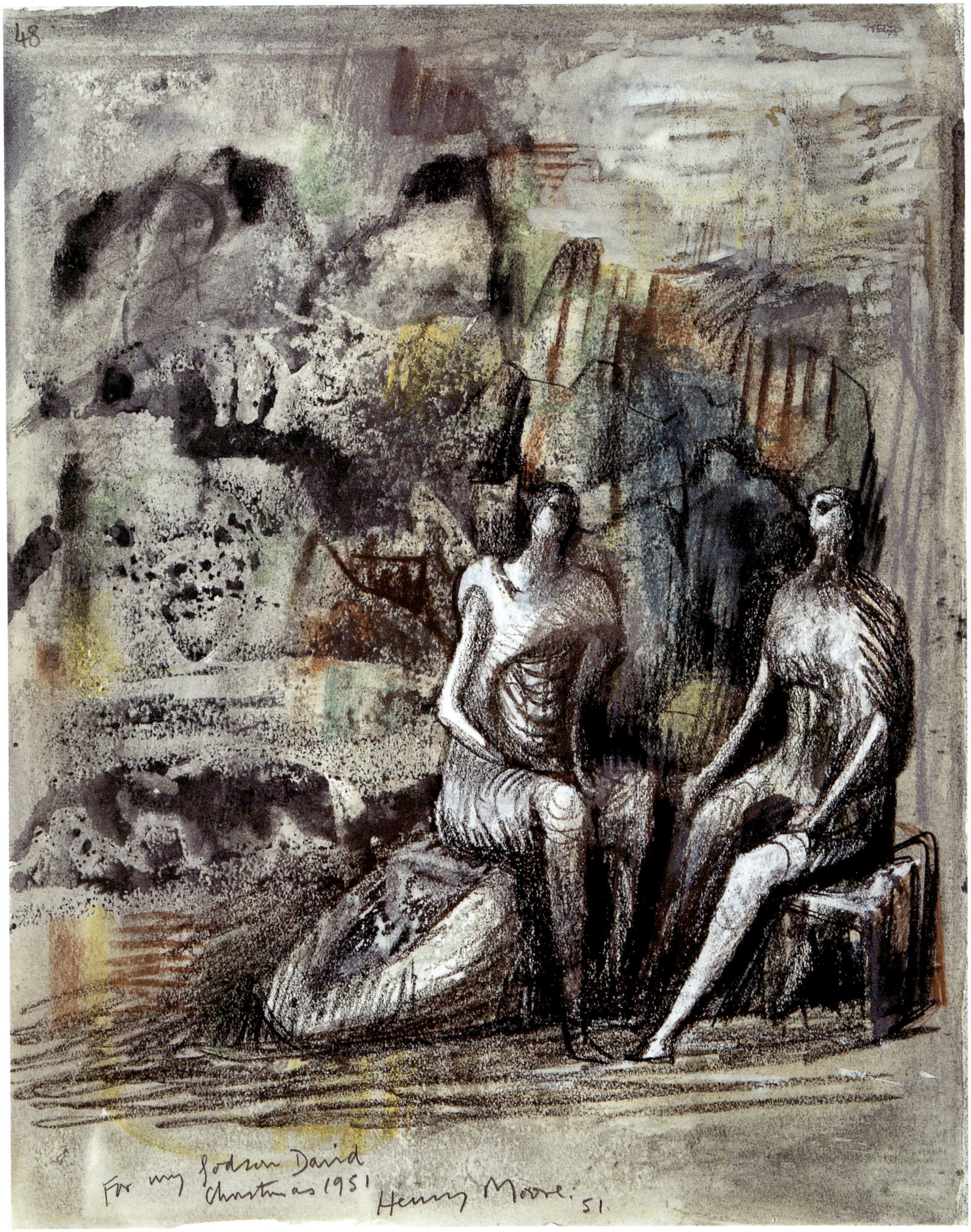
48
For my Godson David
Christmas 1951
Henry Moore. 51.

92.
Warrior with Shield
1953–4
(Photographed in the studio at Hoglands)
Painted plaster on wire support (shield detached)
h.1550mm
The Henry Moore Foundation: gift of the artist 1977
LH 360

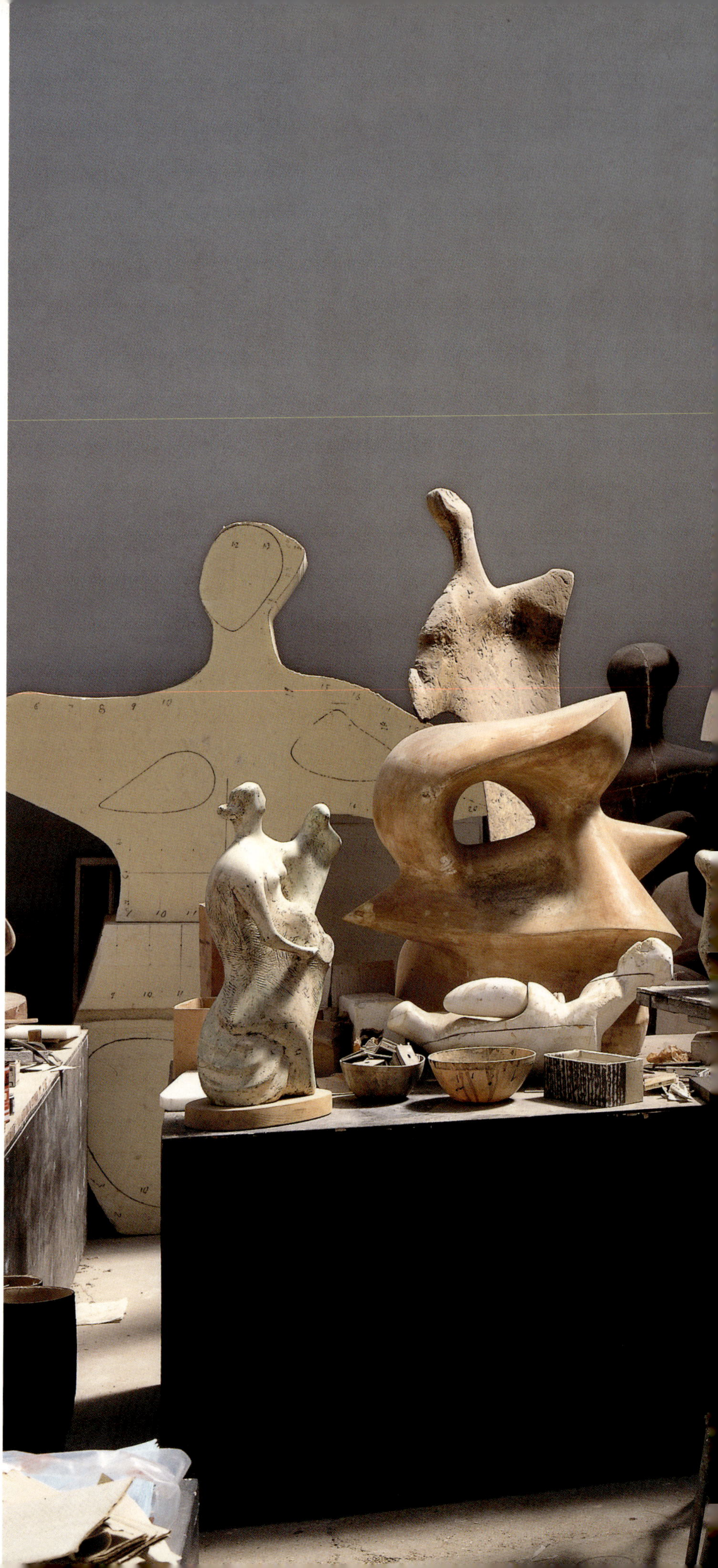

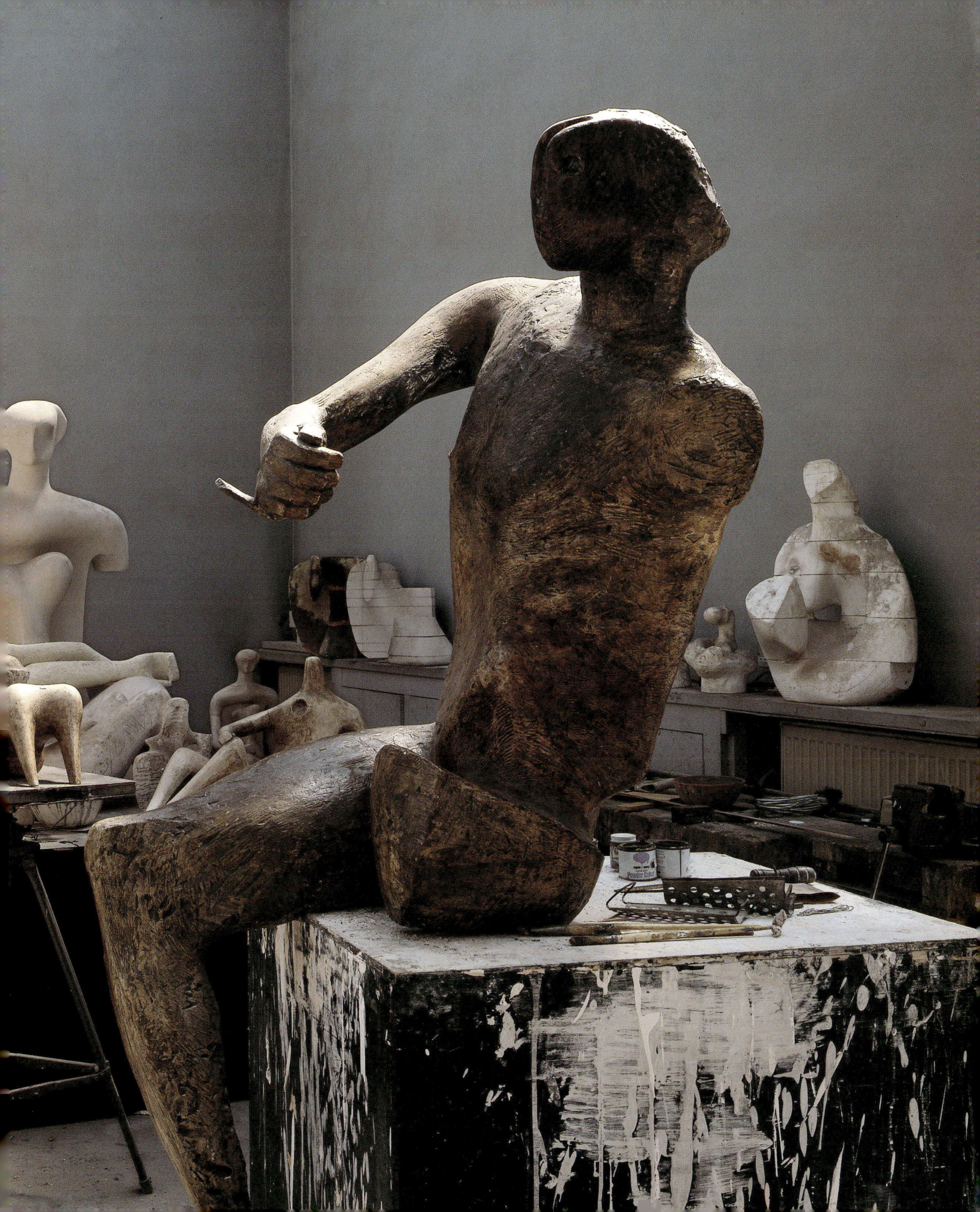

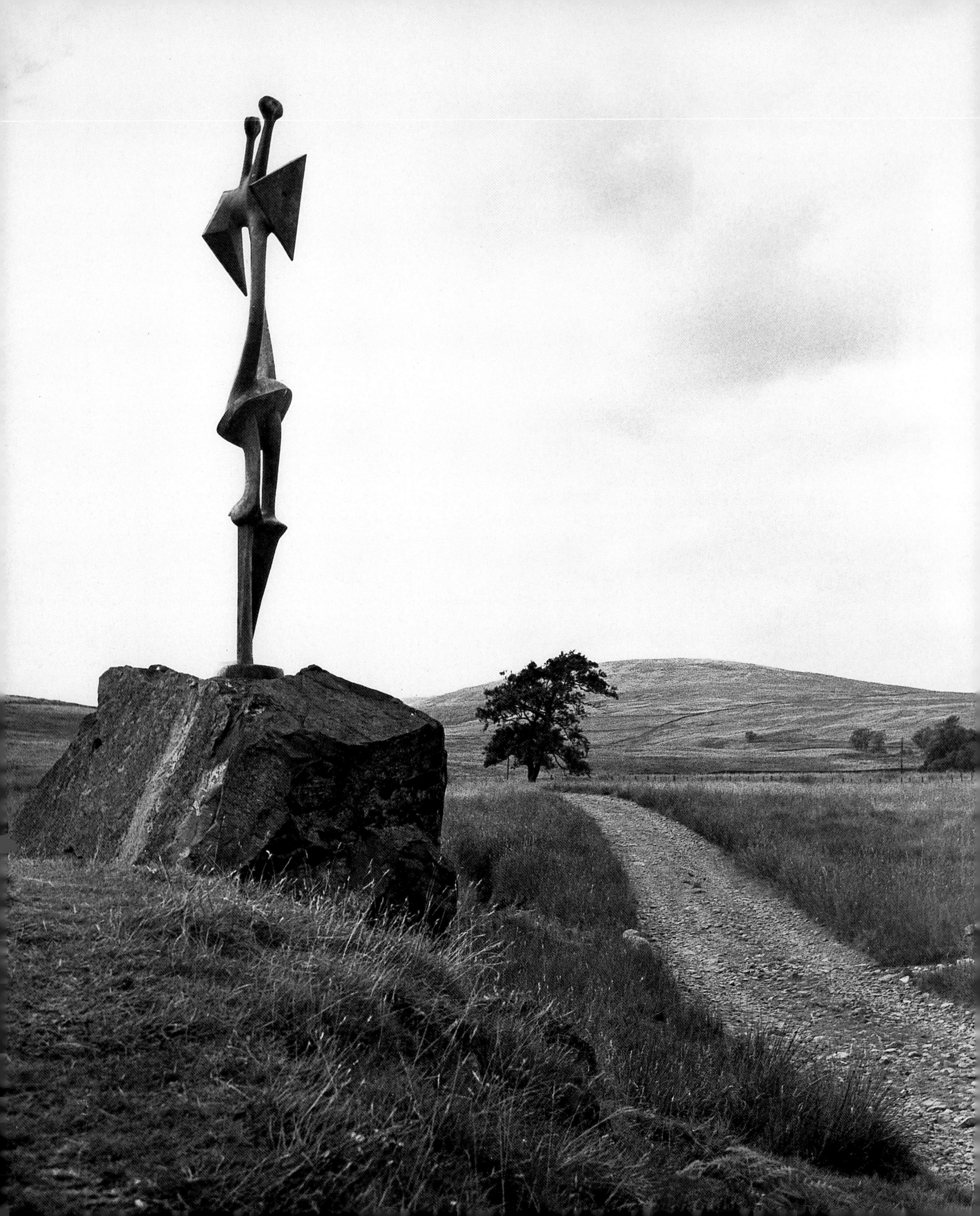

STANDING FIGURES are the exception in Moore's sculpture. There are one or two to be found at the outset of his career, including one (*Standing Woman*, fig. 51) that is clearly of the British Museum tendency filtered through Gaudier-Brzeska. Another, in stone, of 1924 (cat. 93) seems to be an (unfinished?) experiment related very closely to a finished sculpture of two years later (*Standing Girl*, 1926, stone, LH 34). Both are realist in comparison with some of his more private works of the time and one can't help wondering if they were produced at the college, where Moore tended to suppress his more extreme experiments. Cat. 93 is, I think, particularly revealing as the more undeveloped of the two. At this stage in his career, where his commitment to carving did not have quite the solid foundation of technique that time alone could bring, several of his works in their extreme blockishness suggest more than just 'truth to material': there is a hint of anxiety, a worry about actually breaking the stone through inexperienced wielding of the chisel, and this upright sculpture shares that quality. His inherent preference for the solid, the horizontal and the inert, and his instinctive antipathy towards the rendering of movement in stone combined to make a standing figure difficult on several levels for him. Even in his many beautiful life drawings (see cats 94 and 95) his tendency was always to emphasize solidity, inevitably in the broadening of the forms, but also very often in his models' stance – feet well apart, very solid and grounded. His poses tend to deny the likelihood of imminent movement. Cat. 93 is broad, solid and columnar, but the sense of stability is slightly undermined by Moore's decision to bend the right leg forward – a very Grecian note that the more finished version dispenses with. Did its suggestion of imminent movement put him off?

Fig. 51 (below)
Standing Woman, 1923 (LH 5), walnut wood; Manchester City Galleries (Rutherston Loan Collection).

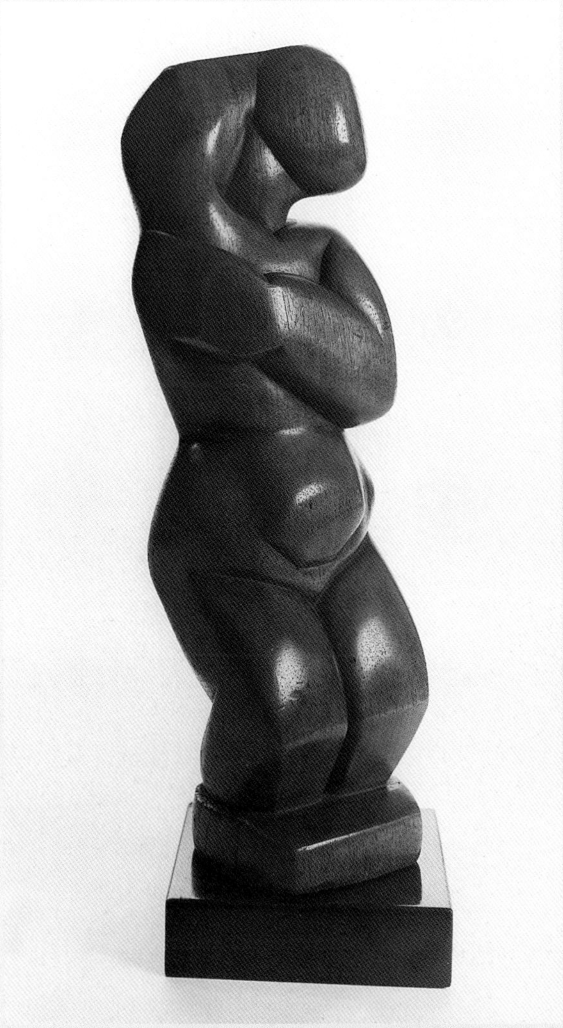

The sheer number of full-length life drawings that exist, no doubt partly a by-product of his fifteen years of teaching, might lead one to expect more attempts at the 'pure' standing figure in sculptural form (as distinct from the more organic 'upright forms') to match all the reclining and sitting figures. In this respect, it is tempting to see significance in the fact that in one of Moore's most famous and odd drawings, the *Crowd Looking at a Tied-Up Object* of 1942 (fig. 52), the hidden object looks very much as if it is a standing figure – did he feel that his audience somehow expected this of him? But even where the drawings show him making the attempt (for instance, there are several family group drawings that feature the man standing), Moore's impulse towards the horizontal usually wins the day.

Except once: the *Three Standing Figures* in Battersea Park (fig. 53), the plaster maquette for which is displayed here (cat. 97; see also fig. 56, p. 170). The installation of this sculpture as part of an open-air sculpture exhibition took place in May 1948, something of an *annus mirabilis* for Moore (he represented Britain at the Venice Biennale the same year). The sculpture was then acquired by the Contemporary Art Society and given to the London County Council for permanent display in the park. Moore always described this sculpture as a culmination of the lessons learned from the shelter drawings experience, and certainly prototypes for the figures can be found there (see cat. 52). The figures are draped, classically, reflecting the mythic quality that Moore had increasingly

Fig. 50 (left)
Standing Figure, 1950 (LH 290), bronze; Glenkiln, Keswick Estate, Dumfries.

The Human Form – Standing Figures

found in his shelter scenes, and their sky scanning suggests something of the anxiety of wartime. They make up a striking, watchful group, and (predictably, by this date) most of the hoop-la that surrounded the opening of the exhibition was focused on them. The usual extremes prevailed. To Patrick Heron, the artist, in his capacity as art critic for the *New Statesman*, the sculpture was 'the greatest work in sculpture or painting to be accomplished in the present century';[41] Epstein, admittedly very bitter about Moore's failure to rally round in support when there was a threat to remove his sculptures altogether from the British Medical Association in 1935, dismissed the whole affair: 'The whole show was really got up to boost Moore and his absurd work.'[42] The sculpture today certainly retains its rather disturbing, listening stillness, but its stylized handling of drapery and its curious mixture of schematic incised features make it look uncomfortably self-conscious – for the first time, one feels that Moore was trying too hard. He certainly never attempted anything similar again. The maquette is truer to the source of inspiration in the shelter figures.

However, the upright form did not disappear from his oeuvre altogether. In fact, in the *Standing Figure: Knife Edge* (fig. 41, p. 89) Moore produced one of his most famous pieces. But the genesis of his other 'standing' figures lay not in his life drawings but in his favourite organic forms. In bones, leaves, trees and stones Moore found an alternative key to the upright figure. As he was a lifelong enthusiast for Stonehenge, it is perhaps not surprising that many of his drawn upright forms are monolithic in style (fig. 54, *Two Upright Forms*). The remarkable *Standing Figure* of 1950 (figs 50, 55), on the other hand, surely derives its taut, wiry frame from bones or possibly thorny twigs, and still looks challenging today – a grand mystery, and a startling reminder that Moore, household name and ultimately establishment figure, never stopped taking risks.

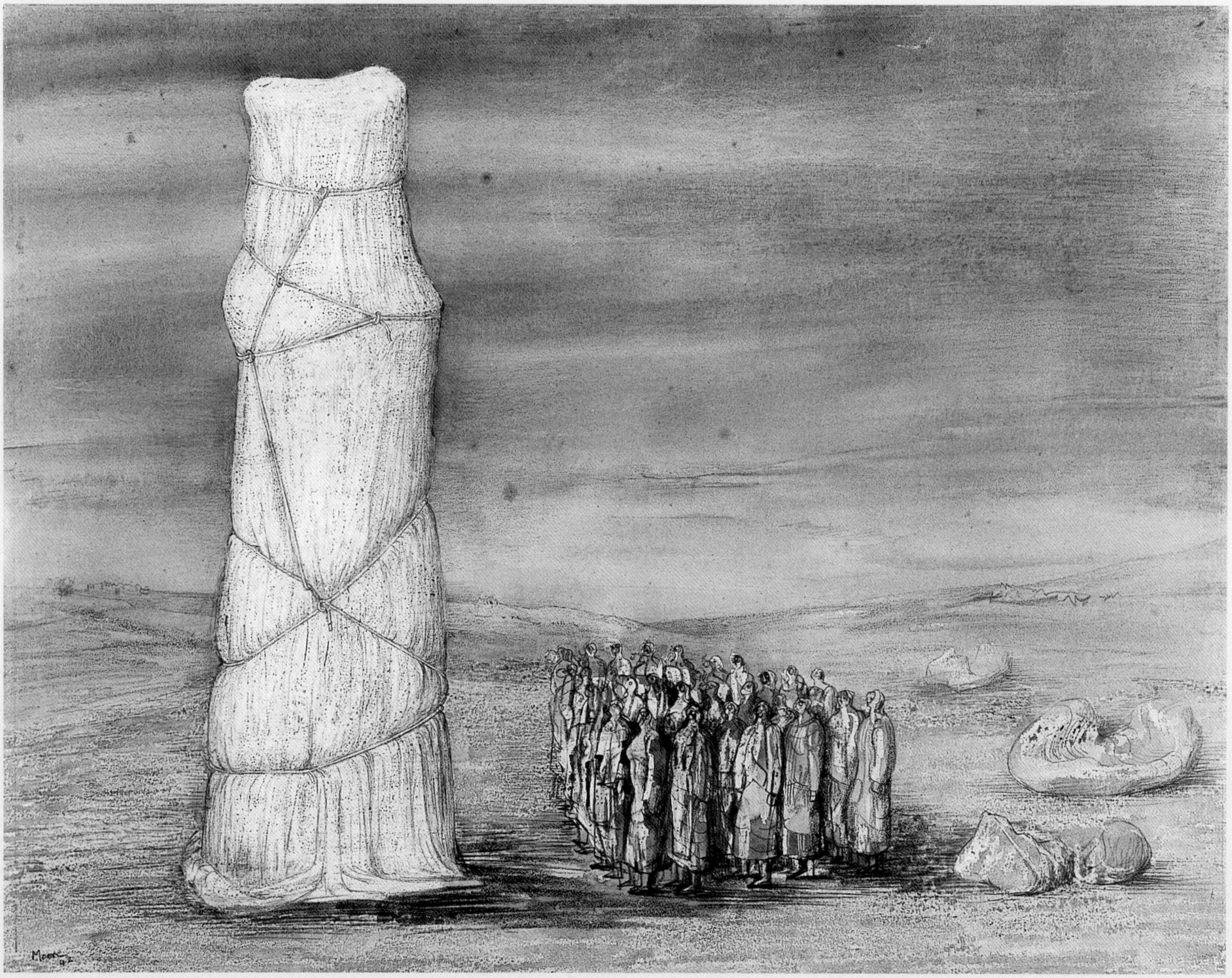

Fig. 53 (right)
Three Standing Figures, 1947–8 (LH 268), Darley Dale stone; Battersea Park, London (gift of the Contemporary Art Society)

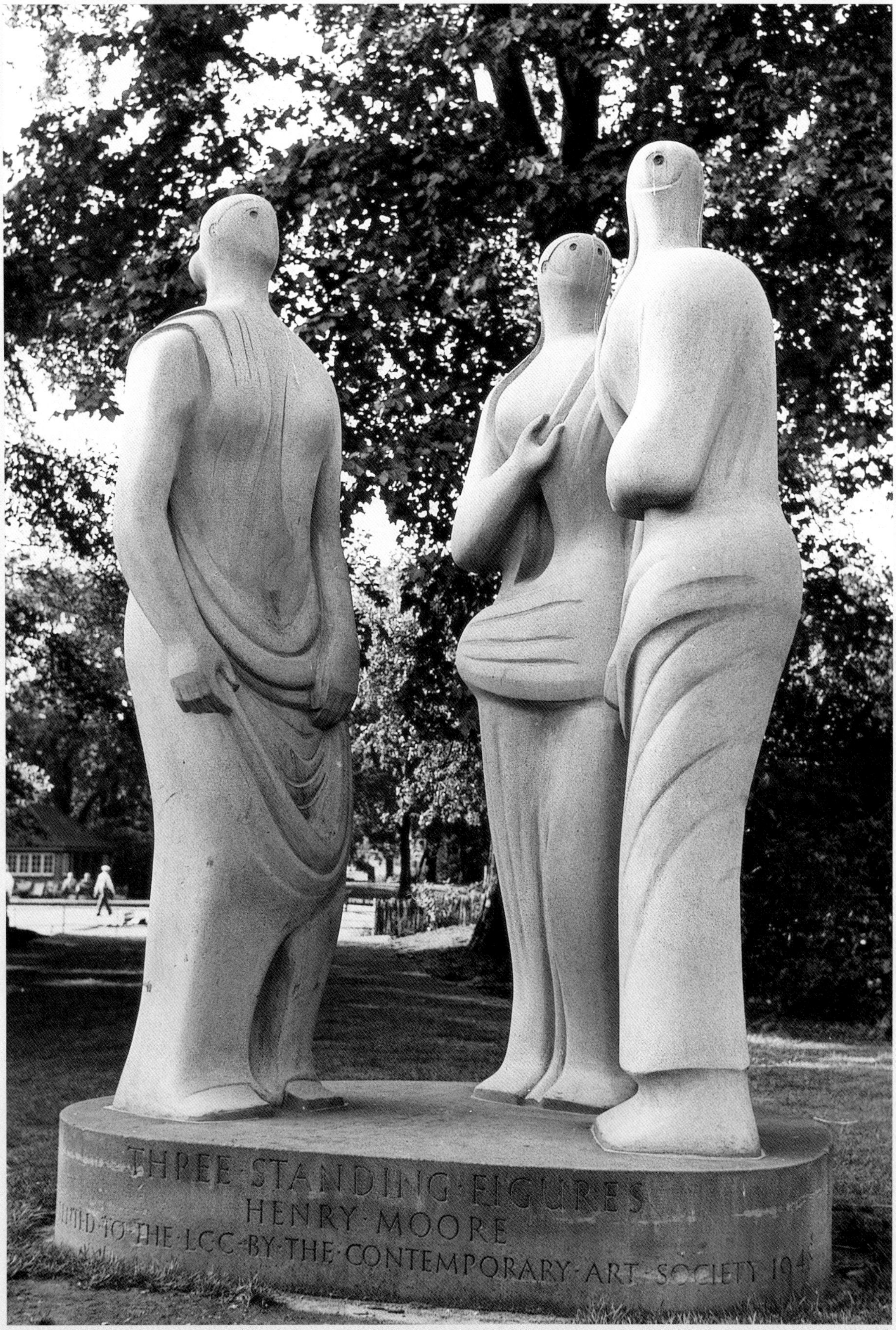

Fig. 52 (left)
Crowd Looking at a Tied-Up Object, 1942 (AG 42.174, HMF 2064), pencil, wax crayon, charcoal (rubbed), watercolour wash, pen and ink; The British Museum: from the estate of Lord Clark.

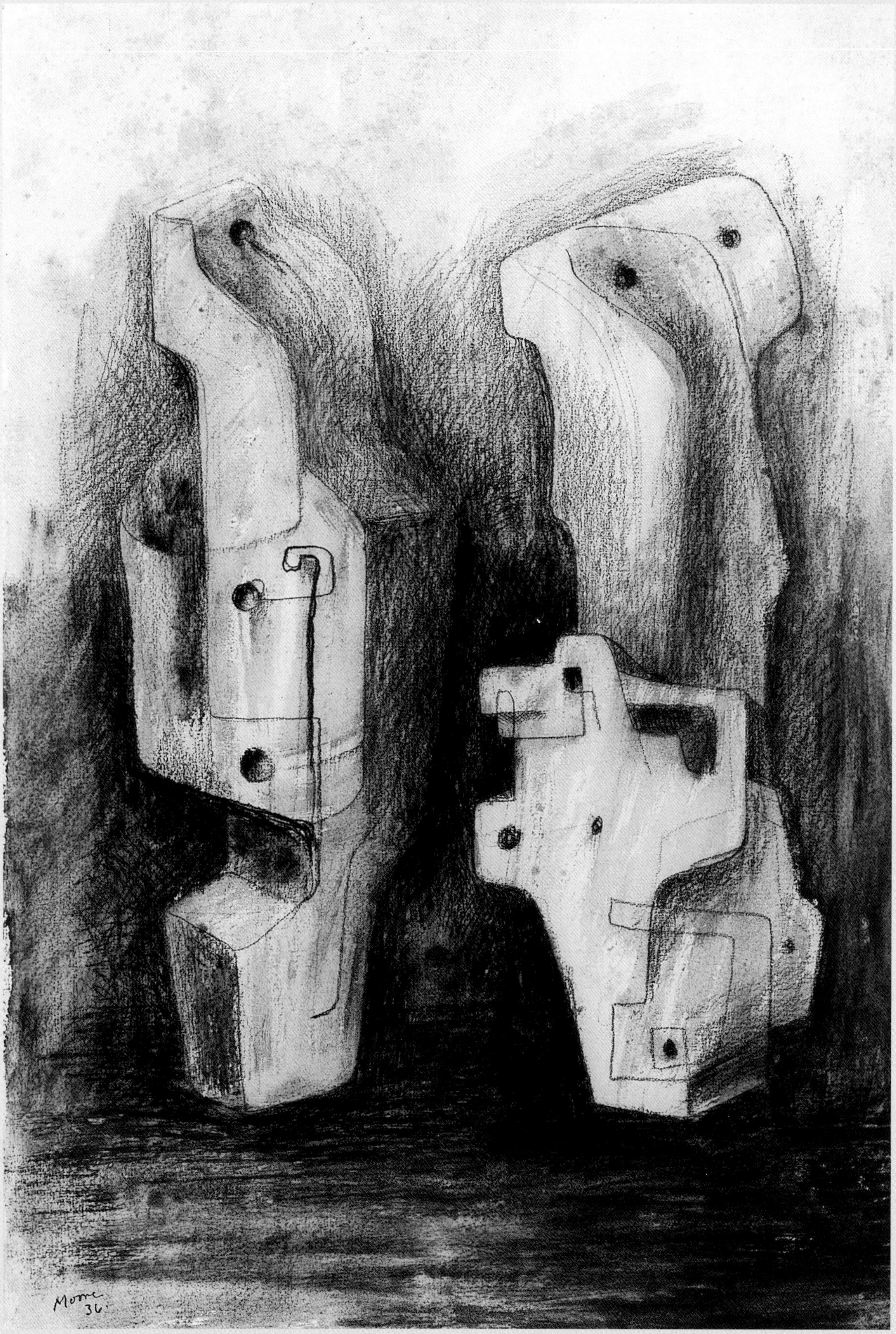

Fig. 54 (left)
Two Upright Forms, 1936 (AG 36.17, HMF 1253), pencil, chalk, wash, pen and ink, wash on cream heavyweight wove; The Henry Moore Foundation: purchased 1998.

Fig. 55 (right)
Another view of *Standing Figure*, 1950 (see fig. 50, p.160).

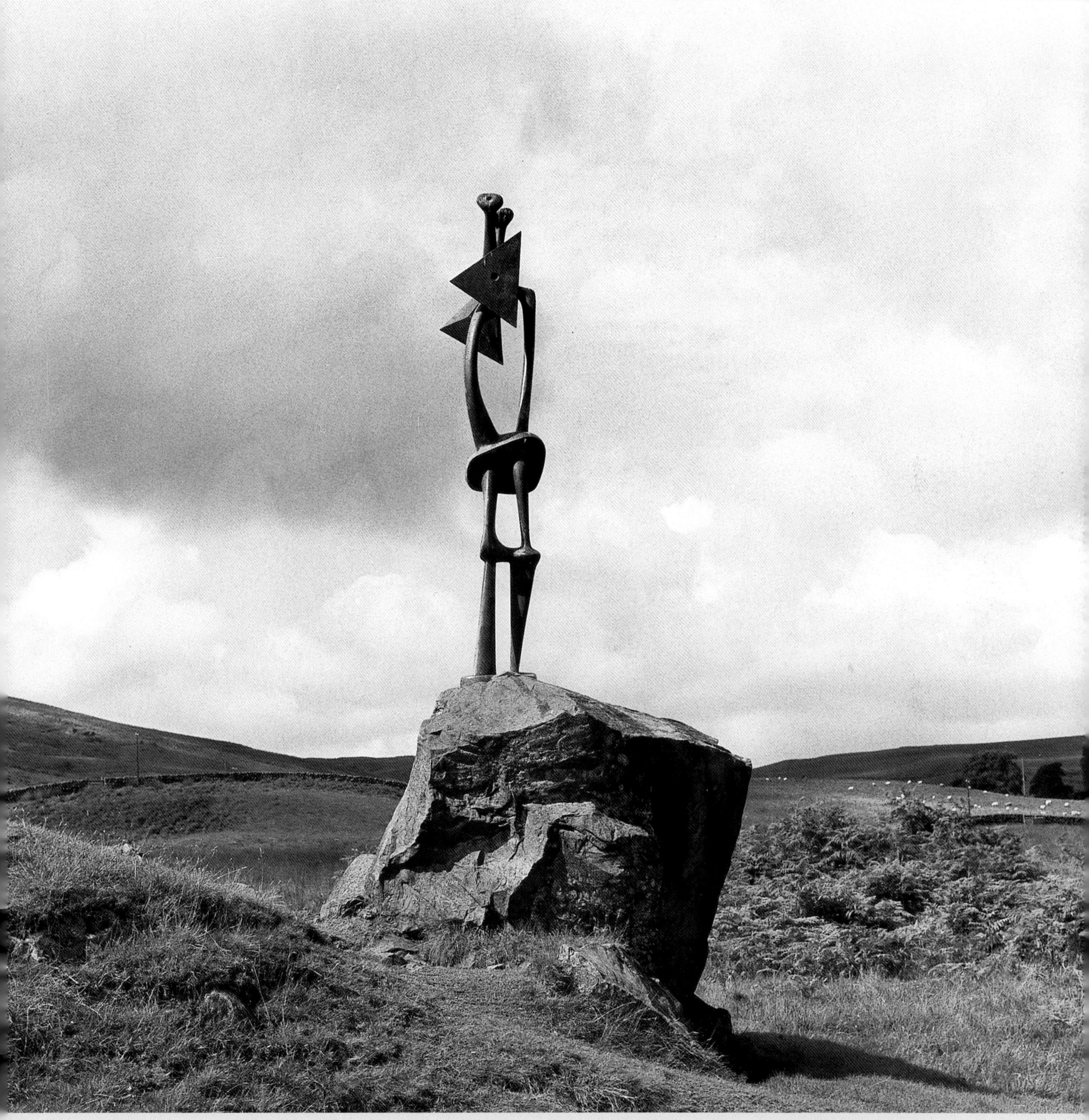

93.

Standing Woman 1924

Portland stone

565 x 137 x 116mm

Private Collection

LH 16

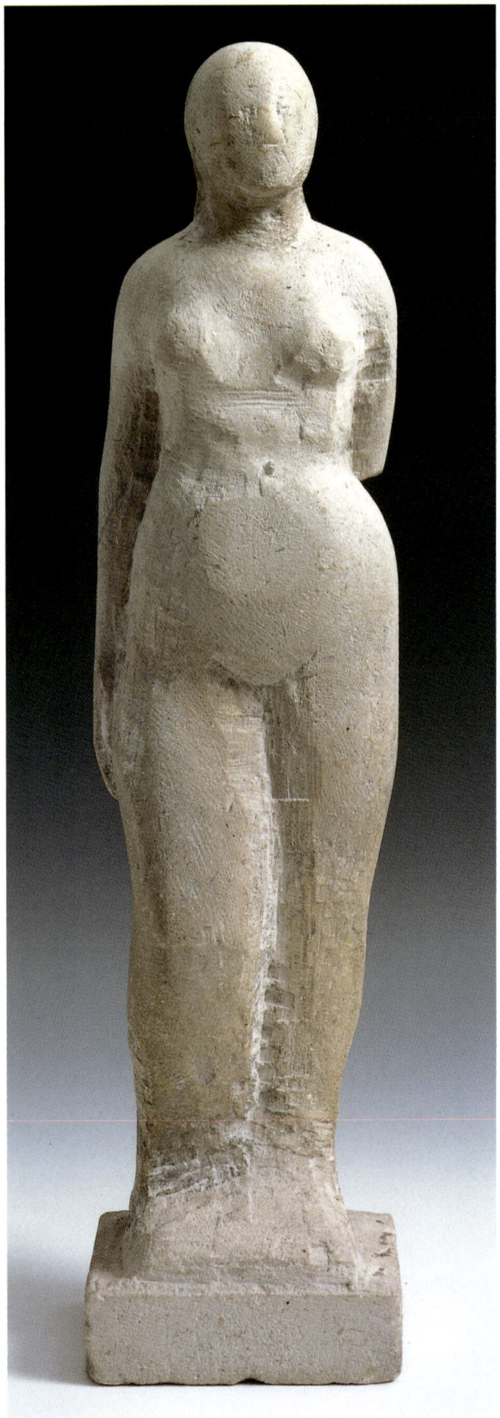

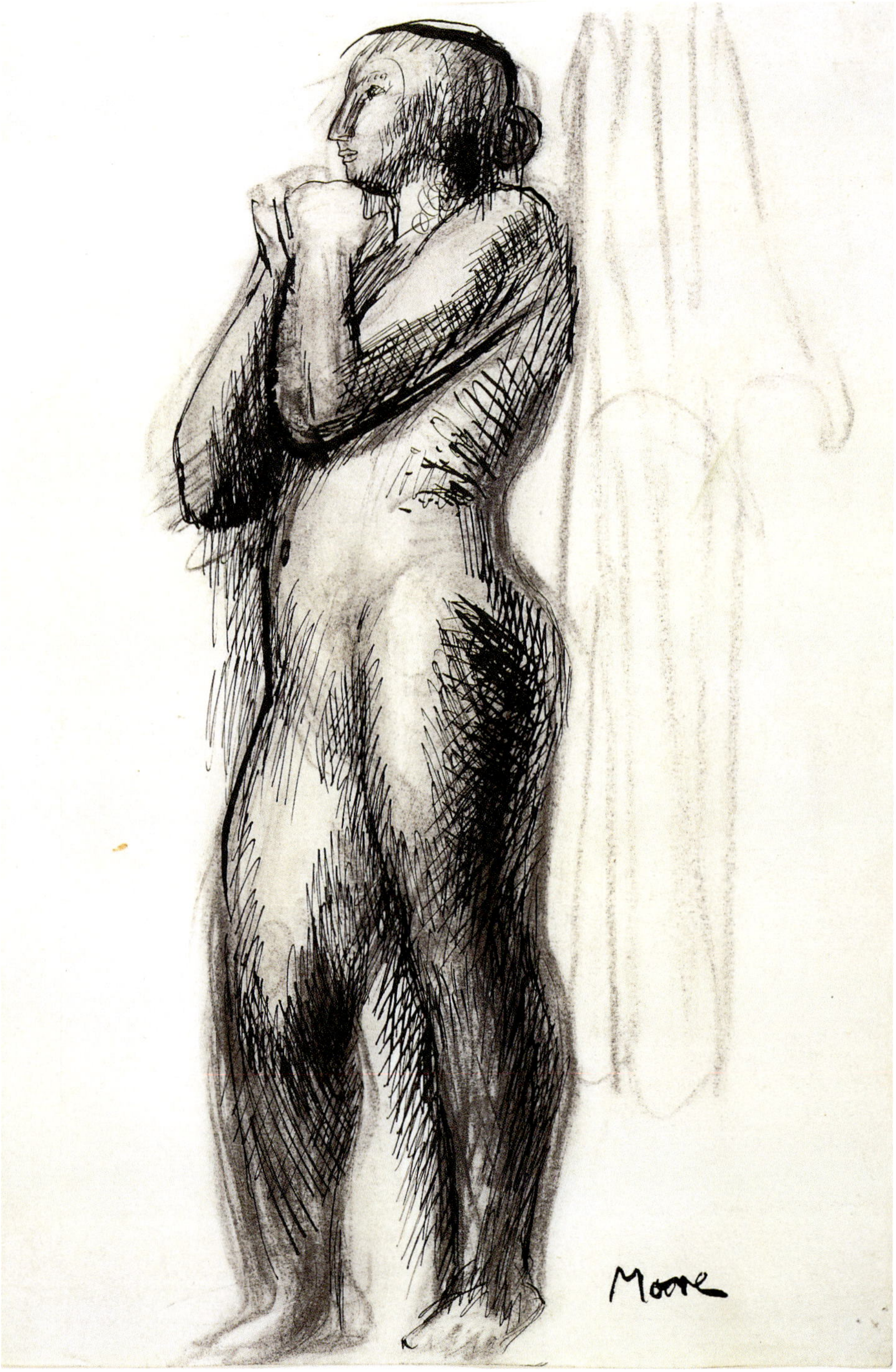

94.
Standing Nude *c.* 1924
Pen and ink, chalk
323 x 214mm
Signed in pen and ink
lower right: 'Moore'
The Henry Moore
Foundation: gift of
the artist 1977
AG 24.24, HMF 234

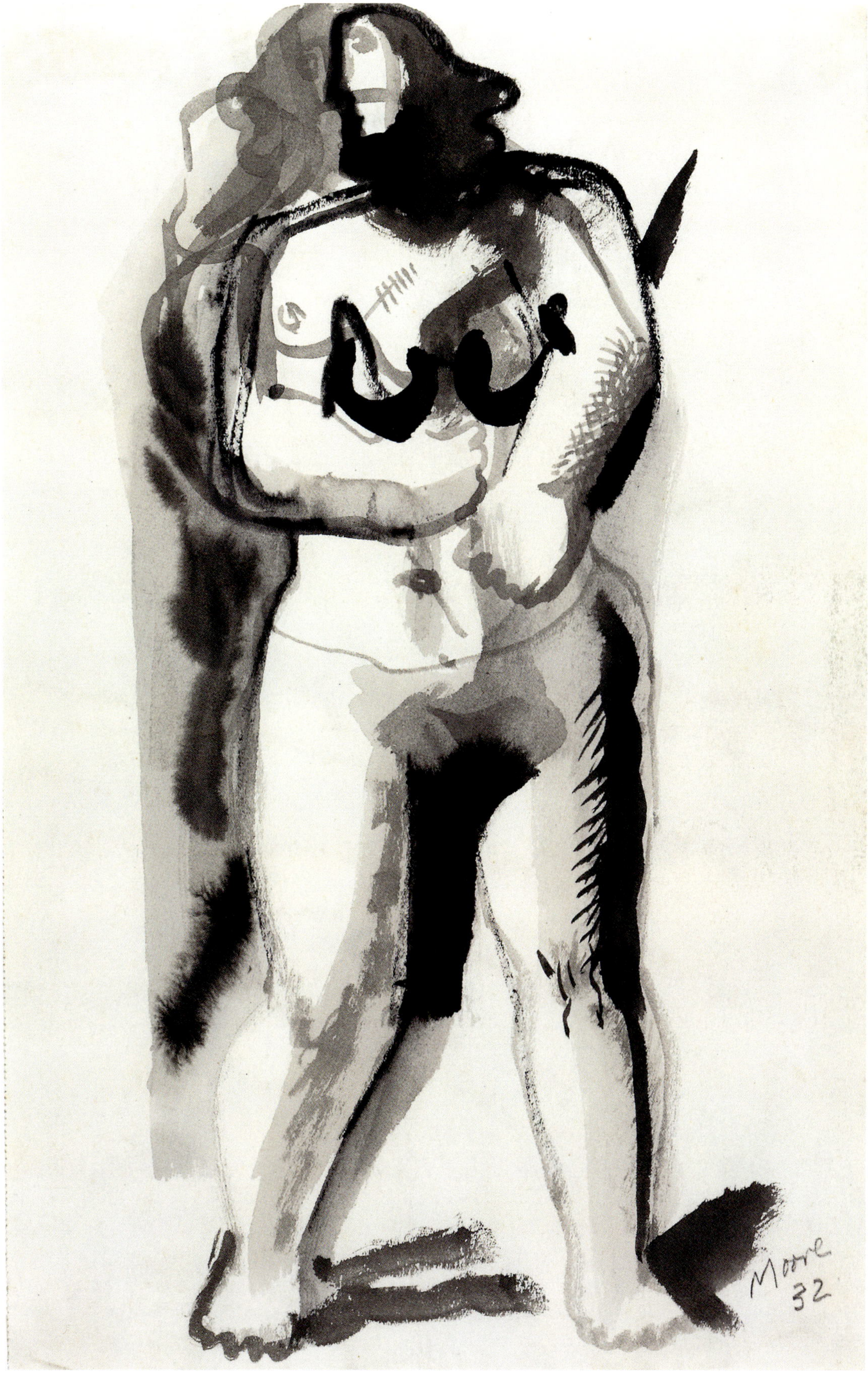

95.
Standing Nude 1932
Charcoal, brush
and ink, wash
365 x 238mm
Signed and dated
in pencil (added later)
lower right: 'Moore / 32'
The Henry Moore
Foundation:
purchased 1980
AG 32.33, HMF 919

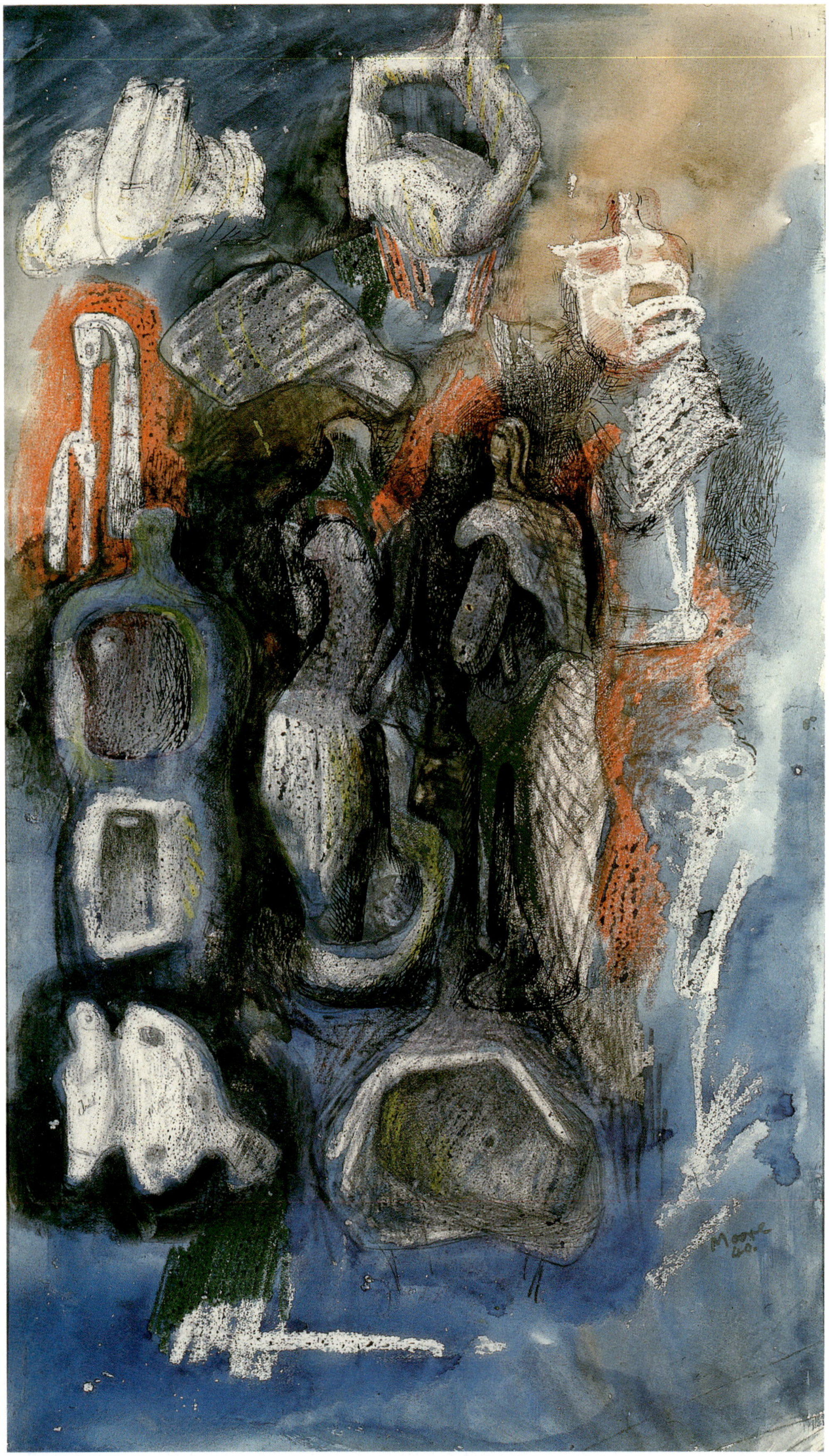

96.
Standing Figures: Studies for Sculpture
1940
Pencil, wax crayon, chalk, watercolour, pen and ink
432 x 254mm
Signed and dated in pen and ink lower right: 'Moore / 40'
Robert and Lisa Sainsbury Collection, University of East Anglia, UEA 92
AG 39-40.38, HMF 1490

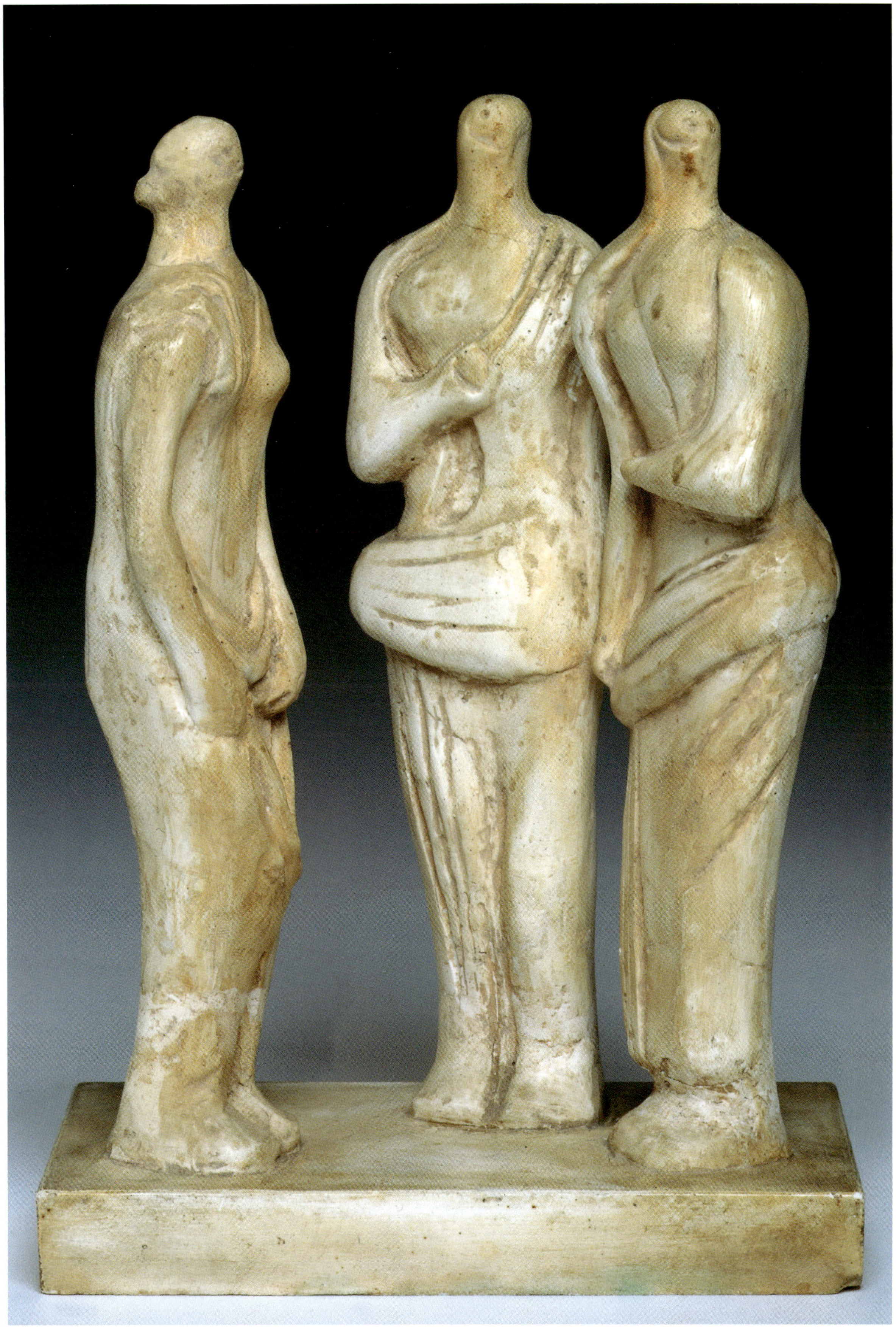

97.
Maquette for Three Standing Figures 1945
Plaster
230 x 116 x 102mm
Private Collection, Switzerland
LH 258

Fig. 56
View of maquettes
including one for
Three Standing Figures.

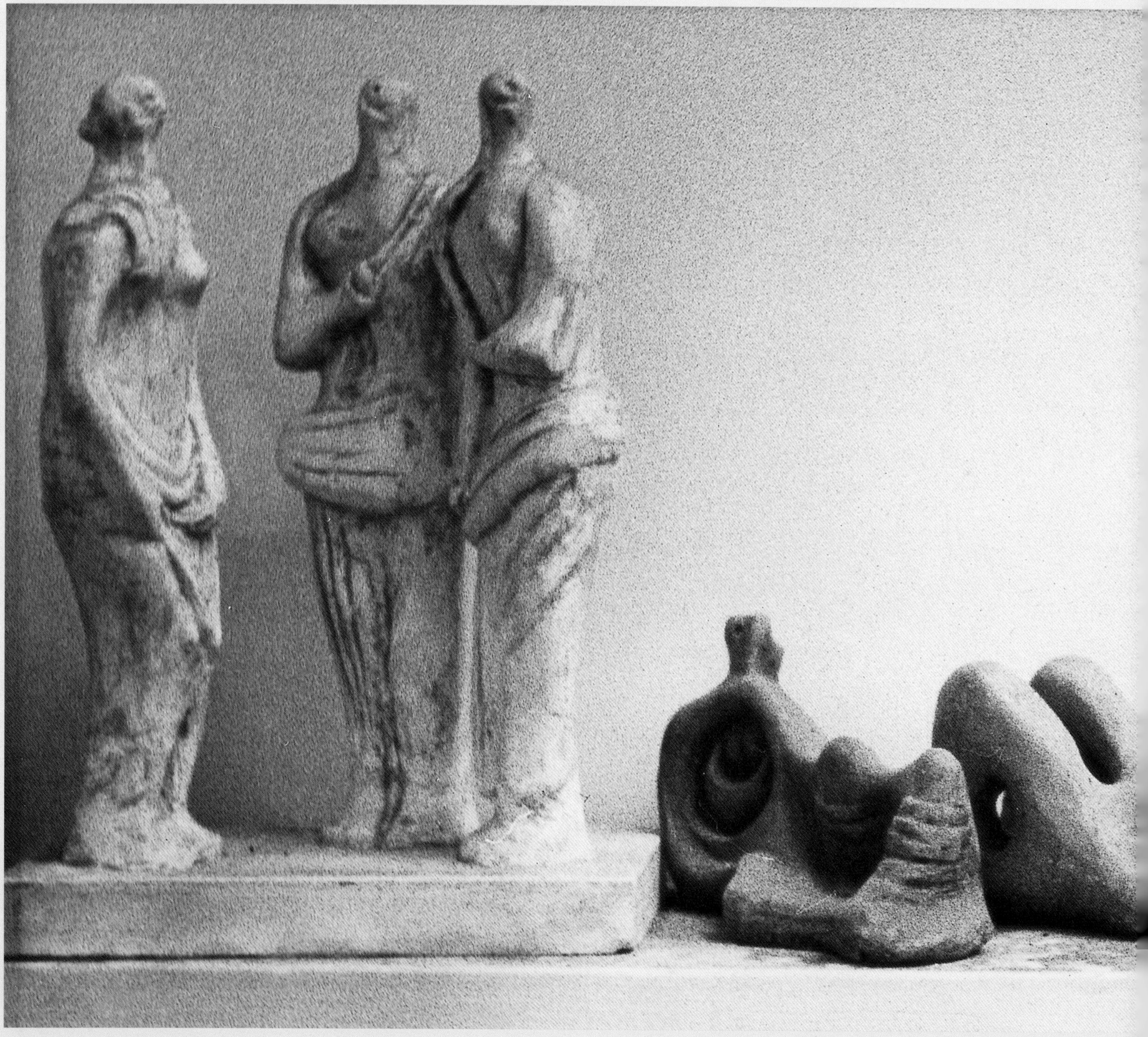

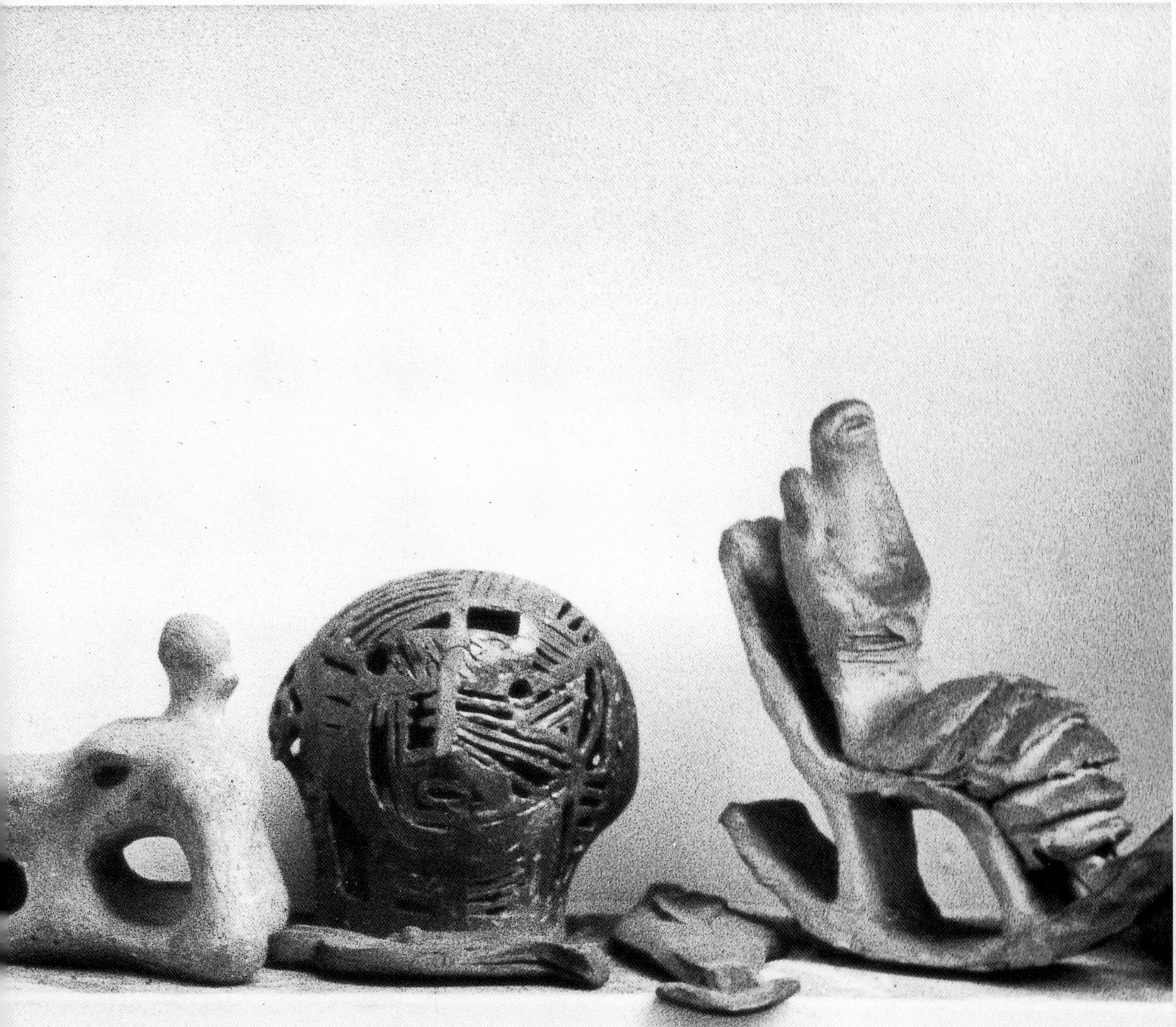

Notes

Henry Moore and the Sainsbury Family (pp. 9–23)

1. Steven Hooper, Director of The Sainsbury Research Unit for the Arts of Africa & the Americas.
2. Hooper 1997, p.xxxvi.
3. Conversation with Steven Hooper 26.4.1996.
4. Approximately £1,950 in today's money.
5. Garrould 1994–2003.
6. Bowness and Sylvester 1986, 1990.
7. Hooper 1997, p. xxx.
8. Ibid., p. xxxii.
9. Ibid., p. xxxii.
10. Ibid., p. xlii.
11. Ibid., p. xliv.
12. Ibid., p. xliv.
13. Ibid., p. lii.
14. Ibid., p. lii.
15. Ibid., p. 99.
16. Ibid., p. xlvi.

Surrealism, Space and String: Henry Moore's *Bird Basket* (pp. 25–33)

1. *Bird Basket* was exhibited at the Tate Gallery, London, in 1968; at the spectacular installation at the Forti de Belvedere, Florence, in 1972; at the Orangerie des Tuileries, Paris, in 1977; and at the Metropolitan Museum of Art, New York, in 1982.
2. Inscribed in pencil on the verso of *Ideas for Sculpture* 1932 (HMF 944), The Henry Moore Foundation: gift of the artist 1977.
3. Art Gallery of Ontario, Toronto: gift of Henry Moore 1974.
4. *Ideas for Sculpture: Transformation Drawings*, 1932 (HMF 950), private collection, UK.
5. Moore referring to the mathematical models in the Science Museum, London, in Hedgecoe 1968, p. 105.
6. See *Ideas for Sculpture* (HMF 845) and *Ideas for Sculpture* (HMF 846), both The Henry Moore Foundation: gift of the artist 1977.
7. See *Four Figures in a Setting*, 1937 (HMF 1307), Peggy Guggenheim Collection, Venice.
8. See *Fundamental Shapes*, *c*.1935 (HMF 1216), and *Ideas for Sculpture*, *c*.1937 (HMF 1336), both pages from Sketchbook B, *c*.1935, The Henry Moore Foundation: gift of the artist 1977.
9. Outbreak of war prevented the print from being editioned.
10. The delegation also included Stephen Spender, William Hayter and Jacob Epstein; see Mitchinson 2001, p. 3.
11. Letter from Moore printed in the *Yorkshire Post,* March 1938, in Berthoud 1987, p. 146.
12. Herbert Read, 'A Nest of Gentle Artists', *Apollo*, September 1962, pp. 536–40.
13. For a vivid description of the myriad Surrealist events associated with the exhibition see Michel Remy, *Surrealism in Britain*, Ashgate, Aldershot, 1999, pp. 73–100.
14. Jean 1980, p. 364.
15. Hedgecoe 1968, p. 105.
16. Man Ray photographed mathematical stringed models on exhibition at the Institut Henri Poincare, Paris, for the Object Issue of *Cahiers d'Art*, XI, nos. 1–2, pp. 7, 9, 11–20; see Christa Lichtenstern, 'Henry Moore and Surrealism', *Burlington Magazine,* vol. CXXIII, no.944, November 1981, p. 651.
17. Martin Hammer and Christina Lodder, *Constructing Modernity: The Art and Career of Naum Gabo*, Yale University Press, New Haven and London, 2000, p. 288.
18. *Henry Moore: Wood Sculpture*, with commentary by Henry Moore and photographs by Gemma Levine, Sidgwick and Jackson, London, 1983, p. 102.
19. Ibid., p. 106.
20. Published slightly earlier as 'The Sculptor Speaks' in the *Listener*, 18 August 1937.
21. For more on this subject see Andrew Causey, 'Henry Moore and the uncanny', in Jane Beckett and Fiona Russell (eds), *Henry Moore: Critical Essays*, Ashgate, Aldershot, 2003, pp. 81–106.
22. Jean 1980, p. 364.
23. Carlton Lake, 'Henry Moore's World', *Atlantic Monthly*, Boston, January 1962, p. 42; quoted in Wilkinson 2002, p. 256.

Catalogue (pp. 35–171)

1. Moore 1981, p. 10.
2. Herbert Read, *Henry Moore: Sculptor*, Zwemmer, London, 1934.
3. Pite's comment was made towards the end of Moore's first year about one of his monthly compositions, on the theme of Night, which he had partly based on an Etruscan tomb at the British Museum (later proved a fake, so Pite was ironically not so far from the truth, in one way at least). The story is told by Roger Berthoud (2003, p. 59).
4. Quoted in Russell 1968, p. 22.
5. Quoted in Hedgecoe 1998, p. 34.
6. 'Primitive Art', *The Listener*, 24 August 1941.
7. Quoted in Hedgecoe 1998, pp. 34–5.
8. Hedgecoe 1968, p. 61.
9. May 1983, interview with Roger Berthoud.
10. Carlton Lake, 'Henry Moore's World', *Atlantic Monthly*, Boston, January 1962, quoted in Berthoud 2003, p. 166.
11. In a letter dated 12 March 1925, quoted by John Rothenstein in *Modern English Painters*: *Lewis to Moore*, London, Eyre and Spottiswoode, 1956.
12. David Finn, 'Photographing with Henry Moore', in Moore 1981, p. 17.
13. To David Sylvester, 1951, quoted in Berthoud 2003, p. 223.
14. Wilkinson 2002, p. 239.
15. *Daily Dispatch*, 3 November 1950, quoted in Berthoud 2003, p. 261.
16. *Financial Times*, 30 October 1950, quoted in Berthoud 2003, p. 261.
17. Hedgecoe 1968, p. 151, quoted in Wilkinson 2002, p. 212.
18. Russell 1968, p. 28, quoted in Wilkinson 2002, p. 212.
19. According to Herbert Read (1965, p. 64).
20. Ionel Jianou, *Henry Moore*, trans. Geoffrey Skelding, Arted, Paris, 1968, p. 29, quoted in Berthoud 2003, p. 106.
21. Richard Cork, 'Overhead Sculpture for the Underground Railway', in *British Sculpture in the Twentieth Century*, exh. cat., Whitechapel Art Gallery, London, 1981, p. 98, quoted in Berthoud 2003, p. 94.
22. Moore 1981, p. 10.
23. Maurice de Sausmarez (ed.), *Ben Nicholson: A Studio International Special*, London, Studio International, 1969, pp. 23–4, quoted in Wilkinson 2002, pp. 161–6.
24. Quoted in Hedgecoe 1998, p. 116.
25. 'This [the use of surface string] does come from the drawings. I don't know if there's anybody else who has used this kind of invention, but I invented at one stage a shorthand way of trying to show in a drawing the sectional line, the form, the shape, without doing shading … well I was dissatisfied with the shape being shown as clearly as I wanted and so I used this drawing … method idea on the sculpture and the strings had to be thin enough not to disrupt or confuse the surface … And to some extent I think it does add an interest and form, it does give the shape more insistence than it would do on an absolutely plain surface.' In conversation with Alan Wilkinson, *c.*1980, quoted in Wilkinson 2002.
26. In conversation with David Mitchinson, 1980, quoted in Wilkinson 2002, pp. 276–7.
27. Moore 1981, p. 8
28. Hedgecoe 1998, p. 38
29. Quoted in Herbert Read (ed.), *Unit One*, London, 1934.
30. Moore 1981, p. 45.
31. According to Ann Garrould (1994–2003, vol. 2, 1998, p. ix), the discovery of this use of wax crayon emerged from the (benevolent) theft of her pack of Woolworth's wax crayons on a visit to her uncle (Moore) in August 1935.
32. The models for cat. 51 are his mother and his niece Ann Garrould, and for cat. 53 his sister Mary and her daughter Ann.
33. Carlton Lake, 'Henry Moore's World', *Atlantic Monthly* 209, no. 1 (January 1962) 39–45, quoted by Dorothy Kosinsky 'Some Reasons for a Reputation', *Henry Moore: Sculpting the 20th Century*, exh. cat. Dallas Museum of Art, 2001, p. 22.
34. Hedgecoe 1998, p. 134.
35. Moore 1981, p. 62.
36. Moore 1981, p. 50.
37. Letter of about August 1925 to Raymond Coxon, quoted in Berthoud 2003, p. 74.
38. Moore 1981, p. 73.
39. Titled *Two Women Seated at a Table* in Ann Garrould's catalogue raisonné and interpreted in more detail in her essay here, p. 19.
40. Letter of 15 January 1955; quoted in Philip James (ed.), *Henry Moore on Sculpture: A Collection of the Sculptor's Writings and Spoken Words*, London, Macdonald, 1966; further quoted in Wilkinson 2002.
41. Quoted in Berthoud 2003, p. 247.
42. Ibid.

Select Bibliography

Bennet, Anita Feldman, David Mitchinson & Margaret Reid, *An Introduction to Henry Moore*, Perry Green, The Henry Moore Foundation (Henry Moore Collections and Exhibitions), 2002

Berthoud, Roger, *The Life of Henry Moore*, London, Giles de la Mare Publishers Ltd, 2003 (revised from the 1st edn, London, Faber and Faber Ltd, 1987)

Bowness, Alan and David Sylvester (eds), *Henry Moore: Complete Sculpture*, 6 vols, London, Lund Humphries, rev. edns 1986, 1990

Cardinal, Roger *et al.*, *Henry Moore: In the Light of Greece*, exh. cat., Andros, Umberto Allemandi & Co., 2000 (in particular the essays: Kyriakos Koutsomallis, 'Henry Moore: from the archaic aesthetic of nature to the organic abstract modernism of art'; Anita Feldman Bennet, 'Rediscovering Humanism')

Compton, Susan, with contributions by Richard Cork and Peter Fuller, *Henry Moore*, exh. cat., London, Royal Academy of Arts published in association with Weidenfeld & Nicolson, 1988 (in particular the essays: Richard Cork, 'An Art of the Open Air: Moore's Major Public Sculpture'; Susan Compton, 'Drawing and Sculpture: A Timeless Art of our Time'; Peter Fuller, 'Henry Moore: An English Romantic')

Garrould, Ann, *Henry Moore Drawings*, London, Thames & Hudson, 1988

Garrould, Ann (ed.), *Henry Moore: Complete Drawings*, 7 vols, London, Lund Humphries, 1994–2003

Hedgecoe, John (ed.), *Henry Spencer Moore*. Nelson, London, 1968

Hedgecoe, John, *A Monumental Vision: The Sculpture of Henry Moore*, London, Collins and Brown, 1998

Hooper, Steven (ed.), *Robert and Lisa Sainsbury Collection, Vol. 1: European 19th and 20th Century Paintings, Drawings and Sculpture*, New Haven and London, Yale University Press in association with University of East Anglia, Norwich, 1997

Jean, Marcel, *The Autobiography of Surrealism* (The Documents of Twentieth Century Art), Viking Press, New York, 1980

Kosinski, Dorothy, *et al.*, *Henry Moore: Sculpting the 20th Century*, exh. cat., Dallas Museum of Art, New Haven and London, Yale University Press, 2001

Mitchinson, David, *Henry Moore: War and Utility*, The Henry Moore Foundation, Much Hadham, 2001

Mitchinson, David, *Henry Moore: Thoughts and Practices*, Perry Green, The Henry Moore Foundation (Henry Moore Collections and Exhibitions), 1999

Mitchinson, David, *et al.*, *Sculpture in the Open Air at Perry Green*, Perry Green, The Henry Moore Foundation (Henry Moore Collections and Exhibitions), 2000

Moore, Henry, *Henry Moore at the British Museum*, London, British Museum Publications Ltd, 1981

Neumann, Erich (translated from the German by R.F.C. Hull), *The Archetypal World of Henry Moore*, London, Routledge & Kegan Paul, 1959

Packer, William, *Henry Moore: An Illustrated Biography*, London, Weidenfeld & Nicolson, 1985

Read, Herbert, *Henry Moore: A Study of his Life and Work*, London, Thames & Hudson, 1965

Russell, John, *Henry Moore*, London, Allen Lane The Penguin Press, 1968

Sweeney, James Johnson, *Henry Moore*, exh. cat., New York, The Museum of Modern Art in collaboration with The Art Institute of Chicago and the San Francisco Museum of Art, distributed by Simon and Schuster, 1946

Wilkinson, Alan (ed. and with an introduction by) *Henry Moore: Writings and Conversations*, Aldershot, Lund Humphries, 2002

Index of Works Exhibited

Page numbers in **bold** refer to catalogue illustrations

Photo credits

The authors would like to thank the following for providing the photographs listed:

Arts Council Collection: cats 30, 79
James Austin: cats 8, 12, 19, 22, 23, 27, 28, 31, 33, 34, 38, 42, 63, 64, 65, 66, 67, 72, 78, 81, 88, 89, 96
British Council: cats 25, 80, 87
British Museum: cats 50–57; figs 8, 52
Darren Chung: cats 26, 46; fig. 13
Brian Coxall: cat. 44
Anita Feldman Bennet: cat. 39
Dennis Gilbert: cat. 92
John Hedgecoe: fig. 38
The Henry Moore Foundation Archive: cats 5, 37, 59, 61, 75; figs 1, 4–7, 9, 11, 13–17, 19–27, 29, 31, 33, 35, 36, 39–44, 46, 48–50, 53, 54–56
Matthew Hollow: cat. 32; figs 3, 10, 12, 28
Errol Jackson: cats 1, 43, 82; fig. 45
Leeds Museums and Galleries: cat. 6
Felix Man: fig. 34
Manchester City Galleries: figs 30, 51
Menor Creative Imaging: cats 21, 68, 69, 77, 85, 86, 95
Michel Muller: cats 2, 7, 9, 16, 18, 24, 40, 41, 45, 49, 58, 60, 70, 71, 83, 94
Museum Conservation Services Ltd: cats 13, 14, 36, 62, 91
National Galleries of Scotland, Picture Library: cat. 15
Michael Phipps: cat. 35
Push One: cat. 73
John Roan Photography, Northampton: cat. 10
Robert and Lisa Sainsbury Collection, University of East Anglia: fig. 2
Julian Stallabrass: cat. 29
Emma Stower: fig. 18
Tate, London 2004: cats 3, 4, 11, 17, 20, 48, 74, 76, 84, 93, 97; figs 32, 37, 42
Wakefield MDC Cultural Services: cat. 47
John Webb: cat. 90